The Columbia Guide to Contemporary African American Fiction

Columbia Guides to Literature Since 1945

The Columbia Guides to Literature Since 1945

The Columbia Guide to the Literatures of Eastern Europe Since 1945, ed. Harold B. Segel

The Columbia Guide to Contemporary African American Fiction

Darryl Dickson-Carr

Columbia University Press
New York

Columbia University Press
Publishers Since 1893
New York   Chichester, West Sussex

The index of this book was made possible by a Research and Creative Activity grant from the Department of English at the Florida State University.

Library of Congress Cataloging-in-Publication Data
Dickson-Carr, Darryl, 1968–
    The Columbia guide to contemporary African American fiction / Darryl Dickson-Carr.
        p. cm. — (Columbia guides to literature since 1945)
    Includes bibliographical references and index.
    ISBN 0–231–12472–4 (cloth : alk. paper)
        1. American fiction—African American authors—History and criticism—Handbooks, manuals, etc. 2. American fiction—20th century—History and criticism—Handbooks, manuals, etc. 3. African Americans—Intellectual life—20th century—Handbooks, manuals, etc. 4. African Americans in literature—Handbooks, manuals, etc. I. Dickson-Carr, Darryl, 1968– II. Title. III. Series.
    PS374.N4D533 2005
    813′.540986073—dc22

                                                        2005045454

Printed in the United States of America

c 10 9 8 7 6 5 4 3 2 1

For Carol

Contents

Preface

The primary goal of this guide is to introduce the reader to the literature, careers, and critical issues surrounding major African American fiction authors published since 1970. This period witnessed an explosion of literary talent from American authors of African descent. As hundreds of these authors made an impressive and permanent mark upon the publishing world, they enjoyed an unprecedented level of attention from academics and critics alike. As a group, these authors clearly owe great debts to previous literary movements, but they have also carved out their own distinctive niches that have irreversibly transformed the landscape of African American literature and its reception in both American publishing and the academy. The reader will be able to trace, whether by randomly sampling this guide's 164 entries or by reading it in its entirety from start to finish, how African American fiction became a centerpiece of American literary history at the end of the twentieth century even as it remained the site of celebration, contestation, diversity, and no small amount of controversy.

Each period within the history of African American literature contains its own loosely definable agenda. Most African American authors have sought to provide at least a glimpse into the varied experiences of African Americans and how those experiences, ranging from the joyous and celebratory to the cataclysmic and horrific, have forced America to transform itself into a nation that better reflects the promises and ideals of democracy. My ultimate goal is to demonstrate how the most recent wave of African American fiction and, to a slightly lesser extent, its criticism best reflect this often-tortured, yet endlessly fascinating transformation.

This guide reviews authors, movements, institutions, and publications that emerged between 1970 and 2000. I begin at 1970 primarily because that year was the crux of a number of major shifts in African American politics. The philosophy of integration and pacifism that Martin Luther King Jr. and the Southern Christian Leadership Conference represented were slowly but inexorably supplanted by African American cultural nationalism beginning in the mid-1960s, inaugurating what is now known as the post–Civil Rights era, which extends until the present. The era that most Americans consider the apex of Civil Rights activism began with the 1954 *Brown v. Board of Education of Topeka, Kansas* Supreme Court decision and ended with the assassination of King, although the fight for Civil Rights truly began many decades earlier, arguably at the end of legal chattel slavery in 1865. The modern push for equality, however, in which King participated and for which he has become a popular icon, arguably began with the *Brown* decision and had its first major victory in the Montgomery, Alabama, bus boycott of 1955. King's assassination in 1968 meant that one of the most important eras in American history—rivaled only by the Revolutionary and Civil wars and the decades leading to them—lost a crucial leader, one who stood on the side of hope and peace. The vacuum he left was filled with many voices questioning the efficacy of the strategy and practice of the nonviolent direct action that defined the modern Civil

Rights movement. Among these voices were many African American intellectuals and writers who constituted the Black Arts Movement.

In African American literary arts, the radicalism of the Black Arts Movement advocated by such luminary writers and critics as Imamu Amiri Baraka (né LeRoi Jones), Hoyt Fuller, Addison Gayle, Nikki Giovanni, Sonia Sanchez, Carolyn Rodgers, Maulana Ron Karenga, and Gwendolyn Brooks brought about a sea change in the literature's scope and content. As we shall see below, debates regarding the merits of pursuing art for art's (or the artist's) sake versus creating socially conscious art have raged for over a century among African American intellectuals. By the late 1960s, though, the latter position of the debate was ascendant as black politics became radicalized in the wake of racism's continuing entrenchment, the demise of African colonialism, and the deaths of such leaders as Malcolm X and Medgar Evers. Literature with a more proletarian or "grassroots" orientation became popular, as did a sort of radical chic. This did not mean that careful artistic craft was in abeyance, but it did mean that someone interested in African American literature in 1970 would have found very little being published that resembled what Richard Wright called, in his famous criticism of the Harlem Renaissance, "humble novels, poems, and plays, prim and decorous ambassadors who went a-begging to white America."[1] Instead, many of African American literature's most prominent artists openly advocated various forms of revolution, from armed conflict to the ideological transformations of cultural nationalism.

Most obviously, 1970 also marked the end of the 1960s, in which the ideological foundations for most of the literature to follow were laid. In 1970 alone, many landmark novels, fiction anthologies, and bibliographies emerged from the writers and editors whose work has attracted extensive critical and popular interest: Ishmael Reed (*19 Necromancers from Now*), Alice Walker (*The Third Life of Grange Copeland*), Toni Morrison (*The Bluest Eye*), Darwin Turner (*Afro-American Writers*). The years immediately following witnessed the publication of many texts that have since ascended to the current African American literary canon: *The Black Aesthetic*, by Addison Gayle (1971); Ishmael Reed's *Mumbo Jumbo* (1972); Charles Johnson's *Faith and the Good Thing* (1974); Toni Morrison's *Sula* (1974), and so on. In short, 1970 marked the beginning of a contemporary flourish that has never truly subsided.

Critical and scholarly attention to African American authors has grown in the last three decades to the point that it is now virtually unthinkable for major literary journals specializing in American literature to ignore black authors. Most critical appraisals and analyses of these authors are now sympathetic, due in large part to the infusion of African American scholars into academia. Regardless of levels of sympathy, the theories of such African American scholars as W. E. B. Du Bois, Toni Morrison, Henry Louis Gates Jr., Barbara Smith, Hortense Spillers, Houston A. Baker Jr., Arnold Rampersad, Audre Lorde, Alice Walker, and Wahneema Lubiano frequently inform most critiques of African American literature. Hundreds of monographs, essay collections, and individual book chapters have been devoted to African American authors since 1970, and since 1996, several major anthologies and critical companions and guides have been published to provide the beginning student of African American literature with quick and easy access to the primary and secondary material in the field. This *Columbia Guide* is but one of these resources and should be considered as much a complement to the others as a gateway to this rapidly expanding world.

---

1. Richard Wright, "Blueprint for Negro Writing," *The New Challenge: A Literary Quarterly* 2, no. 2 (1937): 53.

Each of the entries for different authors, institutions, major publications, and other critical terms opens this world to the reader and suggests a few additional readings that will expand upon the issues the entry raises. My objective is not so much to give a complete biography or history of a subject as it is to touch upon the subject's keynotes. Therefore, instead of reproducing a complete biography of Toni Morrison, which could be found in any one of a handful of sources, it is more productive to discuss a few key events from Morrison's life and career that illustrate why she has been a significant part of contemporary African American literature for the last three decades, then point the reader toward the best biographies.

The reader will also note that some author entries are much longer than others. The length of individual entries is due, as one might expect, to a particular author's eminence in African American literature or, perhaps, to the number and complexity of an author's works. Of course, this rule does not always hold; some authors may very well be major figures in African American *literature*, but since this guide is a resource for African American *fiction*, an author best known for her contributions to poetry or for his critical or journalistic career may be given but a short treatment. In such cases, I have taken pains to acknowledge the author's relevance to other literary forms but have not dwelt on them, unless such attention would help illuminate the author's contributions to prose fiction.

Although this volume is a guide to African American fiction, it is not exhaustive. That is to say, I do not attempt to provide an entry for every African American who has written fiction. With but a few exceptions, I have chosen to exclude at least two identifiable genres from the volume: specialized religious fiction, or fiction written specifically for an audience converted to a particular religion, usually Christianity; and romances. While the overwhelming majority of African Americans profess religious beliefs—most frequently Christian and Muslim, in that order—I assume that those seeking a guide to fiction with an explicitly Christian bent, for example, would have little trouble finding one via such other sources as their clergy or fellow parishioners. This is not to say that the theme of religion may not be found herein. The fact that religion has played and continues to play an essential role in African American communities has inspired countless African American authors to compose stories and novels that draw from and reflect upon black spirituality in all its forms. With few exceptions, though, these works are not necessarily written specifically to proselytize or offer succor for the faithful. Instead, they give us an opportunity to learn about many different aspects of African American life and culture, with religion and spirituality but one part of that mosaic. This guide, then, is for those interested in these aspects as found in African American secular fiction.

I have opted to exclude romance fiction written by African Americans for the simple reason that the numbers of works and authors in this vein are far too numerous and not nearly distinct enough in most appreciable ways to warrant separate entries or close study, despite the fact that this area grew significantly in the last decade or so of the twentieth century. For my purposes, I define "romance fiction" as short stories and novels whose purpose is to explore the terrain of romantic relationships primarily, if not exclusively, for the purpose of entertainment. While these works are certainly popular among an extensive core audience, it is also safe to say that despite the real talent of many writers working in this vein, detailed descriptions of these works would be repetitive and perhaps superfluous. The reader might object that some of the authors included could be classified as writers of romance fiction, to the extent that they write about African American relationships, including love and romance. I argue instead that any author or work included in this guide, including those who might seem to write to a formula or who stick to certain popular generic conventions of romance fiction, at the very least aspire to artistry either by virtue of the careful composition of their writing or by clear attempts to write artistically, politically, and socially challenging art. The few exceptions I have consciously made to this rule, then, are authors who have tried to challenge the limits of their chosen genres and to break out of generic formulae.

"Fiction" will be understood as meaning short stories, novellas, and novels. Unless they are directly relevant to our understanding of fiction or a particular author's oeuvre, the *Guide* will not focus upon dramatic works and poetry. It will, however, discuss and utilize major nonfiction works that have been instrumental in altering the study of African American fiction.

One of the key purposes for this guide, then, is to help the reader make such distinctions. Although I admittedly have my favorite authors within the greater tradition of African American fiction, I have tried to be as objective as possible in my summaries and assessments of different authors. Every author listed has intrinsic value stemming from her or his sincere efforts to write to an intelligent reading audience. As is true of any type of literature, many authors strive toward an eclectic mix of artistic standards or ideological purposes, while others write primarily to entertain, and still others wish to balance the two. In fact, over the course of preparing this guide, it became abundantly clear that many of the most popular African American authors currently writing have a substantial stake in lending a certain degree of social consciousness to their works by incorporating plot lines that confront a number of pertinent social issues. These may range from the drug epidemics of the 1980s and 1990s and the concomitant "War on Drugs" that led to a number of severe social problems; the legacy of the Civil Rights movement in all its cultural, political, and economic implications; the Gay Rights movement, including (but not limited to) the rise of HIV/AIDS and its effects upon African American and gay, lesbian, bisexual, and transgendered communities; the women's movement; racism's continuing impact upon African American communities; and so on. These plotlines may be the crux of some works; in others they might be faintly discernible—or poorly developed—thoughts that do not always affect the overarching plot.

How to Use This Guide

I wrote the alphabetical entries that follow to provide the reader with an introduction to the subject, author, or work at hand. Each author entry in the *Guide* provides: basic biographical information for the author; a summary of the direction, importance, or effects of his or her work; short summaries of minor works; longer discussions of individual works that have had a significant impact upon the literary world, as each case may warrant; and a paragraph or two listing and occasionally annotating the books, essays, or articles that the reader might turn to for more detailed information. These last paragraphs function as bibliographies for individual authors, but they are not meant to be exhaustive catalogues. For many of the newer or younger authors, especially those who began writing in the mid- to late 1990s, the only articles to be found are book reviews. I have opted to exclude listings of book reviews, with two significant exceptions: 1) if the review in question is especially lengthy and informative, or 2) if the author in question is a major figure. Colson Whitehead, for example, promises to become an important author in both contemporary African American literature and the broader historical tradition. Some of the reviews of his two novels help shed light upon his significance and therefore have been included or quoted.

Interspersed with the author entries are terms, subjects, and individual books that have made a deep impression upon the greater field of contemporary African American literature and literary studies. Since I use or refer to many of the terms or subjects freely throughout the remainder of the alphabetized entries, the reader would likely benefit from having relatively brief definitions or histories. Individual books that merit their own entries fit into at least one of several categories. They are either extremely well known, frequently taught at high school and college levels, highly influential, studied regularly by scholars, or—in the estimation of an overwhelming number of professional critics and scholars—the most universally acclaimed. A few scholarly works have made it into this group due to their exceptional impact upon the field of African American literary studies, which grew and developed rapidly in the 1970s and 1980s. The reader is encouraged, however, to refer to this volume's bibliography for a more complete listing of scholarly works.

The bibliography that follows the A–Z section is a listing of anthologies, critical books, book chapters, and articles that discuss the directions African American literature has taken throughout its history, but especially in the twentieth century's last three decades. Most studies of African American fiction published in the last thirty years of the twentieth century consist of either discussions of single authors, a few closely related authors (not all of whom may be African American), and general discussions of African American literary history. I have annotated a number of entries that are particularly outstanding for their ability to shed light on either general African American literary history or the period covered by this volume. Single-author studies are not included.

A Note on Usage of Terms

Before proceeding further, some other commonly used terms warrant definition and clarification. I move interchangeably here between the terms "African American" and "black," with the former term used most frequently. "African American" is the formal term that many native-born Americans of African descent have chosen as the most accurate to describe both their heritage and identity, in the absence of precise genealogies extending back to West Africa. Since relatively few enslaved Africans were allowed to maintain fully their cultural traditions and language in the North American form of slavery, "African American" thus signifies a person whose ancestry is rooted in the African continent and whose phenotype, culture, and legal or personal identity, while containing contributions from European, Semitic, Asian or other peoples, reflects the black African element. This term was intended to replace or clarify such earlier terms as black, Black American (capitalized or not), Afro-American, Aframerican, Negro American (again, capitalized or not), colored, and so on. The identity itself may be a product of conscious self-identification or the sometimes-arbitrary categorization that frequently frustrates those American authors of African descent who might choose to reject some African American cultural traditions. For the sake of brevity, I choose to include under these labels all American-born authors of African descent, as well as those Caribbean authors of African descent who have adopted the United States as their home, whether formally or informally.

On this last point, selecting the authors to be included in this volume, and therefore under the rubric, required making an unsatisfactory but necessary distinction. Although I recognize the obvious fact that the United States of America is certainly not all of the Americas, that blacks in the Caribbean would, in the broadest sense, also be "African American," and that blacks in the United States share some common historical experiences and some common cultural practices, they also have some distinct, complex differences that even the most cursory understanding of Caribbean nations' history would highlight. I would not, therefore, consider an author who lives and works primarily in a Caribbean nation an African *American*, if the latter half of the term means "of the United States," even if that author had spent considerable time in the United States. I should also imagine that a native Jamaican author, for example, would be insulted by my conflating her life and her nation's history with those of black Americans in the same way she might object to the omnibus label "Caribbean writer."

I am also equally comfortable with the term "black" when used as a synonym for African American, since African Americans still accept and use it widely, as do those outside of African American communities. The acceptance of both terms has depended largely upon substantial shifts in African American cultural politics, some of which I discuss below. Except when it is used as part of a proper name or title, though, I do not capitalize "black," again in keeping with current common usage. I do not use decidedly outmoded terms such as "Negro" or "colored" unless, again, I am quoting these terms as part of a name, title, or literary passage. On some occasions I use the term "people of color" as a general descriptor of the major ethnic minority groups in the United States of America, including African Americans, Asian Americans, and Hispanics/Latinos or Chicanos, among others. While the question of *who* or *what* is "African American" is difficult to answer and will be addressed further in various entries within, the definition above serves as a general understanding.

Finally, I tend to place the term "race" in quotation marks to signify the fact that "race" is a commonly accepted but finally problematic term that connotes biological divisions between human beings. Modern science has soundly disproved "race" as a biological reality, yet it remains a social one for millions of people of color in the United States, to say nothing of the rest of the world. "Race" is therefore a falsehood, but it is one that people frequently rely upon to describe phenotypical and cultural characteristics that ultimately transcend "racial" divisions. My quotation marks indicate an ironic usage, which I hope will help inspire the reader to question the term's meaning.

Abbreviations

Some commonly mentioned or cited texts and institutions have been abbreviated after their first appearances in the main body of the entries. These include:

AAR	*African American Review*
BALF	*Black American Literature Forum*
CLA	College Language Association
DLB	*Dictionary of Literary Biography*
NALF	*Negro American Literature Forum*
Norton	*The Norton Anthology of African American Literature*

Acknowledgments

When James Raimes of Columbia University Press first approached me about writing a reference book on contemporary African American fiction, I found the task to be in the abstract a fun, yet challenging one. As I delved further into the project's research and writing, I found that challenge growing but never entirely eclipsing the pleasure. For that, I have to credit James and his immediate successor, Plaegian Alexander, both of whom remained patient and encouraging as I worked out problems in this volume's assembly and composition. Editors James Warren and Juree Sondker were equally professional and indispensable in all their guidance and counsel. Michael Haskell diligently shepherded the manuscript through the copyediting and proofing processes. I extend my gratitude to the entire staff at the press.

Equally important were the patience and encouragement of my colleagues at the Florida State University, where I received a Developing Scholar Award (2002–2003) to help defray the expenses associated with this project. I am indebted to the English department chair, Hunt Hawkins, for granting a course release to ease the writing process, and to the department's office staff—especially Carolyn Morgan—for helping me acquire resources and for protecting my time. I am particularly grateful for the ears of my comrades-in-arms, Christopher Shinn and Barry Faulk, who loaned their empathy and constructive criticism during many late-night sessions at the office. Special thanks go to Lisa C. Lakes, whose assistance in reviewing and correcting the manuscript in the later stages was invaluable. Finally, this volume simply would not have been possible if my wife, Carol Dickson-Carr, had not carved out time and space for me to work on it for long stretches by watching over our daughter, Maya Carr. For that reason, I have happily dedicated this book to her.

The Columbia Guide to Contemporary
African American Fiction

Overview

The three decades between 1970 and 2000 constituted the most productive and successful period in African American literary history. Hundreds of African American authors, including many who were but very young children in 1970, began or continued illustrious writing and publishing careers, transforming the face of American literature itself. Prior to 1970, very few African American authors could hope to sell more than a few thousand copies of their books. By the mid-1990s, sales in the hundreds of thousands for individual works, lucrative film options, and author tours marked by jam-packed readings and signings were commonplace for several dozen writers. Their success has both inspired and enabled hundreds of black authors to begin writing and to create some of the most remarkable fiction of the last quarter century and beyond. The rewards have not been merely financial: African American authors also began winning some of the top literary prizes in the United States and in the world, including the Nobel and Pulitzer Prizes; American Book, National Book, PEN/Faulkner, and PEN/Hemingway Awards; and berths on many publications' "Best of" lists. Book clubs and specialty booksellers, operating either in traditional brick-and-mortar establishments or on the Internet, have proliferated. African American literature is now widely studied at institutions of higher learning worldwide, and key fictional works by contemporary African American authors, particularly Toni Morrison, James Baldwin, Ralph Ellison, Alice Walker, John Edgar Wideman, and Gloria Naylor, may be found on the syllabi of courses in American literature, multiethnic literature, women's studies, sociology, and—naturally—African American studies courses. Before 1970, African American fiction was but a footnote in the estimation of most experts on American literature. By 1980, such prize-winning bestsellers as Alex Haley's *Roots* (1976) and Toni Morrison's *Song of Solomon* (1978) had simultaneously appealed to and sparked widespread interest in African American genealogy and history, along with serious scholarly attention. By 1990, African American fiction had captured great fame and controversy through Alice Walker's *The Color Purple* (1983), Morrison's *Beloved* (1987), Ishmael Reed's *Reckless Eyeballing* (1985), Sherley Anne Williams's *Dessa Rose* (1985), and Terry McMillan's *Mama* (1987), and African American literary studies became one of the most exciting fields in the academy. By 2000, books by African American authors were routinely selling hundreds of thousands, and occasionally millions of copies, an African American had finally won the Nobel Prize in literature (Toni Morrison, 1993), and African American literary studies had become an institution with many stalwart defenders. For today's enlightened student of American literature, African American literature is virtually impossible to ignore.

Not all developments for African American fiction have been so positive. Since Phillis Wheatley published her groundbreaking *Poems on Various Subjects, Religious and Moral* in 1773, critical assessments of African American literature's artistic merits have never been wholly positive, and they have frequently been quite hostile to the direction and purpose of the majority of authors. Two hundred years after Wheatley's first book, African American authors wishing to portray black lives both realistically and sympathetically in works inspired by the Black Arts Movement of the 1960s often met with withering hostility from a critical establishment skeptical of the heightened political consciousness of the early 1970s. As more African American critics have found their independent voices and had their say within recent decades, whether in mainstream publications or from the halls of academia, this situation has changed for the better. Today, however, it is still all too rare for anyone outside of a small but growing group of recent black authors to receive the types of close, careful scholarly examinations their works deserve. Equally troubling is the fact that many of the best authors of the 1970s, including John A. Williams, John Oliver Killens, Fran Ross, Nathan Heard, Clarence Major, Hal Bennett, and William Melvin Kelley, find their best work either out of print entirely or in print for merely the shortest stints. Nevertheless, if it were not for the enormous interest that newer authors had brought to African American literature, these veteran authors and their forgotten classics might never have returned to print at all.

Although the number of African American authors writing and publishing in the 1990s exploded beyond all expectations, this growth had at least as much to do with the desire of publishing houses to capitalize upon the success of such popular authors as Terry McMillan as it was a sign of a new creative spirit among African American writers. Many of the works published in that boom, while certainly accessible, smart, and frequently ambitious, did not always aspire to do much more than provide solid, enjoyable, and entertaining fiction. Of course, this is not necessarily a negative trait. While the public may still obtain most of its dominant images of African Americans from other media—particularly film, music, and television—the ascendance of African American fiction means that more facets of African American life and literary expression now have a chance to be published, read, heard, and appreciated than ever before.

Since 1970, for example, African American women authors have become dominant forces in creating and contributing to the larger tradition after many decades of being virtually silenced by outright neglect from publishers who considered them irrelevant. As with so much literature by and about women, that silence has been broken, giving voice to the infinite complexities of African American women's lives, including women's roles as leaders, creators of culture, mothers, lovers, among many others. These works have therefore helped make various forms of feminist critique available to the public for discussion and helped foster change. Equally important, these works vastly expand a potential medium for women readers of all backgrounds to see their lives and issues alternately represented, affirmed, and challenged. Similarly, black gay, lesbian, and bisexual authors and characters are now almost commonplace in African American literature, brought out of the closets of silence, invisibility, and marginalization that once dominated their identities and desires. Science fiction by such authors as Octavia Butler, Samuel R. Delany, and Tananarive Due has grown in popularity, as has the detective fiction genre best represented by Walter Mosley. These authors have, in turn, placed such issues as class differences, police brutality, slavery, the Civil Rights movement, and the hidden histories of local African American communities into inspired fictional settings that help give new life to a history whose hidden stories are rapidly being rediscovered.

Consider also that popular works have helped to increase the active African American reading audience into the millions through the loyal readerships that such authors as Terry McMillan, Connie Briscoe, Eric Jerome Dickey, E. Lynn Harris, April Sinclair, and Sheneska Jackson enjoy. While readership rates among African Americans remains behind that of other groups,[1] popular fiction has improved it nonetheless. Publishing houses that once dismissed manuscripts by and about African Americans out of a widespread belief that blacks do not read books have been proven wrong time and again. The doors of mainstream publication and distribution may remain open indefinitely to black authors.

Of course, a caveat applies to these upbeat views as well. African Americans still own few presses and therefore have relatively little control over how and where their works are marketed and distributed. These same authors have long struggled with the position of privilege that liberal white Americans, whether embodied by antislavery abolitionists or commercial-press editors, have frequently occupied. This position has historically meant that whites have assumed greater authority to speak on behalf or in support of African Americans than African Americans have had for themselves. In the literary world, this privilege is not merely symbolic; it determines the types of texts that are published or, to be more specific, the types of narratives *about* African American lives that see print. Critics as diverse as Henry Louis Gates Jr., Barbara E. Johnson, W. Lawrence Hogue, and J. Lee Greene have argued that the goal of many African American authors and texts has been, and should be, to avoid the fallacy of seeing value only in those narratives that reaffirm the supremacy of white Western cultures by emulating them and attempting to be "the same."[2] Instead, countless African American authors have used their creative abilities to write against or parody—to "signify upon," in black colloquial terms—the same Western traditions that have attempted to write African Americans out of history. In the contemporary period, these authors have often sought to recover that history, to reclaim and transform it, by positing the diversity, complexity, and inextricability of African American cultures within it.

The purpose of this overview is to participate in this project by highlighting the diversity of African American literature throughout its history. What follows is an attempt to do in a relatively small number of pages what the professor of African American literature typically has to do over the course of a single semester, quarter, or trimester: give a short history of African American literature and of the key historical and literary events that have fed the minds and imaginations of the authors included in this volume's main A–Z reference section. That story includes a history and examination of those events from the 1970s to the 1990s that set that period apart from larger African American literary traditions, while simultaneously writing it into them.

African American Literature Through the 1960s

Even the most cursory glance at the breadth of African American literature reveals two facts: First, African American experiences have varied widely since Africans were forcibly brought to the Americas. Second, these experiences are bound by African Americans' eternal desires to continue surviving and thriving in the Americas. This desire stems primarily from the

1. "Do Blacks Read Books?" *The Journal of Blacks in Higher Education* 20 (Summer 1998): 43.
2. See, for example, Barbara E. Johnson's response to Henry Louis Gates Jr.'s essay "Canon-Formation and the Afro-American Tradition: From the Seen to the Told," in *Afro-American Literary Study in the 1990s*, ed. Houston A. Baker Jr. and Patricia Redmond (Chicago: University of Chicago Press, 1989), 40. W. Lawrence Hogue, *The African American Male, Writing, and Difference: A Polycentric Approach to African American Literature, Criticism, and History* (Albany: State University of New York Press, 2003), extends this argument, as do Johnson, *The Feminist Difference: Literature, Psychoanalysis, Race, and Gender* (Cambridge, Mass.: Harvard University Press, 1997), and Kevin K. Gaines, *Uplifting the Race: Black Leadership, Politics, and Culture in the Twentieth Century* (Chapel Hill: University of North Carolina Press, 1996).

long and extremely difficult period of indentured servitude and chattel slavery (1619–1865), the systems under which the overwhelming majority of African Americans lived and struggled until 1865, when slavery was abolished in the United States with the passage of the Thirteenth Amendment to the United States Constitution.

Both before and after the abolition of slavery, African American literature was a flourishing field. Most of the published literature consisted of nonfiction, with the slave narrative being the dominant form of literary expression until the end of the Civil War in 1865. The prominence of this particular form had everything to do with the cause it supported: the abolition of slavery. Slave narratives were meant to arouse in the reader—often a Northern, white, Christian woman—righteous indignation toward the physical, psychological, and sexual brutalities commonplace under slavery. Ideally, this would in turn arouse support for the abolitionist movement, resulting in the eradication of slavery and the installation of true equality for all Americans. What little fiction existed aided the abolitionist cause as well, as free African Americans saw the artistic development of fictional texts, and the novel in particular, as less important than addressing the ongoing crisis of slavery itself. This does not mean, however, that African American literature lacked artistic ambition and achievement. Many of the most famous autobiographical slave narratives, including *Narrative of the Life of Frederick Douglass, an American Slave, Written by Himself* (1845), Harriet Jacobs's *Incidents in the Life of a Slave Girl* (1861), and *The Interesting Narrative of the Life of Olaudah Equiano, or Gustavus Vassa, the African* (1814) have become bona fide classics in American literature and cornerstones of African American literature and literary studies. The same may be said of the fiction. William Wells Brown's *Clotel; or, The President's Daughter: A Narrative of Slave Life in the United States* (1853), Harriet Wilson's *Our Nig; or, Sketches from the life of a Free Black, in a Two-Story White House, North, Showing That Slavery's Shadows Fall Even There* (1859) were not only the first two novels by African Americans (Brown's was the first but was not published in the United States until 1860) but also two antebellum works that condemned slavery, especially the practice of miscegenation via rape. In addition, such novelists and short story authors as Martin R. Delany, Frances E. W. Harper, and Victor Séjour were notable pioneers of prose fiction and powerful essayists. Each author's fictional subject matter necessarily differed from the others, but autobiographical portrayals of the complexities and common horrors and frustrations of enslaved and free life frequently dominated the field. Both fictional and nonfictional works, then, were explicit vehicles for political and ideological purposes.

Within this group, it is safe to say that proslavery sentiments were understandably nonexistent, except as positions to be soundly rejected. While some nonfiction accounts of slavery looked upon a select few slaveholders as relatively beneficent individuals, such perspectives in a work of fiction would have been unthinkable so long as millions of African Americans remained enslaved. Yet subtle philosophical differences remained among African American authors. The most notable were, and continue to be, between male and female authors or between authors of either gender who advocated more radical or more gradual means to end slavery and other forms of oppression.

These differences amongst antebellum works were the natural forebears of the literature published from the post–Civil War Reconstruction period through at least the Harlem Renaissance. The 1880s and 1890s witnessed the rise of Charles W. Chesnutt, whose highly successful "Conjure Woman" stories blended the conventions of the "local color" genre, with its emphases on the quaintness of provincials and their concomitant dialects, and African

American folklore. Less successful were Chesnutt's later novels and nondialect short works, primarily because they tended to confront contemporary racial issues in ways that were offensive to white sensibilities. Such novels as *The House Behind the Cedars* (1900) and *The Marrow of Tradition* (1901) failed to find a sizeable audience for their complex interrogations of racial definitions and categories at the time, although scholars now consider them perceptive, if flawed classics. Chesnutt's contemporary, Paul Laurence Dunbar (1872–1906), considered the most significant African American poet since the eighteenth century's Phillis Wheatley, wrote several novels and short stories that reflected the same alternating pattern of concern with African American cultures, though most of his novelistic output spent little time dealing with black characters.

A criticism frequently leveled against Chesnutt's and Dunbar's works, as well as those of James Weldon Johnson, James D. Carrothers, and other contemporaries, is whether each author's use of black dialect and inclusion of stereotypical black characters qualified as acquiescence to the generally ugly racial climate of the years between Reconstruction and the Harlem Renaissance. The issue was closely related to the ongoing debates over the direction and strategies of African American political, economic, and social progress that began in antebellum times. Some of the era's most prominent political voices were Booker T. Washington (1856–1915), founder and president of Tuskegee Institute in Tuskegee, Alabama; William Edward Burghardt Du Bois (1868–1963), a founding father of American empirical sociology and one of the most prolific African American activists, essayists, and scholars of the twentieth century; and Ida B. Wells-Barnett (1862–1931), an investigative journalist and political activist.

These figures initiated a debate regarding African American progress in their major non-fiction works. Washington's rise to fame and power, narrated in his powerful autobiography, *Up from Slavery* (1901), was a product of the program of self-help, thrift, business, and practical, vocational education that he instituted at Tuskegee as a model for African American progress. Washington's approach to education, civil rights, and black leadership appealed to a wide cross-section of African Americans and whites, particularly in the South, for its stress upon the manual arts, the importance of friendship between the races, and a more gradual movement towards civic equality. At the same time, Washington stirred controversy for his concession of African Americans' civil rights, particularly as delineated in his famous speech at the Cotton States Exposition in Atlanta, Georgia, in 1895. Known as the "Atlanta Compromise," Washington's address brought him great prestige and power both in the South and in Washington, D.C., on all matters related to African American progress. Simultaneously, however, such rising leaders and intellectuals as Du Bois later argued that Washington's tendency to avoid demands for civil rights, suffrage, and a combination of both industrial and liberal arts education contributed to the rapid disenfranchisement of African Americans in the wake of 1896's landmark *Plessy v. Ferguson* Supreme Court decision, which made segregation of public accommodations legal. Washington, however, was virtually the only African American leader able to work closely with American political figures to help protect African Americans' struggles for equality, frequently behind the scenes. His model of education at Tuskegee, duplicated at hundreds of Negro colleges, also enabled many thousands of African Americans to obtain educations that did contribute to the growth of real economic progress. To this day, Washington remains a controversial figure who helped define a model of African American leadership that remains attractive for its appeals to common principles and optimism.

Du Bois and Wells-Barnett, on the other hand, offered an increasingly popular alternative to Washington's leadership, stressing civil rights, activism, and full citizenship for all African Americans. Du Bois was among the thirty-one founders of the openly anti-Washington Niagara Movement for Civil Rights, which first met at Niagara Falls in Ontario, Canada, on July 10, 1905. Almost four years later, on May 31, 1909, both Du Bois and Wells-Barnett were among those who met in New York City to transform the Civil Rights goals of the Niagara Movement into the platform and bylaws of the National Association for the Advancement of Colored People (NAACP), an interracial organization devoted to radical resistance to segregation and all forms of racial discrimination. The NAACP became much more than an organ of political activity. Via its journal, *The Crisis* (1910–present), originally edited by Du Bois and (by 1919) his indispensable literary editor, Jessie Redmon Fauset, by the latter half of the 1910s the NAACP became one of African America's key sources of fresh literary talent. In addition, Du Bois's classic work *The Souls of Black Folk* (1903), a complex mix of sociology, political critique, history, personal essay, and fiction, was itself an enormous influence upon subsequent debates on African American life, literature, and culture. It includes the crucial essay, "Of Our Spiritual Strivings," in which Du Bois applied the concept of "double-consciousness, this sense of always looking at one's self through the eyes of others, of measuring one's soul by the tape of the world that looks on in amused contempt and pity," to the African American collective psyche. The metaphor of double-consciousness is but one Du Bois employs to argue that "the problem of the twentieth century is the problem of the color-line," an idea that informs all of his early work and has influenced sociologists, writers, and activists through the present. Du Bois's arguments conveyed gracefully the struggle within many African Americans to reconcile the role of pariah that American society imposed upon them with their own culture and feelings of self-worth.

Du Bois's conception had a profound effect upon the fiction of the next significant movement in African American literature, the "New Negro" or Harlem Renaissance (ca. 1919–1940). One of the most prolific and artistically sound collections of literature by and about African Americans to date, it has been surpassed in significance only by the flowering of African American literature and arts that budded in the 1960s and reached full bloom after 1970. The "New Negro" Renaissance was a product of many different elements, all essential, yet none so dominant as to be the single definitive cause. Racial tensions were at one of their highest points since Reconstruction after World War I, in which hundreds of thousands of black soldiers served and fought valiantly, albeit primarily under French command after U.S. military commanders refused to give black soldiers any significant opportunities to prove their abilities. Both the soldiers' valor and the commanders' resistance helped to rally the pride of millions of African Americans who had heard of black soldiers' heroism in that horrendous conflict. The postwar tensions exploded in the "Red Summer" of 1919, which saw thousands of antiblack lynchings and riots in hundreds of American cities and towns as communities throughout the nation attempted to move African Americans back to their prewar status as second-class citizens. This repression combined with the growth of the industrial might of the United States and numerous severe agricultural blights in the South to spur the Great Migration of African Americans from the South to other regions in the nation, but particularly to the urban North. Over the six decades from the 1910s through the 1960s, approximately 7,000,000 African Americans moved from a homeland plagued by racial violence, boll weevil infestations, floods, and fluctuating prices for cotton—the crux of the South's economy—to better economic and cultural opportunities in northern cities where industrial might, decent wages, and more tolerable housing could be found.

The urban cultures that African Americans created in these new environs were the foundations of the Harlem Renaissance and later literary movements, giving them their raison d'être and spirit. Without the Great Migration and the optimism for racial progress that it harnessed and inspired, neither the Harlem Renaissance, the social realism and naturalism of Richard Wright, Ann Petry, and Chester Himes, nor the radicalism of the Black Arts Movement of the 1960s would have been possible. As African Americans moved northward and westward, they took their music, stories, and customs with them, forcing such formerly regional, largely black musical forms as ragtime, the blues, jazz, and—much later—rap and hip-hop to grow and develop, transforming African American and American life and literature in turn. F. Scott Fitzgerald did not call the 1920s the "Jazz Age" for naught; that eternally malleable and continuously evolving musical form gave the decade its soundtrack, eventually becoming America's popular music. The blues, one of jazz's foundations, became a central motif of the works of Ralph Ellison, Sherley Anne Williams, Richard Wright, Toni Morrison, Alice Walker, Chester Himes, Ishmael Reed, J. California Cooper, Clarence Major, Gayl Jones, John Edgar Wideman, Albert Murray, and countless others.

Concomitant with the Great Migration, the death of Booker T. Washington in 1915 meant that the gradualist program of the controversial Tuskegee Institute president would no longer be the dominant ideology influencing the content and tenor of African American politics, educational policy, and intellectual discourse. Such major players of the New Negro movement as Alain Locke, W. E. B. Du Bois, and Langston Hughes argued that the earlier generation of African Americans loyal to Washington represented a type of "Old Negro" who saw African Americans as a sociological "problem" almost as often as whites did and were therefore more accepting of the conditions of legal segregation. The New Negro, in contrast, was a product of a new black urban population, which comprised a class of younger intellectuals and artists who felt free to imagine a future of rapid progress for the African Diaspora as a whole. Literature and other arts would capture this imagination in the spirit of modernity that infused the 1920s. The intellectual exchanges during the Harlem Renaissance, therefore, resulted in a wider dissemination of the full scope of African American political thought, bursting the limits of Washington's program and reaching beyond Harlem into mainstream American discourse.

The founding of the American version of Jamaican Marcus Garvey's Universal Negro Improvement Association (UNIA) in 1916 signified the emergence of the first modern Black Nationalist movement. Garvey and the UNIA aimed to uplift the peoples of the African Diaspora by instilling within them a deep and abiding pride in their history and cultures that would lead to their political, economic, and social independence. This independent and united black nation would then work to end European colonialism of the African continent and recolonize it. Garvey's motto of "Africa for the Africans" was a powerful rallying cry that attracted followers from all classes and backgrounds, from the Caribbean to black Harlem. Garvey also based his movement in Harlem, which meant that he had easy access to and worked closely with some of the best minds of the New Negro movement, at various times including fellow Jamaicans W. A. Domingo and Claude McKay.

Most significant of all, over four dozen novels, anthologies, and books of poetry or short stories emerged in the period, aided by a coterie of new, younger publishers (especially Alfred A. Knopf, Boni & Liveright, Harcourt Brace, J. B. Lippincott, and Harper) who did not share the prejudices against African American authors found at most of the established publishing houses. Such journals as *Crisis*, *Fire!!*, *Opportunity*, *American Mercury*, *The Nation*, *The New Republic*, *The Messenger*, and Alain Locke's seminal collection of fiction, poetry, and essays, *The New Negro* (1925) were responsible for publishing hundreds of stories by the movement's best authors. While some of these journals, particularly *Crisis*, the NAACP's official organ, and *Opportunity* (organ of the National Urban League) existed prior to the movement's most celebrated years in the 1920s, some were either direct products of the era or made special efforts to publish and promote African American authors. *Fire!!* (1926), for instance, was edited by Wallace Thurman, one of the central figures among the Harlem literati, and published works by Langston Hughes, Zora Neale Hurston, and Aaron Douglas, two writers and an artist, respectively, who were among the most celebrated of their time. *Fire!!* had as its express goal the promotion of younger, avant-garde writers who shunned the middle-class aesthetics frequently found in literature published in *Crisis* and *Opportunity*. These journals, however, were just as instrumental in publishing and featuring young writers thanks to the efforts of editor W. E. B. Du Bois and, especially, his literary editor, Jessie Redmon Fauset, an important novelist in her own right.

In contrast, the much older *Nation* (1865–present) aggressively solicited essays and stories from such African American intellectuals and writers as Du Bois, James Weldon Johnson, Walter White, Eric Walrond, Hughes, and George S. Schuyler at the behest of its editor, Oswald Villard. Both Villard and rival John Dewey of *The New Republic* were interested in promoting a sense of American cultural pluralism—that is, the simultaneous independence and interdependence of different ethnic and racial groups—among their readers, and they turned to African American writers and many others to help them achieve this purpose.[1] Together, the movement's literary outlets reveal that African Americans were reevaluating their cultures using ideas and language informed by sociology, political science, anthropology, and a desire to work outside of stereotypical roles.

The writers of the Harlem Renaissance possessed and debated fresh, new perceptions of African Americans' history and potential fortune in America and began to defy whites' and middle-class blacks' definitions of "acceptable" behavior in the arts or in person. Harlem owed its singular place in the African American imagination in the early twentieth century to its being a locus that attracted many of the preeminent black institutions, including the NAACP, the Urban League, the Universal Negro Improvement Association, Father Divine, and virtually every denomination of black church. Consequently, almost every major viewpoint was represented in the movement, including those concerned with artistic production. The debates that arose among Harlem Renaissance luminaries regarding the place of the African American artist still resound today. At the heart of these debates was the question of the African American artist's responsibility to represent her or his community and "race": should the artist serve him- or herself, or a particular ideology?

Although African American literature continued to flourish as the Harlem Renaissance wound down during the Great Depression (1929–1940), it did so with considerably less public fanfare than it had enjoyed in the 1920s. The late 1930s and early 1940s were a period of naturalism in African American fiction, a period in which Richard Wright published his greatest novel, *Native Son* (1940). *Native Son* irrevocably shifted the paradigm for African

1. George Hutchinson, *The Harlem Renaissance in Black and White* (Cambridge, Mass.: Belknap/Harvard University Press, 1995), 209–10.

American writing. Wright's themes of protest, his use of theories espoused by Chicago School of Sociology regarding the marginalization of African Americans within American society, his open confrontation of the hypocrisies of American racial thinking, and his support for Marxist thought catapulted him to the top of the mountain of African American writers. Wright wielded an enormous influence on his contemporaries and protégés, especially novelists Chester Himes, James Baldwin, Ralph Ellison, and Ann Petry, as well as on poet and personal friend Margaret Walker. Each of these authors explored inter- and intraracial discourse before and after World War II, using elements of Wright's naturalistic style. Eventually, however, Wright's advancements became part of African American fiction's mainstream, leading protégé Ralph Ellison to write his magnum opus, *Invisible Man* (1952), as both an homage and reaction to the limits Wright's eminence engendered.

Invisible Man also elicited a new respect for black authorship that would extend through the next few decades, due to Ellison's highly nuanced views of race and its problematic relationship to the idealistic principles upon which America was founded and by which it operates. Centered around the picaresque adventures of its anonymous narrator, *Invisible Man* drew upon, parodied, and paid homage to Ralph Waldo Emerson (Ellison's namesake) and his transcendentalism, Herman Melville, black folklore, American pragmatism, black colleges, modernism, the blues, Sigmund Freud, and the entire history of African Americans. This tour de force novel's artistic achievement earned it a National Book Award, which would not be bestowed upon another African American author until Charles Johnson earned it in 1990 for *Middle Passage*. Moreover, *Invisible Man* is widely recognized as one of the finest novels in canons of both African American and American literature. Ellison died before he could complete the manuscript for his second novel. Yet even when editor John Callahan edited Ellison's manuscripts into *Juneteenth* (1999), the work still caused a considerable stir. Although *Invisible Man* towered over African American literature in the 1960s, it was by no means alone. James Baldwin, who had also been a protégé of Richard Wright, emerged as a powerful novelist in the 1950s, owing to the success of two early works, *Go Tell It on the Mountain* (1952) and *Giovanni's Room* (1956).

If the 1950s was a phase in which African American authors honed and perfected their craft, the mid-to-late 1960s was a period of expansion, of fascinating experimental writing that may be called revolutionary. The 1960s brought with them a comprehension, by both blacks and whites, of black American politics and culture that had not been paralleled since the height of Marcus Garvey's influence in the 1920s and 1930s. The Civil Rights Movement was in full swing and being continually debated by the American public in all of the most dominant media by white and black integrationists, Black Nationalists or separatists (most notably the Nation of Islam and its chief spokesman, Malcolm X), white segregationists and racists, white moderates, and every other group or position that had a stake in the preservation or elimination of accepted racial categories and stratifications. Nowhere did these debates rage more hotly than within the black community itself, which was forced to redefine its own parameters when faced with the possibility that national de jure segregation might actually be eliminated through the efforts of Civil Rights activists and presidential administrations that at least appeared to be sympathetic to the social plight of black Americans.

America in the 1960s became a land of gut-wrenching political turmoil on many different fronts. Between the election—and assassination—of President John F. Kennedy, the beginning of the American phase of the Vietnam War (with the concomitant antiwar movement), the rise of a new brand of feminist political activism, and the Civil Rights Movement, America's mainstream had its work cut out for it in attempting to inculcate radical social change. We now rightly consider the Civil Rights Movement in particular as emblematic of the forefront of the nation's changes; it forced America to confront its appalling oppression and brutal failure to live up to its democratic ideals, the same principles that had been the focus of so much African American literature. Equally important, the Civil Rights Movement ushered in a period of national awareness and appreciation of African American politics and culture unparalleled since the Harlem Renaissance. Its grandest victories and most troubling defeats dominated much of the American discourse on race. In the forefront of the public's consciousness were the rhetoric, actions, and posturing of black and white integrationists, Black Nationalists and separatists, white segregationists and racists, white liberals, and many other groups that had a stake in the elimination or preservation of America's racial caste system. Considering "the centrality of race in shaping American politics and culture," as elucidated by Michael Omi and Howard Winant,[1] the debate encompassed most communities, ideologies, and organizations within the American political spectrum.

In fact, since the late 1960s the terms of the intraracial debate over "racial" and cultural identity, the course of black political organizing and action, and the individuals or organizations that constituted the diverse positions within the debate itself all bore a remarkable likeness to those of the 1920s and 1930s. At the simplest level, the debate raged between those who believed in racial integration as the most effective means of obtaining social justice and civil rights, and those who advocated racial separatism or Black Nationalism as the primary means of reaching complete social, political, and economic freedom. As in any serious debate, of course, numerous individuals and groups supported positions that fell between these poles, sometimes combining their rhetoric and ideologies. Despite the basic goals of civil and human rights and political freedoms that the integrationist and nationalist camps shared, some of the most vitriolic discourse passed between those in the extreme corners of this political and cultural scene. Significantly, the type of support given to particular positions could also be mapped out along regional and class lines. Black Nationalism's strongest support, for example, generally came from the Northern, urban segment of black communities, whereas integration had some of its strongest support among and appealed most often to the disenfranchised Southern African American. The class factor substantially heightened existing conflicts between the two poles, however, as lower-class blacks began to view the middle class as that portion of the community that sought to escape its less fortunate brethren, whether for moral or social reasons. The middle class, on the other hand, tended to view the lower classes as the people who could potentially disrupt or destroy efforts to appeal to the government and the rest of society to implement and enforce civil rights laws and integrative policies, due to their alleged inability or unwillingness to assimilate. This conflict within the black community was not isolated from the rest of society, inasmuch as most of the discussion and arguing occurred in public, via debates between integrationists such as Dr. Martin Luther King Jr. and Ralph Abernathy and such nationalists as Malcolm X, Elijah Muhammad, and, later, Stokely Carmichael.

King, of course, has become an icon of recent American history for his leadership within the larger Civil Rights movement. Both he and Abernethy were crucial figures working for

---

1. Michael Omi and Howard Winant, *Racial Transformation in the United States: From the 1960s to the 1980s* (New York: Routledge, 1986), 6.

the full dismantling of legal segregation and the integration of African Americans into all levels of American life via the Southern Christian Leadership Conference. In contrast, Black Nationalists argued that the very nature of racism (and, in the case of the Nation of Islam, the supposed nature of whites themselves) practically ensured that the overwhelming majority of African Americans would never be allowed to integrate fully into America. Even if this were possible, the argument went, integration into the American cultural and political mainstream amounted to racial suicide or an attempt to jump onto a national ship rapidly sinking from its own corruption, a corruption stemming from its long practice of racial oppression. It would therefore be futile to fight for integration, which seemed to insult the possibility that African Americans could establish and operate their own businesses, schools, community councils, and cultural apparatuses (artistic and publishing ventures, galleries, dramatic troupes and production companies, and the like). Black Nationalists of the 1960s offered instead a call for racial pride that simultaneously echoed strongly and openly honored the example that Marcus Garvey had offered two generations earlier.

The foremost among these in the popular imagination was Malcolm X, who, as the leading minister of the Nation of Islam religious sect (NOI), made frequent appearances on radio and television in the early 1960s, excoriating the leadership, strategies, and goals of the mainstream Civil Rights movement. Malcolm X and other Black Nationalists found the movement's philosophy of nonviolence and its strategic stance in favor of integration too slow and lacking any appreciation of the particular needs of African Americans living in Northern cities, where poverty, unemployment (or underemployment), urban decay, and de facto segregation were more immediate threats to millions of African Americans than the strict, de jure segregation of the South. Malcolm X focused primarily upon racism's effects upon Northern black communities, often through searing indictments of those white and black leaders who appeared either hypocritical or ineffective in terms of their ability to give African Americans dignity and economic independence through the Nation of Islam's program of black pride, thrift, business economics, and racial separatism. This program called as well for African Americans to reject all forms of mainstream political activity—rallying, voting, lobbying, and nonviolent direct action—as irrelevant. This policy made it easier for intragroup rivals to drum Malcolm X out of the NOI after he made pointed remarks about the assassination of President John F. Kennedy, although his ouster had more to do with these rivalries and alleged disloyalty than his insensitivity. Malcolm X then established the Muslim Mosque, Inc., and the Organization of Afro-American Unity (OAAU), modeled after the Organization of African Unity, whose goal was to unite African American groups and leaders for the complete liberation of African Americans from racist oppression and the implementation of full human rights. Although the OAAU never completely got off the ground, when Malcolm X was assassinated on February 21, 1965, he became an instant martyr for Black Nationalism and, by the 1980s, a major cultural icon.

Perhaps most important, the politics and principles Malcolm X espoused and his public persona inspired countless black writers and intellectuals to begin working more assiduously for African Americans' artistic independence. Poet, playwright, and critic LeRoi Jones (who later changed his name to Amiri Baraka), for example, was so moved by Malcolm's assassination that he left his bohemian life in New York's Greenwich Village for Harlem, where he founded the Black Arts Repertory Theater/School, which in turn attracted the talents of such artists as poet Clarence Reed, critic Larry Neal, and musicians and bandleaders Sun Ra and Albert Ayler. It should be noted, though, that LeRoi Jones's artistic vision was also inspired by novelist and critic James Baldwin, whose play *Blues for Mister Charlie* (1964) was a hard-hitting indictment of the current state of race relations. The play also embodied many of the viewpoints espoused by King and Malcolm X and gave Jones many of the ideas used in his own Obie Award–winning play, *The Dutchman*, which premiered barely a month after Baldwin's play opened on Broadway.

One thread runs through all of these events: African American art and politics often inspired each other. The foundation of Jones's Black Arts Repertory Theater/School, which effectively began the Black Arts movement in earnest, meant that African American literature and art would be asked once again to integrate creative ambitions with political ones, although different writers and artists would take different positions within vivid contemporary debates about black life. At the base of these debates were many questions about the popular understanding of black identity and the future of African Americans in a nation that repeatedly revoked the promise of democracy every time it was tentatively offered. That is, how would black people identify themselves from that moment *for* themselves and vis-à-vis the nation? What would be the advantages or disadvantages of a particular sort of identification? If black people perceived themselves as a group that should hold itself apart from the rest of society to form cohesive bonds among themselves, how would that affect their social and economic position? If, conversely, black people attempted to integrate with and possibly assimilate into mainstream American society, would that result in the advancement or destruction of black communities?

These questions were not merely academic; in the late 1960s and early 1970s, African Americans, along with Latinos/Hispanics and poor whites, were being drafted into the United States armed forces and sent to fight in the brutal and unpopular war in Vietnam, where they were maimed and killed in grossly disproportionate numbers and, like so many other veterans returning to the United States, suffered psychologically from their experiences and became addicted to various narcotics. The effect of the war and its psychological aftermath upon black communities was nothing short of devastating, as it saw a substantial portion of an entire generation of youths, many of whom were former or potential community leaders, destroyed physically and mentally. In addition, the violence of the uprisings or riots of the "long, hot summers" of the mid-1960s and after the assassination of Martin Luther King Jr. on April 4, 1968, combined with frequent incidences of police brutality and the government's well-documented surveillance of militant black groups (see the entry on the Black Panther Party for Self-Defense) convinced many African American intellectuals that integration was not only unwise but virtually impossible, as the nation seemed to have declared war on African Americans. Some African American authors saw all of these events as closely connected ways to destroy or drain the spirit of liberation that defined the Civil Rights movement at its best moments. This led many African American authors to write about the conflict in either direct or oblique ways. John A. Williams's *Captain Blackman* (1972), Toni Morrison's *Sula* (1974) and *Song of Solomon* (1978), Ishmael Reed's *Mumbo Jumbo* (1972) and *Flight to Canada* (1976), and Walter Dean Myers's young-adult novel *Fallen Angels* (1989) all make explicit or implicit, symbolic references to the impact of the period's events upon black communities.

The terms of the intraracial debate over racial/cultural identity and the course of black political organizing and action (as well as the parties and organizations who argued for and against specific terms and actions) were remarkably similar to those of earlier decades. Significantly, the type of support given to particular positions could be mapped out along class lines as well; a great deal of Black Nationalism's support came from the disenfranchised (and often urban) component of black communities, whereas integration appealed most often to middle-class black people, though many blacks of the working class and below lent their political support to integration as well. In the writings and work of black artists in particular, though, the debates of the 1960s centered on questions of images and aesthetics that were, according to Hoyt W. Fuller, "about the business of destroying those images and myths that have crippled and degraded black people, and the institution of new images and myths that will liberate them." The "business" of which Fuller wrote was the Black Arts Movement, with its Black Aesthetic school of thought, which rejected the notion that black culture was forever inferior to or dependent on European-centered aesthetics. The Black Arts Movement argued that adherence to such aesthetics was ultimately destructive to blacks of all nationalities, as it required a repudiation of the inherent value of the peoples and cultures of the African Diaspora. According to such critics as Addison Gayle, Amiri Baraka/LeRoi Jones, and Larry Neal, the responsibility of the black artist was to use the word, to use language as a tool invested with the power to transform ideas generated by black people into action, especially revolutionary action.

This new set of narratives was devoted to elevating the most valuable and cherished aspects of the African American and criticizing those who would stand in the way of black progress and empowerment. In essence, then, the Black Arts Movement perceived itself as a direct advocate of the black masses and a staunch adversary to any agency that upheld oppressive stereotypes, whether that agency originated within or outside black communities. Not every African American author subscribed to all the tenets of the Black Aesthetic; Ralph Ellison was perhaps the most famous author to refuse to embrace it, which brought him a great deal of scorn from younger authors. Ellison's refusal was grounded in his belief that "there is an American Negro idiom, a style and a way of life, but none of this is inseparable from the conditions of American society, nor from its general modes or culture," which directly contradicted Black Aesthetic critics' basic assumption of African American difference.[1] Yet the politics that spawned the Black Aestheic influenced a wide sampling of black artists, young and old, including Ishmael Reed, Hal Bennett, William Melvin Kelley, Cecil Brown, and John Oliver Killens. Such younger poets as Nikki Giovanni, Sonia Sanchez, Haki R. Madhubuti (né Don L. Lee), Etheridge Knight, and Jayne Cortez worked to represent the pains of black ghetto life and black life in general, while Gwendolyn Brooks's poetry took on a somewhat more nationalistic tone in the late 1960s.

As Madhu Dubey points out, however, "Black Aesthetic critics, and especially those who wrote on the novel, regarded form as a transparent medium of ideological meaning." The critical problem, then, was that though some 1960s Black Aestheticians were "successfully challenging a formalist aesthetic at one level, by insisting that all art is ideological, Black Aesthetic theorists, by default, allowed the category of form to remain immune and peripheral to the field of ideological analysis." Dubey provides a succinct interpretation and application of Bakhtin's "Discourse in the Novel" as an aid to reading the project of the Black Aesthetic as well as that of black women writers. In Dubey's argument, Black Aestheticians fell into the same trap as the white critics before them of dividing literature among a fallacious form/content split. The problem with the demand for a reflective/realistic aesthetic "is that an exclusive focus on themes helps to maintain the form/content split that usually justifies

1. Ralph Ellison, "Some Questions and Some Answers," in *Shadow and Act* (New York: Vintage, 1995), 271.

a nonideological analysis of literary texts," which was a major failing of white critics. Conversely, a bias toward the content side of this split prevents recognition of the diversity of social and political histories with which specific forms are invested; the realistic, reflective form of literature went relatively unquestioned, becoming an ideal model for all Black art.

Dubey's critique of the Black Aesthetic in her *Black Women Novelists and the Nationalist Aesthetic* is particularly valuable when she demonstrates how even authors heavily influenced by Black Nationalism might simultaneously defy every edict of a nationalist aesthetic yet still be accepted by some of these same nationalists. Dubey offers a piercing example in her recounting of the initial reception of *The Bluest Eye* (1970), by Toni Morrison. Citing Frances Smith Foster's argument that "the prescribed role of black women writers in the . . . 1960s was to destroy negative stereotypes of black women . . . and to affirm the black family and community," Dubey demonstrates that "relationships between black men and women in the novel are driven by violence and sexual perversion." The "black community [in the novel] is equally out of keeping with Black Aesthetic requirements," insofar as it is "committed to white middle-class values, and is divided by color-bias and sexism" and many of the characters are severely pathological, which fits squarely within common stereotypes about African Americans. Yet, Dubey notes, *The Bluest Eye* was among the "most sympathetically received by Black Aesthetic critics," many of whom argued that Morrison's depiction of the destructive nature of "white" values is its most powerful feature, a reading that Morrison encouraged.[1]

Therein lies the contradiction that troubled writers and intellectuals who championed a Black Aesthetic; it was meant to liberate African American authors, critics, and readers from standards that negated African Americans' experiences, yet it was far too easy to accept, excuse, or dismiss an individual work's merits or flaws as the critic saw fit, depending upon his or her particular agenda, rather than see the work as both an artistic and social whole. Moreover, as W. Lawrence Hogue argues, the influence of the Black Aesthetic upon black studies programs and departments or upon faculty in traditional departments who taught African American literature led inevitably to a process of canon formation in which only a small handful of authors and texts were ever discussed at any substantial length in major critical studies.[2]

African American Fiction from 1970 to the Present

The decades following the passage of the Civil Rights legislation in the 1960s and 1970s witnessed enormous and unprecedented transformations in the composition of the African American and mainstream American communities and their respective politics. Economists, political scientists, and sociologists have documented at length the changes within African American communities as de jure Civil Rights and racial integration allowed African Americans greater (though still limited) access to mainstream institutions, professions, and corporations through equal opportunity and affirmative action programs. These new forms of access helped empower a significant portion of African Americans, who

1. Madhu Dubey, *Black Women Novelists and the Nationalist Aesthetic* (Bloomington: Indiana University Press, 1994), 33–34.

2. W. Lawrence Hogue, *The African American Male, Writing, and Difference: A Polycentric Approach to African American Literature, Criticism, and History* (Albany: State University of New York Press, 2003), 42.

quickly found themselves endowed with increased purchasing power and (with the help of antidiscriminatory housing laws) the means to move to the neighborhoods of their choice and to send their children to better schools at the primary, secondary, and college levels in greater numbers than ever before. Thus a new, ever-expanding middle class was created within African American communities. This class's existence, combined with the decidedly antibourgeois slant of Black Nationalism, forced African Americans to try to articulate a new meaning for "race" and its subsequent effects upon black political and economic life, since that life was no longer legally circumscribed, at least not openly.

African American literature has simultaneously absorbed and effected changes in the black political landscape as often and as radically as black people themselves have. Since 1970 in particular, the African American literary tradition has witnessed the ascendance of black women authors, many of whom have helped propel the advancement of African American literary studies overall. Beginning with the Black Studies Department founded in 1968 at San Francisco State College (now San Francisco State University) after extensive student protests, black/Afro-American/African American studies programs and departments grew rapidly at both major and minor universities and colleges nationwide, usually through student-faculty coalitions and activism. Literature of all genres was a foundational component of these programs, with fiction and poetry that supported the Black Nationalism of the Black Arts Movement especially popular. Students of African American history and culture enthusiastically began to rediscover and recover authors who had been locked out of school curricula from kindergarten through Ph.D. programs, and to change American education permanently. The number of black/African American studies programs and departments at American colleges and universities dropped dramatically between 1970 and 1980, with dozens either defunded or absorbed into other departments on their campuses. Nevertheless, as more African American faculty were hired at majority-white institutions in that period, they successfully fought for African American literature courses to be offered regularly and to a lesser, but not insignificant extent, to make study of African American literature part of general American literature courses. Similarly, it is no longer strange for African American fiction to sell hundreds of thousands, even millions of copies, or for the authors and their texts to win awards, fellowships, grants, and internationally renowned prizes. African American fiction is popular reading material and, perhaps most important, has almost become a staple of American university curricula and the subject of hundreds of critical studies. We may even argue, with considerable evidence, that African American literature now possesses a core canon, although, like other literary canons, it is constantly in flux and subject to changes in both cultural climates and taste.

Not surprisingly, the establishment of a canon of sorts has transformed the Black Aesthetic established in the mid-1960s and early 1970s, though it has not necessarily invalidated all of its claims. While the original Black Arts Movement, as the artistic branch of Black Nationalism, was supposed to reflect the masses of African Americans, this particular purpose became more complicated in a black nation that has fractured into several class-divided states. As Madhu Dubey argues, without the "sheer possibility of blackness" that came out of 1960s and 1970s nationalist thought, the focus of contemporary black authors on the black community would be rendered moot; a contemporary text's foregrounding of previously neglected issues more often than not assumes a loosely cohesive black community, albeit one that needs to be more inclusive if it wishes to maintain its cohesion and progress simultaneously.[1] The bonds that would hold such an ideal black community together vary from text to text, but recent African American literature frequently assumes that the term "African American" comprises extremely diverse subject positions—and always has. Rather than relying entirely upon a definition of African American identity that makes the lives and experiences of black males the norm, contemporary African American fiction as a whole affirms the reality of African Americans' experiences even as it reinscribes the experiences of black women, black gays and lesbians, and black people of every class and region as no less "black" because of their differences.

In the works of Alice Walker, for example, we may find examples of her "womanist" aesthetic, which calls for black women to "fearlessly pull out of [themselves] and look at and identify with [their] lives the living creativity" of all black women, especially those rendered nearly voiceless by their class status, and to recognize and recover black women's literature and other forms of creative expression.[2] In pursuit of this aesthetic, Walker was instrumental in reviving the novels of Zora Neale Hurston in the early 1970s, catapulting *Their Eyes Were Watching God* to a new height of celebration for its close attention to women's concerns. Walker's own novels and womanist aesthetic, as well as novels by other black women, especially Toni Morrison, Toni Cade Bambara, Ntozake Shange, Maya Angelou, Gayl Jones, Audre Lorde, Jamaica Kincaid, Gloria Naylor, and J. California Cooper, have helped redefine African American literature so that previously marginalized voices moved to the center. In 1993, when Toni Morrison received the Nobel Prize in Literature, she became the first African American ever to be so honored. Her popular novels—*The Bluest Eye* (1970), *Sula* (1974), *Song of Solomon* (1977), *Tar Baby* (1981), *Beloved* (1987), *Jazz* (1992), and *Paradise* (1996)—combine rich lyricism, the symbolic virtues of modernism, and the politics of the Black Arts Movement for a powerful mix that has made her one of the most frequently studied African American authors in history. Her work as an author and critic helped inspire the career of Gloria Naylor; as an editor at Random House in the 1970s, Morrison helped bring the work of younger African American authors, especially women, into published form. Morrison played a direct hand in the careers of Gayl Jones, Toni Cade Bambara, and Gloria Naylor as editor, mentor, and friend, allowing three major voices of the New Literature to emerge and attract critical attention.

Toni Morrison's role as a pivotal editor in the 1970s highlighted the importance of access to publishers that defined earlier movements in African American literature, most notably the Harlem Renaissance. That movement's success depended largely upon the interest and influence of such new, smaller, and decidedly liberal publishers as Alfred A. Knopf—who has published Morrison's novels from 1970 until the present—and Boni and Liveright. In contrast, African American authors from the 1960s until the present have published with both large, mainstream presses—Doubleday, Random House, MacMillan, Vintage—and smaller presses that have published African American works exclusively: Third World Press, Black Classics Press, and Holloway House. Others, such as Grove, City Lights, or the Free Press, have tended to publish works that mainstream publishers would not, including the

1. Madhu Dubey, *Black Women Novelists and the Nationalist Aesthetic* (Bloomington: Indiana University Press, 1994), 29.

2. Alice Walker, "In Search of Our Mothers' Gardens," in *In Search of Our Mothers' Gardens* (New York: Harcourt Brace, 1983), 237.

speeches of Malcolm X, the writings of Frantz Fanon, and the work of other intellectuals crucial to radical politics in the period.

African American male authors have been no less productive since 1970. Equally as influenced by some precepts of the Black Aesthetic as African American women authors, a new coterie of authors entered into literary canons and found new respectability in the academy. Their work may be classified in any number of ways, ranging from traditionally modernist, to postmodern, to Black Nationalist or Afrocentric. The novels of Leon Forrest—especially *The Bloodworth Orphans* (1977) and *Divine Days* (1992)—and Albert Murray—particularly *Train Whistle Guitar* (1974)—for example, exhibit the influence of their friend Ralph Ellison. Ellison's classic *Invisible Man* may be considered an outgrowth of literary modernism because of its ambiguity, focus upon the inner psyche, extensive allusions to diverse literary traditions and pioneers (particularly Mark Twain, James Joyce, Ernest Hemingway, Fyodor Dostoevsky, and André Malraux), and its attempt to capture the totality of African American experiences through the rhythms and dynamics of such musical forms as the blues and jazz. Both Forrest and Murray take Ellison's cue in all of these respects. John Oliver Killens provided humorous takes on black politics in the early 1970s from a largely nationalistic outlook in which the goals of the Black Aesthetic are most transparent.

On the other hand, Ishmael Reed, Toni Cade Bambara, Clarence Major, Charles Johnson, Toni Morrison, Gayl Jones, and John Edgar Wideman are among the many authors whose work, however widely divergent, has often been described as postmodern, usually because of their tendency to undermine the very genres in which they write and to question the very meaning of such categories as "history" and "truth." Each interrogates traditional ways of constructing narratives and history to highlight how those narratives simultaneously help and hinder our attempts to get at history and experience. The narrator of Toni Morrison's 1992 novel *Jazz*, for example, frequently talks to the reader and doubts her—or its—own ability to tell the story at hand. Many of John Edgar Wideman's novels, including *The Lynchers* (1973), *Philadelphia Fire* (1990), and his Homewood Trilogy (*Damballah* [1981; short stories], *Hiding Place* [1981; novel] and *Sent for You Yesterday* [1983; novel]), tell us about the ways that histories are constructed as much as they tell complexly woven *stories*. In this respect, Wideman is comparable to the late Toni Cade Bambara, whose dense and intricate prose in *Gorilla, My Love* (1972) and *The Salt Eaters* (1980) tells of the wonder and ambiguity in common, everyday lives, while making the reader work for the rich rewards of these inner worlds.

Postmodern African American authors have frequently earned that label for scrutinizing, revising, or subverting popular or foundational genres and authors, particularly the slave narratives and their narrators. The product of their scrutiny has been the neo–slave narrative, which adopts many of the conventions of the slave narratives that defined and dominated early African American literature but uses them to reveal the stories and angles hidden behind the nineteenth-century literary and publication practices to which the original slave narratives had to conform. Many neo–slave narratives emerged in the 1970s as responses, in part, to the controversy surrounding William Styron's *Confessions of Nat Turner* (1967), which numerous African American writers and critics roundly condemned for its questionable reconstruction of slave-insurrectionist Nat Turner's original testimony by focusing upon his imagined psyche and his sexual proclivities. The goal of many neo–slave narratives, then, is to offer a more sympathetic view of enslaved people's lives than Styron seemed to present, using modern literary techniques and understandings of history.

Gayl Jones's *Corregidora* (1975), for instance, reveals the extremes of black women's sexual exploitation under slavery and links it to present-day tensions between men and women, while Ishmael Reed's *Flight to Canada* (1976) seamlessly weaves relatively obscure facts about Harriet Beecher Stowe, the U.S. Civil War, and American and black intellectual politics of the 1970s into a fantastic parody of the conventional slave narrative. Sherley Anne Williams's *Dessa Rose* (1985), Toni Morrison's *Beloved*, and Lorene Cary's *Price of a Child* (1995) use sketches of actual historical events as the bases for powerful novels that reimagine those events, turning them into metaphors for more recent issues in black life. Each of these works has helped broaden our comprehension of a nearly incomprehensible institution; they have also brought immense accolades to African American fiction.

Charles Johnson has also gathered considerable laurels for his heady mix of humor, literary allusion, and philosophy from both Western and Eastern traditions in *Middle Passage* (1990), which won the National Book Award, only the second work by an African American author—*Invisible Man* was the first—to be so honored. His earlier works, *Faith and the Good Thing* (1974), *Oxherding Tale* (1982), and *The Sorceror's Apprentice* (short stories, 1986) fall into the same vein, as does *Dreamer* (1997), a fictional meditation upon the legacy of Dr. Martin Luther King Jr., set in the Civil Rights leader's final days. Most important, this last work shows how the *myth* of King has been created since his assassination, forcing the reader to question whether it was ever possible to know King the person once the icon was created. The defining works of Ishmael Reed and Clarence Major were also genre-crossing and experimental fiction that challenged conventional narrative forms and trends. Reed's *Mumbo Jumbo* (1972), its quasi-sequel *The Last Days of Louisiana Red* (1974), and *Flight to Canada* (1976) each won acclaim and controversy for their satirical views of literary trends and contemporary politics, while Major's *NO* (1973), *Reflex and Bone Structure* (1975), and *Emergency Exit* (1979) completely upset normal reader expectations in terms of their structure and ways of constructing meaning out of their fragmented, episodic formats. In the 1980s and 1990s, Reed and Major began to limit some of the formal innovations of their earlier fiction, but both remained committed to narratives that were political or artistic challenges. Reed's novels *The Terrible Twos* (1982), *Reckless Eyeballing* (1985), *The Terrible Threes* (1987), and *Japanese by Spring* (1992) satirize American politics and current events in African American intellectual and literary life. Major's short story collection *Fun and Games* (1990) and novels *Painted Turtle* (1988), *Such Was the Season* (1987), and *Dirty Bird Blues* (1996) combine experimentalism with Major's deep interest in the place of the blues in African American culture.

Since the 1960s and 1970s, respectively, Samuel R. Delany and Octavia Butler have had brilliant careers as authors of complex science fiction, and their work has won most of that genre's major awards, including the Hugo and Nebula. Each also received all-too-little attention in African American critical circles as part of the tradition of African American fiction in their early years, despite the fact that both frequently published works that offered some of the most sophisticated treatments of issues of race and sexuality. This relative dearth of attention may be explained by the fact that science fiction from African American authors had previously been extremely rare and therefore offered very little context for contemporary critics. In other words, science fiction had previously been considered a largely "white" genre, one closed to most African American authors, despite the tradition of allegorizing racial issues within the field since at least the 1940s. Butler and Delany took this tradition in new directions over their careers, with Butler's Patternist series (1976–1984) and Delany's *Dhalgren* (1975), *Triton* (1977), and Return to Nevèrÿon series (1979–1987), all of which explored the intersections of race, gender, and sexuality through frequently experimental narratives. By the 1990s, both had had all or part of individual issues of major literary journals devoted to criticism concerning their work. Delany was featured in the fall 1996 issue of the *Review of Contemporary Fiction*, and Butler in the winter 1993 issue of *Utopian Studies*. Both were the most prominent authors studied in *Black American Literature Forum*'s special Science Fiction issue (summer 1984).

In the 1980s and 1990s, publishers' interest in African American authors had become keener, as both African American literature and African American literary studies dramatically changed. By the time Johnson Publications shut the doors of its literary-critical magazine *Black World* in 1976, many of the same scholars and thinkers who had developed the Black Aesthetic that the magazine had helped champion were calling it into question. African American women writers now dominated the literary scene, expanding the roster of popularly read and taught African American authors. Prior to the late 1970s, a course on African American literature would rarely move beyond Frederick Douglass, James Weldon Johnson, Richard Wright, Ralph Ellison, James Baldwin, and Gwendolyn Brooks. By 1980, such a course would be more likely to include Toni Morrison, Alice Walker, Zora Neale Hurston, poets Sonia Sanchez and Nikki Giovanni, and other women.

This development was inarguably aided by the rapid inroads that both African American women and men were making into the academy, where they began reinterpreting African American history via feminist, Black Nationalist, gay/lesbian/bisexual, formalist, poststructuralist, New Historicist, Marxist, and many other critical lenses. In addition, such authors as Virginia Hamilton, Rosa Guy, Walter Dean Myers, June Jordan, and Mildred Taylor were regularly winning awards for children's or young-adult fiction that portrayed African American lives positively. Toni Morrison's landmark *Song of Solomon* had won the National Book Critics Circle Award for fiction in 1978. African American authors from previous decades who had been largely neglected, such as Zora Neale Hurston, Nella Larsen, and Jessie Redmon Fauset, had been brought back into print, giving a new generation of readers access to great forgotten works of African American fiction and coincidentally helping African American literary studies to grow. *Negro American Literature Forum* had changed its name in 1977 to *Black American Literature Forum* to reflect the fact that black scholars could extend their work beyond the foundational task of recovering and validating African American history to applying developments within contemporary critical theory to African American literature, in addition to some of the precepts of the Black Aesthetic.[1] Despite coming under attack almost immediately after founding them in the late 1960s and early 1970s, hundreds of American universities still retained black studies programs and departments, giving millions of students potential access to African American history and literature. On an everyday level, the dismantling of legal segregation and the institution of such antidiscrimination policies as affirmative action helped expand the black middle class—those making the American median income or above—from a tiny minority of African Americans prior to the Civil Rights movement to over one-third of the black population of the United States, although African Americans' income remained behind the national median.[2]

1. Joe Weixlmann, "The Way We Were, the Way We Are, the Way We Hope to Be," *Black American Literature Forum* 20, nos. 1–2 (Spring–Summer 1986): 4.

2. Schomburg Center for Research in Black Culture, *The New York Public Library African American Desk Reference* (New York: Wiley, 1999), 258, table 9.7.

The year 1980 also brought a marked shift in racial politics that had its roots in the conflicts of the 1960s and 1970s. When the United States Supreme Court ruled in the *Regents of the University of California v. Bakke* case in 1978, it outlawed strict quotas that employers and educational institutions had put in place to help redress decades of overt discrimination. It also signaled a shift in American attitudes toward racial equality that would reach their high point when Ronald Reagan was elected president of the United States in 1980. For millions of African Americans, Reagan's election portended a backlash against the Civil Rights movement and the affirmative action policies that had its origins in the 1960s. Reagan openly courted conservative Southern white voters who resented legal and economic gains African Americans had made and the loss of legal white supremacy. While the issue of race was far from the only issue that ushered Reagan into office, it certainly played a role in his election and in the policies his administration enacted to roll back many of the changes of the Civil Rights movement and the liberal social policies of previous administrations. The political and social gains that African Americans had obtained during or with the aid of the Lyndon B. Johnson administration's Great Society programs were under attack at the same time that new threats began to hit African American communities: the debilitating recession of 1981; HIV/AIDS, which affected African Americans well out of proportion with the general population; the crack, or rock cocaine epidemic and the concomitant "War on Drugs" that led to skyrocketing incarceration rates for African Americans in the nation's prisons; cuts in Aid to Families with Dependent Children (AFDC) or welfare and similar programs; the loss of jobs and infrastructure in the inner cities; and so on. Many African American intellectuals laid these problems squarely at the feet of the Reagan administration and its policy of benign neglect.

Some African American authors in the 1980s, particularly Samuel R. Delany, Alice Walker, and Ishmael Reed, did try to take account of the immediate effects of the Reagan administration's policies in their fiction and essays. Delany's *Return to Nevèrÿon* (1987) is commonly read as the first novel ever written specifically about the AIDS crisis. The opening pages of Ishmael Reed's *Terrible Twos* (1982) indict the decade's materialism in particular, while his most controversial novel, *Reckless Eyeballing* (1985), accuses black feminists of collaborating with the forces of oppression—in Reed's view, white feminists and powerful racists in general—for the sake of material gain. In the same vein—albeit lacking Reed's critique of feminism—Gloria Naylor's *Linden Hills* (1985) creates a Dantean allegory that questions whether the expansion and enrichment of the black middle class in the 1970s and, to a lesser extent, the 1980s came at the cost of its very soul.

The majority of African American authors in the 1980s, however, were less explicitly political in terms of interrogating the administration in the White House. The artistic goals of the 1970s still captivated new and old authors, especially desires to recover lost stories within African American history, to help create a stronger, more complex black identity, and to explore the possible long term effects of the Civil Rights and Black Power eras upon African America as a whole. This last goal resonated widely as the first generation to grow up without the specter of a seemingly intractable, wholly visible, and thoroughly legal segregation came of age. This younger generation, born since the modern Civil Rights era began with the *Brown v. Board of Education of Topeka, Kansas* decision of 1954 and the ascendance of Martin Luther King Jr. as a leader, came of age in a nation transformed by the legacy of social protest, but it did not always perceive or appreciate the breadth of the changes. The iconic black political heroes of the 1960s were either dead (King, Malcolm X,

Elijah Muhammad, Medgar Evers), had fallen out of the public spotlight, often due to harassment by the government (Huey P. Newton, Elaine Brown, Stokely Carmichael, H. Rap Brown), or had moved into less obviously sensational phases of their lives and careers (Angela Y. Davis, Black Panther Party founders Newton and Bobby Seale, and many others). Political leaders and figures still played key roles in African American politics, of course, as the career of the Civil Rights leader Reverend Jesse Jackson demonstrates. The former lieutenant of Martin Luther King Jr., present when his mentor was assassinated in 1968, made two celebrated bids for the presidency of the United States, in 1984 and 1988, both of which helped galvanize the African American community.

Jackson's political ambitions, however, did not alter the fact that the central problem of the 1980s was how African American life was being marked by greater ambivalence and ambiguity in the absence of Jim Crow; in fact, they threw this situation into relief. This ambiguity, which Charles T. Banner-Haley lists among the "fruits of integration," was embodied in African American literature as an ever-shifting postmodernism.[1] These texts question the way Western versions of history have been constructed, and by whom; revise, update, or parody such traditional literary forms as the travel narrative, slave narrative, romance, and tragedy for the purpose of expanding these forms or showing how they have limited African American forms of expression; and construct experimental texts that dispense with many literary conventions, including linear plots, rules about the mechanical arrangement of text and other media, and the obligation of the author to help the reader construct meaning. Postmodernism was not new to black writers in the 1980s; Clarence Major, Ishmael Reed, Toni Morrison, Ntozake Shange, Samuel R. Delany, and Leon Forrest had already pushed generic limits, with Major arguably the most radically experimental of all. Their fiction consciously resisted easy or linear interpretations, often questioning the boundaries of its own composition and existence, or at least the integrity of the plots and the identities of their characters. African American literature could protest and challenge through its rhetorical stridence, but it was also becoming a site for an expanding artistic freedom as it refused ghettoization.

In the 1980s, this social and artistic ambiguity in black texts merged into a complex, sometimes controversial new state of the arts. The first major defining moment was arguably the publication of Alice Walker's Pulitzer Prize–winning novel *The Color Purple* (1983) and its subsequent transformation into a major motion picture directed by Steven Spielberg. With the film's images often overpowering the novel's complexities, African Americans were split roughly between those who admired Walker for exposing the history of sexual and physical abuse that countless black women had endured and those who believed the film denigrated African American men in general. The controversy was arguably the apex of tensions wrought by the rise of black women authors in the 1970s, as it revealed deep resentment and fears of the new power and influence that these women had finally won through their art. Lost in the furor at times was Walker's masterpiece itself, an epistolary novel in which the protagonist, Celie, tells her story through letters to God and to her beloved sister, Nettie. Celie's story forced readers and viewers to consider gender roles, sexuality, and modern African history in a fluid blend of imaginative lyricism and overtly political messages. Most important of all, Walker helped convince thousands of African American women to take a

---

1. Charles T. Banner-Haley, *The Fruits of Integration: Black Middle-Class Ideology and Culture, 1960–1990* (Jackson: University Press of Mississippi, 1994), xi–xii.

greater interest in literature, paving the way for the massive success of Terry McMillan's *Waiting to Exhale* (1992) nearly a decade later. Walker's novels, short stories, and essays became the foundation of many hundreds of scholarly theses and dissertations, books, and conference panels. Walker also revived interest in the works of Zora Neale Hurston, who had fallen almost completely out of the public eye since her death in 1961. She has been an exemplar of other womanists—black feminists who steadfastly embrace both their ethnic and gender identities—in her determination to show the more intimate sides of black lives as she champions political causes (fighting racism within the women's movement, banning clitoridectomies and genital mutilation, and black sexuality, among others) and tells the hidden stories that a white-male-centered and -driven world frequently silences.

By the late 1980s, and particularly after the publication of her landmark novel *Beloved*, Toni Morrison had become arguably the most important figure in contemporary African American literature due to a number of key factors: her consummate skill in bringing stories of African American women from the background of history into its foreground; the mellifluous lyricism of her prose; the complexities of her characters and plots; a burgeoning interest in feminism in the academy, which owed some of its momentum to Alice Walker's popularity; a growing interest in slavery and other complex or neglected periods and events in African American history; and the combined efforts of scholars of African American literature to establish a canon of literature of the African Diaspora. *Beloved* addressed all of these interests through its revision of the story of Margaret Garner, a refugee from slavery who, in 1857, slew two of her own children rather than see them returned to bondage. When the novel won the Pulitzer Prize for Fiction in 1988, the high esteem with which Morrison was regarded in academic circles was both affirmed and extended via one of the most prestigious awards in American letters. This award helped pave the way for one of the crowning achievements of the contemporary period: the Nobel Prize in Literature awarded to Morrison in 1993.

Alice Walker's and Toni Morrison's success and artistically pathbreaking works of the 1980s were directly responsible for emboldening and establishing the careers of J. California Cooper and Gloria Naylor and helped the enthusiastic critical and commercial reception that greeted the late masterpieces of Paule Marshall (*Praisesong for the Widow* [1983], *Reena and Other Stories* [1983], *Daughters* [1991], and *The Fisher King* [2000]) and Sherley Anne Williams (*Dessa Rose*). Similar to Morrison and Walker, all of these authors created novels in which the narrators often frame their stories in informal, colloquial language, thereby demonstrating the validity of different voices in creating or re-creating African American history.

The late 1980s and 1990s also yielded a number of newer, younger authors whose work, whether influenced by the work of previous generations of African American and white writers or such cultural phenomena as hip-hop, is already carving out a new niche in the African American literary tradition. Novelists Paul Beatty, Trey Ellis, Bebe Moore Campbell, Darryl Pinckney, Walter Mosley, Terry McMillan, Danzy Senna, Colson Whitehead, and Darius James have all had a part in reshaping contemporary African American literature into a "New Renaissance" in African American literature harkening back to and exceeding the Harlem Renaissance of the 1910s through the 1930s in terms of its intellectualism, popularity, and influence. McMillan and Mosley's popular fictions have helped spur widespread interest in African American fiction, thus feeding what Trey Ellis called in 1989 a "New Black Aesthetic," which would leave black artists and writers free to pursue artistic projects that reflect all of their influences, rather than enthralled to a single, overarching vision of "blackness" or black progress.[1]

Ellis's definition of the New Black Aesthetic takes equally from Langston Hughes's declaration of artistic independence nearly sixty-five years earlier in "The Negro Artist and the Racial Mountain" and the many debates over the responsibilities of African American artists to their community that have dominated African American literary criticism ever since, but especially those of the 1960s and 1970s. To paraphrase Henry Louis Gates Jr.'s preface to Greg Tate's *Flyboy in the Buttermilk*, New Black Aestheticians feel but resist "the temptation to romanticize black culture [and] can parody black nationalism because [they have] a real measure of sympathy for it." By the same token, these artists and intellectuals have also learned too much from feminism, the gay rights movement, other liberation struggles, and their own immersion in the complexities of black culture either to "apologize" for it or to excuse the fallacies of its past proponents.[2]

Ellis's argument in "The New Black Aesthetic" stems from the fact that one segment of the first generation of African Americans born during or after the modern Civil Rights Movement—the "Post-Soul" generation—has benefited from the new opportunities that the movement engendered by learning how to move between two cultures: the dominant, or "white," defined by rock 'n' roll music and Caucasian cultural and literary icons; and "black," as defined by rap and hip-hop, jazz, African American literature and history, and so on. The healthy "cultural mulattoes," the core of the NBA, are sufficiently "torn between two worlds to finally go out and create [their] own" (236). Ellis's generation comprises African Americans who find themselves with unprecedented access to middle-class privileges, employment opportunities, and cultural cachet. In fact, the very goal of New Black Aestheticians is to show the degree to which African Americans have already given their "message to the world" or, more accurately, to the world's culture.

The popularity of African American literature in the twentieth century's last two decades ensured that this message would spread rapidly. Terry McMillan played an essential role in this regard as both an author and editor. Her 1990 collection of contemporary African American writing, *Breaking Ice*, remains one of the finest anthologies ever assembled and was a popular hit upon its initial publication. McMillan's breakthrough novel, *Waiting to Exhale* (1992), however, irrevocably changed the way that publishers regarded African Americans as authors and readers. This frequently comic novel about four middle-class black women searching for love and personal peace became a runaway bestseller among American readers of all backgrounds almost overnight and spawned an ever-growing and lucrative trend of novels focusing upon relationships and romance. McMillan used the novel's momentum to leverage a lucrative contract and develop it into an equally popular film, which in turn led to a chart-topping soundtrack album. McMillan's example inspired dozens of African American authors, including Tina McElroy Ansa, Connie Briscoe, Eric Jerome Dickey, E. Lynn Harris, and Sheneska Jackson, to begin writing in the same genre. These novels are often referred to as "Sister Novels" because of their casts of smart, sassy black women and their appeal to a cross-section of upwardly mobile African American women and quite a few men.

1. Trey Ellis, "The New Black Aesthetic," *Callaloo* 12, no. 1 (Winter 1989): 233–46.

2. Henry Louis Gates Jr., foreword to *Flyboy in the Buttermilk: Essays on Contemporary America*, by Greg Tate (New York: Simon & Schuster, 1992), 14.

The authors who create this popular fiction exist alongside their established elders on bookstore shelves but in many cases are marketed quite differently from those who came before them, particularly if they follow the newest trends. For the better part of the 1990s, it was difficult to find novels by and about African American women that did not have cover art echoing Synthia Saint James's dust jacket painting for *Waiting to Exhale*—until McMillan published her next novel, *How Stella Got Her Groove Back* (1996), which spawned its own imitators.

Publishers' advertising campaigns could be equally confusing, as hundreds of books that discussed male-female romantic relationships as but one of many issues suddenly found publishers casting them with the Sister Novel genre, regardless of the content. The novice reader of African American fiction would understandably have a difficult time separating the critically acclaimed artist from the more accessible young lion, if she or he wished to do so. A major grassroots solution to this problem was the book-club phenomenon that swept the nation in the middle of the 1990s, in which people from disparate backgrounds would gather to read and discuss a book assigned to the group. In African American communities in particular, such clubs exploded after *Waiting to Exhale* made more black women and men curious about the literature that people who looked like them were writing. It began to change the demographics of the readership for African American fiction. Throughout American history, the majority of the audience for African American literature has always been nonblack, largely because Caucasians are in the majority and are almost exclusively in control of the publishing industry. African Americans, of course, have always read and been supportive of African American authors. These same authors, however, have faced the same problem that Langston Hughes noted regarding the Harlem Renaissance: "The ordinary Negroes hadn't heard of the Negro Renaissance. And if they had, it hadn't raised their wages any."[1] In other words, African American fiction writers have but rarely enjoyed popular success among African Americans unless, as in the case of Donald Goines in the 1960s and 1970s, they publish with small presses that are marketed to and geared entirely towards representing the lives of the "ordinary Negroes."

These trends continued throughout the 1990s as both authors and publishers continued to feed a growing demand from African American audiences for fiction that reflected the realities of living in the 1990s along the lines of Ellis's New Black Aesthetic. Today, such popular authors as April Sinclair, E. Lynn Harris, Eric Jerome Dickey, Benilde Little, and David Haynes continue to plot novels with similarly middle-class protagonists searching for personal fulfillment and love in an era in which both seem all too fleeting. By the latter half of the 1990s, more authors were moving their foci to other directions in some of the more challenging fiction in recent times. Those challenges could range from characterization and language to formal innovation and philosophical sophistication. The novels *Push* (1996) by Sapphire and *The Coldest Winter Ever* (1999) by Sister Souljah, and most of Jess Mowry's novels throughout the decade (especially *Way Past Cool* [1992]) featured protagonists from America's inner cities that disturb the normal definition of the sympathetic lead. Each author took numerous cues from Richard Wright, to the extent that their characters are meant to discomfit the reader through their heavy use of dialect and current slang. Their protagonists struggle with horrific social ills, including teenage pregnancy, drugs, violence, and despair,

---

1. Langston Hughes, *The Big Sea* (1940; New York: Thunder's Mouth, 1986), 228.

but these novels also suggest that some of the problems within their young characters' lives may find their solutions in a greater faith in and reliance upon communal ties.

The New Black Aesthetic/Post-Soul generation is equally exciting in its formal experimentation. In characteristically postmodern gestures, such newer authors as Jeffery Renard Allen, Melvin Dixon, Edwidge Danticat, Percival Everett, Randall Kenan, James Earl Hardy, Paul Beatty, Darius James, Danzy Senna, and Colson Whitehead try to cross generic boundaries by infusing their narratives with more irony and satire or by incorporating complex philosophical issues that implicitly or explicitly question what African American fiction is. One such example may be found in the work of Percival Everett, who has been publishing critically acclaimed novels and short stories since 1983 but only began receiving widespread recognition with 1999's *Glyph*, simultaneously a spoof of contemporary philosophy and an homage to Laurence Sterne's *Tristram Shandy* (1761). His next novel, *Erasure* (2001), a quasi-autobiographical satire on the contemporary African American literary scene (particularly Sapphire's *Push*), garnered even higher praise, ironically for contributing to the very same scene it ridiculed. Colson Whitehead's widely acclaimed debut novel *The Intuitionist* (1999) is an allegorical meditation upon race, politics, national identity, contemporary critical theory, and the Civil Rights movement's legacy of integration, while its successor, *John Henry Days* (2001) ambitiously reworks the legend of the African American folk hero in its title into a parable for contemporary times. This novel helped earn Whitehead a MacArthur Foundation "Genius" grant in 2002. Jeffery Renard Allen's debut, *Rails Under My Back* (2000), tells an ambitious, epic story of a black family's migration to and from Chicago's South Side over the course of the twentieth century, making Allen one of the most significant African American authors writing on the Windy City since Richard Wright and, in terms of his style and scope, a potential heir to Wright's friend and protégé, Ralph Ellison. Darius James's *Negrophobia* (1992) and Paul Beatty's *White Boy Shuffle* (1996) and *Tuff* (2000) hilariously spoof the crisis in African American leadership of the last thirty years, while Danzy Senna's *Caucasia* (1998) updates and critiques the "tragic mulatto" narrative of a century ago by pointedly removing the tragedy. As a result, Senna is free to create a bildungsroman—a novel of personal growth—that looks carefully at developments in African American life and culture since the 1970s.

Fiction by and about black gay males also made significant impressions upon the African American literary scene in the 1990s. Melvin Dixon's *Vanishing Rooms* (1991), James Earl Hardy's *B-Boy Blues* (1994), Randall Kenan's *Let the Dead Bury the Dead* (1992), and the novels of E. Lynn Harris, particularly his debut *Invisible Life* (1994), each offered some of the most well-received, popular, and often innovative fiction of the period and, via their subject matter, breached one of the long-standing barriers in African American culture and literature. While fiction by or about homosexual black males had certainly appeared in earlier decades—Richard Bruce Nugent's "Smoke, Lilies, and Jade" (1926), Wallace Thurman's *Infants of the Spring* (1934), James Baldwin's *Giovanni's Room* (1956), Hal Bennett's *Lord of Dark Places* (1970), and Samuel R. Delany's *Return to Nevèrÿon* series (1979–1987) being some of the most notable examples—it was only in the 1990s that this subject became more acceptable to a reading public that had not been accustomed to black gay male sexuality. This acceptance owed nearly equal debts to the authors' artistic skills and to generally changing attitudes towards gays and lesbians in American society and to the AIDS crisis that continued to devastate both gay and African American communities in the 1990s. In terms of commercial success, Harris was by far the leader among this group, but all have been the recipients of great critical acclaim and widespread attention in lay and academic circles.

Most of the authors named above wrote from what may be called a Post-Soul viewpoint, often without as heavy an artistic burden as the novels of the previous generation. This is not to imply that Post-Soul artists are any less sophisticated or committed to their art or politics; rather, it is to argue that they are generally less concerned with any single artistic or political agenda than they are with creating art that is true to the enormous complexities of their times and their generation.

Yet the Post-Soul movement is no more the final definition of its era's art than was the Black Arts Movement in the 1960s and 1970s. More established authors, such as Toni Morrison, Charles Johnson, Gayl Jones, Gloria Naylor, and Alice Walker published some of their more challenging and exciting works in the 1990s. Although neither Morrison's *Jazz* (1992) nor *Paradise* (1997) have yet received the same voluminous scholarly treatment or high praise as her earlier *Beloved*, *Song of Solomon*, and *The Bluest Eye*, they helped bring more readers to the fold as they were featured on Oprah Winfrey's Book Club and, in the case of *Beloved*, developed into a major (albeit unsuccessful) motion picture. In 1998, Gayl Jones ended a twenty-year hiatus from the public eye and literary attention by publishing *The Healing* and later *Mosquito* (1999), a seriocomic, epic travel narrative that relies upon dramatic—and often hilarious—shifts in narrative voice. Posthumously, with the help of their respective friends and editors Toni Morrison and John Callahan, the epic, flawed masterpieces on which Toni Cade Bambara and Ralph Ellison had long labored were presented to receptive, albeit mixed reviews. The appearance of Bambara's *Those Bones are Not My Child* (2000) and Ellison's *Juneteenth* (1999) were each greeted with considerable fanfare, but the publication of Ellison's novel in particular became a media event due to the nearly fifty-year gap between *Juneteenth* and his classic *Invisible Man*. At issue as well was the fact that Ellison never actually completed his second novel; the work that Callahan presented to the world was the editor's best attempt—with the blessing of Ellison's widow, Fanny—to make sense of thousands of manuscript and typescript pages, notes, tangents, incomplete episodes, and other ephemera that Ellison had accumulated over forty years of work, using his knowledge of Ellison's artistic vision and philosophical outlook. In both Bambara's and Ellison's cases, the results of their editors' efforts were hailed for their ability to capture the authors' ambitions even as they were lamented for the necessary flaws that arise from shaping an author's work posthumously. Nevertheless, each novel stands as a very worthy conclusion to a distinguished career.

By the time Bambara's and Ellison's final novels became part of the literary scene at the end of the century and the beginning of a new millennium, the epic scope contained within them had become unusual in African American fiction. The current African American fiction scene is as diverse as ever, but the surge of popular fiction that arose after Terry McMillan's success is now the dominant trend, comprising the overwhelming majority of fiction written and bought by a public hungry for narratives that affirm their experiences and ideals. This marketplace of ideas has made for rich opportunities for the reader interested in contemporary African American fiction, but its diversity has also complicated the goal of separating different genres and styles among the fiction for the novice reader. As the preface indicates, the *Columbia Guide to Contemporary African American Fiction, 1970–2000*, is meant to provide the reader with the means to make such separations, to help make distinctions between works of children's and young-adult fiction, experimental novels, short stories, science and speculative fiction, popular Sister Novels, and other genres clearer. It is my hope that this *Guide* will give the authors, movements, institutions, and ideas the respect and consideration they are due and that the reader will join me in admiring one of the most astoundingly fruitful periods in African American literary history.

A–Z Guide to Contemporary African American Fiction

A

African American Review (formerly *Negro American Literature Forum* [1967–76] and *Black American Literature Forum* [1976–1991]) *African American Review* is the official publication of the Modern Language Association's Division on African American Literature and Culture. It rivals *Callaloo* for the title of the top scholarly journal of African American literature. It was first published as a newsletter for public school and university teachers under the auspices of editor John F. Bayliss of Indiana State University in August 1967 as *Negro American Literature Forum*. It changed its name to *Black American Literature Forum* in 1976 and again to *African American Review* in 1992. It remained at Indiana State University for many years with Joe Weixlmann at the helm but is now at St. Louis University. *African American Review* is published quarterly and consists primarily of critical articles on major African American, Afro-Caribbean, and African texts and authors, in that order. Submissions for essays, interviews, poetry, fiction, and book reviews are accepted from scholars in the arts, humanities, and social sciences; affiliation with an institution of higher learning is not required. Most of the journal's contents in a regular issue are devoted to essays, interviews, and book reviews.

The journal has also published a number of issues devoted to special topics or authors: Black South (spring–summer 1993); Black Theatre (winter–summer 1982–1983); Children's and Young-Adult Literature (spring 1998); Contemporary Theatre (winter 1997); Fiction (summer 1989, autumn 1992); Folklore (autumn 1969); Charles Johnson (winter 1996); Literature of Jazz (autumn 1991); Clarence Major (spring 1994); Toni Morrison (summer 2001); Music (summer 1995); Poetry (autumns of 1986, 1987, 1989; summer 1992 [also a Theatre issue]); Protest and Propaganda Literature (autumn 1968); Science Fiction (summer 1984); Wole Soyinka (autumn–winter 1988); Twentieth-Century Autobiography (summer 1990); Women's Culture (autumn 1993, summer 1994); Women Writers (winter 1986, spring 1988, winter 1990, spring 1992).

The journal's original purpose was to help integrate African American literature into American public school and university curricula, in which it was not uncommon to find few or no black authors on students' reading lists. This central purpose still guides the journal, even though its audience has shifted considerably toward the university instructor. *African American Review* has become a vehicle for new and established critics of African American literature to engage in some of their most sophisticated analyses and book reviews. The journal occasionally publishes poetry, short fiction, and excerpts from forthcoming novels. Virtually every major African American literary critic, including no small number of fiction writers, has published articles and reviews in the journal's various permutations. An abbreviated list includes William L. Andrews, K. Anthony Appiah, Michael Awkward, Houston A. Baker Jr., Amiri Baraka, Richard Barksdale, Bernard W. Bell, Susan L. Blake, Joanne M. Braxton, Gwendolyn Brooks, Robert J. Butler, Keith Byerman, Hazel Carby, Wanda Coleman, Thadious M. Davis, Manthia Diawara, Tom Dent, Rita Dove, Frances Smith Foster, Robert E. Fox, Henry Louis Gates Jr., Addison Gayle Jr., Nikki Giovanni, Trudier Harris, William J. Harris, Calvin Hernton, bell hooks, Dolan Hubbard, Charles Johnson, Keneth Kinnamon, Phyllis R. Klotman, Etheridge Knight, Yusuf Komunyakaa, Missy D. Kubitschek, Clarence Major, Nellie Y. McKay, E. Ethelbert Miller, R. Baxter Miller, Toni Morrison, Gloria Naylor, Charles H. Nichols, Aldon L. Nielsen, Arnold Rampersad, Dudley Randall, Ishmael Reed, Kalamu ya Salaam, Valerie Smith, Wole Soyinka, Askia M. Touré, Claudia Tate, Natasha Tretheway, Alice Walker, Cheryl A. Wall, Michele Wallace, Jerry W. Ward Jr., John A. Williams, Richard Yarborough, and many others.

The quality of *African American Review*'s criticism is especially high; most of the essays from the late 1980s and after have either integrated contemporary literary criticism with close scrutiny of major and minor literary and historical texts or, on some occasions, challenged perceived critical hegemonies. To that extent, it is among the most sophisticated and, arguably, one of the most radical records of criticism of African American literature of the last thirty years. Inevitably, the journal itself displays some of its own biases in subject matter, if nowhere else, and they lean toward the more established authors in a de facto African American literary canon. The reader interested in Toni Morrison, Ralph Ellison, Gloria Naylor, Richard Wright, Alice Walker, Charles Johnson, James Baldwin, W. E. B. Du Bois, Charles Chesnutt, Ernest J. Gaines, Rita Dove, and others will rarely have to suffer an issue's being published without essays devoted to at least a few of these august names. This is not necessarily a bad thing; few scholarly journals focusing mostly or exclusively on African American literature and culture remain in print, and prevailing opinions of these authors need to be discussed, questioned, and revised. Yet more obscure names do not receive the amount or frequency of attention they might deserve. This condition, however, is not exclusive to *African American Review*, and the journal remains a crowning jewel of contemporary criticism. One of the best articles about the journal's history was penned by its longtime editor: Joe Weixlmann, "The Way We Were, the Way We Are, the Way We Hope to Be," *BALF* 20, nos. 1/2 (Spring–Summer 1986).

Afrocentricity Afrocentricity, or Afrocentrism, is both a pedagogical method and an ideology first named and delineated by Molefi Kete Asante of Temple University in his books *Afrocentricity: The Theory of Social Change* (1980, revised 1988) and *The Afrocentric Idea* (1989, revised 1998). Afrocentricity's purpose is to examine history, politics, and social and cultural phenomena, including literature, from the perspectives and for the edification of sub-Saharan African cultures and the various peoples of the African Diaspora. As the name implies, then, Africa and black Africans are placed at the center of the world to posit a radical revaluation of each of the aforementioned categories. The descriptor "Afrocentric" has been applied to everything from clothing and lifestyles to sophisticated studies of African, Afro-Caribbean, and African American history and literature. After Asante published his first book on the subject, Afrocentricity grew in popularity among African Americans of different educational and class backgrounds. It has found particular favor in many black studies programs and departments, inasmuch as one of its goals is to persuade students and scholars to reorient their knowledge of history and culture to place the achievements of African peoples in the foreground and center, rather than at the margins.

Afrocentricity is a direct outgrowth of modern Black Nationalism, Negritude, Pan-Africanism, the Black Arts Movement, and the Black Aesthetic that emerged in the 1960s. Arguably, Afrocentricity reached its peak of influence and public attention in the late 1980s and early 1990s, but it remains, under various names, guises, and interpretations, a significant part of African American literary studies.

Asante defines Afrocentricity as "a perspective that involves locating [African American] students within the context of their own cultural references so that they can relate socially and psychologically to other cultural perspectives."[1] In this respect, Afrocentricity is a crucial part of the movement towards multicultural education that arose in the early 1970s. It purports to counter the harmful effects of Eurocentric, or white supremacist, views of world history that either dismiss or minimize the presence of and crucial roles African peoples have played within the development of Western civilization, or entirely independent of it, from ancient times to the present.

Afrocentricity's influence upon and importance to contemporary African American fiction and literary studies are substantially broader. In literary studies, Afrocentric critical approaches might include foci upon the artifacts of and references to sub-Saharan Africa within specific texts; criticism of the Eurocentrism of scholars of African American literature; criticism of Eurocentrism in the works of various fiction authors; comparisons of African Diasporic and sub-Saharan Africa concepts and cultural practices as found within some works; and so on. In contemporary African American fiction itself, Afrocentricity, Afrocentric perspectives and garb, and discussions of the same may be featured in some texts; this is especially true of the Post-Soul or New Black Aesthetic generation of authors. One is apt to find some reflections of Afrocentric thought in the works of such authors as Gayl Jones, Toni Morrison, Gloria Naylor, or Ishmael Reed, all of whom have incorporated explicit references to African cultures, ancient and modern, in their most famous works.

Afrocentricity has also generated more than its fair share of controversy, despite the fact that its precise definition depends largely upon the perspective of the person asked to define it. Since it does have practical implications for primary and secondary education and has been influential in the multicultural education movement, it has been condemned as divisive and "Balkanizing" by its most ardent critics. These criticisms came to the fore primarily due to the publication of Arthur M. Schlesinger Jr.'s *The Disuniting of America* (1991), Mary Lefkowitz's *Not Out of Africa: How Afrocentrism Became an Excuse to Teach Myth as History* (1996), and Dinesh D'Souza's *Illiberal Education: The Politics of Race and Sex on Campus* (1991), to say nothing of such critical essays as Stanley Crouch's "Do the Afrocentric Hustle,"[2] among many others. Afrocentricity's critics tend not only to charge

---

1. Molefi Kete Asante, "The Afrocentric Idea in Education," *The Journal of Negro Education* 60, no. 2 (Spring 1991):171.

2. Stanley Crouch, "Do the Afrocentric Hustle," in *The All-American Skin Game, or, The Decoy of Race: The Long and the Short of It, 1990–1994* (New York: Pantheon Books, 1995), 33–44.

that the model amounts to little more than "cheerleading" for black students and their history but also to accuse Afrocentrists of sloppy, polemical scholarship (an accusation that, while occasionally justified, may apply equally to some of Afrocentricity's critics).

Regardless of the controversy, though, Afrocentricity has undoubtedly offered African American literary studies one way to enliven discussions of the literature itself. It would not be inaccurate to say that Henry Louis Gates Jr.'s *Figures in Black: Words, Signs, and the "Racial" Self* (1987) and *The Signifying Monkey: A Theory of African-American Literary Criticism* (1988) owe as much to Afrocentricity's approach as they do to contemporary poststructuralist theory. Moreover, the theory continues to capture the attention of new and old students of African American literature seeking critical perspectives that enhance our understanding of African American literature as a whole.

Allen, Jeffrey Renard (b. 1962, Chicago, Illinois) *Rails Under My Back* (2000), the first novel by poet and short-story author Jeffrey Renard Allen, attracted many positive notices upon its publication for its ambitious scope. As was true of many works authored by younger African American writers in the 1990s, Rails aspired to the sort of epic, picaresque attempts to capture African Americans' collective condition found in the best works of Paul Laurence Dunbar, Ralph Ellison, Richard Wright, Toni Morrison, and John Edgar Wideman. As do those authors, Allen writes about the Great Migration of African Americans from the South to the urban North that occurred from the early part of the twentieth century well into the 1960s, finding a metaphor for African Americans' search for freedom,

identity, education, and experience in the act of migration itself.

Rails Under My Back is the story of cousins Hatch and Jesus Jones—whose mothers and fathers are sisters and brothers to one another, respectively—and the closely knit Southern families whence they come. Each cousin represents the yin to the other's yang; Hatch is the sensitive soul trying to transcend the restrictions of his homeland and family, while Jesus is righteously angry and bitter about their families' lives. Each also tries to resist the dangers and temptations of growing up African American in the South and the vices of Chicago, with mixed results. In doing so, Hatch and Jesus also try to help keep their larger families' ties and histories together as they face modernity via the city. Allen uses trains, the underground, and gravity as metaphors for these hazards and for the journeys to and from freedom that individual characters undertake. Allen's novel reflects concerns common in many post–Civil Rights novels: What are the hazards or benefits of letting go of traditions that allowed African American individuals, families, and communities to survive generations of legal and customary oppression but that might endanger the identities of each if maintained without revision?

Most initial reviewers note that Allen's ambitions within the novel are often beautifully realized through his poetic language, but some expressed reservations about the novel's organization and cohesiveness. Christopher C. De Santis writes, for example, that *Rails* "contributes a unique and enduring voice" to a long tradition of novels with these themes, but also that it is "difficult" and does not always "weav[e] the many characters' lives together through shifting time and geography in a seamless fashion."[1] Robert Butler calls it "an impressive first

---

1. Christopher C. De Santis, review of *Rails Under My Back*, by Jeffrey Renard Allen, *The Review of Contemporary Fiction* 22, no. 3 (Fall 2002): 169–70.

novel announcing a fresh voice in African American fiction" and compares Allen's work to that of Theodore Dreiser for its ability to revise the picture of the urban environment for a postmodern age with "extraordinary verbal energy." Butler suggests that the novel could have benefited from editorial trimming and further development of some settings and scenes, but praises it overall.

All the Women Are White, All the Blacks Are Men, but Some of Us Are Brave: Black Women's Studies This outstanding 1982 anthology of black feminist essays was edited by Gloria T. Hull, Patricia Bell Scott, and Barbara Smith, three black feminist critics prominent from the 1970s through the 1990s. It ranks as one of the most influential volumes of contemporary feminist thought by women of color, arguably rivaled only by *This Bridge Called My Back: Writings by Radical Women of Color* (1981), edited by Cherríe L. Moraga and Gloria E. Anzaldúa. *All the Women Are White* received the Outstanding Women of Color and the Women Educator's Curriculum Material awards, and it is commonly assigned, whether in its entirety or excerpted, in many African American studies and women's studies courses.

Contributors include the editors and Martha H. Brown, the Combahee River Collective, Erlene Stetson, Alice Walker, Michele Wallace, Mary Helen Washington, Jean Fagan Yellin, and several others. Moreover, many of the foundational essays of contemporary black feminist thought are found here, and each has helped in its own way to shape the direction of African American literary studies from the 1980s onward. This is especially applicable to the numerous African American women authors that became prominent or were otherwise rediscovered in that period; in fact, some of the latter authors owe their renaissance directly to these essays.

While the entire volume is essential to the development of black feminist thought from the 1980s until the present, a few may be specifically mentioned if only because they are more widely known and read than the others. These include: the Combahee River Collective's "A Black Feminist Statement"; Barbara Smith's "Toward a Black Feminist Criticism" and "Racism and Women's Studies"; Gloria T. Hull's "Researching Alice Dunbar-Nelson: A Personal and Literary Perspective"; Michele Wallace's "A Black Feminist's Search for Sisterhood"; Patricia Bell Scott's "Debunking Sapphire: Toward a Non-Racist and Non-Sexist Social Stance" and "Selected Bibliography of Black Feminism"; Alice Walker's "One Child of One's Own: A Meaningful Digression Within the Work(s)—an Excerpt"; and Mary Helen Washington's "Teaching Black-Eyed Susans: An Approach to the Study of Black Women Writers."

Equally important are the teaching resources scattered throughout the volume. Besides Patricia Bell Scott's black feminist bibliography, two collections of course syllabi, one for "General/Social Science/Interdisciplinary" and another for literature courses, provide clear examples of both theoretical and pedagogical strategies for the classroom. These elements are perfect illustrations of black feminism's desire to address more practical concerns, to engage in the sort of work that would enable others to build upon their foundations.

Amistad Magazine Published by Random House in two issues from 1969 to 1971, *Amistad* stands as one of the better "little magazines" to emerge in the wake of the Black Arts Movement, despite its extremely short history. Named after the slave ship on which there was a famous revolt in 1839, *Amistad*, coedited by Charles Harris and fiction writer John A. Williams, was strongly nationalistic and artistically daring. In the spirit of the *Amistad* case, the anthology stood for "revolt, self-determination, justice and freedom," and was meant to be used in "college courses in literature, history, sociology, psychology, education, political science and government, and the arts."[1] In other words, *Amistad* was to address the emergence of black studies as a discipline in American universities and to counter "'intellectual' racism."[2]

The resulting magazine featured essays and fiction, both new and old, by the most prominent African American authors of the Black Arts or Harlem Renaissance movements. Most of the contents consisted of essays by and about African American literature and history; the remainder—about a third—consisted of fiction or other features, such as a portfolio of the photographs of Carl Van Vechten, one of the white patrons of the Harlem Renaissance. Besides the editors themselves, the featured authors included (in alphabetical order): Imamu Amiri Baraka; Haywood Burns; Basil Davidson; George Davis; W. E. B. Du Bois; Addison Gayle; Paula Giddings; Paul Good; Verta Grosvenor; Vincent Harding; Calvin C. Hernton; Langston Hughes; Oliver Jackman; C. L. R. James; Gayl Jones; John Oliver Killens; Toni Morrison; Ishmael Reed; Sterling Stuckey; Carl Van Vechten; Mel Watkins; and Richard Wright. Save for those authors who were deceased—such as Du Bois, Hughes, Van Vechten, Wright—virtually all of these writers went on to become major authors or scholars of African American literature. Notable contributions are an excerpt from *The Bluest Eye*, by Toni Morrison, which had been published the previous year; "D Hexorcism of Noxon D Awful," by Ishmael Reed; "The Return: A Fantasy," by Gayl Jones; and a previously unpublished,

longer version of Richard Wright's seminal essay, "Blueprint for Negro Writing."

Angelou, Maya (b. Marguerite Johnson, 1928, St. Louis, Missouri) Maya Angelou remains one of African American literature's major popular authors, renowned both for her powerful literary skills and her activism. Although Angelou's greatest claims to fame are her six autobiographies, most notably the bestselling *I Know Why the Caged Bird Sings* (1970), her efforts in this area place her squarely within a tradition of stylized autobiography that helps define African American literature as a whole. While her autobiographies are not fictional in the strictest sense, some of them compare favorably to the earlier efforts of Zora Neale Hurston, Frederick Douglass, Booker T. Washington, and Angelou's friend and contemporary, Malcolm X, to the extent that they include an autobiographical persona who functions largely as a fictional character would. Via this persona, the accomplished poet, dancer, singer, actor, choreographer, essayist, and activist frequently reveals a life that has lent itself to dramatic exploits that have involved some of the most illustrious figures in African American life in the latter part of the twentieth century.

Angelou's work is often flamboyant and even controversial; despite its overwhelming popularity with many audiences, *I Know Why the Caged Bird Sings* remains on lists of books banned in high schools for its sexual content and resounding and uncompromising condemnation of racism, particularly racist white Americans. The latter element may be attributed in part to Angelou's first autobiography emerging at the crux of the Black Arts Movement, but it still resonates with new generations of readers, African

1. Charles F. Harris and John A. Williams, introduction to *Amistad* 1 (1969): vii.
2. Charles F. Harris and John A. Williams, introduction to *Amistad* 1 (1969): viii.

American or otherwise. Angelou's popularity led president-elect Bill Clinton to ask her to compose and read the inaugural poem, which was later published in *On the Pulse of Morning* (1993). Poet and critic Wanda Coleman also stirred considerable controversy in 2002 for openly criticizing Angelou's reliance upon cliché and self-aggrandizement in her later memoirs and for her relatively simple poetic forms. Nonetheless, Angelou continues to inspire countless readers ranging from schoolchildren to accomplished academics. She writes and engages in her many activities while teaching at Wake Forest University in Winston-Salem, North Carolina.

Ansa, Tina McElroy (b. 1949, Macon, Georgia) Novelist Tina McElroy Ansa published several well-received and popular novels in the 1990s and 2000s. Her first novel, *Baby of the Family* (1989), attracted warm reviews and respectable sales, due to Ansa's accessible, yet lyrical style. *Baby of the Family* is a bildungsroman (coming-of-age novel) revolving around Lena, who is, not coincidentally, born in a small Georgia town the same year as Ansa. Lena is also born with a caul on her face, which signifies her possession of healing powers in African American folk culture. Young Lena's observations of her middle-class parents' difficult relationship and her adventures within her town's black community create a solid plot, one that has resonated with African American readers, especially those from the South.

Ansa gained significant attention after the publication of *Ugly Ways* (1993), which came in the wake of Terry McMillan's *Waiting to Exhale* and inarguably benefited from the publishing bonanza that novel engendered. Although better written and structured than McMillan's commercial phenomenon, *Ugly Ways* nevertheless found itself classified and marketed in the same category as *Waiting to Exhale* and works by many other authors consciously capitalizing upon that book's trend. *Ugly Ways* recounts the lives of three African American women who return to their small Georgia town of Mulberry after the death of their mother, Mudear, whose power as a matriarch belied the abuse she suffered at the hands of her husband, as her daughters discover in numerous flashbacks. Their conflicts and tensions with one another and their mother's spirit—a major character in her own right—reveal the wittier side of Ansa's writing with imaginative, tightly constructed dialogue. Although the tensions are resolved too easily, the novel succeeds at raising crucial issues regarding personal and familial relationships, which attracted many new readers to Ansa's fiction, thereby giving new life to her earlier novel's sales and her overall significance as a writer. *The Hand I Fan With* (1996), a sequel to *Baby of the Family*, depicts Lena as an adult and her town's new healer and matriarch. Its major foci are the complex spirituality and folk wisdom that inform her community's culture, and male-female relationships, although the male in this case is a spirit, Herman, who acts as a mentor to Lena as her powers come into their own.

Ansa has received some significant critical attention. E. Shelley Reid's article "Beyond Morrison and Walker: Looking Good and Looking Forward in Contemporary Black Women's Stories" (*AAR* 34, no. 2 [Summer 2000]) does not focus a great deal of attention on Ansa, but as she draws primarily upon *The Hand I Fan With*, Reid shows how Ansa's work compares well to her contemporaries and such groundbreaking predecessors as the authors in the article's title.

Artists and Communities Many authors in the Black Arts Movement made the question of their art's place vis-à-vis the masses of African Americans central to their work. This question was not by any means a new one by the time African American artists posed it in the 1960s; authors of the New Negro or Harlem Renaissance in the 1920s and 1930s debated frequently, both in person and in print, whether their art should address the needs or desires of African Americans in general or simply be an expression of the individual artistic sensibility, or "art for art's sake." One might also argue that such activists as David Walker raised the same issue during slavery when they condemned those who failed to use their talents and their words to support the cause of abolition.[1]

Black Arts Movement writers and intellectuals, however, took this debate into other directions as they attempted to create art—poetry, fiction, plays, paintings, sculpture, and so on—that could, on the one hand, reflect the realities of life in predominantly African American communities as those artists perceived them or, on the other hand, bring radical and revolutionary concepts and solutions to those same communities. This is the essence of Hoyt Fuller's definition of a Black Aesthetic, which argues, following Frantz Fanon, that "in the time of revolutionary struggle, the traditional Western liberal ideals are not merely irrelevant but they must be assiduously opposed. The young writers of the black ghetto have set out in search of a black aesthetic, a system of isolating and evaluating the artistic works of black people which reflects the special character and imperatives of black experience."[2] The goal of such

an aesthetic, then, is to erase the boundary that has traditionally separated the artist from the person on the street, to eschew elitism in favor of art that is accessible to the proletariat. Thus Gwendolyn Brooks left her original publisher, Harper & Row, in favor of such smaller, black-owned publishers as Broadside Press and Third World Press so that her poetry—which had become more reflective of Black Nationalist ideas by the late 1960s—could be purchased at lower prices and therefore reach a larger black audience. Theatre companies such as Pennsylvania State University's NOMMO Performing Arts Company and Chicago's Organization of Black American Culture put on performances in smaller theatres; poets Amiri Baraka, Sonia Sanchez, Don L. Lee, or Nikki Giovanni could very well be found reading their work as one of the opening acts to a music concert.

In contrast, some of the same writers of this era, while agreeing with the artist's need to connect with or to be immersed in the community, took issue with the anti-intellectualism they saw in the community. As Alice Walker argues in her essay, "The Unglamorous but Worthwhile Duties of the Black Revolutionary Artist, or of the Black Writer Who Simply Works and Writes,"

> much lip service has been given the role of the revolutionary black writer but now the words must be turned into work. . . . There are the old people . . . who need us to put into words for them the courage and dignity of their lives. There are the students who need guidance and direction. Real guidance

---

1. David Walker, *David Walker's Appeal, in Four Articles; Together with a Preamble, to the Coloured Citizens of the World, but in Particular, and Very Expressly, to Those of the United States of America* (1830; New York: Hill and Wang, 1996), 28ff.

2. Hoyt Fuller, "Introduction: Towards a Black Aesthetic," in *The Black Aesthetic*, ed. Addison Gayle Jr. (Garden City, N.Y.: Doubleday, 1971), 9.

and real direction, and support that doesn't get out of town when the sun goes down. . . . The real revolution is always concerned with the *least glamorous stuff*.[1]

Walker speaks to a long-standing imperative among African Americans to contribute back to the community in much the same way as Fuller did before her, except that she is more concerned with concrete actions than with ideology. Artistic talent must be placed at the service of the community by addressing immediate needs rather than ideals. While this may seem a relatively conservative stance evocative of Booker T. Washington's dicta in favor of utilitarian education and occupations for African Americans in his classic *Up from Slavery* (1901), it is also the epitome of the kind of nationalistic, communal thought that was common in the late 1960s and early 1970s. That is to say, black intellectuals frequently concluded that the Civil Rights movement's primary flaw was its lesser emphasis on economic empowerment as it pressed for political enfranchisement.

Contemporary African American fiction does not always address this last issue, but it frequently probes the complexities of various black communities, largely, one may argue, out of individual authors' wishes to remain closely associated to the very people who are their raisons d'être.

Attica The standoff at New York state's Attica prison in September 1971 remains one of the more shocking events in recent American history. For many African Americans, including more than a few fiction writers, it was a metaphor for the way African Americans have disproportionately suffered abuse at the hands of the American justice system, and therefore the government.

The standoff began as a result of prisoner complaints filed several months earlier about inhumane conditions at the prison, including low pay, shoddy medical facilities and treatment, censorship, routine overt bigotry and brutality from prison guards, and religious intolerance. Most of the prisoners were African American and Puerto Rican, and most of the former were members of the Nation of Islam, who were frequently singled out for unfair treatment. On September 8, 1971, an altercation between two prisoners led to peaceful inmate protests and violent rioting. Three inmates and one guard were killed, and the riots eventually culminated in the inmates' seizing control of the prison, including thirty hostages. For four days, inmates negotiated with state government officials, repeating their earlier complaints and demanding that they be given greater educational and rehabilitative opportunities, visits from religious leaders (especially such Nation of Islam officials as Minister Louis Farrakhan), inspections by doctors and reporters to certify the health of the hostages, and a visit by Governor Nelson E. Rockefeller. On September 13, however, Rockefeller ordered state troopers and prison guards to storm the prison. In the ensuing melee, twenty-nine inmates and ten hostages—some of whom were dressed in inmate uniforms—were killed, and eighty-five prisoners and three hostages were injured. Once the prison was back in the state's hands, the surviving prisoners were brutalized by prison guards for months, regardless of whether they were directly involved in the revolt or not. In sub-

---

1. Alice Walker, "The Unglamorous but Worthwhile Duties of the Black Revolutionary Artist, or of the Black Writer Who Simply Works and Writes," in *In Search of Our Mothers' Gardens: Womanist Prose* (New York: Harcourt Brace, 1983), 130–38; quotations from 133, 135; emphasis in original.

sequent investigations, the state's justifications for the raid, such as allegations of inmates' torture of hostages, were found to be baseless. This led to the surviving inmates and their families filing a class action lawsuit, resulting in an $8 million settlement that later grew to $12 million.

The Attica standoff was a rallying point for many African American activists, who found the government's conduct reprehensible and irresponsible. These activists included a number of authors, such as Ishmael Reed, Toni Morrison, and Amiri Baraka, who wrote essays about the incident and its aftermath and referred to it in their fiction; the prison scene in Morrison's *Beloved* (1987), for example, evokes the torture of the prisoners that occurred after the uprising was quelled. The best sources on the uprising and its impact upon American racial politics would be the following: *The Brothers of Attica* (1973), by Richard X. Clark, edited by Leonard Levitt; *Letters from Attica* (1972) by Samuel Melville, which includes the inmates' complete demands; and *Attica Diary* (1972) by William Coons.

Autobiography Although discussion of the autobiographical form would seem to be inappropriate in a volume discussing fiction, autobiography has been an indelible part of African American literature from its very inception, as African Americans have striven to bear witness to the innumerable trials and triumphs they have experienced individually. The autobiographical slave narrative was by far the most common form of written African American literature in the nineteenth century. In antebellum times, it was intended to help abolish slavery by making the world aware of slavery's physical and psychological horrors. From the end of the Civil War to well into the twentieth century, when the last generation born into slavery passed away, their narratives strengthened already extensive documentation of the "peculiar institution" and its effects upon America and its democratic ideals.

African American autobiography, of course, extends well beyond the slave narrative. From religious testimonials, to oral histories, to book-length texts, autobiography is one of the cornerstones of African American literature. Autobiography's appeal lies largely in its necessary assertion of authentic, usually unmediated experience and thoughtful reflection on that experience. Contemporary African American authors have frequently written first-person narratives using the autobiographical form's generic conventions to help blur the line between fiction and history for at least one of two likely purposes: either to foreground the literary facet of all history and therefore show how history can be constructed; or to demonstrate the possibilities found within fiction, that fiction is but one form of history. This is one of the features of the neo–slave narrative and of postmodernism, both of which are discussed elsewhere in this guide. On a more obvious level, though, it is hardly unusual for authors to base their fiction, especially their earliest efforts, upon personal experiences. African American authors, however, have frequently merged the dual impulses of turning experience into fiction and testing generic boundaries to force their personal experiences simultaneously to transcend and to comment upon historical events.

These impulses may also be guided by the extraordinary influence that African American autobiographies have had in recent years. The autobiographies and memoirs of Malcolm X (*The Autobiography of Malcolm X*, 1965), George Jackson (*Soledad Brother*, 1970), Elaine Brown (*A Taste of Power*, 1992), Eldridge Cleaver (*Soul on Ice*, 1968), Nathan McCall (*Makes Me Wanna Holler*, 1994) have all inspired both critical praise and controversy, but more important, they have been central texts of post–Civil Rights black politics, pushing contemporary audiences to reevaluate recent history through personal testimony.

The list of works and authors that have merged autobiography with fiction since 1970 would be long indeed, but the following is a short list of the better known and regarded among them. All of these texts have in common a protagonist who closely resemble the author or who is, for all intents and purposes, the author. They also use many of the conventions that one would normally expect from fiction or contain passages that either radically reconstruct or imagine the details missing from factual events.

James Baldwin, *If Beale Street Could Talk* (1974) and *Just Above My Head* (1979)

David Bradley, *The Chaneysville Incident* (1981)

Edwidge Danticat, *Breath, Eyes, Memory* (1994)

Randall Kenan, *A Visitation of Spirits* (1989)

Jamaica Kincaid, *Annie John* (1985) and *Lucy* (1990)

Audre Lorde, *Zami: A New Spelling of My Name: A Biomythography* (1982)

Ishmael Reed, *Japanese by Spring* (1993)

Sapphire, *American Dreams* (1994) and *Push* (1996)

Natasha Tarpley, *Girl in the Mirror: Three Generations of Black Women in Motion* (1999)

Alice Walker, *Meridian* (1976)

John Edgar Wideman, *The Homewood Trilogy* (1981–1983) and *Brothers and Keepers* (1984)

John A. Williams, *Captain Blackman* (1972), *Mothersill and the Foxes* (1975), *The Junior Bachelor Society* (1976), *!Click Song* (1982), *The Berhama Account* (1985), and *Clifford's Blues* (1999)

B

Baldwin, James (b. 1924, Harlem, New York City; d. 1987, Saint-Paul-de-Vence, France) James Baldwin is one of the giants of twentieth-century African American literature. Prior to the era covered in the present volume, Baldwin was one of a scant few African American authors—Ralph Ellison, Frederick Douglass, and Langston Hughes were usually the others—taught in American literature courses at elite universities in the United States. Baldwin's inclusion was based largely upon the achievements of his early essays, especially "Notes of a Native Son" and "Many Thousands Gone"; the early novels *Go Tell It on the Mountain* (1954), *Giovanni's Room* (1956), and *Another Country* (1962); the extended, deeply personal essay *The Fire Next Time* (1963); the militant play "Blues for Mr. Charlie" (1964); and his political activism during the Civil Rights movement.

The subsequent Black Arts Movement and the concomitant Black Aesthetics developed within it, however, were less kind to Baldwin in the 1960s and early 1970s. Black Arts Movement artists and intellectuals criticized Baldwin because of his homosexuality, the rhetorical distance from fellow African Americans that Baldwin's first-person-plural essay voice seemed to indicate, earlier criticism of his mentor Richard Wright, his expatriate status, and his vigorous defense of the Civil Rights movement's goals of freedom and equality for African Americans and reconciliation of the "races," the last of which Baldwin saw as essential for the nation's survival. For example, author and future Black Panther Party Minister of Information Eldridge Cleaver condemned Baldwin in his landmark best seller *Soul on Ice* (1968) for the "racial death wish" of homosexuality and for suggesting in *Giovanni's Room* that a white homosexual male could be "an instrument for social change."[1] Therefore, despite the fact that "Blues for Mr. Charlie" was, by Amiri Baraka's own admission, the catalyst and a major inspiration for the Black Arts Movement, and despite Baldwin's being appreciated by such Black Nationalists as Malcolm X,[2] Baldwin found himself virtually irrelevant to the younger African American literary scene of the early 1970s. Some, including Cleaver and Baraka, went so far as to imply that Baldwin was sycophantic towards whites, antiblack, and generally passé.[3]

These criticisms and accusations alienated Baldwin, yet he continued to produce notable fiction from the 1970s until his death in 1987. Two semiautobiographical novels, in fact, came out of this period of relative isolation: *If Beale Street Could Talk* (1974) and Baldwin's last novel, *Just Above My Head* (1979). The former concerns the struggles of a young pregnant woman, Clementine "Tish" Rivers, to free her unborn child's father, Alonzo "Fonny" Hunt, from an undeserved prison sentence. The novel is a sound condemnation of the American criminal justice system, particularly the way it and its agents have aided in the destruction of black families and communities. To the extent that Fonny's own deeply religious family ignores or undermines his efforts to obtain his freedom, the novel is also an indictment of the black bourgeoisie or, more accurately, the bourgeois adherence to Christian churches *as institutions*, rather than as guideposts to social uplift and personal liberation. *Just*

Above My Head, on the other hand, is a complex, extended meditation upon the themes that captivated Baldwin most often: family, sexuality, religion, and the expatriate experience that Baldwin knew so well. It is the story of gospel singer Arthur Montana's tense relationship with his brother Hall, the novel's narrator, which stems from Hall's attempts to deal with his brother's homosexuality and celebrity. Equally important, the novel explores the delicate, intricate relationships between Arthur, his lover Crunch, and Crunch's paramour Julia—a close friend of Hall and Arthur—and her brother Jimmy. Through his narration, Hall attempts to understand his brother and his eventual death, in much the same way that the narrator of Baldwin's classic story "Sonny's Blues" tries to come to terms with his own brother's demons. Many conflicts in the novel resemble events and tensions within Baldwin's own life, to say nothing of themes explored in his earlier novels and plays. Hall Montana, for example, closely resembles both David Baldwin, James's brother, and Baldwin himself, while Arthur closely reflects Baldwin's own situation: an artist, a celebrity, and a gay man, who struggles with the stresses each of these identities brings to his life as they conflict with his own staunchly religious upbringing. These correspondences led Baldwin to comment that *Just Above My Head* brought him "full circle" and was the concatenation of his experiences.[4]

The critical reviews of Baldwin's later fiction followed the patterns of the reviews of his earlier work. They were generally positive but lacked enthusiasm. Most held con-

1. Andrew Shin and Barbara Judson, "Beneath the Black Aesthetic: James Baldwin's Primer of Black American Masculinity," *AAR* 32, no. 2 (Summer 1998): 250.

2. Alex Haley notes that Malcolm X commented that Baldwin was "so brilliant he confuses the white man with words on paper," and that he had "upset the white man more than anybody except The Honorable Elijah Muhammad." Malcolm X and Alex Haley, *The Autobiography of Malcolm X* (New York: Grove Press, 1965), 401.

3. David Leeming, *James Baldwin: A Biography* (New York: Holt, 1994), 304.

4. Mel Watkins, "James Baldwin Writing and Talking," *New York Times Book Review*, September 23, 1979, 3.

siderable reservations about Baldwin's ability to convey the complexities of his settings, although he received extensive admiration for his skilled investigation of his characters' innermost psyches. Some of the criticism focused on Baldwin's continued experiments in including homosexual characters in his novels, which was still daring in the 1970s.

The scholarly literature on Baldwin is both extensive and rich. As a general introduction to Baldwin, his life, and his work, David Leeming's *James Baldwin: A Biography* (1994) is the first and best source to investigate, as Leeming was one of Baldwin's close friends and confidantes. Louis H. Pratt's *James Baldwin* (1978) is less detailed in terms of biographical detail than Leeming's book but takes a careful critical look at Baldwin's oeuvre, albeit obviously without covering Baldwin's last years. Therman B. O'Daniel's collection, *James Baldwin: A Critical Evaluation* (1981), contains essays drawn primarily from *CLA Journal* and *Negro American Literature Forum* (now *African American Review*) and covers all genres and periods of his career. It also has an extensive bibliography of works on Baldwin to date. Pratt's *Conversations with James Baldwin* (1989) fills in some of the gaps left by the earlier volume, as do Fred Standley and Nancy Standley's bibliography, *James Baldwin: A Reference Guide* (1980), and their anthology, *Critical Essays on James Baldwin* (1981).

The journals *African American Review* and *Callaloo* have published many essays on Baldwin's works. One of the latest and best is Robert Tomlinson's "'Payin' One's Dues': Expatriation as Personal Experience and Paradigm in the Works of James Baldwin" (*AAR*, spring 1999), which discusses many of Baldwin's major fictional and nonfictional works and functions as a solid review of the concepts and themes that define much of Baldwin's fiction. D. Quentin Miller's *Re-Viewing James Baldwin* (2000) comprises essays that take somewhat unusual approaches to Baldwin's career, including foci upon gender, film, masculinity, domestic spaces, and photography; its preface is by Baldwin biographer David Leeming. Readers more interested in Baldwin's later works are advised to seek out Lynn Orilla Scott's *James Baldwin's Later Fiction: Witness to the Journey* (2002), which is perhaps the most extensive book-length treatment of this segment of his career. Finally, two recent documentaries of Baldwin's life and literary career, *James Baldwin, Author* (1994) and *James Baldwin: The Price of the Ticket* (1989) are available; the latter is more widely acclaimed.

Bambara, Toni Cade (b. Miltona Mirkin Cade, New York City, March 25, 1939; d. Philadelphia, Pennsylvania, December 9, 1995) Few African American authors of recent years have achieved the degree of critical acclaim that has attended Toni Cade Bambara. The attention afforded Bambara becomes more impressive when we consider the complexity and difficulty of some of her greatest works, especially her masterpiece, *The Salt Eaters* (1980), and her best-known short-story collection, *Gorilla, My Love* (1972). Bambara was also one-third of the triumvirate of major women authors to emerge at the beginning of the contemporary period; the others are Alice Walker and Toni Morrison, the latter of whom was also instrumental in publishing *Gorilla, My Love*. Bambara's place in this group has as much to do with other roles she has played, including her work as a community activist and social worker in Harlem and Philadelphia; as a political activist in such countries as Brazil, Cuba, India, Nigeria, Jamaica, Barbados, Laos, and VietNam; as a documentary filmmaker (*The Bombing of Osage Avenue*, 1986); and as the editor of *The Black Woman* (1970), the first major anthology to tap into the growing demand for African American women's writing. In this last role, Bambara fulfilled one of the ideological goals of many African American women writers in the early 1970s: recovering and representing lost or ignored voices within the individual's community.

Bambara's style, in fact, is deeply immersed in these very same voices, most of which draw frequently on a subtle mix of African American folk culture and womanist goals of giving form to women's voices in a male-dominated milieu. When *The Salt Eaters* was published, in fact, Bambara received immense praise for her careful use of African Americans' "dialect," which she found puzzling. Bambara recounts that she "felt like a fraud" when such praise emerged, as the stories in her book "didn't have anything to do with a political stance. I just thought people lived and moved around in this particular language system. . . . It just seemed polite to handle the characters in this mode."[1] Bambara's attentiveness to the nuances of African Americans' language systems and the ways they link communities combines with more radical experiments with point of view in all of her major fictional works. Beyond *Gorilla, My Love* and *The Salt Eaters*, these include *Tales and Short Stories for Black Folks* (1971; as editor and contributor of one story) and *The Seabirds Are Still Alive* (1977).

Gorilla, My Love is largely autobiographical fiction comprising a preface and fifteen stories in a loosely woven cycle. Through the course of these stories, Bambara paints a portrait of African American communities in the South and North (Bambara's old Brooklyn neighborhood) as sites in which

individuals from different generations learn how to negotiate tensions regarding definitions of black identity, gender, and ideology. Most notable of all is the stories' overarching argument in favor of support among black women in the face of sexism within the community and racism from the society at large. Bambara's second collection of short stories, *The Seabirds Are Still Alive*, is drawn from her experiences traveling to and within the countries of Cuba, Kenya, and Vietnam from 1973 through 1975. These travels altered Bambara both politically and ideologically as a feminist and Black Nationalist, which is manifested in the intense focus on issues of justice for women and children within the stories, as well as symbolic and direct criticisms of white supremacy.

Bambara's masterpiece is *The Salt Eaters*, whose experiments with form and narration make it one of the more challenging works to emerge in the latter portion of the twentieth century. It is the story of Velma Henry and the community whence she comes, which is populated by many characters who weave in and out of the nonlinear plot at a stunning rate. Both Velma Henry and her community seek types of healing, with Velma's coming from healer Minnie Ransom, and the community's in the appreciation of its own richness and diversity. As Ann Folwell Stepford argues, Velma serves as an answer to the eponymous narrator of Ralph Ellison's *Invisible Man* (1952) to the extent that she is placed in the forefront of the reader's vision, rather than rendered invisible.[2] Like the Invisible Man, Velma achieves wisdom by returning to and embracing the mother-wit of her youth, which had been long suppressed in her memories. The complexity,

1. Toni Cade Bambara, "How She Came by Her Name," in *Deep Sightings and Rescue Missions: Fiction, Essays, and Conversations* (New York: Pantheon, 1996), 232.

2. Ann Folwell Stanford, "He Speaks for Whom? Inscription and Reinscription of Women in *Invisible Man* and *The Salt Eaters*," *MELUS* 18, no. 2 (Summer 1993): 17.

cleverness, and rich experimentation of *The Salt Eaters* won it the American Book and Langston Hughes Society awards in 1981 and led to a National Endowment for the Arts Literature Grant (1981). In 1986, the novel was granted the Medallion and Zora Neale Hurston Society awards.

Those Bones Are Not My Child (2000) is Bambara's last novel, published and edited posthumously via Bambara's friend, Toni Morrison. It is a fictional account of life in and around Atlanta, Georgia, at the time of the Atlanta child murders from 1979 to 1982, in which forty African American children and young men were brutally slain. Bambara takes to task official agencies' rush to find both a guilty party and a nonracial explanation for the crimes and links them symbolically to the history of lynching that still haunts Georgia. Reviews of this last magnum opus were mixed; its daunting size—over 600 pages—led such reviewers as Shanna Benjamin to declare that the narrative loses some thrust when Bambara incorporates her extensive research and that it was in need of further editing.[1]

Arguably, the single best introduction to Bambara's life and interests would be *Deep Sightings and Rescue Missions* (1996), also completed posthumously by Morrison. The first third of the anthology comprises six of Bambara's last stories, which stand up well when compared to the best of her work. The remainder of the volume consists of essays, reviews, and an extremely candid and insightful interview, "How She Came by Her Name," conducted by Bambara's friend Louis Massiah shortly before her death. Scholarly books on Bambara's fiction include: Elliott Butler-Evans, *Race, Gender, and Desire: Narrative Strategies in the Fiction of Toni Cade Bambara, Toni Morrison, and*

Alice Walker (1989); Komla Messan Nubukpo, *Through Their Sisters' Eyes: The Representation of Black Men in the Novels of Toni Morrison, Alice Walker, and Toni Cade Bambara* (1987); and Gay Wilentz, *Healing Narratives: Women Writers Curing Cultural Dis-ease* (2000). Notable scholarly journal articles include: Derek Alwes, "The Burden of Liberty: Choice in Toni Morrison's *Jazz* and Toni Cade Bambara's *The Salt Eaters*," *AAR* 30, no. 3 (Autumn 1996); Margot Anne Kelley, "'Damballah is the First Law of Thermodynamics': Modes of Access to Toni Cade Bambara's *The Salt Eaters*," *AAR* 27, no. 3 (Autumn 1993); Farah Jasmine Griffin, "Toni Cade Bambara: Free to Be Anywhere in the Universe," *Callaloo* 19, no. 2 (Spring 1996); Janelle Collins, "Generating Power: Fission, Fusion, and Postmodern Politics in Bambara's *The Salt Eaters*," *MELUS* 21, no. 2 (Summer 1996); Ann Folwell Stanford, "He Speaks for Whom?: Inscription and Reinscription of Women in *Invisible Man* and *The Salt Eaters*," *MELUS* 18, no. 2 (Summer 1993); Imani L. B. Fryar, "Literary Aesthetics and the Black Woman Writer," *Journal of Black Studies* 20, no. 4 (June 1990); George E. Kent, "Outstanding Works in Black Literature in 1972," *Phylon* 34, no. 4 (fourth quarter, 1973).

Beatty, Paul (b. 1962, Los Angeles, California) One of the sharpest wits among of the younger generation of African American writers, poet and novelist Paul Beatty has won virtually universal praise for his hilarious first novel, *The White Boy Shuffle* (1996) and favorable, albeit mixed reviews for his second novel, *Tuff* (2000). A native of Los Angeles, Beatty earned his M.A. in psychology at Boston University and his M.F.A. at Brooklyn College, where his work under the

1. Shanna Greene Benjamin, review of *Those Bones Are Not My Child*, by Toni Cade Bambara, *African American Review* 35, no. 2 (Summer 2001): 338.

direction of preeminent Beat poet Allen Ginsberg led to the publication of two volumes of poetry, *Big Bank Take Little Bank* (1991) and *Joker Joker Deuce* (1994). The *Village Voice* chose the former as one of the best books of 1991. These two books alone earned Beatty a place among a new group of poets who used the rhythms and topical content of rap or hip-hop as the bases for their work.

With his poetic work alone, Beatty had already marked a significant place for himself in African American literature by the mid-1990s, having been featured in numerous profiles and collections. With his satirical *Künstlerroman*, *The White Boy Shuffle*, Beatty created a semiautobiographical, irreverent indictment of the stale, shallow character of 1990s political activism, insincere forms of multiculturalism, and the gross commodification of African American culture. *Tuff*, which fills a similar thematic scope, is a nihilistic, picaresque romp through New York's cultural and political firestorms. Both novels explode innumerable myths about African Americans' alleged pathologies that are too seldom challenged. They have also placed Beatty on the cusp of literary stardom. Where he goes from this point will depend largely upon the quality of his next work.

Given the brevity of Beatty's career thus far, no book-length studies of his work exist. Most critical study consists of book reviews in major newspapers and magazines. This author, however, has written about Beatty's two novels in *African American Satire: The Sacredly Profane Novel* (2001). One of Beatty's early short stories, "What Set You From, Fool?" has been collected in *Next: Young American Writers on the New Generation* (1994), edited by Eric Liu. Excerpts from *The White Boy Shuffle* were also published in Kevin Powell's *Step Into a World: A Global Anthology of the New Black Literature* (2000), a massive, essential anthology.

Before Columbus Foundation The Before Columbus Foundation is a nonprofit educational and service organization cofounded in 1976 by authors Ishmael Reed, Victor Hernandez Cruz, Shawn Wong, and Rudolfo Anaya to promote and disseminate contemporary American multicultural literature. Since 1978, the foundation has recognized the literary achievements of American authors of all backgrounds, primarily through its annual American Book Awards, which are marked by their egalitarian outlook and purpose.

The foundation and its mission are clearly responses to the often controversial decisions that emerge from the National Book, PEN/Faulkner, Pulitzer, and other award committees, whom Reed and other African American authors have accused of elitism, racism, and gender discrimination. The Before Columbus Foundation's recognized books are not designated as the "best" books in a given year; that would connote an elite ranking. Rather, each of the entries named receives an award without any further designation of quality, gender, race, or other characteristic, save for the subcategories of "Children's Book," "Editor," "Journalism," "Special Publishing," and "Lifetime Achievement" awards. The foundation welcomes entries regardless of the author's background or the type, size, and reputation of the publisher.

Past winners of the American Book Award have included Toni Cade Bambara, Derrick Bell, Sandra Cisneros, J. California Cooper, Edwidge Danticat, Angela Y. Davis, Thulani Davis, Don DeLillo, Andrea Dworkin, Trey Ellis, Lawrence Ferlinghetti, Nelson George, Sandra M. Gilbert, Shirley Geok-lin Lim, Chester Himes, Paule Marshall, Terry McMillan, Toni Morrison, Gloria Naylor, and Al Young. In 1992, the foundation also published two major anthologies: *The Before Columbus Foundation Fiction Anthology: Selections from the*

American Book Awards, 1980–1990, edited by Ishmael Reed, Kathryn Trueblood, and Shawn Wong; and *The Before Columbus Foundation Poetry Anthology: Selections from the American Book Awards, 1980–1990,* edited by J. J. Phillips, Ishmael Reed, Gundars Strads, and Shawn Wong.

Beloved Toni Morrison's famed 1987 novel stands as perhaps the most celebrated and widely studied contemporary African American novel. It won the Pulitzer Prize for fiction in 1988 and in all likelihood paved the way for Morrison's being awarded the Nobel Prize in Literature in 1993. It was also made into an eponymous motion picture in 1998, although that film received only modest critical and commercial success. That it did so is not surprising, since *Beloved* is also Morrison's most complex novel and the one that least lends itself to the limits of the film medium. Nonetheless, the novel remains extremely popular, especially on college and university campuses, and has generated dozens of journal articles, book chapters, and entire books. Although many of these discuss the novel in conjunction with other works, quite a few are devoted to the novel alone.

Beloved is based upon the case of Margaret Garner, a runaway slave who slew her infant daughter and attempted to kill her young sons in 1856. The novel centers upon Sethe Suggs who, like Garner, escaped while pregnant into Ohio from brutal, humiliating enslavement on a Kentucky farm, giving birth on the way. She obtains freedom but is pursued and discovered by her former slaveholder, "Schoolteacher." Again, like her model, Sethe slays her infant daughter and attempts to kill her sons, who are saved by her husband's mother; Sethe is jailed for her offense.

In all other respects, the connections between Sethe's and Margaret Garner's cases diverge considerably. Whereas Garner was reenslaved and died an ignoble death (see Steven Weisenburger's *Modern Medea* [1998], which offers a detailed account of Garner's life and the effect it had on the abolitionist movement), Sethe is eventually freed from her physical prison, only to be confined to a psychological one kept by the ghost of her slain daughter. This spirit haunts Sethe's house, 124 Bluestone Road, her family (her sons run away from home, while her daughter, Denver, withdraws from the public), and her conscious and unconscious mind, eventually taking on physical form in the person of "Beloved." As a physical familiar, "Beloved" manipulates Sethe into devoting all of her attentions to futile attempts at making amends with her daughter. This effort slowly devours Sethe until the townsfolk help drive the spirit away.

Beloved may justifiably be cast among other famous ghost stories by American authors, especially Henry James's *The Turn of the Screw* and Edgar Allan Poe's "The Fall of the House of Usher," primarily for its ambiguity. One of the crucial controversies within and surrounding the novel centers upon whether "Beloved" is real or, more likely, a multivalent metaphor for several issues that may haunt African Americans collectively: the legacy of slavery; generational conflicts; the difficulty of progress; the intractability of racism; self-hatred; the silencing of African American voices; women's struggles within the larger African American community; and the struggle to create new possibilities in the face of all of these adversities. The novel may also be read as Morrison's apocalyptic fictional meditation upon the successes and failures of either postbellum black America or of the Civil Rights/Black Power era , to the extent that each period was a crossing point for African Americans, rife with ambiguity and ambivalence. Similarly, each of the novel's characters wishes to confront and overcome the horrors of the past and present yet struggles with her or his desire to nurse pain and hatred, even if it is self-destructive.

These readings are hardly exhaustive, of course, and students of this work are fortunate to have a wealth of secondary materials to supplement or alter them. In fact, except for *Song of Solomon*, no other novel by Morrison has received so much attention from so many different quarters. Steven Weisenburger's aforementioned *Modern Medea: A Family Story of Slavery and Child-Murder from the Old South* (1998) provides an extensive history of *Beloved*'s historical background that opens up new ways of interpreting the novel, although the book is not about *Beloved* per se. A rather perceptive sampling of essays on the novel may be found in *Toni Morrison's Fiction: Contemporary Criticism* (1997), edited by David Middleton. The outstanding essays are Susan Bowers' "*Beloved* and the New Apocalypse," David Lawrence's "Fleshly Ghosts and Ghostly Flesh: The Word and the Body in *Beloved*, and Ed Guerrero's "Tracing 'The Look' in the Novels of Toni Morrison"; each explores some of the major ideas that have captivated Morrison scholars. Barbara K. Solomon's anthology, *Critical Essays on Toni Morrison's Beloved* (1998), stands with Lawrence's edition as one of the most up to date books on Morrison's masterpiece. Its best quality is the inclusion of both reviews and critical essays, including some dissenting voices, such as Stanley Crouch's "Aunt Medea," that take more skeptical looks at the novel's purposes and artistry. Finally, Kathleen Marks's recent *Toni Morrison's Beloved and the Apotropaic Imagination* (2002) brilliantly discusses the way apotropaic acts and rituals—those designed to ward off evil— actually bring on the evil they are meant to negate. Marks applies this notion to Sethe's murder of her infant daughter, of course, and in the process reveals another connection to mythology contained within the text.

Bennett, George Harold (Hal) (b. April 21, 1930, Buckingham, Virginia) Hal Bennett published a series of five well-received novels in the late 1960s and early 1970s that stand among some of the most daring of the Black Arts Movement era. Bennett has also published a novel under the nom de plume Harriet Janeway and five action novels as John D. Revere. Under his own name, Bennett has won a fiction fellowship from the Bread Loaf Writers' Conference (1966), the PEN/Faulkner Award (1973), and he was selected most promising new writer by *Playboy* magazine in 1970 for his story "Dotson Gerber Resurrected."[1] Bennett's first two novels, *A Wilderness of Vines* (1966) and *The Black Wine* (1968) received generally positive reviews upon their publication. Each builds upon the other and forms the thematic foundation for his later, more mature work, with some characters finding their way into the novels of the 1970s. The early novels also introduce the Southern community of Burnside (based upon Buckingham, Virginia), whence most of Bennett's major characters come. Bennett combines this Faulknerian intertextuality—he has repeatedly cited Faulkner as one of his major influences—with foci upon historical legacies, anxieties about black males' masculinity and sexuality, and the often tortuously complex nature of African American identities, to discover ways for African Americans to extract themselves from the trap of self-hatred.

Each early novel contains a noticeable satirical bent, with 1970's *Lord of Dark Places* the most caustic and artistically accom-

1. James A. Miller, "Bennett, Hal," *The Oxford Companion to African American Literature* (New York: Oxford University Press, 1997), 33; Bernard W. Bell, *The Afro-American Novel and Its Tradition* (Amherst: University of Massachusetts Press, 1987), 324.

plished. Bennett's work highlights the ways in which America has simultaneously worshipped and reviled African American sexuality. In particular, Bennett argues strenuously that black males and their phalluses are icons whose presence is undeniable in popular culture, yet they are hated for their ubiquity. Each of his early novels posit the notion that black males must be fully aware of their sexuality within the American milieu if they wish to be liberated. Although Bennett's novels are written in the same picaresque mode as the works of such Black Arts–era authors as Cecil Brown and William Melvin Kelley, they also disregard the Black Arts era's nationalistic image of manhood. His male characters defy any easy sexual categorization, and he regards America as the product of the incestuous confluence of humanity's streams, with the barriers between black/white, North/South, male/female, "queer"/"sissy"/"manly," sacred/profane, formal/vernacular, and normal/taboo constantly in flux throughout the nation's history. While all of his novels explore this ambiguous terrain, it is *Lord of Dark Places* that is most successful in detailing what Bennett describes as "the black American's obsession with filth" that makes African Americans "feel unclean and impure and unworthy and inferior."[1] In this respect, *Lord of Dark Places* essentially revises Ralph Ellison's *Invisible Man*, without Ellison's continuous nods to modernism or the same degree of ambivalence regarding the promises of American democracy that ends Ellison's own masterwork. Bennett's work tells the story of Joe Market, whose incestuous father Titus turns Joe into a Christ figure for the sake of a sham traveling religion in which Joe's body—especially his penis—is worshiped. After Titus is raped and murdered by a Southern police squad, Joe begins a quest to find his identity independent of his father. In the process, Joe

engages in endless sexual exploits with women and men, fights in Vietnam, becomes a father, satirizes the Civil Rights movement and the policies of the Nixon administration, and symbolically becomes a master of all that is profane, yet he never quite finds redemption.

In *Wait Until the Evening* (1974), protagonist Kevin Brittain, a resident of the black community of Cousinsville, New Jersey (introduced in *Lord of Dark Places*), becomes obsessed with death under the belief that murder is the only way that those who possess no sense of identity or self-worth—meaning, in Bennett's corpus, African Americans as a whole—can find meaning and redemption. He strives to become the most horrifying manifestation of white America's fears about African American males possible, a sort of Bigger Thomas writ large. In a particularly Freudian twist, Brittain also attempts to murder his father in Burnside for the ultimate form of redemption.

Seventh Heaven (1976) features protagonist Bill Kelsey, also of Cousinsville, where he finds himself stifled by the limitations placed upon African Americans by both those within the community and the larger society. Like Joe Market, Bill Kelsey explores all that society considers profane, except he takes his psychological sustenance from being a sexual slave or gigolo. He rejects both the Black Nationalism and the colorism of the day as other limitations African Americans place upon one another that destroy whatever sense of self-worth is not already decimated by living in a racist society. Similar to the protagonists of the earlier novels, Kelsey tries to understand himself vis-à-vis his ancestors, the quirks of his community, and by standing on the brink of madness.

Bennett's short story collection, *Insanity Runs in Our Family* (1977), gathers fiction

---

1. Katherine Newman, "An Evening with Hal Bennett: An Interview," *BALF* 21, no. 4 (Winter 1987): 358–59.

Bennett wrote or published from the late 1960s until the book's appearance. The subject matter is diverse, ranging from "The Day My Sister Hid the Ham," a tale of a sister emasculating her brother, to the award-winning "Dotson Gerber Resurrected," an allegorical fable in which an African American man attempts to gain recognition for his murder of a white man. As in his novels, Bennett is interested in seeing the extremes to which African Americans are pushed by their search for redemption. His blunt assessments of African Americans' collective self-esteem, to say nothing of the sexually explicit content of all his novels, might help account for Bennett's remarkably challenging and difficult novels' long disappearance from print. Until 1997, when *Lord of Dark Places* was reprinted, his early novels could not be found in print anywhere;[1] by the end of the millennium, even *Lord of Dark Places* had disappeared from circulation yet again. None of Bennett's other novels have returned to print in the interim in any form.

The almost total absence of Bennett's novels—and of the author himself—from the literary scene, as well as their intense focus on male sexuality, may explain why only a few studies of Bennett's work have emerged in thirty years. Save for the occasional brief mention in various articles and book chapters and short reviews of the reprint of *Lord of Dark Places*, the entire body of critical work on Bennett consists of Ronald Walcott's two-part review of Bennett's novels in *Black World* magazine (1974);[2] a subsection in Bernard W. Bell's *The Afro-American Novel and Its Tradition*; Walcott's entry in the *Dictionary of Literary Biography* (1985), which reproduces much of his *Black World* review; Katherine Newman's remarkable interview, "An Evening

with Hal Bennett" (1987); and this writer's own subsection in *African American Satire: The Sacredly Profane Novel* (2001).

Black Aesthetic, The (1971) Addison Gayle's 1971 anthology was a landmark of the Black Arts Movement for its militant attempt to collect in one place seminal essays establishing new ways of reading African American literature. The critical essays contained therein were concerned with establishing aesthetic standards that neither depended upon nor paid obeisance to rules for writing and reading based in white or European cultures. Most of the essays within *The Black Aesthetic* had been published in various magazines and journals in the preceding five years, but the volume deftly made it easier for scholars and casual readers to gain familiarity with the diversity of critical views emerging at the time. It also comprised some of the foundational essays for the development of African American literature and art in the 1920s, 1930s, and 1940s, as well as for the study of literature from the 1970s until the present. Although structuralist and poststructuralist theories had begun to gain in popularity among academics by the end of the 1970s, *The Black Aesthetic*'s overarching premise underscores African American literary study to the present: African Americans need to create their own aesthetic standards for the appreciation and study of their art and, subsequently, maintain control over these standards.

The essays within *The Black Aesthetic* are divided into five sections: "Theory," "Music," "Poetry," "Drama," and "Fiction." Several essays in the first section are among the most frequently anthologized and quoted: Hoyt Fuller's "Introduction: Towards a Black Aesthetic," Larry Neal's "Some Reflections on

1. Newman, "An Evening with Hal Bennett," 378.

2. Ronald Walcott, "The Novels of Hall Bennett, Part I." *Black World* 23, no. 8 (June 1974): 36–48, 89–97; "The Novels of Hall Bennett, Part II." *Black World* 23, no. 9 (July 1974): 78–96.

the Black Aesthetic," Addison Gayle Jr.'s "Cultural Strangulation: Black Literature and the White Aesthetic," and Darwin T. Turner's "Afro-American Literary Critics: An Introduction." These essays generally agree on several principles: African American literature has been judged by unfair and inappropriate standards developed almost exclusively by white critics; few, if any, white critics have sufficient insight into African American culture to be able to evaluate it as well as African American critics; far more African American critics who possess and read through a black aesthetic are desperately needed to give the literature its due. Not all of the essays in this or other sections are in complete concordance; Julian Mayfield's "You Touch My Black Aesthetic and I'll Touch Yours" is a note of dissent from totalizing or essentialist definitions of a Black Aesthetic. Mayfield argues instead for loose, contingent, and inclusive definitions, if any. Other authors included in this section are Alain Locke, Ron Karenga, and John O'Neal. Of these, Karenga's essay, "Black Cultural Nationalism," is the most controversial. Karenga dismisses the cultural and political significance of the blues, arguing that the blues "teach resignation" and "acceptance of reality," whereas artists should be educated and dedicated to producing art that is "functional" and "collective."[1]

The second section, "Music," comprises landmark essays by Jimmy Stewart, W. E. B. Du Bois, LeRoi Jones (later known as Amiri Baraka), J. A. Rogers, Ron Wellburn, and Ortiz M. Walton. Of these, Du Bois's essay, "Of the Sorrow Songs," taken from his classic *The Souls of Black Folk* (1903), and Jones's essay, "The Changing Same (R&B and New Black Music)," are the more famous and definitive, to the extent that they analyze the

social and political content of African American musical forms sympathetically.

The third section, "Poetry," traces the development of African American literature from the nineteenth century forward. Except for Sarah Webster Fabio's "Tripping with Black Writing," which surveys African American literature's development over many decades, each essay in this section specifies a particular decade or decades as its subject. Langston Hughes's famous work, "The Negro Artist in the Racial Mountain" (1927), is a firsthand argument for a Negro Art in the 1920s and 1930s. In "The Black Aesthetic in the Thirties, Forties, and Fifties," Dudley Randall studies how earlier Black Aesthetics had developed under various pressures. "Toward a Definition: Black Poetry of the Sixties," by Don L. Lee (later known as Haki Madhubuti), outlines trends in that decade. James A. Emanuel's "Blackness Can: A Quest for Aesthetics" surveys twentieth-century African American literary developments but focuses on the 1970s. W. Keoraptse Kgositsile's "Paths to the Future" offers a prescriptive view of African American poetics for the 1970s and beyond. The fourth section, "Drama," consists of essays by Alain Locke, Larry Neal, Loften Mitchell, Ronald Milner, and Clayton Riley. Standouts in this section include Alain Locke's essay, "The Negro and the American Theatre," one of the earliest landmark essays on the subject, while Larry Neal's contribution, "The Black Arts Movement," is one of the best contemporary histories of that artistic period.

The fifth and final section, "Fiction," contains some of the best essays in the book, including Richard Wright's hugely influential—and controversial—1937 essay, "Blueprint for Negro Writing," which argues for an African American aesthetic that defies

---

1. Ron Karenga, "Black Cultural Nationalism," in *The Black Aesthetic*, ed. Addison Gayle Jr. (Garden City, N.J.: Doubleday, 1971), 38, 33, 34.

bourgeois values and serves a collective purpose. "The New Black Literature: Protest or Affirmation," by Hoyt W. Fuller, and "The Black Writer and His Role," by Carolyn F. Gerald, both assert that while much of the writing and art emerging in the late 1960s and early 1970s may be "crude," the nationalistic outlook and attempts by young black artists to move away from Western artistic standards should be applauded.[1] Each of the subsequent essays, by John Oliver Killens, Adam David Miller, Ishmael Reed, and especially Addison Gayle Jr., are once again prescriptive; they argue that African Americans must change, first, their view of themselves based upon their own cultural standards, and then the rest of the nation via literature that reflects a more positive view of African Americans' experiences, which will counterbalance the many extant negative stereotypes. Gayle's essay is remarkable for its strong call for African American authors to eschew a white/black binary that assumes that white is superior and black inherently inferior, thereby requiring African Americans to become the same as whites.

While *The Black Aesthetic* has certainly been immensely influential, two flaws marked its achievements: the dearth of women critics (two) contributing to the volume, and the lack of dissenting points of view, leading inevitably to redundancy when the essays are taken together. Nevertheless, the collective effort offers a strong basis for taking calls for a Black Aesthetic seriously, and it inarguably provided the undergirding for the black studies movement in academia via the essays' calls for a new crop of African American literary critics.

Black American Literature Forum. *See* **African American Review.**

Black Arts Movement/Black Aesthetic The Black Arts Movement and its concomitant Black Aesthetic were the products of debates and struggles in the 1960s regarding Black Nationalism, which was concerned with the control African Americans should have over their economic, political, cultural, and social lives. To participants in these debates, the questions of black control were not simply matters of rhetorical or ideological posturing; the answers were inextricably linked to the well-being of most African Americans. To that extent, they were debated at all levels of black society in the 1960s. In the writings and work of black artists in particular, though, the debate centered on questions of images, social value, and aesthetics; more specifically, they were "about the business of destroying those images and myths that have crippled and degraded black people, and the institution of new images and myths that will liberate them."[2] The premise behind this particular belief and practice was that white Americans' traditional considerations of the cultural value of black people were poisonous if black people themselves ingested such ideas or tried to practice them. The notion that black culture and aesthetics (when black people were granted that much credit by their critics) were forever inferior to or dependent upon European-derived aesthetics would inevitably lead to practices that would cause black people to detest, and perhaps even destroy, themselves. According to critics like Addison Gayle, Maulana Ron Karenga, Amiri Baraka (formerly LeRoi Jones), and Larry Neal, the responsibility of

1. Hoyt W. Fuller, "The New Black Literature: Protest or Affirmation," in *The Black Aesthetic*, ed. Addison Gayle Jr. (Garden City, N.J.: Doubleday, 1971), 346.

2. Hoyt W. Fuller, "The New Black Literature: Protest or Affirmation," in *The Black Aesthetic*, ed. Addison Gayle Jr. (Garden City, N.J.: Doubleday, 1971), 346.

the black artist was to use the word, to use language as a tool invested with the power to transform ideas generated by black people into action, especially revolutionary action. Karenga argues in his 1968 essay "Black Art: Mute Matter Given Force and Function," that it "becomes very important . . . that art plays the role it should play in Black survival and not bog itself down in the meaningless madness of the Western world wasted. In order to avoid this madness, black artists and those who wish to be artists must accept that what is needed is an aesthetic" that would allow for a more balanced assessment of the validity and beauty of black art. Furthermore, "art must expose the enemy, praise the people and support the revolution"; it should be "collective," with the individualism of the artist being a commodity that is "nonexistent," something that African Americans "cannot afford" given the necessity of "committing . . . to revolution and change" on a mass level.[1] Put in Amiri Baraka's terms, the "Black Artist's role in America is to aid in the destruction of America as he knows it" and pursue a "correct" realism that would show America as it is and then guide the reader to the means of destroying it.[2]

While subscribers to the Black Aesthetic were by no means uniform in their views, as we shall see below, the commonalities among their critical enterprises in the late 1960s and early 1970s certainly had a substantial impact upon contemporary trends and continue to affect current African American literature. Two notes from Larry Neal's informative reading of the Black Aesthetic at the time provide a particularly illuminating view: "[In African American literature, the] Word is perceived as energy or force"; "More concerned with the vibrations of the Word, than with the Word itself."[3] In other words, the artist and critic should focus less on wordcraft than on effect, and be devoted to elevating the most valuable and cherished aspects of the African American while criticizing those who would stand in the way of black progress and empowerment. In essence, then, the advocates of the new Black Aesthetic perceived the black artist's role as that of a direct advocate of the black masses and a staunch adversary of any agency that upheld oppressive stereotypes, whether that agency originated within or outside of black communities.

Subsequently, Black Aestheticians found some of the more dangerous agents were white critics, even those who were somewhat sympathetic to black causes. This skepticism toward whites was a direct result of the tenets of various Black Nationalisms, such as this passage from Stokely Carmichael and Charles V. Hamilton's *Black Power* (1967),

1. Maulana Ron Karenga, "Black Art: Mute Matter Given Force and Function," in *New Black Voices: An Anthology of Contemporary Afro-American Literature*, ed. Abraham Chapman (New York: Mentor, 1972), 477–78, 479–90.

2. Imamu Amiri Baraka, "State/meant" (1965), in *The LeRoi Jones/Amiri Baraka Reader*, ed. William J. Harris (New York: Thunder's Mouth Press, 1991), 169–70.

3. Larry Neal, "Some Reflections on the Black Aesthetic," in *The Black Aesthetic*, ed. Addison Gayle Jr. (Garden City, N.Y.: Doubleday, 1971), 14–15. Neal describes his outline as "a rough overview of some categories and elements that constituted a 'Black Aesthetic' outlook," to be further elaborated in a later essay. The outline is apparently designed to provide a cursory history of the mythologies created by African Diasporic peoples and those mythologies' cultural manifestations, both of which led to the Black Aesthetic. Some of the most famous African mythological figures, such as Legba, Urzulie, and shamans, find a place here alongside the cultural figures or phenomena inspiring the Black Aesthetic's ideology in a column on the left (entitled "History as Unitary Myth"), while the basic beliefs of the Aesthetic itself lie in the right-hand column. This article, while somewhat fragmented, provides an excellent summary of what primary cultural forces the Black Aesthetic was intended to embody and push forward to transform not only African American arts but also African American communities in general.

wherein they quote Lewis Killian and Charles Grigg: "Most white Americans, even those white leaders who attempt to communicate and cooperate with their Negro counterparts, do not see racial inequality in the same way that the Negro does." Carmichael and Hamilton conclude "that no matter how 'liberal' a white person might be, he cannot ultimately escape the overpowering influence—on himself and on black people—of his whiteness in a racist society."[1] Hoyt W. Fuller similarly takes white critics to task by arguing that "central to the problem of the irreconcilable conflict between the black writer and the white critic is the failure of recognition of a fundamental and obvious truth of American life—that the two races are residents of two separate and naturally antagonistic worlds."[2] Fuller is essentially rephrasing a common tenet of Black Nationalist belief: all whites, even the most well-meaning ones, are irredeemably tainted by a racist culture, which places them in direct opposition to the wants and needs of black Americans, whether they are conscious of this opposition or not. In a hostile white's eyes, this taint will result in the complete disregard for the value of black literature and culture. A more sympathetic white critic may find some value in black literature but may dismiss any literature that does not appeal to a "universal" aesthetic. The conclusion of the Black Aesthetic, therefore, is that only black artists are capable of creating and judging literature that represents black communities, a literature that would replace negative myths about African Americans with new narratives that extolled the virtues within the community that those outside the community had previously classified as vices.

The move toward making a new aesthetic for African American literature in the 1960s proved, however, to be far more convoluted than its explicators had hoped, leading to marked disagreements between thinkers and writers originally on the same ideological page. Though proponents of Black Nationalism and the Black Aesthetic rightly advocated a revaluation of African American literature and culture, their political rigidity potentially precluded dissent from the definitions of progressive black art outlined above. Specifically, Karenga and Baraka's arguments for revolutionary and lucid writing, positive portrayal of African Americans, and an accent on cultural and political collectivism within the black community was driven just as strongly by Marxist influences as they were by concerns for black progress. These unities could only be obtained by subsuming divergent approaches beneath an overdetermined aesthetic.

In contrast, Hoyt W. Fuller's qualifying statement that "the black writers themselves are well aware of the possibility that what they seek is, after all, beyond codifying" and his acknowledgment that black writers "are fully aware of the dual nature of their heritage, and of the subtleties and complexities" while being "even more aware of the terrible reality of their outsideness, of their political and economic powerlessness, and of the desperate racial need for unity" does not fit the sort of dogmatic position Baraka and Karenga advocate. While Fuller agreed with their imperative need to establish some type of "unity" and "indoctrination of black art and culture," he also understood that some ambivalence in artists' thinking was unavoidable, but it should not be the focus of black art. The focus should instead be on

1. Stokely Carmichael and Charles V. Hamilton, *Black Power: The Politics of Liberation in America*, 61.

2. Hoyt W. Fuller, "Introduction: Towards a Black Aesthetic," in *The Black Aesthetic*, ed. Addison Gayle Jr. (Garden City, N.Y.: Doubleday, 1971), 7.

the form and goal of urban realism, which emphasizes the effects of the stifling urban environment upon the psyche, and on creating art that foments revolutionary thought and action.

Although the ideology, rhetoric, and aims of the Black Arts Movement and the Black Aesthetic were highly controversial and remain so (see this volume's "Overview" for a summary of this controversy), they inarguably had a profound impact upon the artistic direction and content of African American literature since 1970, even in works that explicitly or implicitly eschew its precepts. Objections to Black Aesthetic prescriptions led to two significant outcomes: the eventual rejection of narrow forms of Black Nationalism by the same intellectuals who once embraced them (Nathan Hare, Amiri Baraka, and even Hoyt Fuller; see separate entry on *Negro Digest/Black World*), and the development of the New Black Aesthetic, or "New Fiction" (see separate entries), of the late 1970s through the 1990s, both of which acknowledged their debts to the theorizing of the Black Aesthetic critics of the 1960s and 1970s yet eschewed their more prescriptive gestures in favor of opening up African American fiction, poetry, drama, and criticism to newer, more diverse voices.

The overwhelming majority of scholarly work since the early 1970s that studies works of the period either makes some mention of or directly addresses the precepts of the Black Arts Movement and Black Aesthetics. Therefore, this volume's bibliography is a de facto partial bibliography of works on the subject. A few books beyond those named above and in the bibliography offer particularly close reviews of the movements and their legacies: Winston Napier, ed., *African American Literary Theory* (2000); Kenneth Mostern, *Autobiography and Black Identity Politics: Racialization in Twentieth-Century America* (1999); W. Lawrence Hogue, *Race, Modernity, Postmodernity: A Look at the History and the Literatures of People of Color since the 1960s* (1996); Joyce Ann Joyce, *Warriors, Conjurers, and Priests: Defining African-Centered Literary Criticism* (1994); Madhu Dubey, *Black Women Novelists and the Black Aesthetic* (1994); Houston A. Baker Jr. and Patricia Redmond, eds., *Afro-American Literary Study in the 1990s* (1989); Reginald Martin, *Ishmael Reed and the New Black Aesthetic Critics* (1988); Charles Johnson, *Being and Race* (1985).

Black-Eyed Susans/Midnight Birds: Stories by and About Black Women Edited by Mary Helen Washington, *Black-Eyed Susans: Classic Stories by and About Black Women* (1975) was one of the first anthologies of African American women's fiction published in the contemporary era. It was also easily the first major publication of its kind, as African American women's writing had been largely ignored as a category worthy of scholarly attention. Anthologies of African American women's fiction considered as a discrete subfield were, therefore, virtually unknown. All of the stories contained therein were published after 1960 and often speak to contemporary events and issues. As the subtitle indicates, the stories were particularly concerned with portraying African American women and their greatest concerns, especially in the wake of modern feminism, or what Alice Walker later called "womanism" (see separate entry). Washington later edited another collection, *Midnight Birds: Stories by Contemporary Black Women Writers* (1980); in 1990, both anthologies were combined in a single volume, *Black-Eyed Susans/Midnight Birds*. The twenty stories in the combined volume are written by such authors as Toni Morrison, Ntozake Shange, Sherley Anne Williams, Alexis DeVeaux, and Paulette Childress White. It is especially valuable for Washington's excellent introduction, which places the earlier anthologies within their historical contexts, thereby making a strong case for their essential role in transforming African American literary studies in the 1970s and 1980s.

Black Feminism. *See* **Womanism.**

Black Literature and Literary Theory *Black Literature and Literary Theory* (1984), edited by Henry Louis Gates Jr. and Sunday Ogbonna Anozie, is one of the landmark texts of African American literary criticism of the 1980s, containing essays that helped to create a modern canon of sorts for African American literature, for better or worse. The authors within were heavily influenced by structuralist and poststructuralist poetics as well as the Black Aesthetic of the two previous decades. The volume's purpose, according to Gates's introduction, was to bring contemporary literary to bear upon texts that had been read through primarily political lenses.

Perhaps most important, *Black Literature and Literary Theory* helped serve notice that African American literary studies could no longer be "ghettoized" to the purely political, that they could be subjected to many different kinds of literary criticism. This led in turn to the expansion of African American literary studies' capabilities and repertoire. If the volume has any single major flaw, though, it is the fact that most of the essays weigh in on canonical texts almost exclusively, with Toni Morrison being the only author featured who started publishing after 1970.

Black Nationalism Nationalistic feelings, organizations, and movements among, for, and by African Americans have existed virtually since Africans were captured, im-

ported, and enslaved for the purpose of building a nation that has but reluctantly accepted their descendants. Each form that Black Nationalism has taken in North America over three centuries would take a chapter to define and describe, so it might appear foolish to offer an overarching definition here. Nonetheless, a generic definition might look like this: Black Nationalism in the United States of America is the philosophy that African Americans should be both self-defining and self-determined vis-à-vis the remainder of American society. The forms that such self-definition and self-determination should take are where different types of Black Nationalism diverge wildly, but as with other nationalisms, they might include "demands for territorial cession, political empowerment, or increased cultural autonomy . . . based on a common historical background or cultural heritage."[1]

In the 1960s, Black Nationalism was popularly defined by such groups as the Nation of Islam (especially its onetime national spokesman, Malcolm X, or its spiritual leader, Elijah Muhammad); the Student Nonviolent Coordinating Committee, at least after 1965; the Congress of Racial Equality (again, in the late 1960s, after Floyd McKissick became its leader); and to a lesser degree, the Black Panther Party for Self-Defense, which never considered itself a Black Nationalist organization, despite the fact that many of its members' openly admired Malcolm X. In addition, Dr. Maulana Ron Karenga's US Organization (the "name US actually stands for Black people . . . 'us' as opposed to 'them,' the white oppressors"),[2] founded in Los Angeles in 1966, began as a Black Nationalist self-help group similar in outlook to the Black

1. William L. Van DeBurg, *Modern Black Nationalism: From Marcus Garvey to Louis Farrakhan* (New York: New York University Press, 1997), 2.

2. Scot Brown, *Fighting for Us: Maulana Karenga, the US Organization, and Black Cultural Nationalism* (New York: New York University Press, 2003), 2.

Panther Party. Through US, Karenga developed his Kawaida theory (taken from a Kiswahili term connoting tradition and reason), with its seven principles of Nguzo Saba (Umoja, or unity; Kujichagulia, or self-determination; Ujima, or collective work and responsibility; Ujamaa, or cooperative economics; Nia, or purpose; Kuumba, or creativity; and Imani, or faith); these principles formed the basis of the African American holiday Kwanzaa, which Karenga also invented in 1966. Via Kawaida, Kwanzaa, and various critical essays and books, including *Introduction to Black Studies* (1982), Karenga has been one of the leading progenitors of black cultural nationalism since the 1960s.

Black Nationalism in the 1960s had its most obvious effect in two areas: literary criticism, which saw the rise of a class of African American intellectuals that slowly both complemented and supplanted the dominant voice of white critics in the ongoing struggle to define and describe the literature; and in the craft and content of African American fiction, drama, and poetry. More detailed discussions of these effects may be found in the entries on the Black Aesthetic and the Artists and Communities in this volume, but it would be fair to summarize them as African American authors' and critics' renewed emphases upon the possibilities of black unity and community, economic independence, and cultural richness.

Many writers and critics influenced by Black Nationalism want, on the one hand, to indict America for the gross sins of its past and present with regard to the African Diaspora and its descendants (including those members of the Diaspora who willingly aided and abetted slavery, segregation, and their inimical brutalities), while showing how African Americans might transcend these pasts and form communities defined and determined by their members, rather than by their oppressors.

As with any nationalism, Black Nationalism from the 1960s to the present has been fraught with intense controversy, depending upon the way in which an author, work, or figure defines African Americans, what they should do, and to whom they should do it, especially if "it" means to pursue economic and cultural independence from all things "white," "European," "Western," or whichever term may signify the oppressor. The normal questions that arise regarding such pursuits often ask, first, whether it is possible to sever such ties to the oppressor completely. If so, the question then becomes whether it is either necessary or desirable to do so. Most forms of Black Nationalism take a fairly pragmatic view of these questions; rather than arguing for a complete separation from the oppressor, the goal becomes to create African American–run institutions, organizations, and programs that have as few ties to "white" or governmental obligations as possible, in order for African Americans to see what they can produce of their own volition and according to their specific communal needs.

In the 1960s and 1970s in particular, certain African American authors found some solace in the idea of Black Nationalism and tried to shape their art according to a Black Aesthetic.

The most common expression of Black Nationalist thought in popular culture in the 1980s and 1990s could be found in feature films, R&B music, and hip-hop music and culture. The latter, especially, was the site in which black artists could be most openly critical of white hegemony. Such artists as Run-DMC, Public Enemy, Sister Souljah, Tupac Shakur, Brand Nubians, X-Clan, Professor X, Lauryn Hill, N.W.A., Paris, Mos Def, KRS-ONE/Boogie Down Productions, and Queen Latifah produced albums and CDs that frequently quoted, cited, or were clearly influenced by Black Nationalists new and old: Malcolm X, Elijah Muhammad,

Marcus Garvey, the Nation of Islam (and its subsidiary organizations), the Five Percent Nation of Islam, Minister Louis Farrakhan, Carter G. Woodson, among others.

To the degree that hip-hop culture was a major influence upon those African American authors born after the early 1960s, Black Nationalism was a nearly unavoidable philosophy, regardless of whether some, such as Paul Beatty, Danzy Senna, Trey Ellis, or Darius James, were critical of it. Few younger artists seem to accept 1960s-style Black Nationalism uncritically, but the dearth of authors coming forward to endorse an explicitly or unequivocally nationalist position does not mean that they do not hold to or reveal beliefs in African American cultural or economic independence in their works.

Black Panther Party for Self-Defense When the founders of the Black Panther Party for Self-Defense (popularly known as the Black Panthers) established their organization in Oakland, California, in 1966, they were responding directly to several crucial events in 1960s African American politics: the assassination of Malcolm X; the civil unrest of the "long, hot summers" of 1964 and 1965 and the way they revealed the degree to which economics played a central role in racist oppression; everyday police brutality in black communities; and the rising tide of Black Nationalist sentiment. On this last point, it is important to note that the Black Panthers claimed, credibly, not to be nationalist in either their membership or their goals. It would be more accurate to say that they subscribed to a radical, revolutionary socialism that sought to improve the material conditions in black communities by direct provision of vital services and education. Nevertheless, the original support and admiration they enjoyed—as well as some of the fear and revulsion they endured— came primarily from African Americans. Later, the Black Panthers would receive sub-

stantial financial and logistical support from white philanthropists, but their program of grassroots activism for impoverished African Americans remained at the party's core.

The Black Panther Party's founders were Huey P. Newton and Bobby Seale, who met at Oakland's Merritt College in 1966 and found a common cause in their discontent with both the state of activism on their campus and the inefficacy of the Civil Rights movement with regard to many of Oakland's problems, and in their interest in the idea of Black Power (see separate entry) that Stokely Carmichael of the Student Nonviolent Coordinating Committee (SNCC) had recently extolled. Newton and Seale wrote a "Ten Point Platform and Program" for their new organization, named after the political party that Carmichael had recently started in Alabama. The platform took its impetus from the basic black nationalistic tenet that African Americans should create and control the economy and civic conduct of their own communities, but it also took after self-defense organizations Newton had observed while growing up in Louisiana, with the ideology supplied by a careful reading of Marxist philosophy.

The Black Panther Party immediately found controversy and the enmity of law enforcement officials for its open, albeit then-legal armed patrols of Oakland's streets. As it grew and established chapters in other major U.S. cities, including Sacramento, Los Angeles, Chicago, and New York, it also attracted the attention of the Federal Bureau of Investigation, which infiltrated and helped destroy the organization via its clandestine Counter Intelligence Program (COINTELPRO). The Black Panthers gained in popularity among many African Americans in chapter cities both for its highly public image and the free programs it started, including school breakfasts and ambulance services, but due to internal strife and external harassment, the party was essentially defunct by 1976. Another markedly different organization bearing the same name, founded by ousted Nation of Islam minister Khalid Muhammad in 1998, bears no other relationship to the original Black Panther Party; in fact, the first Black Panther Party's surviving leaders have publicly and vehemently denounced the new organization.

As with the 1971 Attica uprising, the Black Panther Party was an inspirational image for many African American writers and intellectuals. Most of this influence may be seen in literary characters based upon Black Panther Party members and some of the ideals they championed. Mentions and traces of the Black Panthers or their philosophy may be found in Toni Morrison's *Song of Solomon*, John Edgar Wideman's *Philadelphia Fire*, and Alice Walker's *The Color Purple*, but the best source of information would be the biographies of former members, especially Elaine Brown's *A Taste of Power* (1992).

Black Power movement The Black Power movement is, depending upon the historian's or critic's point of view, either the successor to the modern Civil Rights movement or part of it. In either case, Black Power was the form that Black Nationalism took in reaction to the failures and blind spots of the Civil Rights movement. The term itself predates most events of the Civil Rights movement; *Black Power: A Record of Reactions in a Land of Pathos*, Richard Wright's 1954 report on Ghana's independence movement and the anticolonialist mood on the African continent, is the first major literary use of the term. NAACP activist Robert Williams also began using the term to describe the growing need for self-empowerment for African Americans in the late 1950s.

The commonly accepted understanding of the term, however, may be traced to a crucial June 16, 1966, speech by newly elected Student Nonviolent Coordinating Committee (SNCC) National Chairman Stokely Carmichael at a rally stop in Greenwood, Mississippi, during the March Against Fear. Carmichael and other young Civil Rights activists were incensed by what they saw as Dr. Martin Luther King Jr.'s capitulation during and after the events on "Bloody Sunday" in Selma, Alabama, and the nation's resistance to Civil Rights legislation in general. Carmichael's speech culminated in a strident chant—"We want Black Power!"—that he later revised into a political, economic, and cultural credo. The most complete version of Carmichael's ideals were published in *Black Power: The Politics of Liberation* (1967), which he coauthored with Charles V. Hamilton.

In simplest terms, adherents to Black Power rejected the integrationist program of the mainstream Civil Rights movement in favor of a form of Black Nationalism that would give African Americans control over their communities' politics, economics, and cultural apparatuses. As Carmichael and Hamilton write, "we [African Americans] must first redefine ourselves" and "reclaim our history and our identity from what must be called cultural terrorism, from the depredation of self-justifying white guilt."[1] The issue, then, was one of controlling the ways in which African Americans were perceived and understood, especially by themselves, or "full participation in the decision-making processes affecting the lives of black people."[2] Most notably, this included a form

1. Stokely Carmichael and Charles V. Hamilton, *Black Power: The Politics of Liberation* (New York: Grove, 1967), 34–35.
2. Carmichael and Hamilton, *Black Power*, 47.

of cultural nationalism expressed in one portion of SNCC's position paper on Black Power, published shortly after Carmichael's speech:

> Too long have we allowed white people to interpret the importance and meaning of the cultural aspects of our society. We have allowed them to tell us what was good about our Afro-American music, art, and literature. How many black critics do we have on the "jazz" scene? How can a white person who is not part of the black psyche (except in the oppressor's role) interpret the meaning of the blues to us who are manifestations of the song themselves?[1]

The ideas expressed here are directly linked to those found in the manifestoes of the Black Arts Movement, especially Hoyt Fuller's essay "Towards a Black Aesthetic" (1970), which argued that African Americans should develop their own aesthetics to evaluate art produced by other African Americans. For this reason, Fuller, Larry Neal, and other Black Arts critics stressed that the Black Arts Movement should be considered the cultural arm of the Black Power movement, and therefore inseparable in its conceptual outlook. To understand the Black Power movement, then, is to understand the impetuses behind the calls for Black Aesthetics and most African American fiction of the 1970s and 1980s.

As a consequence, literature and scholarship on Black Power are legion. Like the Black Arts Movement and the Black Aesthetic, discussions of the political aspects of post-1970 African American literature routinely make some mention of the Black Power movement and its effects. Several books, however, are crucial foundational texts: Carmichael and Hamilton, *Black Power: The Politics of Liberation* (1967); Lewis M. Killian, *The Impossible Revolution: Black Power and the American Dream* (1968); Richard Newman, *Black Power: A Bibliography* (1969); Dora F. Pantell and Edwin Greenidge, *If Not Now, When? The Many Meanings of Black Power* (1969); James H. Cone, *Black Theology and Black Power* (1969); Robert Lee Scott, *The Rhetoric of Black Power* (1969); James Boggs, *Racism and the Class Struggle: Further Pages from a Black Worker's Notebook* (1973); James McEvoy, *Black Power and Student Rebellion* (1969); Thomas Wagstaff, *Black Power: The Radical Response to White America* (1969); August Meier, ed., *Black Protest in the Sixties* (1970).

Black studies Black studies refers to the systematic study of the history, cultures, and literature of Africa, African America, or other peoples of the African Diaspora. A very young discipline, virtually all of the black, Afro-American or African American studies programs and departments that presently exist at American universities today may trace their origins to student activism of the late 1960s and early 1970s. Prior to 1968, no such program existed at any four-year college or university, although a handful of colleges had individual courses, many of which were popular yet embattled. The students and faculty who began fighting for these programs were heavily influenced by the ideas and leaders of the Black Power and Black Arts movements, which called for African Americans to define and determine their own destinies.

The first such department was founded at San Francisco State College (now San Francisco State University) in 1968 after numerous student protests and petitions of

---

1. Student Nonviolent Coordinating Committee, *Papers, 1959–72* (Sanford, N.C.: Microfilming Corporation of America, 1982), reel 57, item 10, p. 3.

the campus administration. The same pattern followed soon thereafter at many other historically white institutions, such as the University of California's campuses at Berkeley, Los Angeles, and Santa Barbara; campuses of the universities of Illinois, Georgia, Pittsburgh, and Massachusetts; Columbia, Duke, Harvard, New York, Ohio State, Pennsylvania State, Princeton, Stanford, Temple, Tulane, and Yale universities; and many others. A substantial number of historically black colleges and universities (HBCUs) also added black studies programs and departments to their curricula, as no such programs existed on those campuses either, despite the makeup of their student populations. By the end of the 1970s, however, dozens of black studies programs and their faculty had been either dissolved or integrated into other departments on their respective campuses. The relative few that remain still struggle for everything from simple respect to their very existence.

Most of the scholars who formed the core faculties of the first black studies programs and departments included students and intellectuals trained in other disciplines, such as anthropology, history, English, and sociology, who were interested not only in researching African Americans and the African Diaspora but also in transforming their home disciplines. Many still teach black studies courses today, although it has become more common for faculty to reside wholly in traditional departments and teach cross-listed courses. Scholars who have made a significant impact upon black studies, whether directly or indirectly, include: Houston A. Baker Jr.; Molefi K. Asante; Keneth Kinnamon; Richard Barksdale; Toni Cade Bambara; Haki Madhubuti (né Don L. Lee); Henry Louis Gates Jr.; Charles V. Hamilton; Barbara Smith; Elliott Butler-

Evans; Hortense Spillers; Hoyt Fuller; Larry Neal; and Maulana Ron Karenga. The latter's book, *Introduction to Black Studies* (1982), is a significant early textbook in the field, along with Barksdale and Kinnamon's *Black Writers of America* (1972).

Several foundational journals of literature and criticism arose directly out of the black studies, Black Power, and Black Arts movements; most of them are still active. These include the *Journal of Black Studies* (bimonthly; 1970–present); *African American Review* (quarterly; 1967–present); *Callaloo* (quarterly; 1976–present); *The Western Journal of Black Studies* (quarterly; 1977–present). Although it was founded in 1940, decades prior to the Black Arts Movement, Atlanta University's *Phylon* (quarterly; 1940–present) is an excellent source of scholarly information about African American history and culture. It regularly features essays about fiction and other forms of literature by African Americans in nearly every issue. Most essays, however, concern literature written prior to 1970.

Black Writers of America: A Comprehensive Anthology When Richard Barksdale and Kenneth Kinnamon published *Black Writers of America* in 1972, they did more than add a new anthology to the hundreds of collections of African American literature that have emerged since the nineteenth century; they presented what may rightly be called the first major anthology to make it possible to teach African American literature survey courses without assigning multiple texts. As its preface notes, it is "inclusive enough to satisfy the needs of a two-semester survey course, but its selections . . . could constitute a semester's or a quarter's work."[1] In other words, the claim to comprehensiveness in the anthology's subtitle is quite sup-

1. Richard Barksdale and Keneth Kinnamon, *Black Writers of America: A Comprehensive Anthology* (New York: Macmillan., 1972), xi.

portable. Its publication was especially timely, as hundreds of black studies programs and departments were being created in the early 1970s.

Black Writers of America was originally modeled on the 1941 anthology *Negro Caravan*, edited by Sterling Brown, Arthur P. Davis, and Ulysses Lee, which Barksdale and Kinnamon had originally planned to update. They soon decided, however, to create an original anthology that extended the breadth and depth of previous anthologies, some of which did not recognize or acknowledge any African American literature prior to the poetry of Paul Laurence Dunbar.[1] As a result, Barksdale and Kinnamon played a significant role in redefining the term "African American literature" so that folklore, song lyrics, and oratory—all products of the oral tradition in African American culture—would be included. This had an irreversible and positive effect upon attempts to create an African American canon over the next thirty years.

Black Writers of America thus collects representative work from sixty-six authors, as well as dozens of folktales, spirituals, work songs, prison songs, blues lyrics, breakdowns, gospel songs, and so on. It is divided into six major periods, beginning in the eighteenth century and ending with the post-WWII generation. Each period is further divided; it begins with "major writers," followed by generic divisions: history, autobiography, poetry, "race politics," folk literature, oral accounts, and several others.

From its publication until 1996, when the *Norton Anthology of African American Literature* emerged, *Black Writers of America* was the only major comprehensive anthology available. It was not easily available, though, as the clothbound volume cost about $60.00 by the 1990s. A $39.00 paperback version was not issued until 1997, certainly long after it was needed, and after the publication of the *Norton Anthology of African American Literature*, which inarguably made *Black Writers of America* obsolete, if time had not already done so. In addition, Macmillan Publishing Company, the original publisher, did not permit Barksdale and Kinnamon to update the anthology to accommodate new authors and perspectives. Naturally, the anthology became as outdated as its predecessors.

One could very well argue, however, that even before the appearance of the *Norton Anthology*, *Black Writers of America* was simply dated. It is clearly a product of a specific political and social epoch in African American history, as signified by several elements. The volume foregrounds the fact that it was created during the late 1960s' and early 1970s' strong, male-centered Black Nationalism. Beyond the title—the authors are *Black*, not Negro, writers of America—each author is pointedly identified as Black with a capital B, a bold assertion of the then-new importance given to "Blackness." White Americans are "the white man." One major section is entitled "The Black Man in the Civil War: 1861–1865" and contains a subsection, "Two Black Women Serve and Observe," that effectively minimizes the presence and role of African American women in that particular struggle. The final subsection contains speeches and writings from three "Racial Spokesmen," Martin Luther King Jr., Malcolm X, and Eldridge Cleaver, whose essay "To All Black Women, From All Black Men" serves as the only significant acknowledgement of women's role in African American history and culture in this subsection. Perhaps most troubling, of the sixty-six writers collected, only fifteen are women, excluding the probability that some of the anonymous

---

1. Dolan Hubbard, "An Interview with Richard K. Barksdale," *BALF* 19, no. 4 (Winter 1985): 140.

authors of the folk literature included in each section were women.

Many of the author biographies also filter that author's achievements through a lens that focuses upon his or her ability to come to terms with a somewhat anachronistic African American identity. Generally, Barksdale and Kinnamon applaud authors and other figures for their capacity to stand up to or defy "the white man" or otherwise aid in African American liberation, "revolution," and expression of a monolithic "Black Experience." Authors who express some ambivalence about their identity, such as Countee Cullen, are chided for not "approaching the rhetoric of Blackness."[1]

The criticisms noted here are not mere matters of outmoded terminology. While it would be fair to say that *Black Writers of America*'s oversights reflect the inevitable problems of canon building in general and anthologies in particular—differing and historically specific criteria for inclusion and exclusion of authors—they also reflect blind spots in African American cultural nationalism that affected the way the literature has been received and perceived. As Calvin Hernton has noted, regarding the issue of women's place in assessments of African American literary history, many contemporary male African American critics consider it "an offense" for black women "to struggle on their own, let alone achieve something of their own," whereas black men are allowed and expected to do precisely that.[2] This view seems to color *Black Writers of America*'s organization and editorial policy.

Another issue kept this anthology from reaching its full potential: the publisher forbade the editors to revise their own anthol-

ogy.[3] If Barksdale and Kinnamon's landmark text still reflects the tenor of its time, whether to its credit or detriment, the editors cannot be blamed in this regard. Instead, they should be credited for assembling a groundbreaking, if inevitably flawed, insight into the whole of African American literature.

Bluest Eye, The Toni Morrison's first novel (1970) is also one of the most frequently assigned and discussed of her six published to date. It is also one of the most frequently banned books in the United States, most likely due to its horrifying depiction of a young African American girl molested by her father. That girl, Pecola Breedlove, lives a life of psychological misery as she sees how frequently her parents and other elders, but especially her mother, pay homage to the idea of white supremacy, often in unconscious ways. The actions of the adults in Pecola's world are shaped by encounters with racism that damage, even break their spirits. Eventually, the pain stemming from both this hatred and a general absence of love and meaningful human connections leads Pecola's father, Cholly, to molest her, which in turns drives Pecola insane, as she wishes for blue eyes and whiteness to save her from her own psychological hell.

The Bluest Eye marks not only the beginning of Toni Morrison's career as a published author but also the inauguration of numerous themes and approaches that would occupy many African American authors from the 1970s onward: a focus on the black family's troubled history; the power of racial stereotypes that devalue African Americans' beauty and feelings of

1. Barksdale and Kinnamon, *Black Writers*, 529.

2. Calvin Hernton, "The Sexual Mountain and Black Women Writers," *BALF* 18, no. 4 (Winter 1984): 142.

3. Chester J. Fontenot Jr., review of *The Norton Anthology of African American Literature* and *Call and Response: The Riverside Anthology of the African American Literary Tradition*, CLA Journal 41, no. 4 (June 1998): 483.

self-worth; the degree to which many African Americans ironically subscribe to these stereotypes, consciously and unconsciously; the power and danger of African American sexuality in the popular mind and among African American communities; and the complicated nature of black women's relations with black men and white women and men.

The literature on *The Bluest Eye* is quite extensive. Most scholarly studies may be found in books on Morrison's corpus as a whole; see separate entry on Morrison. The following are among the most notable essays focusing primarily or largely on the novel:

Barbara Christian, "Community and Nature: The Novels of Toni Morrison," *Journal of Ethnic Studies* 7, no. 4 (Winter 1980); Patrice Cormier-Hamilton, "Black Naturalism and Toni Morrison: The Journey Away from Self-Love in *The Bluest Eye*," *MELUS* 19, no. 4 (Winter 1994); John Duvall, "Naming Invisible Authority: Toni Morrison's Covert Letter to Ralph Ellison," *Studies in American Fiction* 25, no. 2 (Autumn 1997); Phyllis R. Klotman, "Duck and Jane and the Shirley Temple Sensibility in *The Bluest Eye*," *Black American Literature Forum* 13, no. 4 (Winter 1979); Jane Kuenz, "*The Bluest Eye*: Notes on History, Community, and Black Female Subjectivity," *AAR* 27, no. 3 (Autumn 1993); Rafael Pérez-Torres, "Tracing and Erasing: Race and Pedagogy in *The Bluest Eye*," in *Approaches to Teaching the Novels of Toni Morrison*, ed. Nellie Y. McKay (New York: Modern Language Association, 1997).

Blues, Ideology, and Afro-American Literature: A Vernacular Theory

Often mentioned in conjunction with *The Signifying Monkey*, by Henry Louis Gates Jr.(1988), Houston A. Baker's *Blues, Ideology, and Afro-American Literature* (1984) is one of the crucial books of African American literary criticism to be published in the 1980s. Baker's positing of the blues as a foundational form that informs much of African American literature was a logical outgrowth of his critical positions of the early 1970s, which were deeply influenced by the Black Arts Movement and the Black Aesthetic that were its theoretical underpinning. *Blues, Ideology, and Afro-American Literature*, however, took Baker's criticism in new directions with its conscious incorporation of poststructuralist literary theory in conjunction with affirmative analyses of the blues, with the former often serving to help validate the latter. This move and the book as a whole were quite controversial at the time, as they went against one of the precepts of the very Black Aesthetic of which Baker was a champion in the early 1970s. That is to say, the Black Arts Movement and its Black Aesthetic eschewed any appeals to European or Euro-American standards, arguing instead for the validity of African American and African Diasporic cultures on their own terms. Moreover, the Black Aesthetic demanded that African American texts be accessible to African Americans in terms of both their language and cultural grounding. By drawing heavily upon the theories of Karl Marx, G. W. F. Hegel, Roland Barthes, Michel Foucault, Hayden White, Frederic Jameson, Clifford Geertz, and several others, Baker broke with these major precepts while arguing strenuously and convincingly for the sophistication and complexity of the blues form in ways that satisfy the demands of both African American cultural theories and, ironically, the strictures of frequently biased European traditions. Baker also assailed the formalist bases of such peers as Gates and Robert Stepto as inadequate to explore the nuances of African American literature and culture.

Despite the controversy, Baker's book has remained one of the foundational theoretical texts of the contemporary period. Several contemporary reviews and articles stand out for their careful reading of the book and its importance: Arnold Rampersad, "The Literary Blues Tradition," *Callaloo* 24 (Spring-Summer 1985); Joe Weixlmann, "The Way We Were, the Way We Are, the Way We Hope to Be," *BALF* 20, nos. 1/2 (Spring-Summer 1986); and R. Baxter Miller, "Baptized Infidel: Play and Critical Legacy," *BALF* 21, no. 4 (Winter 1987). Most important of all, however, would be the great debate held in the pages of *New Literary History* between Baker, Gates, and Joyce Ann Joyce over the role of critical theory and the authenticity of contemporary African American critics and criticism in *NLH* 18, no. 2 (Winter 1987), which immediately galvanized scholars in African American literary studies. Two excellent responses to the debate are Joyce's "The Problems with Silence and Exclusiveness in the African American Literary Community," *Black Books Bulletin: WordsWork* 16 (Winter 1993–94) and Theodore O. Mason's "Between the Populist and the Scientist: Ideology and Power in Recent Afro-American Literary Criticism, or, 'The Dozens' as Scholarship," *Callaloo* 36 (Summer 1988). The *NLH* articles are also collected in Winston Napier's anthology, *African American Literary Theory* (2000).

Bradley, David (b. September 1950, Bedford, Pennsylvania) Novelist and short story author David Bradley authored two of the finest works in the contemporary era in the 1970s and early 1980s. The first, *South Street* (1975), is set in Philadelphia's black community. It features Adlai Stevenson Brown, a young black poet who moves to the titular South Street and becomes involved in the community's life via the three major set pieces, Lightnin' Ed's Bar, the Elysium Hotel, and the Word of Life storefront church. The characters that populate the community and Brown's shifting relation-

ships with them provide the crux of the novel's plot; it is primarily a novel about the street and its quirkier denizens, all of whom weave in and out of one another's lives and stories. The details of their lives and stories, combined with Bradley's lyricism and cadence, provide one of the more remarkable works of the mid-1970s. Between the publication of *South Street* and his second novel, Bradley also published a number of short stories: "The Happiness of the Long Distance Runner," *The Village Voice* (August 1976); "Assignment No. 4: The Business Letter," *Tracks* (Spring 1977); "Eye Witness News," *Tracks* (Spring 1978); and "City of the Big Sleep," *Signature* (August 1979).

In the main, though, Bradley's reputation rests almost entirely upon his classic second novel, *The Chaneysville Incident* (1981), a historical work that fits perfectly into the neo–slave narrative genre (see separate entry). It won the PEN/Faulkner Award in 1982 and became a Book-of-the-Month Club Alternate Selection. The incident mentioned in the title is one based upon an actual event in Bedford County, Pennsylvania, in which thirteen escaped slaves, once caught, asked to be killed rather than taken back into slavery; their request was granted. Bradley turns this event, remembered by many African Americans in the community yet forgotten in the official history, into the mystery at the heart of the novel. Protagonist John Washington wishes to discover who the slaves were, how they came to that spot in Bedford County, who killed them and why (beyond their request), what occurred afterwards, and why this history has been hidden for so long. The novel's perspective shifts into the past at many points to provide the slaves' perspective and therefore to create a slave narrative for them, one including the sorts of details frequently excluded from classic, traditional narratives. Inasmuch as the novel is based upon an incident with which Bradley was personally familiar—his mother kept and wrote records of it, and Bradley was of that community and possibly descended from the slaves at its center—it blurs the boundaries between fact and fiction. This is, in fact, Bradley's clear intent, as the novel questions how official history, which often excludes African American perspectives or simply lies about them, is formed and made official in the first place.

Since 1981, Bradley has been working on the follow-up to *The Chaneysville Incident*, but it has yet to appear, although Bradley has published many book reviews and a number of nonfiction essays. He also edited a reference work, *The Encyclopedia of Civil Rights in America* (1998). The scholarship on Bradley and especially *Chaneysville*, on the other hand, has been deservedly extensive, resulting in close studies in at least two books and dozens of scholarly articles. The extant books include: Kamau Kemayo, *Emerging African Survivals: An Afrocentric Critical Theory* (2003), and Martin J. Gliserman, *Psychoanalysis, Language, and the Body of the Text* (1996). Significant journal articles include: Jay Clayton, "The Narrative Turn in Recent African American Fiction," *American Literary History*, 2, no. 3 (Autumn 1990); Charles Johnson, "Whole Sight: Notes on New Black Fiction," *Callaloo* 22 (Autumn 1984); Susan L. Blake and James A. Miller, "The Business of Writing: An Interview With David Bradley," *Callaloo* 21 (Spring-Summer 1984); Klaus Ensslen, "Fictionalizing History: David Bradley's *The Chaneysville Incident*," *Callaloo* 35 (Spring 1988); Matthew Wilson, "The African American Historian: David Bradley's *The Chaneysville Incident*," *AAR* 29, no. 1 (Spring 1995); Edward Pavlic, "Syndetic Redemption: Above-Underground Emergence in David Bradley's *The Chaneysville Incident*," *AAR* 30, no. 2 (Summer 1996); Philip J. Egan, "Unraveling

Misogyny and Forging the New Self: Mother, Lover, and Storyteller in *The Chaneysville Incident*," *Papers on Language and Literature* 33, no. 3 (Summer 1997); Missy Dehn Kubitschek, "'So You Want a History, Do You?': Epistemologies and *The Chaneysville Incident*," *The Mississippi Quarterly* 49, no. 4 (Fall 1996); Helen Lock, "'Building Up from Fragments: The Oral Memory Process in Some Recent African-American Written Narratives," *College Literature* 22, no. 3 (October 1995); Cathy Brigham, "Identity, Masculinity, and Desire in David Bradley's Fiction," *Contemporary Literature* 36, no. 2 (Summer 1995); W. Lawrence Hogue, "Problematizing History: David Bradley's *The Chaneysville Incident*," *CLA Journal* 38, no. 4 (June 1995); and Martin J. Gliserman, "David Bradley's *The Chaneysville Incident*: The Belly of the Text," *American Imago* 43, no. 97 (Summer 1986).

Briscoe, Connie (b. December 31, 1952) Novelist Connie Briscoe stands among the better writers to emerge in and benefit from the strong wave of interest in African American fiction that arose in the early 1990s after the publication of Terry McMillan's *Waiting to Exhale* (1992). Her first novel, *Sisters and Lovers* (1994), for example, sold nearly 500,000 copies in cloth and paperback combined in its first two years, while her second, *Big Girls Don't Cry* (1996), had an initial print run of 100,000 in cloth.[1] Briscoe is not, however, a mere imitator of McMillan in either style or content. Although her novels primarily discuss African American women's concerns with romantic relationships, careers, and family, Briscoe makes highly topical threads about contemporary racial politics inextricable parts of her plots, which are peopled with far more realistic characters than may be found in many other post-McMillan works.

1. Malcolm Jones Jr., "Successful Sisters: Faux Terry Is Better Than No Terry," *Newsweek*, April 29, 1996, 79.

Sisters and Lovers, for example, tells of three sisters, Beverly, Charmaine, and Evelyn, who spend a great deal of time ruminating over their relationships with their spouses and partners but also have considerable problems that arise from sexism, despite being otherwise fairly successful in their careers, and from everyday life in Washington, D.C., and environs. *Big Girls Don't Cry* (1996) is even more topical; it is set during the early 1960s, which was a crucial time in the Civil Rights era. Middle-class protagonist Naomi Jefferson becomes interested in African Americans' greater concerns after her brother dies working for the movement. Naomi's problematic romantic encounters in college parallel some of her later struggles with workplace discrimination, which allow Briscoe to delve into the importance of the Civil Rights movement and affirmative action as a policy. The historical novel *A Long Way from Home* (1999) is based upon Briscoe's own genealogy. Set during slavery, the novel revolves around the young house slave Clara, who works in the home of former president James Madison. In a plot that recalls the life of Harriet Jacobs,[1] Clara finds her own life and those of her half-white children—especially daughter Susan—thrown into chaos after Madison dies. The novel chronicles Susan's search for her own genealogy and identity as someone who can pass for white yet is all too aware of her heritage. Briscoe has been nominated for a National Book Critics Circle Award and a NAACP Image Award (2000).

Brown, Cecil (b. July 3, 1943, Bolton, North Carolina) Author, poet, critic, and essayist Cecil Brown is best known for *The Life and Loves of Mr. Jiveass Nigger* (1969), a rollicking, picaresque satire of American attitudes toward black male sexuality as well as its lack of appreciation of African American literature. Since the publication of *Life and Loves*, however, Brown's output as a fiction writer has been frustratingly sparse, with but two novels and a handful of short stories to his credit. Most of Brown's published work has consisted of literary criticism, book reviews, and nonfiction during his long tenure as a lecturer at the University of California at Berkeley and Merritt College in Oakland, California.

The Life and Loves of Mr. Jiveass Nigger is a picaresque novel and satirical bildungsroman that examines the exploits of George Washington, a young African American expatriate living in Copenhagen, as he fulfills and explodes the stereotype of the "black stud" or "bad nigger" who defies the accepted racial order despite the dangers of doing so. Not only is Washington "the cussinges' man ever born," full of lusts, obscenities and lies, but his modus operandi is to be a "jiveass nigger," which means to superficially honor the authorities and social mores that guided the early part of his life while subtly subverting them through trickery and deceit. This behavior is an extension of Washington's singular personality; he possesses "the almost fanatical ability to remain *different* against all odds," to be able to walk in both high- and low-brow worlds.[2] The novel switches between scenes from Washington's youth and events in Copenhagen, where he continually hustles money and women for his own benefit, to feed both himself and his cynicism regarding absolute truths and stabilities. His exploits also give him many opportunities

1. Harriet Jacobs (writing as Linda Brent), *Incidents in the Life of a Slave Girl, Written by Herself*, ed. Jean Fagan Yellin (1861; Cambridge, Mass.: Harvard University Press, 1987).

2. Cecil Brown, *The Life and Loves of Mr. Jiveass Nigger* (New York: Farrar, Straus Giroux, 1969), 12; italics in the original.

to pontificate on the limits facing African American authors.

Brown spent most of the 1970s writing short stories, essays, criticism, and screenplays. The best known of the latter is the Richard Pryor comedy *Which Way is Up?* (1977), cowritten with Carl Gottlieb, Lina Wertmüller, and Sonny Gordon. Brown's experiences in Hollywood provided the background of his next novel, *Days Without Weather* (1983), which features the exploits of Jonah Drinkwater, a cantankerous, failed comedian working in Los Angeles. One of Drinkwater's uncles is a hack writer in Hollywood who ekes out a living by compromising, and therefore destroying, any script by African American writers that is too militant. Brown also published his memoir, *Coming Up Down Home: A Memoir of a Southern Childhood*, in 1993, and he continues to write essays. His history of the legend of African American folk hero Stagolee, *Stagolee Shot Billy*, was published in 2003.

Despite the notoriety engendered by his first novel, scholarship on Brown is quite sparse, with most information on his work consisting of the inevitable book reviews and mentions in retrospectives of African American literature of the late 1960s and early 1970s. This writer devotes part of a chapter of *African American Satire: The Sacredly Profane Novel* (2001) to *The Life and Loves of Mr. Jiveass Nigger*.

Bunkley, Anita Richmond (b. September 29, 1944, Columbus, Ohio) Anita Richmond Bunkley is one of the better-known names in the subfield of African American romance fiction to achieve prominence in the latter half of the 1990s. Like her peer, detective-fiction author Walter Mosley, Bunkley imbues her chosen genre with cautionary tales and social realities that allow her to be simultaneously true to generic conventions

yet topical. The results are works that are highly entertaining yet historically informative and ultimately provocative. They have in common an interest in African American history and heritage, including current events that resonate with Bunkley's large, loyal audience.

Between 1989 and 2000, Bunkley published five novels, coauthored two short-story collections, and authored one nonfiction book, *Steppin' Out with Attitude: Sister, Sell Your Dream!* (1998). The anthologies, *Sisters* (1996) and *Girlfriends* (1999), comprise short stories about the friendships and bonds among groups of African American women authored by Bunkley and writers Sandra Kitt and Eva Rutland. *Emily, the Yellow Rose* (1989) tells the story of Emily West, the former slave whose romantic saga inspired the popular song, "The Yellow Rose of Texas." In her 1997 article, "'The Yellow Rose of Texas': A Different Cultural View," scholar Trudier Harris credits Bunkley's novel with placing West's life within its proper historical context, showing how the heroine helped the United States achieve victory in the U.S.-Mexican War (1846–1848).[1]

Black Gold (1994), also set in Texas, tells of the jealousies, romances, and conflicts between two rival African American families. *Wild Embers* (1996), set during World War II, follows the story of Janelle Roy, an African American nurse who endures a series of crises due to the vagaries of racism. She eventually becomes an Army nurse working with the legendary Tuskegee Airmen, the highly decorated all-black flying unit, and falls in love with one of its more handsome members. *Starlight Passage* (1997) tells of doctoral student Kiana Sheridan's quest for her heritage, which leads the text into an exploration of the case for reparations for slavery. *Balancing Act* (1998) veers a bit from Bunkley's normal fare, as it

---

1. Trudier Harris, "'The Yellow Rose of Texas': A Different Cultural View," *Callaloo* 20, no. 1 (Winter 1997): 8–19.

sidesteps the romantic plot elements in favor of an indictment of environmental racism. The novel tracks black media professional Elise Jeffries's dilemmas as she is torn between the demands of her marriage, her desire to protect her community, and being an effective employee of the firm whose actions threaten that community's existence.

Butler, Octavia Estelle (b. June 22, 1947, Pasadena, California) Speculative (or science) fiction author Octavia E. Butler is, along with Samuel R. Delany, one of the premiere African American writers in the genre. For that matter, she is one of a very small handful of African Americans, and even fewer African American *women*, in a field that has historically been dominated by white males. Her achievements, of course, extend beyond her identity; Butler is widely acknowledged as a major writer in speculative/science fiction, to say nothing of African American literature. Her novels and novellas have earned her extensive and consistent acclaim, resulting in science fiction's top honors, including the 1984 and 1985 Hugo Awards for the short story "Speech Sounds" (1983) and for the novella "Bloodchild" (1984), respectively, and the 1984 Nebula Award, also for "Bloodchild." Butler also received a MacArthur Foundation Genius Grant in 1995.

Butler's fiction is linked and united by a number of common themes, characters, and metaphors. She is concerned primarily with exploring the origins of dystopian societies that function via hierarchies defined by ethnicity or race, economic class, ability, gender, sexuality, or other qualities. Butler takes an intense look in particular at the way such hierarchies inevitably devolve into forms of oppression or slavery for those others who either lack the preferred characteristics or who are paradoxically connected to the elite through blood or genetic ties. These themes are most apparent in her earliest works, the "Patternist" series, which comprises six novels or novellas published between 1976 and 1984. They are *Patternmaster* (1976), *Mind of My Mind* (1977), *Survivor* (1978), *Kindred* (1979), *Wild Seed* (1980), and *Clay's Ark* (1984). The series chronicles a civilization governed by elite telepaths attempting to engineer a supreme race and enslave those who lack their abilities. The best known of these (that is, outside of science fiction circles) is *Kindred*, a powerful meditation on slavery, miscegenation, and cultural development and mixing. *Wild Seed* follows in the same vein, concentrating primarily on the way slavery operates both physically and psychologically.

Clay's Ark serves as a somewhat transitional work between the Patternist series and the Xenogenesis Trilogy, which comprises *Dawn* (1987), *Adulthood Rites* (1988), and *Imago* (1989). These novels construct metaphors of addiction, with the trilogy in particular presenting a postapocalyptic vision of humanity in which an alien species integrates itself with *homo sapiens* for its further destruction. The only way humanity can hope to survive is by cooperation and the elimination of hierarchies, but its genetic programming and addictions make this nearly impossible. *Parable of the Sower* (1993) is also concerned with slavery to drugs, but it emphasizes the way drugs oblige the addict to become a slave in both the economic and spiritual realms. Its protagonist, Lauren Olamina, leads a religious sect whose Earthseed philosophy is meant to show its followers how to live in the world in a way that is ethically sensitive to the individual's body, environment, society, and world in practice. For their beliefs, Olamina and her followers are persecuted and, in 1998's *Parable of the Talents*, cast into concentration camps. Other works by Butler include *"Bloodchild" and Other Stories* (1995), which contains Butler's best short fiction, while *Lilith's Brood* (2000) collects the Xenogenesis Trilogy in one volume.

As might be expected, Butler's fiction has been discussed extensively in journals and magazines devoted to science fiction and fantasy, but she has also won a permanent place in scholarly publications. Butler is frequently classed as the author of neo–slave narratives, since so many of her novels reconfigure slavery's meaning in new contexts, allegorically comparing the peculiar institution to contemporary conditions in which African Americans and other groups live. She is also considered a key figure in contemporary feminist fiction to the extent that her novels probe the boundaries of gender definitions and the meaning of sexual orientations. Several journals, in fact, have devoted all or part of discrete issues to Butler's work. The winter 2003 issue of *Utopian Studies* (14, no. 1), a special issue on "Afrofuturism," features two articles on Butler, while *BALF*'s Science Fiction Issue (18, no. 2, summer 1984) includes three articles, including a bibliography. Maria Holmgren Troy's *In the First Person and in the House: The House Chronotope in Four Works by American Women Writers* (1999) places Butler in the company of Harriet Jacobs, Marilynn Robinson, and Elizabeth Stoddard.

C

Cain, George M. (b. 1943, New York, New York) Harlem author George M. Cain is known for his one book, *Blueschild Baby* (1971), a heavily autobiographical novel—the protagonist's name is George Cain—that tells of the harrowing nature of drug addiction and racism. Due to its focus on the path

to freedom from slavery, it is a revision of the slave narrative form and therefore merits classification as a neo–slave narrative as well. *Blueschild Baby*'s complex portrait of Harlem life made it stand out from many African American–authored novels of the early 1970s. Harlem is more than a symbol; it is a real community, with many different groups and classes making it a living, breathing space amidst its problems.

Callaloo (1976–present) *Callaloo* is one of two major journals of African American literature and criticism to emerge in the wake of the Black Arts Movement; the other is the *African American Review*. It was founded in 1976 by Charles Henry Rowell in Baton Rouge, Louisiana. Its primary goal is, according to Rowell, is to publish "literature and literary and cultural studies of the African diaspora . . . in addition to printing pieces of visual art, interviews, and articles dealing with cultural politics."[1] In practice, this means that *Callaloo*'s editorial policy has been to include writers of African descent from all parts of the globe, although the majority of contributors to and subjects discussed within the journal have been African American. It also means that a reader is more likely to find fiction, poetry, and author interviews in *Callaloo* than in its rival and contemporary, *African American Review*, which reserves more of its space for literary studies. Both, however, have contributed significantly and indispensably to the development of recent scholarship on African Diasporic literatures.

In pursuit of its primary goal, *Callaloo* has published many articles written in the original languages of its contributors. It has also published a number of special issues devoted entirely to the literature of Haiti (spring and summer 1992); the literature of

1. Charles Henry Rowell, introduction to *Making Callaloo: Twenty-five Years of Black Literature* (New York: St. Martin's Griffin, 2002), xix.

Guadeloupe and Martinique (winter 1992), Native America literatures (winter 1994); Puerto Rican women writers (summer 1994), African-Brazilian literature (fall 1995); Eric Williams and the postcolonial Caribbean (fall 1997); Caribbean literature from Suriname, the Netherlands Antilles, Aruba, and the Netherlands (summer 1998); and the literature and culture of the Dominican Republic (summer 2000).

The fiction writers published in *Callaloo* between 1976 and 2000 are some of the best that contemporary African American and African Diasporic literatures have had to offer. They include: Octavia Butler, Edwidge Danticat, Samuel R. Delany, Rita Dove, Trey Ellis, Ralph Ellison, Percival Everett, Leon Forrest, Thomas Glave, Wilson Harris, Charles Johnson, Gayl Jones, Randall Kenan, Helen Elaine Lee, Nathaniel Mackey, John McCluskey, Terry McMillan, Caryl Phillips, and John Edgar Wideman. Some of these authors were published for the first time in *Callaloo* or premiered excerpts from major works in the journal's pages. In addition, a number of special issues have been dedicated to the work of emerging or younger authors: fiction (autumn 1984); emerging women writers (spring 1996); and two special issues on emerging male writers (winter and spring 1998).

Other special issues include numbers on Ernest J. Gaines (May 1978), women poets (February 1979), Jay Wright (autumn 1983), Larry Neal (winter 1985), recent essays from Europe (autumn 1985), Richard Wright (summer 1986), Nicholas Guillen (spring 1987), "Post-Colonial Discourse" (autumn 1993), Maryse Condé (summer 1995), Sterling A. Brown (fall 1998), the European response to John Edgar Wideman (summer 1999), Nathaniel Mackey (spring 2000), and a memorial to Melvin Dixon and Audre Lorde (winter 2000).

Besides the original issues of the journal itself, readers interested in contemporary African American fiction may find *Callaloo's* twenty-fifth anniversary anthology, *Making Callaloo: Twenty-five Years of Black Literature* (2002) the best introduction to the fiction and poetry published in that time. Scholars should also note that through 1989 and issue 41, *Callaloo* was numbered sequentially; since 1990 and with volume 13, it has been divided into yearly volumes, with quarterly issues within each volume receiving their own numbers, 1 through 4.

Call and Response: The Riverside Anthology of the African American Literary Tradition

Although *Call and Response* (1998) was in production around the same time as the *Norton Anthology of African American Literature*, it was published some months after its competitor entered the market, which led to its being overshadowed. Like its rival, though, *Call and Response* represents a significant leap forward for anthologies of African American literature targeted for the academic-textbook market and is in some ways superior in terms of its production values, organization, pedagogical uses, and editorial outlook. General editor Patrician Liggins Hill, along with her editors, Bernard W. Bell, Trudier Harris, William J. Harris, R. Baxter Miller, Sondra A. O'Neale, and Horace Porter, explicitly chose to present African American literature "according to the Black Aesthetic, a criteria for black art developed by Americans of African descent," which means that "African American literature is a distinct tradition, one originating in the African and African American cultural heritages and in the experience of enslavement in the United States and kept alive beyond slavery through song, sermon, and other spoken and written forms." The editorial policy, then, "enables [the editors] to give equal place to the oral and written dimensions of African American literature" via "poetry, fiction, drama, essays, speeches, letters, autobiographies, sermons, criticism, journals, and folk literature from secular songs to rap." Their goal, therefore, is greater inclusiveness.[1]

The editors not only assembled what is arguably a more diverse set of texts but also concentrated their efforts less on classifying authors temporally (although they certainly do so) and more on scholarly, yet accessible discussions of authors' significance to African American literary traditions and to their chosen genres. For example, in the case of such African and African American folk genres as slave songs, secular work songs, and gospel music, the editors opted to write headnotes that show in intricate detail how these forms are structured in terms of their cadences and rhythms. For other modes and genres, the scholarship is no less meticulous. A typical section header includes a title (e.g., "Tell Ole Pharaoh, Let My People Go"), a temporal classification ("African American History and Culture, 1808–1865), and two subtitles indicating the general direction of literature and conditions for African Americans during that period ("The Explanations of the Desire for Freedom"; "Repression and Racial Response"). Each author receives a headnote with a short biography and a broad generic classification; the headnotes for genres and subgenres define each, with examples. The anthology also includes a CD with musical and poetic selections and speeches by authors included in the book.

Reviews of *Call and Response* have not, unfortunately, been as common as its better-known competitor, but one of the best is Julia Eichelberger's, published in *Mississippi Quarterly*'s winter 1999 issue. Eichelberger notes, quite accurately, that "each [anthol-ogy] is governed by a different story. One, the *Norton*, is the story of American adaptation and subversion, of 'signifying' upon the social and aesthetic ideals of the Enlightenment and the American experiment in democracy. The other, *Call and Response*, is a story of survival and revival, of an African diaspora that refused to disappear, and of this diaspora's growing consciousness of its own distinctive voice and vision." Eichelberger goes on to trace the ways in which the anthologies are indeed complementary in their organization, outlook, and selections.[2] Chester Fontenot's review in the June 1998 issue of *CLA Journal* is certainly the equal of Eichelberger's. Fontenot questions the very project of canon formation and traces the history of African American literary anthologies and their stated missions; he then offers a thorough comparison of the anthologies' strengths (e.g., full-length works in the case of the *Norton*; better bibliographies and more hard-to-find works in *Call and Response*). Fontenot also criticizes both texts for failing to pay enough attention to hip-hop and rap's diversity but finally concludes that although each anthology is problematic in its own way, they inarguably "fill the void created by the lack of a comprehensive collection since the publication of [Keneth Kinnamon and Richard Barksdale's] *Black Writers of America* [1972]."[3]

Campbell, Bebe Moore (b. 1950, Philadelphia, Pennsylvania) Although she began successfully writing and publishing in the late 1980s, novelist Bebe Moore Campbell has become associated with the wave of writers who entered the literary world in the

1. Patrician Liggins Hill, preface to *Call and Response: The Riverside Anthology of the African American Literary Tradition* (Boston: Houghton Mifflin, 1998), xxxiii.

2. Julia Eichelberger, review of *Call and Response: The Riverside Anthology of the African American Literary Tradition*, ed. Patrician Liggins Hill, *Mississippi Quarterly* 53, no. 1 (March 1999): 111.

3. Chester Fontenot, review of *Call and Response: The Riverside Anthology of the African American Literary Tradition*, ed. Patrician Liggins Hill, *CLA Journal* 40, no. 4 (June 1998): 477–93.

wake of Terry McMillan's runaway best-seller, *Waiting to Exhale* (1992). This is largely due to the fact that her first novel, *Your Blues Ain't Like Mine* (1992) was published the same year as McMillan's breakthrough. This association is also somewhat unfortunate, as the quality of Campbell's work generally exceeds that of many later writers in terms of its sophistication and overall quality. The only significant connection between Campbell and these authors is the broad subject of interpersonal relationships between African American men and women. Unlike many of her peers, however, Campbell frequently experiments with storytelling techniques and points of view and has a greater range of affect. She is nonetheless an extremely popular author who has benefited from both the quality of her art and strong promotion especially—and ironically—after McMillan.

Although Campbell's first two books, *Successful Women, Angry Men: Backlash in the Two-Career Marriage* (1987), and *Sweet Summer: Growing up with and Without My Dad* (1989) are nonfiction, they presage many of the characteristics of Campbell's fiction, to the extent that both reflect upon the changes in African American communities and communal bonds both during and after the Civil Rights movement. This concern is illustrated equally well in *Your Blues Ain't Like Mine*, a semiautobiographical narrative offering a witty and frequently startling story about the way that "race" and African Americans' roles in American society have changed dramatically in the latter half of the twentieth century. It is set in both rural Mississippi and urban Chicago in part to help highlight the tensions and conflicts among African Americans but also to show the degree to which racism is still very much part of American society. It tells of the murder of a young Chicagoan African American, Armstrong Todd, who is accused of flirting with a young white woman while in Mississippi. His case is clearly based upon that of Emmett Till, whose brutal murder in 1955 outraged African Americans and a good portion of the American public. Via Todd's fate, Campbell ponders how the Till case would be handled in post–Civil Rights America, with devastating results.

Brothers and Sisters (1994) is set in 1992 Los Angeles after the April 29 acquittal of the four white officers accused of brutalizing black motorist Rodney King, when the city exploded in the largest urban uprising since the Watts Riot of 1965. The protagonist is Esther Jackson, a middle manager at the novel's main location, a local bank where members of the city's diverse communities converge to discuss the many tensions across the lines of neighborhood, ethnicity, gender, and class that led to the verdict and its aftermath. Campbell's fiction has also been included in such anthologies as *New Bones: Contemporary Black Writers in America* (2001), *Wild Women* (1997), *Streetlights: Illuminating Tales of the Urban Black Experience* (1996), and *Breaking Ice: An Anthology of Contemporary African American Fiction* (1990).

Campbell's fiction has garnered a respectable amount of scholarly attention in addition to critical accolades and popular sales. Not only are her books are regularly reviewed in key literary journals dedicated to African American or ethnic American literature (*African American Review*, *Callaloo*, *MELUS*), but Campbell is also an accomplished reviewer and critic herself, having published dozens of reviews for the *New York Times* and made regular appearances on National Public Radio as a commentator. Campbell was interviewed in the fall 1999 issue of *Callaloo* (22, no. 4), and has been profiled in *Dictionary of Literary Biography Volume 227: American Novelists Since World War II* (2000). In addition, three scholarly articles have appeared that feature close analyses of Campbell's fiction: E. Shelley

Reid's "Beyond Morrison and Walker: Looking Good and Looking Forward in Contemporary Black Women's Stories," in *AAR* 34, no. 2 (summer 2000); and Christopher Metress's "'No Justice, No Peace': The Figure of Emmett Till in African American Literature," in *MELUS* 28, no. 1 (spring 2003).

Canon formation M. H. Abrams defines the most commonly accepted meaning of the term "literary canon" to be "those authors who, by a cumulative consensus of critics, scholars, and teachers, have come to be widely recognized as 'major,' and to have written works often hailed as literary classics. The literary works by canonical authors are the ones which, at a given time, are most kept in print, most frequently and fully discussed by literary critics and historians, and most likely to be included in anthologies and in the syllabi of college courses."[1] Abrams's definition has been applied to African American literature since the 1970s for the purpose of creating a standard list— the Greek word "*kanon*" means measuring rod—of significant African American writers who could be upheld as signs of continuous achievement and excellence.

Perhaps more important, such a standard could enable teachers of African American literature to cite, and therefore teach, a litany of greats via literary anthologies. This last desire led to the publication of several successful major anthologies—*Black Writers of America*, the *Norton Anthology of African American Literature*, and *Call and Response: The Riverside Anthology of the African American Literary Tradition*—whose implicit and explicit purposes were to help form canons.

Forming a canon of any particular type of literature is inherently problematic, for the simple reason that any criteria used to determine what should belong in a particular canon are inevitably subjective and the product of a particular historical moment, regardless of the number of thoughtful scholars who contribute their opinions. As a result, it is all too common for deserving texts to be excluded from such lists, even as less deserving texts accompany the accepted and cherished classics. In literary studies, then, the act of canon formation is nothing if not at least a little controversial in any era. In recent decades, as scholarly definitions of "classic" or merely great literature have opened up to be more inclusive, with women and people of color being the main—and intentional—beneficiaries, this process has become even more difficult, as critics and scholars have collectively struggled to expand different canons while not completely discarding their mainstays. The acrimony that resulted from often fierce disagreements about what great literature is developed into what is now known as the "Culture Wars" of the 1980s and 1990s, which pitted the avatars of a more European- and male-centered canon against proponents of various types of multiculturalism. While this binary opposition is somewhat oversimplified, it describes in general terms where the dividing lines were drawn. In the United States, the stakes were ultimately about control, but not simply of long book lists; rather, the issue may be fairly described as one of control of cultural capital itself, of the hearts and minds of an educated populace still coming to terms with the transformations that the politics of the 1960s initiated in the academy. One of these transformations, of course, was the creation of black studies courses, programs, and departments, many of which had to struggle for their very existence, particularly at some of the nation's more prestigious public universities.

Part of this struggle was directly tied to a problem that had vexed African American

1. M. H. Abrams, *A Glossary of Literary Terms, Seventh Edition* (New York: Harcourt Brace, 1999), page 29.

scholars since the nineteenth century. That is to say, one means by which African Americans might hope to achieve social, economic, and political equality in the United States is to dispel the common racist myth that African Americans, due to their alleged intellectual inferiority, have not written great literature and therefore cannot ever become part of the American cultural mainstream. Put another way, the myth argues that African Americans have contributed nothing to American or world civilization.

Such early African American intellectuals as David Walker, Henry Highland Garnet, Frederick Douglass, Frances E. W. Harper, Martin R. Delaney, Booker T. Washington and, most prominently, W. E. B. Du Bois did much to refute this myth, citing the greatness of ancient and modern figures from the African Diaspora. As the modern academy developed in the late nineteenth and early twentieth centuries, so did various types of pseudo-scientific racism that informed educators' views of African Americans and therefore led to their exclusion, both as students and as professors, from all but a scant few of the most prestigious campuses. Consequently, early scholars' attempts to extol the past accomplishments of the African Diaspora and to encourage future ones found few outlets. This exclusion, incidentally, was linked to the emphasis on vocational, rather than liberal arts education for African Americans that Booker T. Washington of the Tuskegee Institute advocated, despite Washington's own efforts to bring black accomplishments to the forefront of the public's mind. The relative dearth of African American fiction writers published by major presses was simultaneously a symptom and product of racist exclusion.

By the time the Harlem Renaissance began producing a coterie of talented young artists, though, it was quite possible for such major anthologies as James Weldon Johnson's *Book of American Negro Poetry* (1922) and V. F. Calverton's *Anthology of American Negro Literature* (1929) to be compiled and produced. Each of these anthologies, as have all others that followed them, have either implied or asserted that "the world does not know that a people is great until that people produces great literature and art," and that "no people that has produced great literature and art has ever been looked upon by the world as distinctly inferior," as Johnson does in the preface to his landmark volume.[1]

Nonetheless, deciding what "great literature and art" are for African Americans has been fraught with contention. The most vigorous debates have centered upon questions regarding both form and content. To be more specific, critics have frequently asked whether African American artists should aspire to emulate and improve upon acknowledged European and American masters or incorporate expressions of the rich folk heritage the African Diaspora has produced. As far as content is concerned, the divisions are more complicated; most have to do with the black artist's responsibility to African Americans as a whole, as well as his or her obligation to adhere to any particular artistic or political standard. During the Harlem Renaissance and the pre-WWII years, these questions dogged virtually every major African American intellectual and artist from W. E. B. Du Bois, Langston Hughes, Alain Locke, and George S. Schuyler to Zora Neale Hurston, Richard Wright, Sterling Brown, and many others. After the war, James Baldwin, John Oliver Killens, Ralph Ellison, Lorraine Hansberry, and Harold Cruse developed into some of the more vocal participants in the process of canon formation, debating the very purpose of African American literature and therefore

1. James Weldon Johnson, *The Book of American Negro Poetry* (New York: Harcourt Brace, 1922), 9.

which texts should be held up as the standards.

Since the mid-1960s, the question of canon formation has been inextricably tied to the Black Arts Movement, its concomitant Black Aesthetic, and the subsequent creation of black studies programs, whose scholars became the de facto creators and defenders of a new, loosely defined, and ever-shifting literary canon. With the publication of Keneth Kinnamon and Richard C Barksdale's *Black Writers of America* (1972), the idea of canon formation was transformed considerably. As Chester J. Fontenot Jr. writes, *Black Writers of America* "exploded the process of canon formation in challenging the 'literariness' of all cultural texts. [It] included . . . a balanced mixture of consciously and unconsciously literary texts from the African American tradition," with a "healthy portion of poems, plays, short stories, excerpts from novels, critical essays, political speeches, discursive writings, folklore, sacred and secular songs, and sermons" that demanded that "the African American literary tradition [be] judged . . . from within its own dialogic system."[1] In other words, *Black Writers of America* ensured that no anthologies published since 1970 that claimed to be comprehensive could exclude any the genres that Barksdale and Kinnamon included. It forced editors to relinquish the idea that African American literature mattered only to the extent that African Americans produced literature acceptable according to European-derived definitions of "literature" and canonicity.

The example that *Black Writers of America* set, in fact, was the basis for the two major comprehensive anthologies of the 1990s: *The Norton Anthology of African American Literature* (1997) and *Call and*

Response: The Riverside Anthology of the African American Literary Tradition (1998) (see separate entries for each anthology.) Both anthologies were meant to update *Black Writers of America*, whose publisher prevented the editors from revising their own anthology.[2] Both succeeded in that role, albeit in different ways, based upon different editorial outlooks stemming from debates regarding African American literary study that captivated the field in the 1980s and 1990s. Some of these debates often revolved around questions of gender or, more specifically, the degree to which women were included in or excluded from both canons and the process of creating them. More often , though, one of the central debates in African American literary studies concerned the place of contemporary literary theories and whether they fostered elitism. The many facets of this broad debate are too complex to outline in detail here, but a series of exchanges in 1989 in *American Literature* between critics Henry Louis Gates Jr. and Houston A. Baker Jr., on the one hand, and Joyce Ann Joyce on the other represent the essence of the discussion. The exchanges and many ancillary debates may be found in Winston Napier's excellent collection, *African American Literary Theory: A Reader* (2000). Inarguably, however, as a greater number of African American authors publish popular fiction, the question of canon formation is sure to remain a contentious one.

Cary, Lorene (b. November 29, 1956, Philadelphia, Pennsylvania) The three novels of memoirist and novelist Lorene Cary stand among the best of those to emerge in the 1990s, in terms of both the quality of Cary's writing and attention to the concerns

---

1. Chester Fontenot, review of *Call and Response: The Riverside Anthology of the African American Literary Tradition*, ed. Patrician Liggins Hill, *CLA Journal* 40, no. 4 (June 1998): 483.

2. Fontenot, review of *Call and Response*, 483.

of the Post-Soul generation of African Americans. Prior to her matriculation at the University of Pennsylvania (B.A., 1977; M.A., 1978) and the University of Sussex (M.A., 1979), Cary attended the predominantly white St. Paul's preparatory school in New Hampshire, an experience that formed the basis of her first book, the memoir *Black Ice* (1991). At St. Paul's, Cary found herself confronting racism and sexism alike in a supposedly integrated institution, prompting her to turn those experiences into a subtle, clever narrative that stands in a class with such creative memoirs as John Edgar Wideman's *Brothers and Keepers* (1984) and *The Woman Warrior* (1975), by Asian American Maxine Hong Kingston. Along the way, Cary uncovers the ambivalence that many middle-class African Americans feel toward the goal of integration itself. *Black Ice* emphasizes Cary's desire for her generation and those to follow to embrace their identities as African Americans even as they improve their lot in life. In short, Cary's memoir updates W. E. B. Du Bois's 1903 definition of double-consciousness (first delineated in *The Souls of Black Folk*) for the 1990s. Much of Cary's reputation as an author rests upon *Black Ice*. It has received numerous glowing reviews and is frequently mentioned as an exemplar of contemporary African American fiction. In 1992, the American Library Association designated it a Notable Book, while Colby College bestowed an honorary doctorate upon her the same year.

Cary's first novel, *The Price of a Child* (1995) is a neo–slave narrative that both adopts and revises the conventions of the slave narrative genre that dominated African American literature's first century. *The Price of a Child* is based upon the true story of Jane Johnson, a woman who escaped from enslavement the same way as protagonist Virginia Pryor, by being rescued by abolitionists while traveling with her master aboard a ferry. The novel's richness arises from Cary's crisp prose and simultaneous attention to historical accuracy (particularly in her portrayal of the abolitionist movement and the Underground Railroad) and the slave narrative's conventions (the physical brutality of slavery; the enslaved's dark moment of the soul that precipitates the quest for freedom; and an emphasis upon the slave's genius). Cary also creates slaveholders who are both horrifying and human, thereby building a degree of sympathy that ironically makes them even more horrific. Virginia's attempts to be a mother in the face of a brutal institution recalls Toni Morrison's *Beloved* (1987) and Gayl Jones's *Corregidora* (1975), just as her doubts about the meaning of freedom compare to those of Raven Quickskill in Ishmael Reed's *Flight to Canada* (1976) or Cary's own *Black Ice*.

Cary's third novel, *Pride* (1998) is a more straightforward and accessible contemporary novel in the vein of Terry McMillan or Eric Jerome Dickey, focusing on the tight-knit friendship shared by four middle-class African American women. As they search for greater meaning and affirmation in their lives, their bonds are put to the test by disease, death, and personal betrayals in their romantic relationships. Although not as artistically accomplished as her earlier works, *Pride* is Cary's most commercially successful novel. Although Cary has not yet been the subject of a detailed critical article, the high regard her first two books have earned virtually guarantees that such careful studies are forthcoming.

Chant of Saints: A Gathering of Afro-American Literature, Art, and Scholarship This anthology (1979) edited by poet-critic Michael S. Harper and scholar Robert B Stepto is, after Barksdale and Kinnamon's *Black Writers of America* (1972), one of the best anthologies of African American literature and criticism of the 1970s. It both capped the decade's burgeoning developments in professional African American literary criticism and presaged what was to come in the 1980s. As the subtitle indicates, *Chant of Saints* blends primary literature, some art and photography, and rigorous scholarship, including essays and interviews. The literary selections include poetry and fiction by Chinua Achebe, Ralph Ellison, Leon Forrest, Ernest J. Gaines, Harper, Robert Hayden, Gayl Jones, James Alan McPherson, Toni Morrison, John Stewart, Frederick Turner, Derek Walcott, Alice Walker, Sherley A. Williams, and Jay Wright. The volume's collages and paintings are by Romare Bearden (who is also the subject of an essay by Ralph Ellison) and Richard Yarde, respectively; its photographs are by Lawrence Sykes; the sculptures are by Richard Hunt. Personal and critical essayists include Kimberly W. Benston, Mary F. Berry and John W. Blassingame, Sterling A. Brown (to whom the entire volume is dedicated), John F. Callahan, Melvin Dixon, Ralph Ellison, Albert Murray, Stepto, Robert Farris Thompson, Alice Walker, Sherley A. Williams, and Wilburn Williams Jr. Interviewees include Leon Forrest, Gayl Jones, Toni Morrison, and Derek Walcott.

Chase-Riboud, Barbara (b. June 26, 1939, Philadelphia, Pennsylvania) Novelist, poet, and sculptor Barbara Chase-Riboud began her career in fiction writing relatively late but sparked great interest and controversy from the start. Her first novel, *Sally Hemings* (1979), drew heavily upon historical records to imagine the life and circumstances of the real Sally Hemings, an enslaved woman who had a romantic relationship with Thomas Jefferson and likely bore several of his children. The novel foregrounded the fact that miscegenation has always been part of American history, up to and including one of the most revered Founding Fathers. It also offered an alternate view of ambivalent,

yet ultimately racist remarks Jefferson had made about African Americans and slavery in his *Notes on the State of Virginia* (1785) and helped encourage the efforts of Jefferson's African American descendants to be recognized fully as part of the family. It was the quality of Chase-Riboud's writing, however, that won *Sally Hemings* the Janet Heidinger Kafka Prize for Best Historical Novel by an American Woman in 1979, which in turn helped inspire Chase-Riboud to write a sequel, *The President's Daughter* (1994), about Harriet Hemings. This novel reignited controversy over the relationship between Jefferson and Hemings, albeit not to the same degree as in 1979. Chase-Riboud started another sequel in the saga, but it has yet to appear.

The stature of Chase-Riboud's accomplishments as a writer parallels that of her efforts in poetry and sculpture. In the latter art, Chase-Riboud was a major figure in Europe before Toni Morrison edited and helped publish her first book of poems (*From Memphis and Peking*) in 1974. In all three fields, Chase-Riboud possesses a passionate interest in discovering historical figures—usually women and men of African descent—and events that have been long ignored, obscured, or silenced precisely because they trouble the way Americans and the West think of themselves. For this reason, Chase-Riboud is normally counted as one of the more prominent authors of neo–slave narratives (see separate entry), akin to her mentor Morrison, David Bradley, Gayl Jones, Sherley Anne Williams, and Ishmael Reed. In all of these novels Chase-Riboud's attention to the details of historical documents, language, and context allows them to compare well to the standard histories they parallel, while her desire to provide her subjects' perspectives distinguishes them to the same degree. For example, Chase-Riboud's second novel, *Valide: A Novel of the Harem* (1986) contains many parallels to *Sally Hemings*; it tells the story of a Martinican women sold into slavery in the Ottoman Empire, eventually becoming part of the harem of Sultan Abdulhamid I and rising to the rank of *valide*, thereby becoming the most powerful woman in the country while still a slave. In her latest novel, *Hottentot Venus* (2003) Chase-Riboud recovers the history of Sarah Baartmann, a South African woman who was lured from her homeland and put on display, naked, in a freak show in London's Piccadilly Circus and later had her genitalia dissected and preserved as signs of African ugliness. *Echo of Lions* (1989) recounts the famous *Amistad* incident in 1839, in which a group of Africans, led by Sengbe (a.k.a. Joseph Cinqué) rebelled against the crew of the Spanish slave ship en route to bondage, steered to Long Island, and eventually won their freedom in a case that went to the Supreme Court. When dancer Debbie Allen and Steven Spielberg produced and directed the film *Amistad* in 1997, Chase-Riboud sued the production for copyright infringement, attracting considerable media attention and controversy among scholars about the ownership and depiction of African Americans and their history, which rivaled the furor over the film version of Alice Walker's novel *The Color Purple*. Chase-Riboud, however, later dropped the charges, finding that the producers committed no wrongdoing.

Most appreciations of Chase-Riboud's work consist of contemporary reviews, but several key journal articles and books have emerged as well, although the latter discuss her sculpture, rather than her fiction. The better journal articles include Ashraf H. Rushdy, "Representing the Constitution: Embodiments of America in Barbara Chase-Riboud's *Echo of Lions*," *Critique* 36, no. 4 (Summer 1995), 258–81; and "'I Write in Tongues': The Supplement of Voice in Barbara Chase-Riboud's *Sally Hemings*,"

Contemporary Literature 35, no. 1 (Spring 1994), 100–136.

Children of the Night: The Best Short Stories by Black Writers, 1967 to the Present This 1995 collection, edited by novelist Gloria Naylor, is one of the most carefully edited and organized collection of short fiction to emerge in the 1990s. It represents Naylor's desire to place the range of African American experiences in a revelatory context in which those experiences may be seen in an affirmative light. This goal is revealed both in Naylor's preface and the four thematic sections: "Remembering . . . ," "Affirming . . . ," "Revealing the Self Divided . . . ," and "Moving On. . . ." The subject matter ranges from pieces that examine slavery's effects upon the African American body and psyche to lyrical analyses of the inner self, classism, colorism, the meaning of African heritage, community diversity and unity, and so on. The collection is remarkable for its ability to capture the range and gist of African American short fiction over a quarter century without either being too dogmatic or too diffuse.

Virtually every major African American author published since 1967 is represented in this collection. These include: Samuel R. Delany, Sherley Anne Williams, John Edgar Wideman, Jewell Parker Rhodes, Maya Angelou, Toni Cade Bambara, James Baldwin, Terry McMillan, Clarence Major, Edwidge Danticat, James Alan McPherson, Charles Johnson, Alice Walker, and Ralph Ellison. A handful of newer or lesser-known authors are also present.

Childress, Alice (b. October 12, 1920, Charleston, South Carolina; d. August 14, 1994, Long Island, New York) Actor, playwright, essayist, and novelist Alice Childress was one of the most influential dramatists in African American history. Her many plays stand as provocative monuments to the richness, complexity, and diversity of African

American life and demonstrate Childress's nearly unrivalled command of language. Although Childress's works of fiction were not quite as popular as her well-known and highly acclaimed plays, they were also highly significant contributions to the African American literature in the postwar era, especially in the 1970s, and won many awards. Childress's works are generally written for a young-adult audience but resonate with adults as well. Her first novel of the contemporary period, *A Hero Ain't Nothin' But a Sandwich* (1973), was popular enough to be made into a film starring Cicely Tyson and Paul Winfield. It is the gritty tale of Benjie, a thirteen-year-old heroin addict, who forces the adults in his community—especially Butler, his stepfather—to pay closer and earlier attention to the needs of the younger generation of African Americans, rather than providing models of behavior after the world has begun taking its toll. It won the Jane Addams Peace Association and Lewis Carroll Shelf Awards, a National Book Award nomination, and Outstanding Book of the Year and Best Young Adult Book citations from the *New York Times* and American Library Association, respectively. *A Short Walk* (1979), an adult novel, uses the life of protagonist Cora James to review the difficulties of African American life from the beginning of the twentieth century, through the Harlem Renaissance, ending in the Civil Rights movement. *Rainbow Jordan* (1981), another novel for young adults, is somewhat similar to the earlier *Hero*; it is a coming-of-age story in which the girl Rainbow finds herself drawing upon many different mother figures to help her form her identity. *Those Other People* (1989) is the story of Jonathan Barnett, a seventeen-year-old gay high school computer instructor who attempts to intervene on behalf of his school's two black students, only to be confronted by homophobia and pressure from those in power above him. Childress's other general awards include the Radcliffe Graduate Society Medal (1984) and the Harlem School of the Arts Humanitarian Award. (1987).

Most of the extant scholarship on Childress is concerned with her plays rather than her fiction. A handful of books and articles discussing her career and individual works, however, are valuable studies of her oeuvre: La Vinia Delois Jennings, *Alice Childress* (1995); Christy Gavin, *African American Women Playwrights: A Research Guide* (1999). Relevant articles: Olga Duncan, "Telling the Truth: Alice Childress as Theorist and Playwright," *The Journal of African American History* 81, nos. 1–4 (1996); Elizabeth Brown-Guillory, "Alice Childress: A Pioneering Spirit," *SAGE* 4 (Spring 1987); Mary Helen Washington, "New Lives and New Letters: Black Women Writers at the End of the Seventies," *College English* 43, no. 1 (January 1981); Judy Richardson, "Black Children's Books: An Overview," *The Journal of Negro Education* 43, no. 3 (Summer 1974).

Cleage, Pearl (b. December 7, 1948, Springfield, Massachusetts) Playwright, essayist, and novelist Pearl Cleage is best known for her prolific and award-winning plays and provocative essays, all of which take incisive looks at social issues from personal and proudly womanist perspectives. Her debut novel, *What Looks Like Crazy on an Ordinary Day* (1997) received immense attention due to being one of the first books by a noncanonical African American author featured in Oprah Winfrey's Book Club. The novel's protagonist, Ava Johnson, returns to her Michigan home from Atlanta and finds herself helping members of her family heal from various hurts and abusive relationships. Despite the subject matter, Cleage's novel approaches serious issues with wit and humor. In 2001, Cleage published her second novel, *I Wish I Had a Red Dress*, about social worker Joyce Mitchell, sister to *What Looks Like Crazy*'s Ava Johnson.

Through Joyce's work and personal search for love and passion, the novel confronts a number of the issues facing African American communities and particularly black women at the turn of the twenty-first century, including domestic violence, drugs, and a lack of real love in a cold world. *Some Things I Never Thought I'd Do* (2003) is the story of Regina Burns, a recovering addict who tries to reconnect to the fuller, richer life she formerly enjoyed before her last relationship ended and addiction consumed her. Regina's search for fulfillment requires faith in herself as a woman first, one who can be loved by the man she desires, Blue Hamilton, be responsible for her destiny again, and become a significant player in her community.

Virtually all scholarly attention given to Cleage has examined her plays not her fiction. Cleage and her plays have been reviewed and examined many times in *AAR* and *Callaloo*, but such publications rarely even mention her fictional works. The extant criticism of Cleage's drama, however, is excellent. The winter 1997 issue of *AAR* (31, no. 4) reviews and discusses several of Cleage's plays among those of many other playwrights, as does that journal's winter 2003 issue.

College Language Association The College Language Association (CLA) is a professional organization founded in 1937 at LeMoyne College in Memphis, Tennessee by ten scholars at historically black colleges and universities (HBCUs). The College Language Association was intended as a racially integrated response to the Modern Language Association of America, which did not welcome African American members at that time. Its membership presently comprises independent scholars, faculty, and graduate students in English and foreign languages at HBCUs and predominantly white institutions.

The CLA's mission is to promote scholarship and professional standards among and its members, publish essay collections and bibliographies, support creative writing, and maintain directories of its members, past and present.[1] The association sponsors annual contests in creative and scholarly writing for students at the institutions where members teach; publishes the *CLA Journal*, a quarterly featuring members' critical articles and book reviews; and holds an annual convention open to all members. The convention's location changes from year to year, but it generally remains in cities in the American South and therefore closer to most HBCUs. Information about the organization may be found at http://www.clascholars.org.

CLA Journal (**1957–present**) *CLA Journal* is the quarterly organ of the College Language Association, first published in 1957. It features members' and subscribers' critical articles and book reviews. Since publication in *CLA Journal* is limited to members of the organization, it does not possess quite the same cachet as such competing journals as *African American Review* or *Callaloo*, but it has served and continues to serve as an important and high-quality forum for new and established scholars. The journal publishes articles on language and literature, book reviews and literary criticism, and news and reports pertaining to the association. It places no restrictions on the type of subjects its contributors write, but since many of its members are interested in African American literature, a subscriber will find many articles on texts from the African Diaspora. See also College Language Association.

1. *CLA Journal* 46, no. 3 (March 2003): v.

Color Purple, The Alice Walker's third and most famous novel (1982) is inarguably one of the greatest works of American fiction in the late twentieth century, and perhaps one of the most controversial. It is written in an epistolary format, in which the protagonist and narrator, Celie, writes to God and, later, her sister Nettie about her travails. Celie is raped by her purported father and bears two children by him, both of whom he sends away for adoption. Celie is eventually married off to Mr. —— (whose name is eventually revealed as Albert) when Nettie refuses Mr. ——'s advances. This marriage of convenience becomes entirely miserable for Celie after Nettie runs away to escape Mr. ———'s overtures. Celie eventually finds spiritual and sexual sustenance in her husband's former lover, Shug Avery, who helps her discover her sexuality, her voice, her identity, and therefore her will to leave Albert, start her own business, and, much later, reunite with Nettie and her long-lost children. The novel's engaging and innovative quality is a product of the way Walker turns the epistolary form into a subtle, sensitive, and moving analysis of gender issues among African Americans. Its discovery and indictment of community secrets, including spousal abuse, incest, and homosexuality between African American women led to the controversy. The novel's critics have frequently condemned it for its alleged disloyalty to the premises of black aesthetics, specifically the idea that black art should celebrate the beauties of African American history and culture rather than emphasize the ways in which they fail to meet ideals. In other words, Walker has been accused of betraying African Americans, and African American males in particular, with this novel. It must be emphasized, however, that two major factors contributed to these criticisms.

First, Walker's novel was a runaway bestseller and recipient of the 1983 Pulitzer Prize, the American Book Award, and many other honors. It therefore found great national and international popularity, which meant that Walker's portrayal of African Americans, including Celie's occasionally harsh, albeit understandable, criticisms of specific African American males—chiefly Mr. ——, her husband—became popular among a predominantly white audience. To such critics as Ishmael Reed, whose novel *Reckless Eyeballing* mercilessly and transparently satirizes *The Color Purple*, this amounted to a betrayal of African American males and their contributions to literature (including, naturally, Reed's).

Second, much of the criticism that arose regarding the novel resulted from its conversion into the 1985 motion picture of the same name, directed and coproduced by famed director Steven Spielberg. The film departed from the novel in a number of crucial aspects, in part because the treatment Walker wrote for the screen was never used. The film minimized Celie and Shug's deeply intimate, sexual relationship, excluded Celie's reconciliation with Mr. ——, deemphasized his ultimate redemption, and contained an idyllic scene of Shug's rapprochement with her estranged father that was never part of the novel and again minimized the essential importance of the bonds between the women in the novel. Moreover, Spielberg's depiction of African Americans occasionally bordered on common stereotypes that evoked many African American's memories of Hollywood's earlier days. *In The Same River Twice: Honoring the Difficult* (1996), her memoir of the experience of collaborating on the film, Walker writes that

> it was said that I hated men, black men in particular; that my work was injurious to black male and female relationships; that my ideas of equality and tolerance were harmful, even destructive to the black community. That my success, and that of other black women

writers in publishing our work, was at the expense of black male writers who were not being published sufficiently. I was "accused" of being a lesbian, as if respecting and honoring women automatically discredited anything a woman might say. I was the object of literary stalking: one black male writer attacked me obsessively in lecture, interview and book for over a decade, to the point where I was concerned about his sanity and my safety.   (22)

The film clearly had a cultural impact that extended far beyond the book; the question of whether works in any medium that cover ground similar to *The Color Purple* are "harmful" still echoes in critical circles. Walker has astutely noted, however, that the most curious quality of the novel's harshest critics is that they tend to ignore the suffering of the novel's women and children for the sake of vilifying Walker's alleged disdain for its men. Based upon Walker's own ruminations, it is clear that the novel's goal, ultimately, is to show how rich, complex, and loving the bonds between women can be, must be, when males attempt to silence their voices and ignore their feelings or identities.

Criticism of *The Color Purple* notwithstanding, analyses of the book have been fittingly rich and complex. Several splendid critical books and dissertations have been devoted to Walker's work as a whole and may be found in the entry under her name; most of the extant material devoted solely to *The Color Purple* may be found in critical journal articles. One book, Walker's aforementioned *The Same River Twice*, is an especially helpful tome that not only provides an account of the process that went into making the film version but also reveals what Walker wanted the characters to represent. Walker has much to say about the controversy that surrounded the book and the film and refutes many of her harshest critics. In addition, her essay

collection, *In Search of Our Mothers' Gardens: Womanist Prose* (1984), surveys the political thought that informs *The Color Purple* and, most important, contains the essay "Writing *The Color Purple*." Henry Louis Gates Jr. and K. Anthony Appiah's *Alice Walker: Critical Perspectives Past and Present* (1993) is not only one of the first places to look for reviews and essays on Walker in general, but also a compendium of some of the more insightful essays on *The Color Purple* alone. Michele Wallace's *Invisibility Blues: From Pop to Theory* (1991) contains her essay "Blues for Mr. Spielberg," which contrasts the print and film versions of the novel. Wallace creates a careful critique of the novel's virtues as a feminist/womanist text, as well as its flaws as a prescriptive for African Americans' concerns, gendered or otherwise.

Colter, Cyrus (b. January 8, 1910, Noblesville, Indiana; d. May 2002, Evanston, Illinois) Novelist, short-story writer, and poet Cyrus Colter started writing rather late in his life—1970—but produced a number of novels and short stories in the next quarter-century that stand among the most respectable of the period. Due to his reliance upon dense prose at a time when the Black Arts Movement and its Black Aesthetics were demanding that African American authors write with clarity, Colter did not receive as much attention for his work as he deserved. Nevertheless, the Northwestern University professor emeritus continued to write until his death in 2002 and to serve as a member of the Illinois Commerce Commission.

Many of Colter's works are set in Chicago and, like the works of earlier Chicago author Richard Wright, fall into the realm of naturalist, social-realist fiction. Colter's first book, *The Beach Umbrella* (1970), comprises fourteen stories set in Chicago in which the characters try to find love and self-worth through material possessions rather than self-examination, ultimately leading them to disappointment and despair. It was chosen for publication after it won the first Iowa School of Letters Award for Short Fiction in 1970. It also won awards from the Chicago Friends of Literature and the Society of Midland Authors.[1] Colter's first novel, *The River of Eros* (1972) is the story of Clotilda Pilgrim, who owns a boardinghouse and takes care of her grandchildren, Lester and Addie. Through Clotilda's encounters with her grandchildren and boarders, she discovers that her difficulties in life are due to her unwillingness to confront her past, in which she had an illicit affair that eventually produced her daughter and grandchildren. As with the characters in *The Beach Umbrella*, Clotilda is undone by her lack of self-examination.

The Hippodrome (1973) is an allegorical novel that compares the nature of sexuality and the structure of religion, specifically their implicit complementarity. It is the story of Jackson Yeager, a writer of religious pamphlets and essays, who, while carrying his wife's head in a sack and evading the police, is offered refuge by Bea, who runs a hippodrome in which African Americans hold sexual orgies for white onlookers. Yeager is forced to choose whether to become part of the spectacle or risk capture. He is eventually ejected from the hippodrome and forced to consider how much of his life and experience has been real and how much the product of fantasy and subconscious anxieties. *Night Studies* (1980), winner of the Carl Sandburg Award, focuses primarily upon John Calvin Knight, the leader of the Black People's Congress; the wealthy black woman Mary Dee Adkins; and Griselda Graves, a young woman who is unknowingly passing for white. Their intertwined stories, which form a long section recount-

ing African American history beginning with the Atlantic slave trade, reveal the interdependence of the "races" in the United States as well as the nation's inability to escape its past with regard to racial issues.

A Chocolate Soldier (1988) resembles *Night Studies* to the extent that it attempts to discover why Africans were enslaved and scattered throughout the world. It is an experimental work, playing with narrative voices and time shifts as a way of matching the novel's query into the collective African American past. It concerns "Cager" Lee, who kills a rich white woman and spends the rest of the novel seeking redemption for his anger and confusion as a black man. *The Amoralists and Other Stories* (1990) comprises eighteen stories set in Chicago and revolving around African Americans of different classes who must make crucial decisions that will either leave them free or trapped by their pasts. Colter won the *Triquarterly* Award in 1991, partly for his work in *The Amoralists*. *City of Light* (1993) is the story of Paul Kessey, a wealthy African American who travels to Paris to found the Coterie, a movement with Black Nationalist aims similar to those of the Négritude movement (see separate entry) and Marcus Garvey's Universal Negro Improvement Association (UNIA) of the 1910s through 1930s. The novel criticizes Kessey's dream as being guided by his sense of guilt and self-hatred.

Colter has been the subject of a few scholarly studies in major literary journals. A special section of the autumn 1991 issue of *Callaloo* was devoted to Colter's extant fiction; it includes two analytical articles by Gilton Gregory Cross and Reginald Gibbons, a bibliography, and an excerpt from *City of Light*. Key articles include: Graham Clarke, "Beyond Realism: Recent Black Fic-

1. Helen R. Houston, "Cyrus Colter," *DLB* 33:50.

tion and the Language of the 'Real Thing,'" *BALF* 16, no. 1 (spring 1982);

Combahee River Collective The Combahee River Collective was a group of black feminists who began meeting in 1974 to formulate ways of engaging in "political work within our own group and in coalition with other progressive organizations and movements."[1] Some of their members include critics Barbara Smith, Sharon Page Ritchie, Cheryl Clarke, Margo Okizawa Rey, Gloria Akasha Hull, and Demita Frazier. Their foundational essay, "A Black Feminist Statement," also known as the "Combahee River Collective Statement," was first published in 1977 and has since been reprinted in many different womanist and feminist anthologies. It gained some of its best exposure in *Home Girls: A Black Feminist Anthology* (1983), edited by one of its members, Barbara Smith. According to Duchess Harris, the Collective's activities included generating support for Kenneth Edelin, a black doctor in Boston arrested for performing a legal abortion; defending Ella Ellison, a black woman wrongfully accused of murder; picketing the Third World Workers Coalition to see that black laborers would be hired to work on a high school in Boston's black community; and bringing local and national attention to the murder of twelve African American women in the Boston area in 1979.[2] The Collective eventually drifted apart largely due to personal differences and geographic distances that grew as the members' careers evolved. Most of the former members continue the same sort of political work that the Collective initiated from academia.

The Collective's statement is as much a declaration of political aims and goals as it is a response to the sexism and homophobia, both overt and covert, of the Black Power and Black Arts movements and the black middle class, as well as the racism and sexism of America in general. As the Collective succinctly put it, their politics defined them as "actively committed to struggling against racial, sexual, heterosexual, and class oppression." They saw "as [their] particular task the development of integrated analysis and practice based upon the fact that the major systems of oppression are interlocking" and that black and other "Third World" women (that is, women of color) suffered from all of the major systems of oppression. To achieve these goals, the members of the collective wished to develop an antiracist politics to counter the racism within many white feminist organizations, and an antisexist politics to counter the sexism of black and white men. They wished to do so, however, without either the biological determinism or sexual separatism found within some radical lesbian feminist groups. Instead, the Collective wished to "struggle together with black men against racism, while ... also struggl[ing] with black men about sexism" as they "examined the multilayered texture of black women's lives."[3]

The Combahee River Collective's statement has become one of the crucial texts in defining black feminism since 1970 and therefore stands as a major pillar of many contemporary African American writers'

1. Combahee River Collective, "A Black Feminist Statement," reprinted in *Feminist Frameworks: Alternative Theoretical Accounts of the Relations Between Women and Men*, ed. Alison M. Jaggar and Paula S. Rothenberg, 2nd ed. (New York: McGraw Hill, 1984), 202.

2. Duchess Harris, "'All of Who I Am in the Same Place': The Combahee River Collective," *Womanist Theory and Research* 3, no. 1 (1999); http://www.uga.edu/~womanist/harris3.1.htm.

3. Combahee River Collective, "A Black Feminist Statement," 202, 203, 206, 205.

and critics' work, as Elliott Butler-Evans has demonstrated.[1] The crucial links between sexism, racism, and homophobia that the Collective identified resonate in authors as different in style and scope as Toni Morrison, Alice Walker, Bebe Moore Campbell, Gloria Naylor, Sapphire, Ntozake Shange, April Sinclair, Tina McElroy Ansa, Audre Lorde, and Terry McMillan, among many others. Also see the separate entry on womanism.

Cooper, J. California (birthdate unknown, Berkeley, California) With her first short-story collection, *A Piece of Mine* (1984), playwright, short-story writer, and novelist J. (Joan) California Cooper immediately garnered attention as part of the New Black Renaissance (or "New Literature") of the 1980s. Cooper has since split her energies largely between novels and short fiction, publishing five additional collections of the latter, although she also continues practicing her first love, writing plays. Cooper's strength is the short story, although she has also published three novels, *Family* (1991), *In Search of Satisfaction* (1994), and *The Wake of the Wind* (1998). Cooper's stories are folksy and intimate morality tales that compare favorably to the best work of such progenitors as Zora Neale Hurston and particularly such peers as Alice Walker, Gloria Naylor, and John Edgar Wideman. Cooper's narrators' words should be read aloud; she carefully writes the cadences of her characters' natural speech into the narrative, stripping it of layers of artifice. Cooper's protagonists, usually women, struggle toward self-discovery in the face of extensive abuse from the men in their lives and the criticism of families and friends who fail to comprehend and appreciate the protagonists' complex identities as women. It is only through processes of self-discovery, whether through

religion and spirituality, sexuality, or physical removal from harmful environments and relationships, that her protagonists are able to overcome their situations.

A Piece of Mine comprises twelve stories set in a small town in which the characters, almost exclusively African American, overcome personal hardships by gaining a new moral compass. As in many of Cooper's stories, the narrators are mature women in the community who act as its sources of wisdom and common sense. The collection *Homemade Love* (1986), which won a Before Columbus Foundation American Book Award in 1989, comprises thirteen short stories. All of them focus upon the difficulties that the female protagonists encounter as they make the transition from adolescence into young womanhood, adulthood, then maturity. Each finds herself following a path similar to that taken by her own parents, with each generation losing a sense of its need for domestic and spiritual fulfillment. *Some Soul to Keep* (1987) consists of five stories set in the deep South. Each is written in the same vein and with the same themes as *A Piece of Mine*, with foci upon the centrality of family, a strong spiritual life, and a clear moral direction for the characters as they mature, marry, and experience loss and heartbreak and redemption.

Cooper's first novel, *Family* (1991) follows this pattern as well, with a marked difference: it is a neo–slave narrative (see separate entry) that helps illustrate how slavery made the pursuit of all the typical goals of her stories' characters—family, love, security, and spirituality—either extremely difficult or impossible. Simultaneously, Cooper reiterates that enslaved Africans were far from simple passive victims of slavery; they found innumerable ways of deceiving slaveholders so that they could survive and escape the

1. Elliott Butler-Evans, *Race, Gender, and Desire: Narrative Strategies in the Fiction of Toni Cade Bambara, Toni Morrison, and Alice Walker* (Philadelphia: Temple University Press, 1989), 39–41.

institution's physical and psychological holds. Cooper manages to incorporate elements from Mark Twain's *Pudd'nhead Wilson* (1894; the plot device of switched white and black infants), Toni Morrison's *Beloved* (1987; the theme of infanticide), and other novellas and novels about slavery, but in the most seamless way possible. As the novel's title implies, family is all; it is narrated by the spirit of Clora, who escaped slavery by committing suicide and attempting to poison her children. Some of her half-black, half-white children escape slavery by passing; Always, who is too dark to pass, endures the physical and sexual horrors of being an enslaved woman. Eventually, Always bears children who grow up to enjoy freedom, only to find themselves in a nation that still embraces racism. The novel is more pessimistic than many of Cooper's earlier and subsequent works, but it is also one of her best.

Cooper's next two story collections, *The Matter Is Life* (1991) and *Some Love, Some Pain, Sometime* (1995), continue the work of her earlier short stories. The latter is arguably the stronger text, due to Cooper's renewed focus upon romance in long-term relationships. Cooper's second novel, *In Search of Satisfaction* (1994), is a moral allegory set in the fictional town of Yoville, New York, from the postbellum years through the 1920s. The children of Josephus Josephus, a former slave, and his rich white mistress seek their identities between the hedonistic and spiritually bankrupt world defined by the rich Krupt and Befoe families and the pursuit of God and salvation. Cooper's third novel, *The Wake of the Wind* (1998), is another historical novel set in the postbellum era. Its protagonists, Mordecai and Lifee, are former slaves married under bondage, who find love in the postemancipation period and struggle to set up a stable homestead in the face of the brutalities of lynching and segregation during and after Reconstruction. *The Future Has a Past*

(2000) is a story collection about women who battle low self-esteem as they seek love and fulfillment, despite having been told repeatedly that they are worthy of neither.

Scholarly attention to Cooper's work has been extensive. She is the subject of the following books and book chapters: Elizabeth Ann Beaulieu, *Black Women Writers and the American Neo-Slave Narrative: Femininity Unfettered* (2000); Wolfgang Karrer and Barbara Puschmann-Nalenz, eds., *The African American Short Story 1970–1990: A Collection of Critical Essays* (1997); Barbara J. Marshall, "Kitchen Table Talk: J. California Cooper's Use of Nommo—Female Bonding and Transcendence," in *Language and Literature in the African American Imagination*, ed. Carol Aisha Blackshire-Belay (1992); a relevant journal article is E. Shelley Reid, "Beyond Morrison and Walker: Looking Good and Looking Forward in Contemporary Black Women's Stories," *AAR* 34, no. 2 (Summer 2000).

Corregidora Gayl Jones's first novel, originally published in 1975, is frequently considered her best and most complex. It stands as one of the finest novels to emerge in the 1970s, and certainly among the best that African American women authors have produced in recent decades. Ashraf Rushdy classifies *Corregidora* as one of many neo–slave narratives (see separate entry) published in the wake of William Styron's *The Confessions of Nat Turner* (1967), which many African American authors and critics condemned for its problematic and frequently racist depiction of a major figure in African American history. Aside from a number of declamations against the novel, many African American authors responded via fiction to foreground the degree to which whites have repeatedly mediated and subsumed African Americans' voices and views.

Corregidora tells the story of blues singer Ursa Corregidora who, when she is but five years old, is pulled aside by her grandmother and told how Ursa's grandmother and great-grandmother were raped and forced to act as concubines for the same slavemaster, Corregidora, the family's namesake. Through his acts, Corregidora is both Ursa's grandfather and great-grandfather. If the horror of this situation weren't enough, Ursa discovers that many of the African American men she knows share some of Corregidora's contempt for women, if not his precise transgressions. Both sets of knowledge and experience inform the blues and show, by extension, the breadth and depth of African Americans' pain and the way it is passed on through the generations, usually by women, and often against their will.

Critical treatments of *Corregidora* are both plentiful and wonderfully sophisticated, with a flood of articles and critical essays published in the late 1990s and early 2000s alone, perhaps due to the publicity surrounding the death of Gayl's husband in 1997. Most recent is Gil Zehava Hochberg's "Mother, Memory, History: Maternal Genealogies in Gayl Jones's *Corregidora* and Simone Schwarz-Bart's *Pluie et vent sur Télumée Miracle*," *Research in African Literatures* 34, no. 2 (Summer 2003), which uses Jones's and Schwarz-Bart's novels to show how mother-daughter relationships are foregrounded in contemporary African American and African women's writing in general. Hochberg's article is based in part on Madhu Dubey's "Gayl Jones and the Matrilineal Metaphor of Tradition," found in *Signs* 20, no. 2 (Winter 1995). Maryemma Graham's "Living the Legacy: Pain, Desire and Narrative Time in Gayl Jones' *Corregidora*" focuses upon Ursa's association of sex with pain due to her ancestors' experiences, while Ashraf H. A. Rushdy's "'Relate Sexual to Historical': Race, Resistance, and Desire in Gayl Jones's *Corregidora*," *AAR* 24, no. 2 (Summer 2000), examines the way in which Ursa Corregidora becomes her mother,

grandmother, and great-grandmother—and how they become her—through hearing their stories, a common motif in Jones's work. Innovative readings on the question of the (un)reliability of memory, testimonial, and silence in the making of history within the novel may be found in Elizabeth Yukins, "Bastard Daughters and the Possession of History in *Corregidora* and *Paradise*," *Signs* 28, no. 1 (Autumn 2002); Adam McKible, "'These Are the Facts of the Darky's History': Thinking History and Reading Names in Four African American Texts," *AAR* 28, no. 2 (Summer 1994); Amy S. Gottfried, "Angry Arts: Silence, Speech, and Song in Gayl Jones's *Corregidora*," *AAR* 28, no. 4 (Winter 1994); Richard Hardack, "Making Generations and Bearing Witness: Violence and Orality in Gayl Jones's *Corregidora*," *Prospects* 24 (1999); and Jennifer Cognard-Black, "'I Said Nothing': The Rhetoric of Silence and Gayl Jones's *Corregidora*," *NWSA Journal* 13, no. 1 (Spring 2001).

Crouch, Stanley (b. 1945, Los Angeles, California) Stanley Crouch is best known as an exceedingly intelligent, yet occasionally truculent critic of social issues, music—especially jazz—and literature. He is also one of the most influential and devoted aficionados and critics of jazz music to emerge in the last quarter of the twentieth century. A long-time contributor to New York's *Village Voice*, the Los Angeles native has published three books that collect essays he has written for the *Voice*, the *New York Daily News*, and many other periodicals. These include *Notes of a Hanging Judge: Essays and Reviews, 1979–1989* (1991); *The All-American Skin Game, or, The Decoy of Race: The Long and the Short of It, 1990–1994* (1997); and *Always in Pursuit: Fresh American Perspectives* (1998). His social-issue and jazz criticism have earned him a number of awards, the most prominent being a MacArthur Fellowship (1993). Like Harlem Renaissance journalist, author, and critic George S. Schuyler before him, Crouch is nothing if not iconoclastic, provocative, and perpetually audacious, but he is neither boring nor pat.

Crouch's famous contrariness began in the early 1970s, when he was among the many young artists influenced by the Black Arts Movement. His first volume of poetry, *Ain't No Ambulances for No Nigguhs Tonight* (1972), is full of complex verses that demonstrate the influence of modernism's avant-garde. Some of the verses fit the militant mode that Crouch later rejected and actively condemned as he established his career as a critic, as the volume's title indicates, but remain complex and subtle.

In 2000, Crouch published his long-awaited first novel, *Don't the Moon Look Lonesome: A Novel in Blues and Swing*. The novel centers upon the relationship between Carla, a white jazz singer from South Dakota, and her tempestuous relationship with Maxwell, an African American saxophone player. Carla's central problem is that she wishes to be fully steeped in the blues idiom, but the myth of "race" stands in her way. The novel's course takes it through New York literary society and disquisitions on the problems of racial ideologies.

Reviews of *Don't the Moon Look Lonesome* have been both limited in number and mixed, at best; no critical articles studying the novel have yet appeared. Michael Thelwell's review in *African American Review* was both an admittedly ad hominem attack upon Crouch and a complete dismissal of the novel, save for a few "engaging, original, and skillfully drawn characters" and "the occasional passage of inspired, nicely achieved prose" among "a Sahara of arid, malformed" writing.[1] The anonymous reviewer for *The Economist* judged the text more a "passionate polemic" than a novel, one that "captures America's particular zest and, even in discontented times, its underlying confidence."[2] The review in *Library Journal* is perhaps most judicious; it notes that "Crouch is at his best when writing about [jazz]," that his "descriptions have a flow that makes the reader feel as though he or she is listening to a blues band or gospel choir," and that "some of the dialog is talky and the main characters distant."[3] Overall, then, it may be fair to say that critics have deemed Crouch's debut as inauspicious, so far as its artistic quality is concerned. Given the many enemies Crouch has created over the years, though, it is doubtful whether any future novels, which may very well improve upon the first, will receive the credit they might deserve. Nonetheless, Crouch's reputation as an incisive, if blunt, critic of the contemporary African American cultural scene is assured.

Cultural Nationalism In African American intellectual history, cultural nationalism asserts the intrinsic value of African American culture. It frequently assumes that African Americans and whites have separate values, cultures, histories, and ways of living in and perceiving the world and that art and other cultural expressions are clear reflections of these differences. In addition, a few cultural nationalists regard African Ameri-

1. Michael Thelwell, review of *Don't the Moon Look Lonesome: A Novel in Blues and Swing*, by Stanley Crouch, *AAR* 36, no. 1 (Spring 2002): 171.

2. Review of *Don't the Moon Look Lonesome: A Novel in Blues and Swing*, by Stanley Crouch, *The Economist*, 15 July 2000, 14.

3. Ellen Flexman, review of *Don't the Moon Look Lonesome: A Novel in Blues and Swing*, by Stanley Crouch, *Library Journal* 125, no. 6 (April 2000): 129.

can culture as superior to "white" culture, whether implicitly or explicitly.

Although African American cultural nationalism is commonly connected to the struggles of the 1960s and 1970s, the more recent form is, like those struggles, a culmination of many years—decades—of theorizing about art and literature. Some of the most heavily anthologized essays of the Harlem Renaissance era, including Langston Hughes's "The Negro Artist and the Racial Mountain" (1926), Alain Locke's "Youth Speaks" (1925), and Richard Wright's "Blueprint for Negro Writing" (1937), are nothing if not calls for or records of nationalistic feeling and a degree of cultural pride among African American artists. Accordingly, these same essays were included in *The Black Aesthetic* (1971), edited by Addison Gayle Jr., to undergird that volume's theoretical basis.

Accordingly, cultural nationalism since 1970 has found a number of expressions inextricably tied to the Black Aesthetic that emerged in the 1960s. This bent owes as much to earlier theories as it does to an often pungent strain of vulgar Marxism. In fact, one of the most straightforward, if controversial definitions of this genus of black cultural nationalism, Maulana Karenga's essay "Black Cultural Nationalism" (1968), was also included in *The Black Aesthetic*. In that essay, Karenga argues vociferously against the validity of the notion of "art for art's sake" for the black artist, since "black art, like everything else in the black community, must respond positively to the reality of revolution."[1] Art must be "useful," which means that it must correspond with the black community and serve its needs, not those of the individual artist, whom Karenga insists must be a "personality" within the larger collective rather than expressing his or her "indivi-

dualism," which is a luxury that, in fact, "does not exist," since all artists are part of a larger cultural context. Karenga goes on to dismiss the blues as being irrelevant in face of the coming revolution, due to its alleged nostalgia.[2]

Not surprisingly, Karenga has taken a sound critical drubbing for the last comment, but he was neither the only critic to hold that opinion, nor the only one to come under fire for it. Karenga and others sought to tie African American culture to sub-Saharan Africa through a Marxist lens in order to stress a communal bond. If their glee toward the prospect of an impending revolution seems misplaced now, we would do well to remember that the climate of violence and unrest in the late 1960s made a physical revolution seem not only likely but inevitable within a matter of years. Even those cultural nationalist critics who were not as strident as Karenga made cases for the differences between "white" and "black" culture and reified the right of African American authors *not* to serve a "universal" goal of appealing to a wider—read: whiter—mass audience.

To attempt to devise a complete bibliographic record of discussions of black cultural nationalism here would be foolish indeed, as that task would require listing the majority of African American literary criticism published in the last thirty years. On the other hand, one may safely offer a few exemplary texts in a broad stylistic and contextual range that will inevitably provide links to a larger body of texts. *The Black Aesthetic* is, of course, the best single-volume contemporary reflection of 1970s cultural nationalism, but it is out of print and not readily available to most readers, unless they have access to university libraries. One

---

1. Maulana Karenga, "Black Cultural Nationalism," in *The Black Aesthetic*, ed. Addison Gayle Jr. (Garden City, N.Y.: Doubleday, 1971), 32.
2. Karenga, "Black Cultural Nationalism," 33, 35, 37.

recent anthology, however, collects many essays that track the arguments for and against black cultural nationalism: *African American Literary Theory* (2000), edited by Winston Napier. Napier collects essays by virtually every major African American literary critic of the twentieth century, but strangely, Karenga is not represented, although many of the authors included in *The Black Aesthetic* are.

The reader with access to a better library possessing extensive journal holdings should attempt to find and peruse the later years of *Negro Digest*, renamed *Black World* (1970–76), which was the premiere forum for African American cultural and literary criticism after Hoyt Fuller assumed the editorial reins in 1961. Many of the essays in *The Black Aesthetic*, in fact, were originally published in *Negro Digest* and *Black World*.

D

Danticat, Edwidge (b. January 19, 1969, Port-au-Prince, Haiti) Novelist and short-story author Edwidge Danticat is one of the major figures among the younger generation of African American writers. Her first two books, the novel *Breath, Eyes, Memory* (1994) and the short-story collection *Krik? Krak!* (1995) caused major ripples in the literary world. The buzz surrounding Danticat was due not only to her relatively young age but also her extraordinary skill in depicting life in Haiti, despite the fact that she emigrated to the United States from the island nation (controlled at the time by dictator Jean-Claude "Baby Doc" Duvalier) when she was

four years old.[1] Danticat's fiction consists of deeply lyrical, semiautobiographical journeys into the ambivalence of the immigrant, particularly her desires for a homeland that is ever changing, albeit not always in positive ways. To be more specific, Danticat is interested in the position the immigrant holds between the new and old lands and what that "in-between space," which is "between history and memory, the vernacular and the official, fiction and fact," means as her characters shape their identities.[2]

Breath, Eyes, Memory, which was originally Danticat's master of fine arts thesis at Brown University, is the story of narrator Sophie Caco, a young Haitian girl who finds herself trying to establish a place for herself in a family of strong-willed women who believe deeply in familial, religious, sexual, and cultural traditions. Sophie's chastity and sexuality are tightly controlled in much the same way that Haiti is itself under strict control and the threat of terror by its dictatorship. When Sophie joins her estranged mother Martine in New York, she has to reestablish her relationship with her even as she serves as a conduit between her mother and their homeland and attempts to adjust to a very different, often traumatic life in the United States. Danticat explores her themes of the immigrant's strange status as well as the alternating benefits (storytelling, language, familial bonds) and problems (abuse, humiliation, repression) of passing on certain traditions from generation to generation among a family's women.

The ten stories of *Krik? Krak!* revolve around life in Haiti under the Duvalier regime. To the extent that their lives are almost completely circumscribed by Duvalier's security forces, the protagonists of

1. "Two Blacks Named Among America's Most Promising Young Novelists," *Journal of Blacks in Higher Education* 12 (Summer 1996): 111.

2. Kelli Lyon Johnson, "Both Sides of the Massacre: Collective Memory and Narrative on Hispaniola," *Mosaic* 36, no. 2 (June 2003): 76.

each of the stories find or imagine ways to escape physically and mentally from official as well as internal repressions. *Krik? Krak!* received extensive praise upon initial publication; it made many publications' "best of" lists, and received the Pushcart Prize in 1995 and a nomination for the National Book Award that same year. It also won awards from *The Caribbean Writer*, *Seventeen*, and *Essence* magazines. *The Farming of Bones* (1998) is a historical novel recounting, in part, the 1937 massacre of 15,000–18,000 Haitian laborers at the orders of Dominican Republic dictator General Rafael Trujillo Molina. At its heart, though, the novel is also an account of the history of race and class relations in Haiti from its very origins. The protagonist and narrator, Amabelle, finds herself and her children persecuted, scarred, or killed along with virtually all other Haitians in the country in the genocidal purge, which had as much to do with racial and cultural distinctions as political ones. As with so many other contemporary African American novels, *The Farming of Bones* is about recovering lost episodes in history or, to be more accurate, episodes that the residents of the country—to say nothing of the rest of the world—would like to forget. Danticat is also the editor of two collections: *The Beacon Best of 2000: Great Writing by Women and Men of All Colors and Cultures* (2000); and *The Butterfly's Way: Voices from the Haitian Dyaspora* [sic] (2001).

Interest in Danticat, scholarly and otherwise, has been especially impressive in view of her relatively short career. Her stories are collected in Elaine Campbell and Pierrette Frickey, eds., *The Whistling Bird: Women Writers of the Caribbean* (1998); Daniel Halpern, ed., *The Art of the Story: An International Anthology of Contemporary Short Stories* (1999); Rosemarie Robotham, ed., *The Bluelight Corner: Black Women Writing on Passion, Sex, and Romantic Love* (1999);

Kevin Young, ed., *Giant Steps: The New Generation of African American Writers* (2000); and Kevin Powell, ed., *Step into a World: A Global Anthology of the New Black Literature*, as well as many major anthologies designed for college curricula. She is profiled in Jonathan Bing, ed., *Writing for Your Life #4* (2000); and Harold Bloom, ed., *Caribbean Women Writers* (1997). Danticat's work is also studied in Adele S. Newson and Linda Strong-Leek, *Winds of Change: The Transforming Voices of Caribbean Women Writers and Scholars* (1998).

Delany, Samuel R. (b. 1942, Harlem, New York City) Samuel R. Delany is one of the most celebrated, prodigious, and prolific science- (or speculative-) fiction authors in history, one of very few successful and well-known African American writers of the genre, and the first to garner significant exposure, acclaim, and impressive sales. Of this small group, only Octavia Butler has rivaled Delany in terms of fame and praise. A former child prodigy (he began writing at a young age and published his first novel when he was only twenty years old), Delany has won the science-fiction industry's most coveted awards, including the Hugo, the Nebula, and the Pilgrim Award for excellence in science fiction criticism (1985), as well as the Bill Whitehead Memorial Award for Lifetime Excellence in Gay and Lesbian Literature (1993). Delany is often classified with science fiction's "New Wave" of the 1960s, although he disputes that notion, generally resisting such categorizations but also arguing that he is closer to such authors as Harlan Ellison and Theodore Sturgeon. He is also an accomplished poet, lecturer, gay rights and AIDS activist, and perceptive social critic.

Between 1962 and 2000, Delany published twenty-six books of fiction. This list comprises nineteen novels, three short story collections (*Driftglass*, 1971; *Distant Stars*,

1981; *Driftglass/Starshards*, 1993); a book consisting of three novellas (*Atlantis: Three Tales*, 1995); and two graphic novels (extended comic books), *Empire* (1980, illustrated by Howard Chaykin) and *Bread and Wine* (1999, illustrated by Mia Wolff). Delany's last novel, *Hogg*, was published in 1995; from that point until the end of the millennium, he concentrated on nonfiction, specifically social and literary criticism. The only books of fiction that emerged in the latter half of the 1990s were reprints from Delany's later period (1970 to the present). One hastens to add, however, that although Delany is best known for his fiction, he has earned extensive acclaim as a perceptive, incisive, and lyrical critic. This is due, in part, to Delany's wise refusal to recognize the artificial line dividing literature and criticism. Even *1984*, a collection of letters from late 1983 through early 1985, artfully combines both of these intellectual projects into a memoir that owes as much to epistolary fiction as it does to William S. Burroughs's *Naked Lunch* (1952). He has also written criticism under the noms de plume K. Leslie Steiner and S. L. Kermit, who also appear as scholars contributing essays and other intellectual material in his books; *Tales of Nevèrÿon* contains a fine example of the pseudonyms' role.

Delany's fiction, most notably his work from the early 1970s forward, is remarkable for its insistence upon maintaining all of the author's personal and intellectual identities—male, African American, gay, intellectual, science-fiction writer, literature professor—at once while telling extraordinarily complex, multilayered, and utterly gripping stories. In his Return to Nevèrÿon series (1979–1987), for example, Delany often prefaces individual chapters with complex epigraphs from such philosophers, literary critics, historians, and psychologists as Julia Kristeva, Luce Irigaray, Roland Barthe, Jacques Derrida, Rodolphe Gasché, Edward

Said, Jane Jacobs, Marguerite Yourcenar, Shoshana Feldman, Fernard Braudel, and many others; these same chapters respond to or illustrate some or all of the abstract ideas found within the epigraphs. Many of his characters have been known to launch into extended monologues and conversations on art, metaphysics, politics, sexuality, and gender identity without distracting significantly from the narrative. Delany has also experimented with narrative forms and pushed the science-fiction genre past its normal limits. His 1975 novel *Dhalgren* best illustrates all of Delany's skills and most of his themes. It may safely be considered his magnum opus. As fellow science fiction writer William Gibson writes in his foreword to the 1996 reprinting, *Dhalgren* is a highly experimental novel that fits in well with the types of literary experiments now associated with postmodernism, surfiction, or the "New Fiction" of the 1960s. As is true of so many works associated with this movement, *Dhalgren* repeatedly defers and denies the reader's normal expectations regarding narrative structure and voice, chronological order, and realism or the nature of the real. It is the tale of a young man named the Kid, a poet, romantic, and gang leader who lives in the fictional city of Bellona, whose own reality, in fact, is completely disrupted by civil disturbances, manmade catastrophes, and environmental disasters. In the simplest terms, *Dhalgren* may be described as a product of and metaphor for the social and civil conflicts of the 1960s and 1970s, but it would be better to say that it beggars description altogether as it interrogates such commonly accepted dichotomies as sanity/insanity, truth/fiction, literature/scholarship, gay/straight, male/female, and so on. 1977's *Triton* (also published as *Trouble on Triton*) follows in *Dhalgren*'s conceptual and artistic footsteps, albeit with a greater emphasis on sex and sexuality.

The Return to Nevèrÿon series is, after *Dhalgren* and *Triton*, Delany's most complex and accomplished body of work. It comprises four books—*Tales of Nevèrÿon* (1979), *Neveryóna* (1983), *Flight from Nevèrÿon* (1985), and *Return to Nevèrÿon, or The Bridge of Lost Desire* (1987) (which is part of the series, but also may stand alone)—the Return to Nevèrÿon saga is a swords-and-sorcery fantasy set in an ancient, prehistorical, and preliterate society that plays with constructions of sexuality and gender. The series asks how humankind went from barter systems to cash economies, which might be read as an allegory regarding the eventual rise of capitalism. In the third volume, Delany produced what may rightfully be called the first AIDS novel ever published. Its "The Tale of Plague and Carnivals" section is the novel's most explicit attempt to allegorize the AIDS crisis that was rapidly decimating gay communities in American cities in 1984 and 1985 (a period and phenomenon chronicled in *1984*).

Delany's other post-1970 novels include *Stars in My Pocket Like Grains of Sand* (1984), which continues the artistic experimentation begun in *Dhalgren* and *Triton*, and *They Fly at Çiron* (1995). Although Delany is best known for science fiction, he has also dived into other genres, including erotica or pornographic fiction (*Tides of Lust*, 1973; *The Mad Man*, 1995 [revised 1996]; *Hogg*, 1995; *Bread and Wine: An Erotic Tale of New York*, 1999); quasi-autobiographical fantasy (*Atlantis: Three Tales*, 1995;), and several memoirs (*Heavenly Breakfast*, 1978; *Times Square Red, Times Square Blue*, 1999). As with Delany's criticism, his memoirs are practically as good as his fiction and contain many of the same elements—extreme eloquence and intelligence, strong narrative devices, frank language—as his fiction; they should not be ignored.

Scholars have studied Delany's fiction and criticism extensively in both article and book form, with Delany standing as one of his own best critics. To date, twelve books

and eight dissertations have been written on Delany's fiction; of those, six books and six dissertations have been devoted to Delany alone, while the rest discuss him vis-à-vis other authors. Students of Delany's fiction are encouraged to begin with *The Review of Contemporary Fiction*'s fall 1996 issue (vol. 16, no. 3), the latter half of which is dedicated to Delany's fiction. From that issue, James Sallis, "Samuel R. Delany: An Introduction," Robert Elliot Fox, " 'This You-shaped Hole of Insight and Fire': Meditations on *Dhalgren*," and Marc Laidlaw, "*Dhalgren*: The City Not Yet Fallen, the Novel Still Unread" (a meditation on the power of Delany's masterwork for readers who have never actually read it, including the article's author), are three standouts that help to demystify Delany's oeuvre. Later that year, Sallis edited select essays from that issue as *Ash of Stars: On the Writing of Samuel R. Delany* for the University of Mississippi Press. The contributing Delany scholars include Robert Elliot Fox, Jean Mark Gawron, David N. Samuelson, Ray Davis, and Kathleen L. Spencer. The critical outlooks vary widely, but this adds to the collection's riches. Michael W. Peplow and Robert Bravard, *Samuel R. Delany: A Primary and Secondary Bibliography, 1962–1979* (1980), despite its being woefully outdated, is valuable because Peplow and Bravard both worked with Delany to assemble the book (Bravard is one of Delany's close friends and correspondents). Robert Elliot Fox, *Conscientious Sorcerers: The Black Postmodernist Fiction of LeRoi Jones/Amiri Baraka, Ishmael Reed, and Samuel R. Delany* (1987) places Delany's work in conversation with that of two other major authors of challenging, fantastic African American fiction, and it is judiciously informed by Fox's knowledge of black science fiction.

Of Delany's own books on his work, the aforementioned *1984* is indispensable, as are *The Jewel-Hinged Jaw: Notes on the Lan-*

guage of Science Fiction (1977), *The American Shore: Meditations on a Tale of Science Fiction* (1978), *The Motion of Light in Water: Sex and Science Fiction Writing in the East Village, 1957–1965* (1988, rev. 1993), and *Silent Interviews: On Language, Race, Sex, Science Fiction, and Some Comics* (1994). True to form, each of these critical works combines sophisticated readings of contemporary literary theory with Delany's reflections on the ways critics have received his works and the makeup of his audience along ideological, political, sexual, racial, and gender lines. Delany is, in the end, arguably his own best critic.

Demby, William (b. December 25, 1922, Pittsburgh, Pennsylvania) Poet, journalist, and novelist William Demby is best known for his poetry and a handful of novels published while in self-imposed exile in Rome from 1947 to the end of the millennium, although Demby spent substantial stretches of time in the United States for employment purposes. His early novels, *Beetlecreek* (1950) and *The Catacombs* (1965) are considered inventive minor classics. *Love Story Black* (1978) is a satirical novel narrated by Professor Edwards, an author who is virtually identical to Demby himself. Edwards begins working on a biography of eighty-year-old entertainer and virgin Mona Pariss with the aid of a paramour, scholar Hortense Schiller (cf. African American critic Hortense Spiller). Edwards's chronicling of Pariss's life eventually teaches him about the true nature of love.

Due to his long exile and irregular record with publishers (*Love Story Black* was published by Ishmael Reed's Reed Publishing Company, which limited its audience), Demby's books remain out of print, which has led in turn to virtually no extensive critical attention. Only one major article on Demby's work, Joseph C. Connelly, "William Demby's Fiction: The Pursuit of Muse," *NALF* 10, no. 3 (Autumn 1976), has been published in the last thirty years, and it is too early for *Love Story Black* to be included.

De Veaux, Alexis (b. September 24, 1948, New York City) Poet, playwright, fiction writer, essayist, editor, and educator Alexis De Veaux is best known as an author of many books of juvenile fiction, placing her in the company of such other African American writers in this genre as Virginia Hamilton, Rosa Guy, Jess Mowry, and Walter Dean Myers. An editor at *Essence* magazine from 1978 to 1990, De Veaux was also instrumental in gaining exposure for many younger or newer writers emerging in that period. She has been especially important for encouraging and supporting lesbian writers of color.

De Veaux's two major fictional contributions are *Na-Ni* (1973), *Spirits in the Street* (1973), and *An Enchanted Hair Tale* (1987). *Na-Ni* is an award-winning children's book about the existence of evil in the world, as young Harlemite Na-Ni tries to make the new bicycle her mother promised her fit into the block of 133 Street where she lives. *An Enchanted Hair Tale* is the story of young African American Sudan, who learns to take pride in his hair's uniqueness and beauty. *Spirits in the Street*, De Veaux's only novel of adult fiction, is an emotionally charged record of Harlem of the late 1960s and early 1970s, when tensions over many issues, including the Vietnam War, Watergate, Richard Nixon, the imprisonment of Angela Davis, drugs, police brutality, school desegregation, and crime were at their height.

Dickey, Eric Jerome (b. July 7, 1961, Memphis, Tennessee) Similar to such peers as Omar Tyree, Sheneska Jackson, and Benilde Little, Eric Jerome Dickey established himself in the latter half of the 1990s as a writer of popular fiction that benefited from the inroads established by Terry McMillan's success. Dickey has been extraordinarily prolific, publishing at least one novel every year since 1996, with virtually all of them charting high sales, generating mostly positive reviews, and satisfying a loyal, primarily African American audience. Dickey's popularity is due not only to his chosen focus on romance and relationships but also to his realistic yet humorous characterizations, settings, and plots. Moreover, Dickey weaves social commentary into his fiction, taking note of intraracial prejudices along class and color lines that often have deleterious effects upon modern African American relationships and family situations. As a result, Dickey has been a consistently bestselling author.

Dickey's debut, *Sister, Sister* (1996) is auspicious as an entry into the "Girlfriend" or "Sister Novel" genre (see separate entry) that became immensely popular in the latter half of the 1990s. It concerns the relationship between sisters Valerie and Inda, who slowly discover the infidelities and indiscretions of the men in their lives, eventually becoming friends with the fiancée of Valerie's boyfriend, Raymond, and sharing their hilarious and damning insights about romance. *Friends and Lovers* (1997) is set in Los Angeles and concerns two professional African American men, Tyrel and Leonard, and the two women, Debra and Shelby, with whom they become romantically involved. *Milk in My Coffee* (1998) covers much of the same territory as its predecessor, though Dickey develops his characters and situations in more depth. The novel focuses primarily upon African American engineer Jordan Greene and white artist Kimberly Chavers, who must confront the prejudices of their respective communities as their romance blooms. The tension is heightened as Jordan deals with tragedies within his family and the legacy of racism in his small Tennessee town.

Cheaters (1999) concerns the lives of several buppies (black urban professionals) living in Southern California, especially Stephan, a resolute ladies' man whose family past makes it difficult to find and keep love. His story is woven with those of Chante, a single, female accountant, and Darnell, a struggling writer whose wife does not support his work. Each is forced to deal with her or his false understandings about the nature of love and fidelity; that is, they require hard work. *Liar's Game* (2000) also focuses upon broken relationships and infidelity, but via divorced protagonist Vincent Calvary Browne Jr., his former wife, his child, and his new partner, Dana Ann Smith, the novel focuses as well upon issues of child custody, family structure, violence, police brutality, and intraracial differences, particularly between black Africans and African Americans.

Dixon, Melvin (b. 1950, Stamford, Connecticut; d. 1992, New York City) Until his death of AIDS-related complications in 1992, Melvin Dixon was a prominent young poet, novelist, critic, and activist. His first novel, *Trouble the Water* (1989), is the story of Jordan Henry, a successful history professor at a northern college who returns to the South after his grandmother's death to sort out the family's legacy. Haunted by his grandmother's dreams for him to avenge his mother's death in childbirth by killing his father, Jordan is forced to confront his family's entire complex past, which is symbolized through travel metaphors, African Diasporic folklore, and references to the blues. Dixon's second novel, *Vanishing Rooms* (1991), made a significant impact not only in African American literary circles but also in gay, lesbian, bisexual, and transgendered communities for its frank and occasionally graphic depiction of the horrific prejudices, discrimination, and violence—

both physical and psychological—that black gay men often endure. It comprises several intertwined plots centered upon the murder of a gay white man, Metro, by a gang of homophobic thugs. Metro's black lover, dancer Jesse Duran, seeks answers regarding Metro's murder and past via Ruella, a black woman he befriends, and Lonny, a young man who helped murder Metro. Dixon's descriptions of Metro's past, especially his rape in prison, are sometimes graphic, but the novel is ultimately a devastating indictment of society's ignorance and hatred of gay men.

Dixon also authored an excellent book of literary criticism, *Ride Out the Wilderness: Geography and Identity in African American Literature* (1987). *Vanishing Rooms* received an extensive critical treatment in Vivian May's essay "Reading Melvin Dixon's *Vanishing Rooms*: Experiencing 'The Ordinary Rope that Can Change in a Second to a Lyncher's Noose or a Rescue Line,'" *Callaloo* 23, no. 1 (Winter 2000).

Dove, Rita (b. August 28, 1952, Akron, Ohio) Poet and novelist Rita Dove is one of African American literature's brightest stars of the 1980s and 1990s as a result of her outstanding, complex poetry, which earned her the distinction of being named the seventh poet laureate (formerly consultant in poetry) of the United States by Congress for 1993 through 1995, the first African American to serve in that capacity and the youngest person to date. This led in turn to Dove being named a special consultant in poetry by the Congress from 1999–2000. Her many awards include: Fulbright Scholar at Universität Tübingen, 1974–1975; the Pulitzer Prize for Poetry in 1987 (for *Thomas and Beulah*); Ohio Arts Council Grant, 1979; Fellowship, National Endowment for the Arts (NEA), 1978 and 1989; Guggenheim Foundation fellowship, 1983–1984; the *Callaloo* Award,

1986; Lavan Younger Poet Award from the American Academy of Poets, 1986; General Electric Foundation Award, 1987; Ohio Governor's Award, 1988; Bellagio Residency at the Rockefeller Foundation, 1989; Mellon Fellowship at the National Humanities Center, 1988–1989; Fellowship at the Center for Advanced Studies, 1989–1992); Phi Beta Kappa Poet, 1993; the NAACP Great American Artist Award, 1993; Renaissance Forum Award, Folger Shakespeare Library, 1994; Duke Ellington Lifetime Achievement Award, 2001.

As a poet, Dove is best known for her technical discipline, mastery of poetic traditions, and fluidity. Her productivity in fiction has not been nearly as prolific as her poetic accomplishments (eight books since 1980), but it has generated very respectable attention and reviews. In 1985, eight of Dove's short stories were collected and published as *Fifth Sunday: Stories*, the inaugural number of the *Callaloo* Fiction series. The stories' subjects are varied, but each is an invariably complex musing on African American lives in a number of settings, including churches, weddings, and street scenes involving unorthodox characters. Her first novel, *Through the Ivory Gate* (1992), is a semiautobiographical *Künstlerroman* about a young black artist, Virginia King, who returns to Akron, Ohio, to teach young children about the value of art and creativity as she delves into and overcomes the pain of memories nestled in her childhood and adolescence. The novel received solid reviews, although some found it rather conservative in its plotting and characterizations.

To date, the only study of Dove's fiction beyond book reviews and interviews is Malin Pereira's essay, "'When the pear blossoms / cast their pale faces on /t he darker side of the earth': Miscegenation, the Primal Scene, and the Incest Motif in Rita Dove's

Work," in *AAR* 36, no. 2 (Summer 2002). Pereira's interview with Dove in *Contemporary Literature* 40, no. 2 (Summer 1999) also discusses *Through the Ivory Gate*. Notable appreciations and profiles of Dove's career include: Judith Pierce Rosenberg, "Rita Dove," in *Belles Lettres: A Review of Books by Women* 9, no. 2 (Winter 1993); "Dove, Rita" in *Current Biography* 55, no. 5 (May 1994); and Helen Vendler, "Rita Dove: Identity Markers," in *Callaloo* 17, no. 2 (Spring 1994). Interviews with Dove are collected in Earl G. Ingersol, ed., *Conversations with Rita Dove* (2003), part of Greenwood Press's Literary Conversations series.

Du Bois Institute for Afro-American Research, Harvard University The Du Bois institute was founded in 1975 and named after legendary scholar W. E. B. Du Bois, the first African American to earn a Ph.D. from Harvard University. The program of the Du Bois Institute for Afro-American Research comprises numerous missions and functions: it offers ten to fifteen fellowships annually to promising and established scholars in all areas within the larger field of African and African American Studies; it houses and supports the W. E. B. Du Bois Society, which invites secondary-school students to the institute to study with its faculty; from 1991 until 2003, it housed the second major iteration of the journal *Transition* (see separate entry); the institute acts as a site for many different programs, including AIDS initiatives, a slave-trade database, working groups, National Endowment for the Humanities seminars, art projects and databases, and so on. The crux of the institute, however, is its fellowship program.

While many of the scholars awarded the fellowships study African American fiction, the institute's name has become nearly synonymous with stellar scholarship in African American literary studies, due largely to the reputation of its current director, Henry Louis Gates Jr., one of the most notable scholars of the field in recent years. Although the institute had done well for the first eighteen years of its existence, it came into considerable fame in 1991 after Gates, previously of Duke University, accepted the director position and began luring a "dream team" of key scholars to Harvard. These included philosophers Cornel West and K. Anthony Appiah, sociologist William Julius Wilson (long associated with the University of Chicago), legal scholar Lani Guinier, Orlando Patterson, Evelyn Higginbotham, Lawrence Bobo, Kimberly Dawson, and many others.

Due, Tananarive (b. 1966, Miami, Florida) Journalist and novelist Tananarive Due, the daughter of Civil Rights activists, is one of the most artistically successful members of the Post-Soul generation, concerned as she is with the problems facing African Americans who are the heirs of the Civil Rights era's legacy. Her work plumbs many formative experiences in the lives of African Americans of that generation, thereby showing how many different moments and trials contribute to the complex psyches and worldviews of her subjects. She also stands as one of the few African American novelists, contemporary or otherwise, to write successful and critically acclaimed science or speculative fiction.

Due's first novel, *The Between* (1995), blends African and African American folklore, horror, suspense, and fantasy to portray the struggle for personal identity and meaning in the lives of African Americans living in south Florida. It tells the story of Hilton James, a middle-class social worker whose life is disrupted after his wife, the first African American judge in Miami, receives death threats after she convicts a racist. Hilton begins to have horrific dreams that he is living in different realities and experiencing fates in which he may or may not die.

exploded in the 1980s and 1990s. All of these novels, along with Ellis's short stories, are implicit expressions of Ellis's essay, "The New Black Aesthetic" (see separate article) which, as a partial response to the strictures of Black Aesthetic of the 1960s, argues that no racial label, whether foisted upon African Americans by whites or fellow African Americans, will suffice to describe the full spectrum of black culture. Its thesis is almost identical to Langston Hughes's famous 1925 essay, "The Negro Artist and the Racial Mountain" (Ellis even quotes a key phrase from Hughes's conclusion) in its assertion of the artist's independence from aesthetics guided more by politics than the artist's desire to express his interpretation of reality.[1]

This philosophy is perhaps best expressed in Ellis's debut novel, *Platitudes*, a parody of conventions or clichés in recent African American literature. Ellis's narrative is a mock *Künstlerroman* in which a young black artist, Dewayne Wellington, struggles to tell the story of his social, racial, and artistic awakenings through the eyes of his postmodern subjectivity, even as another, female artist, Isshee Ayam cajoles him to see himself as part of a traditional black community by writing his story in a rural context that focuses more on black women. This particular convention parodies the subject matter and settings through which Zora Neale Hurston, Alice Walker, and Toni Morrison achieved some of their greatest literary triumphs.[2]

The narrative's tension rests upon the male protagonist's desire to write his story free of the *platitudes* of contemporary fiction, a desire that is continually undermined as he finds himself using every available cliché, but only for the sake of commenting upon the impossibility of originality when every previous literary movement has already preempted a new aesthetic. Thus, for example, the narrators continually call attention to the process and impetuses behind the narrative's formation, as when Dewayne writes one chapter about a scene in a movie theater in which signs on the movie screen reflect the interactions between the narrative's main characters.[3] Ellis portrays the socialization of post–Civil Rights African Americans as being closely linked to both the new black middle-class dynamic that has emerged in the last three decades and to the fixtures of mainstream popular and intellectual cultures. Ellis thus lampoons such icons as standardized tests, popular music, and contemporary literary theories for their tendency to be blindly accepted and followed without thought to their social relevance.

If Ellis was attempting to create a space for a new generation of black writers in *Platitudes*, his second novel, *Home Repairs*, is less ambitious. Both books are novels of growth, but the latter is more a bildungsroman than a *Künstlerroman*, more autobiographical, and more comedic than satirical. As a result, *Home Repairs* also lacks some of the first novel's sharp wit and thematic focus and seems less developed than its predecessor. Arguably, its greatest value is as an example of the New Black Aesthetic that Ellis champions, to the extent that Ellis's protagonist, Austin McMillan represents the type of "cultural mulatto" discussed in Ellis's essay.

Ellis's third novel, *Right Here, Right Now*, shares only the epistolary format with the earlier works. Its extended satire on the self-help, inspirational-speaker, and lurid talk-show industries, with a touch of the O. J.

1. Trey Ellis, "The New Black Aesthetic," *Callaloo* 12, no. 1 (Winter 1989).

2. Some of Ayam's titles: "*Chillun o' de Lawd, Hog Jowl Junction,* and *My Big Ol' Feets Gon' Stomp Dat Devil Down*": see Trey Ellis, *Platitudes* (New York: Vintage, 1988), 110.

3. Ellis, *Platitudes*, 150–51.

Simpson controversy thrown into the plot, is both biting and successful. Narrator Ashton Robinson is an African American inspirational speaker who eventually begins his own process of self-discovery. As did its predecessors, *Right Here, Right Now* received a number of favorable reviews.

Ellis has also written a number of short stories. The best of these is "Guess Who's Coming to Seder," originally published in *Black American Literature Forum* in 1989. "Guess" is a hilarious send-up of both Sidney Poitier's famous 1967 film and the state of black-Jewish relations in the late 1980s. He has also written several screenplays and teleplays, including (uncredited) *The Inkwell* (1994) and *The Tuskegee Airmen* (1995). To date, little has been written on Ellis outside of book reviews, and he has not yet been assigned extensively, partly because his earliest work was out of print for almost a decade. Nevertheless, Ellis may easily be considered a key figure in the African American literature of the last twenty years, if only for articulating a crucial aspect of the issues captivating the post–Civil Rights generation.

Ellison, Ralph (b. 1914, Oklahoma City, Oklahoma; d. 1994, New York City) Ralph Ellison has inarguably attained the status of a giant of African American and American literature, for both the work he published during his lifetime and the extensive second novel he never actually completed and published. Until the late 1990s, Ralph Ellison's literary reputation rested primarily upon his National Book Award–winning first novel, *Invisible Man* (1952), a widely acknowledged American classic and an indispensable landmark in African American literature. Ellison's many essays on diverse subjects have been almost equally as successful and influential, with each offering further evidence of the universalist thesis that has guided Ellison's work since the 1940s. The story of a young African American man who searches for the meaning of his invisibility to both himself and the greater American society, *Invisible Man* is considered one of the most accomplished and important novels in the post–World War II period, a distinction bestowed upon the work in a *Book Week* magazine poll in 1965 and reinforced innumerable times ever since via its many accolades and popularity in high school and college courses.

Ellison's work has emerged from the sentiment expressed in *Invisible Man*'s closing line: "Who knows but that, on the lower frequencies, I speak for you?" This is an expression of the argument that African Americans are at the very center of American culture, that they speak, write, and perform from it, and that their destiny is inextricably tied to that of the rest of the nation. The novel's unnamed, picaresque protagonist's search for identity underscores the argument, as he slowly realizes that his visibility depends upon his acknowledgment of every aspect of his past, in much the same way that Americans, whether of African descent or not, must acknowledge and confront their interdependence in pursuit of the nation's democratic ideals. This same notion brought Ellison a great deal of criticism from many quarters, especially the American left wing and American Black Nationalists in the 1960s, who thought the novel's ambivalence and ambiguity were attempts to dodge the necessity of political action. Although this reading has been criticized several times, not least by Ellison himself,[1] it

---

1. See Ellison, "The World and the Jug," in his *Shadow and Act* (1964), 107–43; and T.V. Reed, "Invisible Movements, Black Powers: Double Vision and Trickster Politics in *Invisible Man*," in *Fifteen Jugglers, Five Believers: Literary Politics and the Poetics of American Social Movements* (Berkeley: University of California Press, 1992), pp. 58–86.

is one of the major divisions among the novel's critics and readers. It was during the 1960s and 1970s, in fact, that *Invisible Man* truly became canonized within the African American literary tradition via numerous journal articles, book-length studies, and anthologies.

While *Invisible Man* inarguably thrust Ellison into literary stardom, the delay in publishing his second novel caused no small amount of consternation for both his critics and admirers, and it tormented Ellison as well. This frustration was driven in part by Ellison's rare, yet widely heralded publication of several excerpts from the enormous manuscript and the fact that he had lost a substantial portion of the only copy of his manuscript—over three hundred and sixty pages, by Ellison's own estimation—to a house fire in 1967. Although Ellison labored intermittently until the end of his life to complete his magnum opus, he died in 1994 with over two thousand manuscript pages left unfinished and without any clear indication of the shape they were ultimately supposed to take. The manuscript promised to be an even more ambitious meditation on race and American identity than *Invisible Man*, one that would highlight the common identity that Americans of all backgrounds share, despite differences that often seem insurmountable. In the absence of Ellison's directions, though, the possibility of this novel ever seeing light died with him. Nonetheless, Ellison's friend and literary executor, John F. Callahan, undertook the monumental task of organizing parts of Ellison's countless chapters, notes, and vignettes into *Juneteenth* (1999; see separate entry), which received extensive praise, as well as great controversy, particularly due to the inevitable difficulties of posthumously extracting an author's intentions.

Ellison also wrote and published eleven short stories during his lifetime. Eight of these were published before *Invisible Man*,

two were published several years after the novel, and another in the 1960s. Most of these have been reprinted in various publications over the years, but the single best source of them would be *Flying Home and Other Stories* (1996), edited by John Callahan. While Ellison was working on the second book, he released eight excerpts from the work in progress, many of which were fine short stories in their own right. Most of these have been incorporated into *Juneteenth*.

Scholarship on Ellison is among the most extensive for any African American author; *Invisible Man* is, arguably, *the* preeminent novel of African American literature in the twentieth century. Scholarly studies of Ellison's short fiction are not as plentiful, but the relative few that exist are of high quality. Most study the short fiction in conjunction with *Invisible Man*. The first to be mentioned are Ellison's own essay collections, which contain essays and speeches that address or expand many of the issues in his fiction, including *Invisible Man* and its reception: *Shadow and Act* (1964) and *Going to the Territory* (1986). Due to the fanfare surrounding *Juneteenth*'s publication, most of the contemporary reviews of the novel serve as excellent scholarly studies. Other key critical works include: Kimberly W. Benston, ed., *Speaking for You: The Vision of Ralph Ellison* (1987), which contains an updated version of Robert G. O'Meally's exhaustive bibliography of works by or on Ellison as of 1986; Jacqueline Covo, *The Blinking Eye: Ralph Waldo Ellison and His American, German, and Italian Critics, 1952–1971* (1974); Robert G. O'Meally, *The Craft of Ralph Ellison* (1980); J. M. Reilly, ed., *Twentieth-Century Interpretations of* Invisible Man (1970); Edith Schor, *Visible Ellison: A Study of Ralph Ellison's Fiction* (1993), which includes an annotated bibliography of sources on Ellison and issues related to his fiction; Joseph T. Skerrett Jr., ed. "Ralph

Ellison and the Example of Richard Wright," *Studies in Short Fiction* 15, no. 2 (Spring 1978), 145–53. The March 1970 issue of *CLA Journal* (number 13) is devoted entirely to Ellison.

Everett, Percival (b. 1956, Fort Gordon, Georgia) A graduate of the University of Miami and Brown University, Percival Everett is one of the better-kept secrets among contemporary African American authors. He has published fourteen novels since the early 1980s. Virtually all of them have attracted considerable praise, but few have received anything close to the attention they deserve. His first work, *Suder* (1983), brought him a D. H. Lawrence fellowship from the University of New Mexico, while *God's Country* (1994) helped garner a Lila Wallace–*Readers Digest* Fellowship at the Woodrow Wilson Foundation. In 1992, Everett was William Robertson Coe Chair in American Studies, University of Wyoming. His other works include *Walk Me to the Distance* (1985), *Cutting Lisa* (1986), *The Weather and Women Treat Me Fair* (short stories; 1987), *For Her Dark Skin* (1989), *Zulus* (1990; winner of the New American Writing Award), *The One That Got Away* (1992), *Big Picture* (short stories; winner of the PEN/Oakland–Josephine Miles Award for Excellence in Literature) and *Watershed* (both 1996; *Watershed* was republished in paperback form in 2003), *Frenzy* (1997), *Glyph* (1999), *Grand Canyon, Inc.*, and *Erasure* (both 2001; *Erasure* won the Hurston/Wright Legacy Award for Fiction and the Hillsdale Prize for Fiction). In the 1990s, Everett began publishing his short stories and novel excerpts frequently in *Callaloo*, one of the leading literary journals.

Glyph brought Everett an unprecedented amount of critical attention for its ingenious satire of academia and contemporary trends or fads in critical literary theory. These notices led in turn to extensive atten-

tion for *Erasure*, an extended satire of faddishness in literary publishing, especially in the case of African American authors. Ironically, the novel's lampooning of simplistic categories and of African Americans' occasional fetishization of "authenticity"—literary, cultural, or otherwise—instantly made *Erasure* into a significant work of African American fiction and probably helped *God's Country* and *Watershed*, two of his earlier novels, be reprinted in paperback for the first time in 2003. Although the same courtesy has yet to be extended to the rest of Everett's corpus, interest in his more recent novels seems likely to correct this state of affairs, as are future works he has planned.

Everett's narrative craft is frequently reminiscent of Toni Cade Bambara's, to the extent that he is deeply conversant with different narrative voices and outlooks, although he is really a contemporary of Michelle Cliff, Randall Kenan, and Clarence Major in terms of his style and outlook on history. Everett's mixing of genres and concern with the conflict between tradition and modernity also takes a clear cue from the innovations of such literary modernists as William Faulkner, Ralph Ellison, and Albert Murray. In keeping with Everett's eschewing of the numerous categories frequently assigned authors, it should be noted that his individual works always transcend the categories in which critics and publishers normally place them, due perhaps to the satirical and comedic elements within them. *Glyph* and *Erasure*, for example, lampoon intellectual fads, thereby disrupting the academy's narrative of itself, while *God's Country*, *Watershed*, *Grand Canyon, Inc.*, and *The One That Got Away* undermine versions of American history—especially the Western or frontier narrative—that ultimately serve the purpose of maintaining the supremacy of both racism and capitalism, especially with regard to African Americans and various Native American peoples. *Suder* begins—superficially—as a baseball novel about a washed-up player, but it quickly morphs into a farcical quest for identity and meaning that involves everything from the drug trade to jazz and innumerable pop-culture references. *Walk Me to the Distance* uses a Hemingwayesque prose style for a study of eccentric characters struggling to make a life in a Wyoming backwater, while *Zulus* mixes postapocalyptic science fiction and comedy into disciplined, yet experimental fiction that compares well with the work of Samuel R. Delany. Everett's short stories cover all of the ground found in his novels, with all of the inevitable economy of form and structure one expects from the mode.

Fair, Ronald L. (b. October 27, 1932, Chicago, Illinois) Novelist and poet Ronald L. Fair became one of several African American authors in the late 1960s and early 1970s who wrote largely experimental fiction. For this reason, he is often discussed in the same breath as Clarence Major and Ishmael Reed. His debut novel, *Many Thousand Gone* (1965), is a speculative and satirical narrative that posits a Southern community that had never freed its slaves, while *Hog Butcher* (1966; republished as *Cornbread, Earl, and Me* in 1974) indicts racism in Chicago in ways similar to those found in Richard Wright's *Native Son*. In the 1970s, Fair returned to speculative fiction with *World of Nothing* (1970), which comprises two novellas, *Jerome* and *World of Nothing*. In the first, the eponymous protagonist becomes a Christ figure due to his ability to foresee evil events and is later crucified for the danger his talent poses to his mother. The novella *World of Nothing* features a first-person narrator, his friend Red Top, and a lengthy cast

of characters who dance into and out of the narrative in the pattern of a blues or jazz improvisation. Set in Chicago, the narrative's loose structure allows Fair to illustrate many different themes in order to flesh out Chicago's diversity. The collection *World of Nothing* won second prize from the National Institute of Letters in 1971.

Fair's third novel, *We Can't Breathe* (1972), won a Best Book Award from the American Library Association that same year for its depiction of the generation of African Americans who were born in the South and moved to the North during the Great Depression. As with many other novels that re-create the migration of African Americans to Chicago, the novel highlights the racism in that city as a way of showing that racism is not simply a Southern problem; its Northern manifestations are just as insidious. The five featured characters, Ernie, George, Willie, Jake, and Sam, struggle to survive in extreme poverty and a community that is full of every possible vice. When World War II begins, the boys see first- and secondhand how Northern racism operates via the segregated and unequal conditions African Americans face in housing and jobs. The boys are also forced to decide how to survive psychologically, whether through independence and militancy or assimilation.

Scholarship on Fair is relatively limited, due perhaps to the absence of any books of fiction since *We Can't Breathe*. Fair also published two books of poetry, *Excerpts* (1975) and *Rufus* (1977). The following are the most notable journal articles: George E. Kent, "Struggle for the Image: Selected Books by or About Blacks During 1971," *Phylon* 33, no. 4 (fourth quarter, 1972); Elizabeth A. Schultz, "The Insistence Upon Community in the Contemporary Afro-American Novel," *College English* 41, no. 2 (October 1979).

Ferrell, Carolyn (b. 1963, Brooklyn, New York) Short-story author Carolyn Ferrell is a graduate (1984) of Sarah Lawrence College, where she earned a bachelor's degree in creative writing and a Fulbright Scholarship, which she used to study abroad and pursue a musical career as a violinist for four years. Ferrell has published her stories in many different periodicals, including *Callaloo*, *The Literary Review*, and *Fiction*, which led to a number of awards and honors. These include berths in *The Best American Short Stories 1994* and *Best American Short Stories of the Century* for her masterpiece, "Proper Library." Ferrell also won the 1997 *Los Angeles Times* Art Seidenbaum Award for First Fiction and the *Ploughshares* John C. Zacharis Award for *Don't Erase Me* (1997), her first short story collection.

Ferrell's stories are based largely upon the lives of young people she met during her work with literacy programs in the Bronx and Manhattan. Each story subtly probes the intersecting lives of neighborhood residents of different ages, genders, sexualities, crossroads, and racial or ethnic backgrounds, but particularly African American youths trying to obtain freedom through education in a school system and culture that places immense obstacles in their paths. Their pursuits, however, are never divorced from their other identities and desires, which makes Ferrell's New York a site of identities and voices whose complexity and nuances seldom find their way into mainstream media.

Files, Lolita (b. circa 1964, Fort Lauderdale, Florida) Author Lolita Files emerged in the late 1990s as one of many younger authors of "Sister Novels." Her novels *Scenes from a Sistah* (1997), *Getting to the Good Part* (1999), and *Blind Ambitions* (2000) are perhaps perfect examples of the genre, with hip, young black urbanites in a nearly relentless, but consistently humorous cycle of partying, loving, and career-climbing. *Scenes from a Sistah* revolves around the exploits of Armistice "Misty" Fine and her best friend,

Reesy Snowden, as they grow up in and travel between Ft. Lauderdale, Florida, Atlanta, and New York City; *Getting to the Good Part* is a sequel to the first novel. *Blind Ambitions* introduces three new characters, women who struggle to make a living in the fast-paced, corrupt bacchanalia of Hollywood, all the while trying to maintain both their integrity and romantic lives.

All of Files's novels are good, rollicking reads that play well to contemporary African American audiences, but they seldom rise above the level of entertainment. Files's postmillennial novel, *Child of God* (2001) is more challenging material, exploring such as issues of sexuality, incest, and other taboos, and it is altogether more daring artistically and structurally than her previous works.

Flowers, Arthur R. (b. 1951, Memphis, Tennessee) Novelist and essayist Arthur R. Flowers is known for his politically charged and powerful fiction, which incorporates the language, local or regional nature, and rhythms of the blues. A student of John Oliver Killens's writing workshops, Flowers is interested in using major events in African American history to show the resiliency of African Americans as a whole while indicting the conditions that have forced such flexibility. His first novel, *De Mojo Blues: De Quest of High John De Conqueror* (1985) is set in the early 1970s, when three Vietnam veterans return from the conflict and try to restart their lives in the Black Power era in different occupations. One of the protagonists, Tucept HighJohn, embodies and revises the African American folk character High John De Conqueror, a mainstay of New Orleans hoodoo conjuring, eventually becoming a true conjure man. He helps raise the consciousness of his Vietnam friends' capacity for self-actualization, thereby occupying a role similar to that of conjure man Papa LaBas of Ishmael Reed's *Mumbo Jumbo* (1972). *Another Good Loving Blues* (1993) allows Flowers to take on the role of griot or narrator as he tells the story of conjure woman Melvira Dupress and her partner, Lucas Bodeen, a blues man, who illustrate the difficulties African Americans faced during the Great Migration of the twentieth century, in which some three million African Americans moved north and west from the South between 1910 and 1960. *Mojo Rising: Confessions of a Twenty-first Century Conjureman* (2001) is Flowers's memoir, chronicling the adventures as a conjure man and blues musician that provided much of the material for his two novels.

Two scholarly essays on Flowers's novels have appeared: Patricia R. Schoeder, "Rootwork: Arthur Flowers, Zora Neale Hurston, and the 'Literary Hoodoo' Tradition," *AAR* 36, no. 2 (Summer 2002); and Deborah Smith Pollard, "African American Holyground in *Another Good Loving Blues*," *CLA Journal* 44, no. 1 (September 2000).

Forrest, Leon (b. January 8, 1937, Chicago, Illinois; d. November 6, 1997, Evanston, Illinois) Novelist, editor, and critic Leon Forrest was among the most complex of the writers to begin writing in the wake of the Black Arts Movement. Forrest stood apart from many of the period's authors in openly embracing artistic ambitions over political ones, although his novels and short stories constantly include implicit and explicit commentaries upon the long-standing pattern of transcendence and declension that defined African American history in his view. He maintained a long, close friendship with Toni Morrison, who edited his first novel. Each of his four novels—*There Is a Tree More Ancient Than Eden* (1973), *The Bloodworth Orphans* (1977), *Two Wings to Veil My Face* (1984), and *Divine Days* (1992)—builds and draws upon the characters, situations, and themes of its predecessor to create an extensive epic that Forrest consciously modeled upon the achieve-

ments of James Joyce and Forrest's friend Ralph Ellison.

Forrest's ideas in all of his novels were shaped by a number of key factors, not the least of which was his upbringing on Chicago's South Side by parents who represented a combination of ethnic (black and New Orleans Creole) and religious (Protestant and Catholic) backgrounds. The cultural mixture of these formative years helped convince Forrest of the fact of America's multivalent ethnic, cultural, and religious composition. It also stood in contradistinction to Forrest's later experiences as a soldier in the army, and as an associate, then managing editor at *Muhammad Speaks*, the official organ of the Nation of Islam, a black nationalist religious sect. Forrest spent over half a dozen years at the newspaper, which gave him a privileged view of the NOI's inner machinery. Although Forrest came to disagree strongly with the NOI's views, he also understood their appeal to many African Americans. In the end, however, Forrest found that the richness of his early years spoke more accurately to America's past and promise. Nevertheless, he parlayed the tension between these different positions into his novels, most clearly in his last, *Divine Days*. All of Forrest's novels are set in fictional Forrest County—pun intended—which bears a strong resemblance to Chicago's Cook County. Forrest consistently weaves together black and white family histories and cultural markers (food, recreation, music, politics, and so on) as a metaphor for the American experience itself. In the spirit of Ralph Ellison's query at the end of *Invisible Man* (1952)—"Who knows but that, on the lower frequencies, I speak for you?"—Forrest asks whether African Americans and white Americans really do speak to and for one another as estranged members of the same national family.

There Is a Tree More Ancient Than Eden earned extensive praise upon its initial publication. It is the first novel in what would become a trilogy by introducing the fictional Forrest County and semiautobiographical protagonist Nathaniel Witherspoon, whose mother's death provides the impetus for existential angst and extensive plumbing of his consciousness. The Bloodworth family, southern whites who once owned and helped beget Nathaniel's ancestors, and a number of other characters recur and are expanded through the next two novels. *The Bloodworth Orphans* elaborates on the history of the Bloodworth family, using their relationship vis-à-vis the Witherspoon family as a metaphor for the heritage and history of African Americans. The Bloodworth family's disownership of the black branch of their family signifies the many ways in which African Americans have been denied their true place in American history, what Ralph Ellison called "dispossession" in *Invisible Man*. In *Two Wings to Veil My Face* (1984), Nathaniel Witherspoon is haunted by his grandfather's advice to "trouble, remember, and reveal," which recalls the contrasting advice that Ellison's Invisible Man received from his dying grandfather to "live with your head in the lion's mouth . . . overcome 'em with yeses, undermine 'em with grins, agree 'em to death and destruction."[1] Witherspoon soon learns about his troubled genealogy; his grandmother Sweetie has no biological ties to him, while his grandfather had an affair that helps to illustrate simultaneously the fickle nature of love and the need to be resilient when love is either at an ebb or absent.

Forrest's last novel, *Divine Days*, is the acme of his artistic career as well as the culmination and conclusion of his prior works. In fact, it would be fair to say that *Divine Days* both revises and comprises all of his earlier novels. At 1,135 pages, it is undoubtedly the longest of all his works and one of the longest novels in American fiction in general. Similar to Irish author James Joyce's masterpiece, *Ulysses* (1922) and magnum opus *Finnegans Wake* (1939), to say nothing of Ralph Ellison's Joycean *Invisible Man* or John Barth's *Sot-Weed Factor* (1960), Forrest attempts a complete portrait of the concerns and issues that have helped to define all that is simultaneously virtuous and problematic within African American history and identity. Like its literary models, the narrative of *Divine Days* is cyclical, often returning to earlier events in the narrative or to moments in his earlier novels. Its epic retelling of one week in 1966 in the life of Joubert Aintoine Jones draws events from the Bloodworth trilogy, Forrest's own life and experiences (especially his work with the Nation of Islam), the entire arc of early African American history from slavery to freedom, the Black Power era, and trends in African American literature, culture, and art since the 1960s. Its central motif is a question that tests the differences between generations, eras, "races," and classes: "How can you destroy what we created?"

Scholarship on Forrest, especially on the enormous *Divine Days*, has been limited but thoughtful and thorough. The only extant book on Forrest is an anthology (albeit a strong one), John G. Cawelti, *Leon Forrest: Introductions and Interpretations* (1997), which includes an extensive bibliography. Dana Williams, "Preachin' and Singin' Just to Make It Over: The Gospel Impulse in Leon Forrest's Bloodworth Trilogy," is the most comprehensive assessment of Forrest's early works to date and possibly the harbinger of the first single-author, book-length study of Forrest's fiction as a whole. Other notable sources include: *Callaloo* 16, no. 2 (Spring 1993), which contains a special section on Forrest; Leon Forrest and Madhu Dubey, "The Mythos of Gumbo: Leon For-

---

1. Ralph Ellison, *Invisible Man* (1952; reprint, New York: Vintage, 1995), 16.

rest Talks about *Divine Days*," *Callaloo* 19, no. 3 (Summer 1996); Charles H. Rowell and Leon Forrest, "'Beyond the Hard Work and Discipline': An Interview with Leon Forrest," *Callaloo* 20, no. 2 (Spring 1997).

Foster, Sharon Ewell (b. May 9, 1956, Marshall, Texas) Novelist Sharon Ewell Foster writes fiction intended primarily for the Christian community, but she has also won recognition for her novels' ability to fuse a deep spirituality with harrowing portrayal social issues. Her first novel, *Passing by Samaria* (2000), is set in Mississippi and Chicago in 1919, one of the worst years of racial violence in American history. It centers upon young, black Alena Waterbridge, who discovers a friend's lynched body in Mississippi and is consequently sent north by her parents to save her life. Once in Chicago, she becomes involved in the city's black community and witnesses the racial violence that affects that city during a horrible riot. Alena eventually embraces her faith and learns the power of forgiveness. *Ain't No River*, published in early 2001, indicts both materialism and employment discrimination against African Americans.

G

Gaines, Ernest J. (b. January 15, 1933, Oscar, Louisiana) Novelist and short-story author Ernest J. Gaines is one of the most distinguished and steadily prolific African American authors of recent years. He is best known for *The Autobiography of Miss Jane Pittman* (1971), but such later novels as *In My Father's House* (1978), *A Gathering of Old Men* (1983), and *A Lesson Before Dying* (1993) have earned at least as much praise as his breakthrough novel and a raft of awards and fellowships.

Gaines's novels and stories are set primarily in the American South, specifically Louisiana's rural African American communities. Each novel is either set in or connected to the town of Bayonne, St. Raphael Parish, Louisiana, where African American, Creole, Cajun, and Caucasian cultures interact, mix, and confront each other. Gaines's focus upon Bayonne, St. Raphael Parish, and the South in general has earned him an increasingly common place within Southern literature courses in American universities. One of Gaines's major goals as a writer is to reinsert African Americans into their rightful place in Southern history, as was true of many African American authors who began publishing in the 1960s. His sympathetic portrayal of African Americans in and from the South certainly sets him apart from such white peers and predecessors as William Faulkner and Robert Penn Warren, but he is also as true to the vagaries and eccentricities of Southern life as any other writer from the region. Gaines's perspicacious and nuanced view of his subjects has earned him a Wallace Stegner Award (1957–1958), a Guggenheim Fellowship (1973–1974), a MacArthur Foundation "Genius" grant in 1993, and a special issue of the journal *Callaloo* (1, no. 3, May 1978) devoted to his works. *Callaloo* also bestowed a special citation upon Gaines at the Modern Language Association's annual convention in 2001 as part of its twenty-fifth anniversary celebration.

Gaines's early novels, *Catherine Carmier* (1964) and *Of Love and Dust* (1967), and his short story collection *Bloodline* (1968) introduce not only the setting that concerns the remainder of his works but also the themes of silence and repression brought about by the South's and the nation's obsession with racial categories. His novels since 1970 are arguably his best and most mature, with several bona fide classics among them. The undisputed masterpiece among these is *The Autobiography of Miss Jane Pittman* (1971), which is often categorized as a neo–slave narrative (see separate entry) for its 110-year-old, first-person narrator and protagonist, who was born in antebellum 1852 and lives into the tumultuous Civil Rights era. The novel is told as if Miss Jane is speaking to an editor recording her life, thereby emphasizing the importance of orality in African American culture and literature. The length of Miss Jane's life and the clarity with which she recalls her experiences allow her to record and remark upon many of the major developments in African American and American history from the Civil War until the novel's present. The novel is invested in showing the ways in which the different groups living in St. Raphael Parish established their identities along racial lines, with most of the attention going to African Americans, who, like Miss Jane Pittman herself, must name themselves, stave off violent assaults upon both their persons and their communities, and reinvent themselves as the nation slowly crawls toward progress. This is best expressed through the violent deaths of Miss Jane's adopted son Ned, already orphaned by racial violence, and Jimmy Aaron, a Civil Rights activist. The absurdity of racial distinctions and their repressive effects are ultimately indicted, but the novel emphasizes that the fight against even the worst forms of degradation and discrimination must never cease. *The Autobiography of Miss Jane Pittman* was also made into a popular film for television in 1974, starring Cicely Tyson as Miss Jane.

In My Father's House (1978) is perhaps the least popular and artistically successful of Gaines's novels, qualities attributable to its startling departure from the cautious optimism of *The Autobiography of Miss Jane Pittman*. The protagonist, Philip Martin, is a prominent Civil Rights activist who finds that both he and his community now question the efficacy of nonviolent, integrated protest and actions. Philip's haunting

queries act as metaphors for a parallel quest for peace with his past, in which he fathered an illegitimate son who reappears as a member of the Nation of Islam. Martin's struggles with both his son and his past do not flow as well as the action of the earlier novel but still offer sufficient opportunity to take a retrospective look at the successes and failures of the Civil Rights era.

A Gathering of Old Men (1983) is structured as a detective novel of sorts, with the detectives being the nine men of the title, each of whom has an opportunity to narrate a section of the novel and therefore unravel the plot's mystery. The latter concerns the murder of Beau Botan, a Cajun work boss on the plantation of the Marshall family. As the local sheriff tries to find the killer, he discovers that many people, especially African Americans who had been subjected to numerous horrors under both de jure and de facto segregation and racial discrimination, have more than enough motive to murder Botan and are willing to pay for his death, regardless of their innocence. As the Boutan family plans its traditional violent vengeance upon the town's black population, they soon discover that the old ways no longer work in the post–Civil Rights era, in which violence is more destructive to those who commit it.

A Lesson Before Dying (1993), set in Bayonne in 1948, is narrated by Grant Wiggins, a black schoolteacher who is called upon to act as the amanuensis for Jefferson, a young black man falsely accused of robbing a local liquor store. At his trial, Jefferson's incompetent defense attorney uses a racist defense in front of the all-white jury, arguing that Jefferson's African heritage makes him capable of spontaneous, random violence but not intelligent enough to plot a robbery. As a result, Jefferson is sentenced to death, but his mother is determined that her barely literate son find a way to define and express himself fully through mastery of language so that he may also die with dignity, despite the vagaries of a racist system. As Jefferson completes his journal indicting the failures of democracy—his name is an ironic commentary upon Thomas Jefferson's ambivalent attempts to define democracy for the nation—he transforms his community and the narrator himself. *A Lesson Before Dying* won the National Book Critics Circle Award in 1993.

The scholarship on Gaines is extensive; the majority of the articles on his novels are found in *Callaloo*, *African American Review*, *CLA Journal*, *MELUS*, and *American Literature*, in that order. Since Gaines is from Louisiana and *Callaloo* was long based at Louisiana State University, that journal has routinely published excerpts from Gaines's novels in progress and is the single greatest source of regular scholarship; its entire May 1978 issue (number 3) is devoted to Gaines's work and should be among the first consulted. Books on Gaines's fiction include: Valerie Melissa Babb, *Ernest Gaines* (1991); David C. Estes, ed., *Critical Reflections on the Fiction of Ernest J. Gaines* (1994); Herman Beavers, *Wrestling Angels Into Song: The Fictions of Ernest J. Gaines and James Alan McPherson* (1995); Karen Carmean, *Ernest J. Gaines: A Critical Companion* (1998); and Mary Ellen Doyle, *Voices from the Quarters: The Fiction of Ernest J. Gaines* (2002).

Key critical articles include: Jack Hicks, "To Make These Bones Live: History and Community in Ernest J. Gaines's Fiction," *BALF* 11, no. 1 (Spring 1977); John W. Roberts, "The Individual and the Community in Two Short Stories by Ernest J. Gaines," *BALF* 18, no. 3 (Autumn 1984); Mary Ellen Doyle, "Ernest Gaines' Materials: Place, People, Author," *MELUS* 15, no. 3 (Autumn 1988), and "Ernest J. Gaines: An Annotated Bibliography, 1956–1988," *BALF* 24, no. 1 (Spring 1990); Wolfgang Lepschy, "A

MELUS Interview: Ernest J. Gaines," *MELUS* 24, no. 1 (Spring 1999).

"Girlfriends' Book." *See* **Sister Novel.**

Goines, Donald (b. December 15, 1937, Detroit, Michigan; d. October 21, 1974, Detroit, Michigan) During his short career, Donald Goines was one of the most popular African American fiction authors, due largely to his novels' accessible style and street-savvy subject matter. Between the publication of his first novel, *Dopefiend*, in 1971, and 1975, when his last two novels were published after Goines's violent death, he attracted and maintained his sizeable audience by writing about subjects he knew all too well from his own experience: the lives and perspectives of heroin addicts and drug dealers; gambling, pimping and prostitution; armed robbery; and various forms of street hustling. He spent approximately six years of his life in prison for offenses committed in several of these occupations. By the time *Dopefiend* was published, Goines had been arrested fifteen times or more and was addicted to heroin from 1955 until his death.[1] All of these experiences gave Goines's writing a gritty realism that few writers could match, but they also led to his early death at age thirty-six, when he and his wife were shot in their Detroit home. The identity of their two assailants has yet to be determined.

All of Goines's novels document the life of street hustlers engaged in just about every type of illegal business imaginable. Goines was largely inspired by Iceberg Slim, the former pimp and street hustler whose books were—and still are—highly popular in many African American communities. Like Slim, Goines frequently condemns the very behavior he is depicting and offers a number of both straightforward and implicit social

1. Greg Goode, "Donald Goines," *DLB*, vol. 96:96, 98.

commentaries along the way in a double-voiced style (that is to say, a mix of urban African American and standard English) that pulls few punches. His appeal rests upon offering an indictment of racism and the hypocrisy of the American middle and upper classes, arguing that the underclasses must scrabble under the worst circumstances to survive in a world that is known only in the most oblique way by most of the nation. *Dopefiend: The Story of a Black Junkie*, for example, follows the downfall of Teddy and Terry, two middle-class African Americans seduced into heroin addiction, including virtually every vice and behavior in which hardcore addicts participate. The same may be said of *Whoreson: The Story of a Ghetto Pimp* (1971), in which Whoreson Jones, the progeny of a black prostitute and unknown white father, rises to the level of a major pimp by becoming utterly ruthless, thereby sacrificing most of the attributes that are normally accorded to middle-class respectability in America. *Black Gangster* (1972) uses the life of another street hustler to show how everything from different types of street crime to the Black Nationalist politics of the late 1960s and early 1970s are vices that can be hustled to the right people if one is clever and cynical enough; *Street Players* (1973) repeats many of the same themes. *White Man's Justice, Black Man's Grief: Crime Partners* (1973) is largely an exposé of the racial inequities of the American justice system, while *Black Girl Lost* (1973), *Eldorado Red* (1974), and *Never Die Alone* (1974) cover much of the same territory found in Goines's earlier novels. *Swamp Man* (1974) is somewhat unusual, in that it imagines the implications of a lusty interracial relationship between a black woman and a white man. With the exception of the posthumous *Inner City Hoodlum* (1975), the remainder of Goines's novels were published under the pseudonym of Al C. Clark to avoid flooding the market with too many books under the

author's given name. Four of these novels constitute a series featuring the exploits of militant protagonist Kenyatta, who first appeared in *White Man's Justice, Black Man's Grief*; the others are *Death List, Kenyatta's Escape* (both 1974), and *Kenyatta's Last Hit* (1975). Over the course of the series, Kenyatta develops into a major revolutionary figure in Detroit. *Daddy Cool* (1974) and *Inner City Hoodlum* again cover much of the same ground of Goines's earlier work, although deeper human bonds and emotions do appear in the former novel, in which a hit man feels enormous regret after his daughter is seduced into the world of prostitution.

Golden, Marita (b. April 28, 1950, Washington, D.C.) Memoirist, essayist, and novelist Marita Golden has established herself as an influential and prolific figure on the contemporary African American literary scene. In 1990, Golden founded the nonprofit Zora Neale Hurston/Richard Wright Foundation, which annually awards prizes to writers of African descent in the categories of fiction, debut fiction, nonfiction, and contemporary fiction. Many newer or younger African American writers of the 1990s have either won an award from the Hurston/Wright foundation, or have been named as finalists. A recent anthology, *Gumbo: A Celebration of African American Writing* (2002), co-edited with novelist E. Lynn Harris, collects stories and novel excerpts from many of the Hurston/Wright award winners. The proceeds from its sales also benefit the foundation.

Golden's first autobiography, *Migrations of the Heart* (1983), uses her experiences coming of age in the 1960s and in the changing African American communities of the 1970s to reflect upon issues that affected the nation as well as Golden herself. Golden's subsequent memoirs and essay collections have followed *Migrations*'s combination of fluid, clever prose and personal experience and its focus upon addressing contemporary social issues. The titles of two of her most popular works, *Saving Our Sons: Raising Black Children in a Turbulent World* (1995) and *A Miracle Every Day: Triumph and Transformation in the Lives of Single Mothers* (1999), demonstrate this most effectively; both arose directly from Golden's experiences raising her family.

Golden's contributions to contemporary fiction consist of four novels to date. The first, *A Woman's Place* (1986), is based upon a few of Golden's own experiences in the 1960s and 1970s. It revolves around three black women, Faith, Crystal, and Serena, who meet at a predominantly white college in the late 1960s and form strong bonds through their mutual interest in political activism and in finding their identities as women. Each discovers that she must learn to take possession of that identity rather than to surrender it to men who have been acculturated to view women as mere objects to be possessed and controlled.

Long Distance Life (1989) is set in Washington, D.C., and concerns the journey of Naomi Johnson, who moved as a young woman from a hard life of sharecropping in North Carolina to the nation's capitol to raise her family. Naomi watches as the fortunes of her family wax and wane over four generations, decaying as they move further from the traditions and spirituality that Naomi represents. Golden uses the connections and conflicts between Naomi, her daughter Esther, and their respective husbands to symbolize changes in African American communities over time and through major historical epochs. In addition, Golden tells a quieter tale of the extent to which the novel's women and men need one another; each of the major male characters dies too young, thereby allowing Golden to show how the novel's women struggle in their absence. Golden seems equally concerned with showing this struggle and af-

firming her women's inner strength, although that character comes with a tragic price.

And Do Remember Me (1992) tells how Civil Rights activist Jessie Foster escaped from her father's sexual molestation to become part of the zeitgeist of the greatest social movement of the 1960s. As Jessie witnesses the triumphs and tragedies of the movement, she also begins an acting career and befriends Macon, a young black college professor at an historically white university, who encounters the virulent racism common at that time. Macon and Jessie's respective stories link the Civil Rights movement to present-day "race" relations, arguing implicitly that the struggle that the Civil Rights movement represented never truly ended but has waned due to a dearth of knowledge about that struggle on both sides of the racial divide.

In *The Edge of Heaven* (1998), Golden experiments with form and perspective to create a postmodern novel about the Singletary family, in which the mother, Lena, is estranged from her daughter Teresa during Lena's stint in prison for an accounting scandal. When Lena is released, she soon realizes that her family's bonds have always been strained due to the absence of deep love and the presence of alienating modern conveniences—television, automobiles, and other material items—and deep family secrets in their lives. All of these elements threaten to destroy the family unless they can find paths to redemption and forgiveness.

Gomez, Jewelle (b. September 1948, Boston, Massachusetts) Poet, critic, activist, and novelist Jewelle Gomez began writing and publishing her poetry in the late 1970s after being inspired by the poetic works and performances of Audre Lorde, Nikki Giovanni, and Ntozake Shange. Although most of her output consists of poetry and criticism, Gomez's novel and short-story collection have earned considerable attention and acclaim. All of her writing is marked by an interest in and attention to the possibilities of helping women to transcend sexism, especially the ignorance and abuse that it brings. Gomez's first novel, *The Gilda Stories* (1991), is superficially a vampire story set in antebellum New Orleans, but it is also a remarkable revision of the vampire motif within the horror genre. In fact, it is barely a horror story in the traditional sense, as the true horror comes from the circumstances of slavery whence The Girl runs into the care of the eponymous Gilda, the main vampire in question. Gilda acts as a savior, maternal figure, and lover to The Girl long before she bites her. As with traditional vampire narratives, that act is eroticized, but the eroticism is deeply infused with love, as Gilda gives The Girl her name and a greater sense of identity. The novel earned high praise for Gomez from several quarters but especially from the gay, lesbian, bisexual, and transgendered community, which applauded the possibilities of sexual and gender identity the novel offered, earning Gomez a Lambda Award (1991). Gomez's work also appeals to some aficionados of science/speculative fiction. Gomez's first short-story collection, *Don't Explain: Short Fiction* (1998) comprises a number of sketches and longer stories that fit into the science fiction and fantasy genres, including one that continues Gilda's saga. The previous year, Gomez also coedited the collection *Best Lesbian Erotica 1997* with Tristan Taormino.

To date, a number of scholarly articles have been published both by and about Gomez: Judith E. Johnson, "Women and Vampires: Nightmare or Utopia?" *The Kenyon Review* 15, no. 1 (Winter 1993); Elyce Rae Helford, "The Future of Political Community: Race, Ethnicity, and Class Privilege in Novels by Piercy, Gomez, and Misha," *Utopian Studies* 12, no. 2 (Spring 2001); Gomez, "Speculative Fiction and Black Lesbians," *Signs* 18, no. 4 (Summer 1993); and "Talking About It: Homophobia in the Black Community, a Dialogue Between Jewelle Gomez and Barbara Smith," *Feminist Review* 34 (Spring 1990).

Gordon, Howard (b. March 11, 1952, Syracuse, New York) Short-story writer Howard Gordon is the author of one collection, *The African in Me* (1993). The volume comprises nine stories set in the African American community of Syracuse, New York. Many delineate the ways in which racism, difficult family dynamics, and anger affect the lives of the characters. Gordon has had stories printed in the following collections: "After Dreaming of President Johnson," in Gloria Naylor, ed., *Children of the Night: The Best Short Stories by Black Writers, 1967 to the Present* (1995) and in *The Souls of Black Folk and Related Readings* (1998); "The Playground of Hostility," in *Imagining America: Stories From the Promised Land*, ed. Wesley Brown and Amy Ling (1992); "My Lucy," in *Rites of Passage: Stories About Growing Up by Black Writers from Around the World*, ed. Tonya Bolden (1994); "I Can't Find My Blackface," in *Streetlights: Illuminating Tales of the Urban Black Experience*, ed. DorisJean Austin and Martin Simmons (1996); "Someone is Screaming" in *Preventing Violence in Schools: A Challenge to American Democracy*, ed. Joan Burstyn (2001).

Greenlee, Sam (b. July 30, 1930, Chicago, Illinois) Novelist, poet, and nonfiction author Sam Greenlee became famous via his bestselling novel, *The Spook Who Sat by the Door* (1969). The novel tells of an African American, Dan Freeman, who fawns his way into being hired by the CIA as a token black in the wake of the Civil Rights and Black Power movements; he then uses his knowledge to become a revolutionary. Written as a militant indictment of racism and cynicism within the United States government,

Greenlee's novel was a major influence upon African American fiction and culture of the 1970s and later turned into a popular Blaxploitation film in 1973. It underscores the difficulty, if not impossibility, of African Americans achieving true equality in post–Civil Rights America. His only other novel was *Baghdad Blues: The Revolution That Brought Saddam Hussein to Power* (1976; reprinted 1991), the semiautobiographical adventures of a U.S. intelligence bureau operative stationed in Iraq at the time of the coup mentioned in the subtitle. It is remarkable for its prescient view of the Hussein regime's nature and role in the region.

Grooms, Anthony (b. January 15, 1955, Louisa County, Virginia) Poet, short-story writer, and novelist Anthony Grooms made a significant mark upon the literary scene with his first book of poems, *Ice Poems* (1988). His two book-length contributions to contemporary African American fiction, *Trouble No More* (1995; short stories) and *Bombingham* (2001) have also been successes. In addition, *Trouble No More* won the 1996 Lillian Smith Award for Fiction, while *Bombingham* has won universal praise for its combination of lyricism, complex characters, and a delicate balance of history, politics, and a focus on simple humanity.

Trouble No More's stories are remarkable for all of these reasons but also for their attention to the extreme diversity within African American communities. Their narrators and protagonists are frequently youths living during or after the Civil Rights movement, attempting to make sense of a world in which their ordinary wants and needs come into conflict with racism or difficult family circumstances. Grooms's stories highlight the fact that African American communities are never monolithic, always comprising people allied to divergent factions but with their own personal and political problems that often parallel one another.

Grooms's first novel, *Bombingham*, illustrates this point perfectly. *Bombingham* takes its title from a nickname that members of the black community of Birmingham, Alabama, gave the city after more than twenty unsolved bombings of African American homes and institutions had occurred in the 1950s and 1960s. The novel's protagonist, Walter Lee Burke, is a soldier in the Vietnam War attempting to discover when he lost his humanity and compassion. He traces this loss back to 1963, the year when the Civil Rights movement had began to turn the corner of popular support, in part due to the horrific bombing of Birmingham's Sixteenth Street Baptist Church, in which four African American girls were killed and many others were injured. Even as the city's African American community, Civil Rights leaders, and the world at large galvanizes around the event, eleven-year-old Walter Lee must also cope with his mother's devastating, slow death from cancer. The tragedies parallel each other, creating an elaborate metaphor for the wrenching shift in the nation's view of African Americans, while keeping the humanity of black people in the light.

Grooms's work has also garnered a Sokolov Scholarship from the Breadloaf Writing Conference, the Lamar lectureship from Wesleyan College, and an Arts Administration Fellowship from the National Endowment for the Arts.

Guy, Rosa (b. September 1, 1925, Trinidad) Novelist Rosa Guy wrote a series of stories intended primarily for young adults and juveniles from the 1960s through the 1980s. She was a cofounder of the Harlem Writers Guild (along with John Oliver Killens) in 1951 and a member of the Committee for the Negro in the Arts in the 1940s. Most of her novels are set in Harlem and focus upon the difficulties of coming of age in that environment. The best-known of these are her earliest works, a trilogy comprising *Friends* (1973), *Ruby* (1976), and *Edith Jackson* (1978). Each novel studies conflicts within African American and African Diasporic communities via the Cathy and Jackson families of Harlem. *Friends* explores class differences and conflicts between African Americans and black Caribbeans, while *Ruby* focuses upon Ruby Cathy's heartbreak in the wake of her mother's death. It was selected as the Best Book for Young Adults by the American Library Association in 1976. *Edith Jackson* follows the eponymous protagonist's struggles after her father leaves the family, allowing the novel to comment upon the modern state of the American family.

Guy is also widely known for writing the exploits of young black detective Imamu Jones in another trilogy consisting of *The Disappearance* (1979), *New Guys Around the Block* (1983), and *And I Heard a Bird Sing* (1987). Each of the Imamu Jones novels is both an exemplary work of suspense and an exposé of the problems of drugs, alcoholism, and abuse found in many urban African American communities. Other works include: *Mirror of Her Own* (1981), about an upper-class white family and its conflicts over love, infidelity, and addiction, and *Mother Crocodile* (1983; a children's book adapted from an African American folktale). *A Measure of Time* (1983) is an adult novel apparently—and loosely—based upon the life of millionaire beauty product manufacturer Madame C. J. Walker. Set in Montgomery, Alablama, and Harlem, the protagonist, Dorine Davis, goes from poverty in the South to riches in Harlem yet maintains her humanity. *Paris, Peewee, and Big Dog* (1984), *My Love, My Love, or The Peasant Girl* (1985), and *Billy the Great* are more examples of Guy's juvenile fiction. The first and third are tales of friendship, while *My Love, My Love* adapts Hans Christian Andersen's "The Little Mermaid" for the Antilles in a tale of racial prejudice. It was in turn adapted into the Broadway Musical *Once on This Island* in 1990 and nominated for eight Tony Awards. *The Ups and Downs of Carl Davis III* (1989) is juvenile fiction centering upon the titular protagonist's attempts to share his African American heritage and history with his indifferent schoolmates. *The Music of Summer* (1991) is an adult novel about intraracial prejudice along color and class lines, while *The Sun, the Sea, a Touch of the Wind* (1995), also an adult novel, is based in part on Guy's own time in Haiti in the early 1970s. Its protagonist, painter Jonnie Dash, travels to the impoverished island nation to escape her New York environment and background and to restore her artistic vision by painting the local citizenry, but she finds herself shocked and outraged by the poverty that surrounds her.

For her efforts, Guy has become one of the leading voices in contemporary African American juvenile fiction and is routinely listed among the genre's most important authors of the twentieth century. Guy is included in *The Oxford Book of Children's Stories* (1995) and *Calling the Wind: Twentieth-Century African-American Short Stories* (1994). Scholarly attention has followed, primarily in the 1990s, as the field of juvenile fiction garnered more attention. Key articles include: Vera R. Edwards, "Telling Tales: The Pedagogy and the Promise of African American Literature for Youth," *AAR* 28, no. 1 (Spring 1994); Elizabeth Schafer, "'I'm Gonna Glory in Learnin': Academic Aspirations of African American Characters in Children's Literature," *AAR* 32, no. 1 (Spring 1998).

Haley, Alex (b. August 11, 1921, Ithaca, New York; d. February 21, 1992, Seattle, Washington) Alex Haley is best known for two major contributions to African American literature: *The Autobiography of Malcolm X* (1965), which has become perhaps the most important and influential autobiography of an African American in the last fifty years; and *Roots* (1976), a novel based upon Haley's own genealogy. *Roots* was a critically acclaimed best-seller upon its publication. The following year, it also won the Pulitzer Prize and became a major phenomenon when it was transformed into the first of two television miniseries on the ABC network. The *Roots* miniseries became one of the highest-rated shows ever to air on television, with between one-third to nearly one-half of the American population tuning in each week, and won countless accolades. Surveys and polls taken in the succeeding decades name *Roots* as one of the best and most successful miniseries of all time. It also stirred a national interest in genealogy, especially among African Americans. This interest only became stronger when *Roots: The Next Generation*, the sequel to the first miniseries, was produced in 1979.

Roots is the saga of Kunta Kinte, a Mandinka from what is now Gambia, who is kidnapped from his African home and enslaved in Virginia. Kunta Kinte's adherence to the beliefs and traditions of his African upbringing, as well as his determination to pass them on to his descendants (especially his daughter, Kizzy), were inspirational odes to the power of black pride, which is where both the book and the series gained much of their appeal to African Americans. Haley was later criticized for sloppy historical research in the book and accused of plagiarizing substantial portions of it. Nevertheless, no other single work of African American literature has reached an audience as great as the book and miniseries' combined numbers.

Haley also wrote a novella, *A Different Kind of Christmas* (1988), in which a slave-holder's son learns to despise slavery to the point of joining the abolitionist movement. Another novel, *Alex Haley's Queen* (1993), was left unfinished at Haley's death but later edited for publication by David Stevens.

Hamilton, Virginia (b. March 12, 1936, Yellow Springs, Ohio; d. February 19, 2002, Yellow Springs, Ohio) Novelist Virginia Hamilton was one of the most prolific and influential authors of juvenile fiction in African American literary history. She was the author of several modern classics of fiction for young people: *Zeely* (1967), *The Planet of Junior Brown* (1971), *M. C. Higgins, the Great* (1974), and *The People Could Fly* (1985, republished 2000; retold African American folktales). Hamilton's reputation rests upon her ability to create richly poetic juvenile fiction for and about African Americans, with emphases upon the possibilities for survival and success despite the burden of racist discrimination and upon characters who are fully three-dimensional and complex.

The Planet of Junior Brown (1971), which won the Newbery Award in 1971, tells the story of Junior Brown, an obese musical prodigy, and his fellow eighth-grader, Buddy Clark, who protects Junior from many of the persecutions of his world. *M. C. Higgins, the Great* (1974), winner of the National Book Award, the Newbery Medal, and the *Boston Globe/Horn* Book Award (all 1974), is the captivating story of young M. C., who wishes to save his family's home from destruction by the mining company that is destroying the land around him. *Justice and Her Brothers* (1978), *Dustland* (1980), and *The Gathering* (1980) form a science fiction trilogy centered upon a young girl, Justice, and her twin brothers, all of whom attempt to save the Earth from an evil force.

Other works by Hamilton include: *The Girl Who Spun Gold* (2000); *Bluish* (1999); *Second Cousins* (1998); *The Bells of Christmas* (1997); *A Ring of Tricksters* (1997); *When*

Birds Could Talk and Bats Could Sing (1996); *Her Stories* (1996); *Jaguarundi* (1995); *Plain City* (1993); *Drylongso* (1992); *The All Jahdu Story Book* (1988); *The Mystery of Drear House: The Conclusion of the Dies Drear Chronicle* (1987); *A White Romance* (1987); *A Little Love* (1984); *Sweet Whispers, Brother Rush* (1982); *The House of Dies Drear* (1968). *Time Pieces: The Book of Times* (2002; semi-autobiographical fiction about a black family's migration) was published posthumously. Among her many awards, Hamilton also won a MacArthur Foundation "Genius" Grant in 1995.

Scholarly work on Hamilton is extensive; she is among the most frequently cited African American authors in her chosen genre. Key books and book chapters include: Nina Mikkelson, *Virginia Hamilton* (1994); Millicent Lenz, "Virginia Hamilton's Justice Trilogy: Exploring the Frontiers of Consciousness," in *African-American Voices in Young Adult Literature: Tradition, Transition, Transformation*, ed. Karen Patricia Smith (1994), 293–310. The entire Spring 1998 issue of *African American Review* (32, no. 1) is dedicated to children's literature, with significant attention paid to Hamilton's work; that issue should be consulted first. Scholarly articles include: Roberta Seelinger Trites, "'I Double Never Ever Never Lie to My Chil'ren': Inside People in Virginia Hamilton's Narratives," *AAR* 32, no. 1 (Spring 1998); Gail Sidonie Sobat, "If the Ghost Be There, Then Am I Crazy?: An Examination of Ghosts in Virginia Hamilton's *Sweet Whispers, Brother Rush* and Toni Morrison's *Beloved*," *Children's Literature Association Quarterly* 20, no. 4 (Winter 1995–1996); Janice Hartwick Dressel, "The Legacy of Ralph Ellison in Virginia Hamilton's Justice Trilogy," *English Journal* 42 (November 1984).

Hardy, James Earl (b. 1966, Brooklyn, New York) Novelist and poet James Earl Hardy's debut novel, *B-Boy Blues: A Seriously Sexy, Fiercely Funny, Black-on-Black Love Story* (1994), won resoundingly positive reviews and wide attention for its engaging, humorous, yet unflinchingly honest portrayal of black gay males' lives. Although Hardy has been compared to author E. Lynn Harris, another popular black gay author who writes about black, middle-class, closeted gay men, those connections are virtually the only ones the authors share. Whereas Harris's novels are divided between "straight" and gay characters and written for a mass "straight" audience, Hardy's focus squarely on black gay men, especially the "B-Boys," the streetwise, break dancing, members of hip-hop culture, and Caucasians are relegated to the margins of the novels' worlds. *B-Boy Blues*'s protagonist, Mitchell Crawford, desires and eventually enters into a relationship with one such B-Boy, Raheim, who represents the height of masculinity for him. The novel reveals the complexities within African American culture along lines of sexuality, class, and gender as Mitchell must come to terms with both his lover's machismo and the son he brings with him.

Although it was not a bestseller, *B-Boy Blues* was popular enough to warrant the creation of a series of additional books based upon Mitchell's experiences. *Second Time Around* (1996) picks up where *B-Boy Blues* ends, with Mitchell now deeply ensconced in his relationship with Raheim. The novel also delves further into the analyses of the conflicts within African American communities about gays, particularly gay men, especially the silencing and blatant discrimination they encounter. *If Only for One Nite* (1997) finds Mitchell reminiscing about the affair he had with Warren, his high school gym coach, during his class reunion. These memories turn into a rekindled affair in the present. Hardy continues Mitchell's saga in *The Day Eazy-E Died: A B-Boy Blues Novel* (2001) and *Love the One You're With* (2002).

No scholarly articles on Hardy's novels exist thus far, but since he is a major figure in contemporary gay fiction, that is sure to change. Hardy is profiled in Robert L. Pela, "James Earl Hardy," *The Advocate: The National Gay and Lesbian Newsmagazine*, September 17, 1996; and interviewed in Greg Herren, "Frank Words from James Earl Hardy about Racism, Homophobia, Hip-Hop, and Shopping at Macy's," *Lambda Book Report* 10, no. 2 (September 2001).

Harris, E. Lynn (b. 1956, Little Rock, Arkansas) A former computer salesman for IBM, E. Lynn Harris began publishing his popular series of novels with *Invisible Life* (1994). Each of Harris's novels has since hit the best-seller lists and sold at least 100,000 copies, thereby making him one of the most popular African American authors of the 1990s and 2000s. All of Harris's novels focus on similar themes: romantic relationships, whether between African American men and women or between African American men; secrets within those relationships, particularly secrets regarding hidden sexual desires or orientations; the construction of masculinity and (false) gender identities; and color consciousness among African Americans. The content of his novels is semiautobiographical; Harris discovered he was bisexual in college but remained in the closet for many years for fear of losing his employment.

Harris's novels are typically populated by middle-class, African American professionals and athletes who find their personal and romantic lives troubled by secrets from the past. In *Invisible Life* and its sequels, *Just As I Am* (1995) and *Abide With Me* (1999), protagonist Raymond Tyler, a former college football star and successful lawyer, is forced

to confront his own bisexuality as past men he has slept with come back to haunt him as he tries to maintain his relationship with his fiancée, Nicole. After a great deal of consternation, Tyler chooses his male lovers and, eventually, a gay identity over his heterosexual life, but in the process his struggles raise a number of questions about the way African American communities deal or fail to deal with the fact of homosexuality within social and religious institutions. In *And This Too Shall Pass* (1996), Harris again explores sexual identity but also addresses substance abuse and the treatment of women in contemporary African American communities.

Despite the challenge his novels pose in foregrounding these questions, they occasionally suffer from a degree of sameness in basic plot structure and a tendency to classify characters too quickly into neat stereotypes. The sequels to *Invisible Life* and *Not a Day Goes By* (2000) particularly reflect this problem, although Harris attempted to include slightly different (but still black, middle-class, professional) characters in *If This World Were Mine* (1997). Nevertheless, Harris's largely African American audience is attracted to his novels because of their reliably consistent exploration of African American sexuality and sexual identities. In a period in which the rapid and epidemic spread of AIDS among African Americans has forced many communities within the larger group to ask hard questions about sexuality, Harris's novels help answer some of those questions. Harris's reward, beyond impressive sales, has been mixed, but overall positive reviews. Most reservations about his work have to do with "stilted dialogue" and charges that Harris's plots are "soap opera material."[1] On the other hand, Harris has also been commended for creating "a

---

1. Review of *And This Too Shall Pass*, *Publishers Weekly*, January 29, 1996, 84; review of *Just As I Am*, *Publishers Weekly*, January 24, 1994, 41.

body of diverse characters, a group of friends and family members who admirably demonstrate a continuity of love and support,"[1] and his undeniable ability to expose his readers to the complexities of gay men's lives. Thus far, however, Harris's novels have not received notable scholarly treatment.

Harris has also published a short story in the collection *Got to Be Real: Four Original Love Stories* (2000) and coedited, with Marita Golden, *Gumbo: A Celebration of African American Writing* (2002), an anthology benefiting the Hurston/Wright Foundation and collecting a wide variety of African American fiction, almost all of it from the 1980s and 1990s. Authors gathered in the anthology include Bertice Berry, Bebe Moore Campbell, Lorene Cary, Pearl Cleage, J. California Cooper, Edwidge Danticat, Eric Jerome Dickey, David Haynes, Ravi Howard, Mitchell Jackson, R. M. Johnson, Terry McMillan, Walter Mosley, Danzy Senna, John Edgar Wideman, Shay Youngblood, and the editors.

Haynes, David (b. 1955, St. Louis, Missouri) Since the early 1990s, Minnesotan teacher and novelist David Haynes has published a diverse series of novels that take a witty, often satiric view of contemporary African American culture, especially as lived among the black bourgeoisie. All of his novels are narratives of self-discovery and growth, with a healthy dose of irony. The first, *Right By My Side* (1993) is the story of African American teen Marshall Field Finney, whose mother left him and his father to discover herself, which led in turn to the emergence of Marshall's own identity and will. The novel was cited by the American Library Association as one of the Best Books of the Year for Young Adults and won the Minnesota Voices Project award. In *Somebody Else's Mama* (1995), Paula and Al Johnson, a middle-class African

American couple living in an all-black town in Missouri, find themselves trying to cope with the reemergence of Al's elderly mother into their busy lives. In the process, the family is forced to deal with its fragmentation (linked to the situation of the larger African American community) as its fortunes have changed, thereby resolving some generational differences. *Live at Five* (1996) is a satire concerning the fortunes of African American TV newscaster Brandon Wilson, whose condescending supervisors send him into the poorest community in St. Paul, Minnesota, to create a superficial report on the people living therein. When Brandon falls in love with one of the residents, the novel takes on some of the elements of romance, but at its heart it offers a scathing indictment of American media when Brandon's new love, Nita, undermines the original purpose of the report.

Heathens, also published in 1996, is a series of vignettes told from several different points of view within the middle-class, African American Gabriel family as it tackles a number of personal and familial crises. It also won the Minnesota Voices Project award. *The Gumma Wars* (1997) is the first volume of Haynes's series of fiction for young adults. It centers upon the adventures and travails of a multiethnic middle-school clique, the West Seventh Wildcats; *Business as Usual* (1998) is the series' next installment. *All American Dream Dolls* (1997) is a comedic farce akin to the previous year's *Live at Five*, with a young African American advertising executive, Athena Deneen Wilkerson, taking a role similar to Brandon Wilson's in the earlier work. After a number of personal crises, Wilkerson returns to her mother's house, only to find that her family's dynamics have changed as both her mother and her adolescent, beauty-queen half-sister Ciara make life extremely dif-

---

1. Review of *Abide With Me*, *Library Journal*, September 15, 1999, 128.

ficult. These difficulties are compounded when Deneen becomes enamored of a beauty pageant coach whose career seems to depend upon Ciara's failure.

Haynes has also coedited *Welcome to Your Life: Writings for the Heart of Young America* (1998) with Julie Landsman. The anthology collects short stories—fictional and nonfictional—about growing up in the 1990s. One scholarly article has been written on Haynes: Daylanme K. English, "Somebody Else's Foremother: David Haynes and Zora Neale Hurston," *AAR* 33, no. 2 (Summer 1999). He was also picked as one of *Granta's* "Best Young American Writers" in 1996.

Heard, Nathan (b. November 7, 1936, Newark, New Jersey) Novelist and English professor Nathan Heard is one of numerous writers who began publishing in the late 1960s and early 1970s and who have been almost entirely neglected in the intervening decades. Heard's first novel, *Howard Street* (1968) is a gritty classic of urban realism heavily influenced by Richard Wright, James Baldwin, and Norman Mailer. A high school dropout who later served time in prison for armed robbery, Heard established a place for himself among the most important writers to emerge from the 1960s in spite, or perhaps because of these challenges. In prison he began to read hungrily works by Wright, Baldwin, Mailer, Langston Hughes, Jean Genet, Malcolm X, and Amiri Baraka, among others.[1] Inspired by these writers' examples and a desire to make a living as a professional writer, Heard began writing *Howard Street* in prison in 1963 but was unable to find a publisher until 1968. Upon its appearance, *Howard Street* became a best-seller; it has gone through some fifteen printings since its initial publication, although most of its sales were generated in its first few years in print. *Howard Street* gained

both favorable and unfavorable notice for its nonjudgmental, even favorable portrayal of African American street life, particularly the shadow economy: pimps, sex workers, drug addicts, winos, hustlers, and so on. The novel's—and Heard's—refusal to judge the characters' morality led to several harshly negative reviews, but it was generally received as an authentic portrayal of the environment familiar to millions of urban African Americans.

Heard's newfound celebrity and the growing black studies movement in American universities led to appointments at Fresno State College in California (now Fresno State University) and Rutgers, where he wrote and published his second novel, *To Reach a Dream* (1972). An example of urban realism similar to *Howard Street*, *To Reach a Dream* tells the story of Bartholomew (Bart) Kedar Enos, who aspires to be a hustler, gigolo, and street celebrity, all to realize his manhood. As in *Howard Street*, Heard focuses successfully upon depicting the language, sounds, smells, and harsh realities of urban African America, although his character development sometimes leaves much to be desired. *A Cold Fire Burning* (1974) takes on a different subject, albeit one familiar within African American fiction: interracial sexual tensions and unions and the degree to which they symbolize both the worst excesses of racism and the greatest possibilities across racial lines. *When Shadows Fall* (1977) centers upon the illicit drug trade and its effects upon African American communities. Heard is particularly concerned with the extent to which the drug trade fuels cynicism and self-interest at a time when African Americans could use a greater communal consciousness. As Richard Yarborough notes, however, *When Shadows Fall* went almost completely unnoticed when it was initially published, coming

---

1. Richard Yarborough, "Nathan C. Heard," *DLB*, 33:110–11.

as it did from the soon-defunct pulp publisher Playboy Press; it is extremely difficult to find. Heard's most recent novel, *House of Slammers* (1983), however, garnered considerable praise and notice from such major African American reviewers and authors as Mel Watkins, Cecil Brown, and John Edgar Wideman upon initial publication. Based largely upon Heard's experiences in prison, *House of Slammers* is one of the most brutal depictions of the American penal system and its crushing effects upon the individual ever published, and one of the more remarkable African American novels of the early 1980s. Nevertheless, it soon went out of print and is also somewhat difficult to obtain.

Critical assessments of Heard's novels have been sparse, to say the least. Save for contemporary reviews of his novels and entries in reference books, the only significant critical assessments of Heard's work are Eric Beaumont, "The Nathan Heard Interviews," *AAR* 28, no. 3 (Fall 1994): 395–410; and a chapter on *Howard Street* in W. Lawrence Hogue, *The African American Male, Writing, and Difference: A Polycentric Approach to African American Literature, Culture, and Theory* (2003). Both sources, however, are fairly solid; Beaumont's interview with the author, while wide ranging, focuses directly upon his literary works and their development, while Hogue's study of *Howard Street* is a definitive appreciation of the novel's challenge to middle-class African American values. No one, however, has yet studied Heard's later novels in depth. *Howard Street*, *To Reach a Dream*, and *A Cold Fire Burning* are available from Amok Books, although only *A Cold Fire Burning* is in print.

Herron, Carolivia (b. July 22, 1947, Washington, D.C.) Novelist and children's literature author Carolivia Herron attracted national attention in 1998 for her children's book,

Nappy Hair (1997), about a young black protagonist who learns to appreciate her natural hair texture. It was not the book or its subject matter that caused a furor at first but rather the fact that a white teacher in New York City opted to read it to her predominantly black classroom. A number of the school's parents decried a situation they perceived as a condescending white teacher reading a racist text to her charges, despite Herron's vociferous plaints to the contrary. The teacher was eventually dismissed from her position. The controversy brought issues regarding self-hatred and the troubled history of the term "nappy" to the fore of discussions within African American communities. Although the controversy was ultimately short-lived, it overshadowed Herron's earlier achievement, the novel *Thereafter Johnnie* (1991), which received strongly positive reviews upon its initial publication. The novel's protagonist, Johnnie Snowdon, endures life as a mute until puberty, when she begins to discover the history of the incestuous relationship between her mother and grandfather that resulted in her birth and that torments her existence. Her quest for truth crosses the bildungsroman form with the themes of Gayl Jones's *Corregidora* (1975) and Hal Bennett's *Lord of Dark Places* (1970), both of which use incest both in literal and metaphorical ways to explore African American history.

Hip-hop/rap Inarguably, hip-hop culture and rap music are among the most critical influences upon African American authors born after the early to mid-1960s. It is little wonder, in fact, that this grouping is often called the "hip-hop generation," since it either invented, innovated, or embraced both the music and the culture, which ranges from dance ("break dancing" or "street dancing"), clothing, graffiti, and a lexicon of terms that now run so deeply in the American mainstream that it is amazing to remember that most music critics dismissed this still-controversial phenomenon as a mere fad well into the 1980s. In African American literature, all aspects of hip-hop culture have inspired and galvanized such "Post-Soul" authors as Lisa Jones, Greg Tate, Paul Beatty, Darius James, Trey Ellis, and Danzy Senna, all of whom are interested in locating the younger black generation vis-à-vis the preceding one, with hip-hop and rap functioning as a major marker of difference.

Hip-hop arose out of the youth culture of the housing projects of the South Bronx in New York City in the early 1970s, a place and time situated in the wake of the political struggles of the 1960s. Such famous disc jockeys as Kool Herc, Grandmaster Flash, Afrika Bambaataa, Breakout, and many others began attracting large followings at house parties and parks for their skills mixing and, later, scratching records with flair. As these followings grew and began paying more attention to the DJ than to dancing, some DJs, most notably Kool Herc and Afrika Bambataa, began to "rap" while performing. This rapping was derived directly from the "toasts" common in Caribbean cultures; Kool Herc was Jamaican and drew upon dancehall music and its traditions, as well as the rhythms of black singers such as James Brown, in his performances. Many imitators followed, exhorting crowds in increasingly creative ways between beats and choruses. Hip-hop culture was also indelibly linked to trends in dancing and fashion, as well as to sophisticated graffiti art and other aspects of urban-black-youth culture.

Outside of the New York and New Jersey areas, though, this culture was largely unknown until 1979, when the Brooklyn group the Sugar Hill Gang, released a single, "Rapper's Delight" (derived from an earlier record, "DJ's Delight"), which caused a national sensation, effectively bringing more attention to other New York DJs and rappers (called MCs—for Master of Ceremonies—

in hip-hop parlance) and to hip-hop culture in general. This inspired countless teenagers, especially African American ones, to begin emulating the musical, dance, and fashion styles coming from the movement. Break dancing, which fused many dance styles, including those of James Brown and such soul acts as the Temptations, with contemporary moves found in New York discotheques, had developed as another diversion during street parties; by the early 1980s, youths across America could be found emulating and passing on moves.

All of these elements combined to capture the imagination of young African Americans coming of age from the late 1970s until the present. Although critics almost universally dismissed each aspect of hip-hop culture as a fad, rap and break dancing were enormous influences on music throughout the 1980s. Hip-hop, like incarnations of jazz music before it, represented youthful rebellion and a simultaneous homage to and rejection of the previous generation's aesthetics. It was also the epitome of postmodernism, to the extent that it crossed a number of cultural barriers and musical genres and influences, was difficult to define, and always implied an ironic relationship to everything it absorbed or incorporated. Regardless of whether this absorption occurred via the practice of "sampling" earlier music, sounds, or references to popular culture, it connected to millions of young people (and no small number of their parents) primarily because the artists who developed the music grew up with the same popular culture as their fans.

Naturally, an enormous amount of controversy has dogged rap from the beginning. The sine qua non of rap is aggressive, often hyperbolic braggadocio about the MC's abilities in "freestyling," or rapping extemporaneously. Given this aggression, the fact that males dominate the genre and that many lyrics either demean women or appear to do so, critics have accused rap of fostering sexism, misogyny, and violence in general. Popular images and stereotypes regarding African American males and their sexuality have played a role in these criticisms as well. As Tricia Rose notes in her groundbreaking *Black Noise: Rap Music and Black Culture in Contemporary America* (1994), the controversies that swirl around rap concern the music's imagined or real influence on its audience, which became predominantly white by the late 1980s and early 1990s. In addition, Rose writes,

> rappers engage [these debates] in contradictory ways. Some rappers defend the work of gangster rappers and at the same time consider it a negative influence on black youths. Female rappers openly criticize male rappers' sexist work and simultaneously defend the 2 Live Crew's right to sell misogynist music. Rappers who criticize America for its perpetuation of racial and economic discrimination also share conservative ideas about personal responsibility, call for self-improvement strategies in the black community that focus heavily on personal behavior as the cause and solution for crime, drugs, and community instability.[1]

In other words, the responses to the many arguments surrounding rap from the very artists who create it is extremely complex. This underscores rap's postmodernity to the extent that postmodern artists and works question the very means by which they create and are created, as well as the ideologies they contain. This has caused the genre to transform and grow many times over, with many different trends, fads, styles, and subgenres emerging over the years. These may range from heavily jazz-influenced rap to the more hardcore "gangsta" rap. The latter has received the most media attention and record company promotion by far, which raises the issue of who actually owns or controls rap.

These issues parallel similar issues in contemporary African American fiction, where hip-hop has found particular resonance among the "Post-Soul" generation of authors, or those born since 1960. Many of these younger artists grew up listening to rap music and made it part of their literary soundtracks or, in the cases of fiction writers Paul Beatty, Darius James, Omar Tyree, Sheneska Jackson, Jake Lamar, and Eric Jerome Dickey, incorporated it into the rhythms and referentiality of their texts. Equally important, many younger writers grew up with the same pop cultural or African American icons that inspired hip-hop's development, often because they grew up in the same cities and neighborhoods, watched the same television programs, listened to the same music or, quite simply, are in or near the same age range as rappers. Paul Beatty's novels and poetry are especially adept at incorporating hip-hop sensibilities and rhythms, and the entire "poetry slam" movement, in which poets use their best poems in competitive performances, owes part of its development and flavor, if not its invention, to hip-hop. Equally important, however, are the parallels between contemporary African American fiction and hip-hop: both are products of the politics of the Civil Rights and post–Civil Rights era; both are now read largely by white audiences; both enjoyed a "renaissance" or "golden age" in the late 1980s and early 1990s, once sales of selected titles soared and mainstream media began taking notice; both have struggled with questions of gender issues; both struggle with questions

1. Tricia Rose, *Black Noise: Rap Music and Black Culture in Contemporary America* (Middletown, Conn.: Wesleyan University Press, 1994), 1–2.

regarding the nature of art or, to be more specific, the relationship between art, politics, and commerce. Perhaps the strongest parallel is the degree to which both contemporary African American fiction and hip-hop speak to African Americans' concerns in the post–Civil Rights era.

Information on hip-hop and rap's development is easily available. Numerous national magazines have sprung up around hip-hop alone (*Black Beat, Vibe, The Source, Rap Pages, Right On!, XXL*, and so on). Each has its own style and culture but is also attuned to developments within the music, the media, and the music industry. In short, an extensive education on hip-hop may be had through these magazines alone.

At first, the academic world was neither kind nor prolific with its interest in rap music and its culture, but in the 1990s and 2000s many scholars began coming around to both rap's legitimacy as a musical art form and hip-hop's cultural significance as both grew in popularity. The product was an impressive tide of extensive studies of hip-hop and rap. One of the first books on rap is David Toop's *The Rap Attack: African Jive to New York Hip Hop* (1984; reprinted in 1991 as *Rap Attack 2: African Rap to Global Hip Hop* and revised in 2000 as *Rap Attack 3*), while the first analyses of rap's coming importance to the academy came from leading African American critic Houston A. Baker Jr. in 1993: *Black Studies, Rap, and the Academy* and *Village Voice* cultural critic Greg Tate's *Flyboy in the Buttermilk* (1992).

The single best book-length analysis of hip-hop and rap's cultural significance, however, would be Rose's *Black Noise* (1994). Rose engages most of the debates about rap directly, using a fluid yet accessible pastiche of contemporary literary theory. Some of Rose's early work on the subject may be found in Michele Wallace and Gina Dent's *Black Popular Culture* (1992), one of the best collections of criticism on African American popular forms. The volume also contains essays by the editors, Rose, Baker, Greg Tate, Manthia Diawara, Valerie Smith, Manning Marable, Stuart Hall, Cornel West, and many others on a variety of subjects under the book's rubric, but many essays either touch upon or discuss at some length hip-hop and rap. In a similar vein are Michael Eric Dyson's meditative analyses of rap, *Between God and Gangsta Rap: Bearing Witness to Black Culture* (1996), which examines the eternal conflict between the sacred and the profane in black culture, including that conflict's paths in rap music; *Holler If You Hear Me: Searching for Tupac Shakur* (2001) reviews the life, career, politics, and enormous influence of one of rap's greatest MCs; *Open Mike: Reflections on Philosophy, Race, Sex, Culture, and Religion* (2003) collects essays on various subjects, including an excellent piece on preaching and rap rhetoric. Veteran music and culture critic Nelson George's *Hip Hop America* (1998) also examines the culture's growth.

Histories of hip-hop culture and rap music also abound: Bakari Kitwana's *The Hip Hop Generation: Young Blacks and the Crisis in African American Culture* (2002) is a thorough cultural history on hip-hop and its politics, influence, and future, while Mark Anthony Neal's *Soul Babies: Black Popular Culture and the Post-Soul Aesthetic* (2002) links everything from 1970s soul music, to the Civil Rights/Black Power eras, to the rise of hip-hop/rap and the Post-Soul movement within African American literature in the 1990s. Adam Krim's *Rap Music and the Poetics of Identity* (2000) works a similar vein as the books by Rose, Neal, and Kitwana, as does William Eric Perkins's collection, *Droppin' Science: Critical Essays on Rap Music and Hip Hop Culture* (1996), with essays by Perkins, Tricia Rose, Robin D. G. Kelley, Juan Flores, and several others. Gail Hilson Woldu wrote an extraordinary essay on rap for the collection *American Popular Music:*

New Approaches to the Twentieth Century (2001), edited by Rachel Rubin and Jeffrey Melnick. Another collection that places rap in its musical context is *African American Jazz and Rap: Social and Philosophical Examinations of Black Expressive Behavior* (2001). R. Christopher Corley also wrote a dissertation, "Voices from the Margins: Rap Music as Contemporary Cultural Production and Sexual Politics in New York City" (Florida State University, 1998), investigating, similar to Tricia Rose, rap's emergence from the sexually complex B-boy culture.

Hopkinson, Nalo (b. 1960, Jamaica) Short-story writer and novelist Nalo Hopkinson is one of a small but critically acclaimed group of African American authors publishing speculative fiction, which encompasses horror, fantasy, magical realism, and science fiction (for which "speculative fiction" has become an accepted synonym). The other notable black authors who have published in this genre are Octavia Butler, Samuel R. Delany, Ronald L. Fair, Jewelle Gomez, Walter Mosley, and Hopkinson's contemporary, Tananarive Due.

Hopkinson's first stories appeared in 1993 and soon attracted enough attention to guarantee the author a spot in the 1995 Clarion Science Fiction and Fantasy Writers' Workshop at Michigan State University. Hopkinson entered the novel's manuscript she started at the workshop in the Warner Aspect First Novel Contest, which she won in 1997. This led to the publication of *Brown Girl in the Ring* (1998). Set in twenty-first-century Toronto, the novel centers upon Ti-Jeanne Baines, a young woman of Caribbean descent and a single mother. In a city whose urban sprawl and abandonment of the inner city have made it a virtual postapocalyptic wasteland, Ti-Jeanne must eventually learn about the rich depths of her heritage, especially Obeah spiritual practices, to survive both physical and psychological dangers.

Brown Girl in the Ring also won the *Locus* Award for Best First Novel (1999) and the John W. Campbell Award for Best New Writer (1999).

Hopkinson's next novel, *Midnight Robber* (2000), is set on the planet Toussaint, which has been colonized by Caribbeans who have created a prison planet in New Half-Way Tree, an alternate universe. This is where the novel's young protagonist, Tan-Tan Habib grows up, as she struggles against her incestuous father. Through immersion in the magic rituals and lore of her Caribbean past, Tan-Tan eventually becomes a Midnight Robber, or a version of Three-Finger Jack, a folk figure who champions the poor against the rich. *Midnight Robber* was a finalist for the Hugo, Nebula, Philip K. Dick, and James Tiptree, Jr. Awards in 2001.

In 2001, Hopkinson published *Skin Folk*, a collection of fifteen of her short stories, ranging from science/speculative fiction and erotica to more conventional fiction. It includes the celebrated "Slow Cold Chick," "Riding the Red," and "Greedy Choke Puppy." Most of the stories incorporate the same Caribbean folk elements that marked Hopkinson's first two novels, including "Tan-Tan and Dry Bone," a story about the heroine of *Midnight Robbers*. *Skin Folk* won the World Fantasy Award in 2003. *The Salt Roads*, a novel, appeared in 2003. Similar in many ways to Hopkinson's earlier novels and stories, *The Salt Roads* is set in early nineteenth-century Saint Domingue (present-day Haiti), where the African-Caribbean *loa* (goddess) of love and sexuality, Ezili, inhabits the bodies of various women to help them come to terms with their identities as women and sexual beings in a society that devalues both. Hopkinson is also editor of *Whispers from the Cotton Tree Root: Caribbean Fabulist Fiction* (2000), and *Mojo: Conjure Stories* (2003).

Although Hopkinson's work has not been the subject of scholarly articles per se, she is one of the primary subjects of Candra K.

Gill's dissertation, "Beyond Boundaries: Counter-Discourse and Intertextuality in Nalo Hopkinson's *Brown Girl in the Ring* and Colson Whitehead's *The Intuitionist*," written in 2002 (Northern Michigan University). She has also been interviewed in the leading journals of African American literature: Diane Glave, "An Interview with Nalo Hopkinson," and Jene Watson-Aifah's "A Conversation with Nalo Hopkinson" *Callaloo* 26, no. 1 (Winter 2003); and Gregory E. Rutledge, "Speaking in Tongues: An Interview with Science Fiction Writer Nalo Hopkinson," *AAR* 33, no. 4 (Winter 1999).

J

Jackson, Sheneska (b. 1970, Los Angeles, California) Sheneska Jackson's novels are written primarily in the vein of the popular relationship/romance fiction that found its audience in the latter half of the 1990s, the authors of which include Omar Tyree, Eric Jerome Dickey, E. Lynn Harris, and Rosalyn McMillan. Jackson has stated in interviews that she was initially inspired to write after attending a lecture by author Terry McMillan,[1] and her three novels of the 1990s, *Caught Up in the Rapture* (1996), *Li'l Mama's Rules* (1997), and *Blessings* (1998), reflect the influence McMillan's later novels (especially *Waiting to Exhale*) had upon her. All of Jackson's works may be classified as Sister or "Girlfriend" Novels, with their cohorts of characters struggling to cope with life as black women in search of fulfillment and love, including scenes in which these same women trade humorous war stories about their relationships with men and family members. As with other novels in this sub-

genre, though, Jackson also reflects seriously upon a number of social issues. This is especially true in *Blessings*, in which four black women working at a beauty shop share their concerns about adoption, the issue of abortion, and the trials of motherhood. In *Li'l Mama's Rules*, Madison, the title character, contracts HIV after a string of sexual encounters driven by the pain stemming from an absent father. *Caught Up in the Rapture*, Jackson's debut, also offers a realistic portrait of life in modern Los Angeles as protagonists and recording artists Jazmine Deems and Xavier Honor attempt to find a better life than is available to them in the city's South Central community.

James, Darius (b. 1962, New Haven, Conn.[?]) Novelist, performance artist, and critic Darius James has spent most of his creative energies on the latter two avocations, but he has unquestionably been an avant-garde practitioner in all three. His history of Blaxploitation films, *That's Blaxploitation! Roots of the Baadasssss 'tude (Rated X by an All-Whyte Jury)* (1995) traces the genre's developments with incessant wit but also with great reverence for the better examples of 1970s black films. The humor of *That's Blaxploitation!* comes directly from James's strong interest in popular culture. His only novel, the satirical *Negrophobia* (1992), which earned the praise of many critics, including master satirist Ishmael Reed, is one of the most singular works of recent fiction, African American or otherwise. Both the novel and James himself may safely be classified as part of the "Post-Soul" or New Black Aesthetic generation of writers due not only to James's age but also to his ambivalence toward the black politics and culture of the 1960s and 1970s. His criticism and fiction reveal an extensive knowledge of

---

1. "Rookie's Rapture: Sheneska Jackson Hits It Big with a First Novel," *People Weekly*, June 10, 1996, 125.

African American history, but James refuses to consider this history as sacrosanct, and therefore above criticism.

Written in the form of a screenplay, *Negrophobia* is one of many scatological novels to emerge from the American literary scene since William S. Burroughs's *Naked Lunch*, and arguably the most continuously grotesque fictional work in African American literature. James wrote it to be "as ugly and gross as racism itself,"[1] to make both repulsive to his readers. *Negrophobia* is the narrative of Bubbles Brazil, a young white woman with an acute case of the condition referred to in the title, who embarks on numerous hallucinogenic, picaresque adventures in New York City after casting a voodoo spell on herself. In the course of these adventures, Bubbles confronts her fear of African Americans via almost every negative stereotype available. James manages to satirize, parody, lampoon or otherwise offend and rhetorically decimate most of the major figures in African American history, art, literature, music and politics within the past century. The novel seems consciously to take the dizzying historical referentiality of some of Ishmael Reed's most experimental novels to their logical ends. Whereas Reed's novels seek to shed light on contemporary political and social events in American, especially African American politics, James's novel forces his readers to confront, digest, and perhaps purge themselves of the most offensive racial and racist images and ideas extant.

In *That's Blaxploitation!* James writes, "nowhere is it written [that] Black people cannot take back the images of racism and use them as a weapon against those who oppress them" (5). A reader who had not yet encountered *Negrophobia* would find this argument useful for limning the novel's basic premise; James focuses most of his text on utilizing and flouting stereotypical images of African Americans to keep his audience off-balance. This subtle critique proved to be a self-fulfilling prophecy. When the cloth version of *Negrophobia* was published in 1992, its jacket, which depicted a scantily clad white woman with a gigantic Sambo figure standing over her shoulder, was protested by the employees of the book's publisher, Citadel Press. James said, in response to the protest, "I understand that these images were once oppressive. But I think we are at the stage where we can look at these images and not feel threatened. . . . All kinds of black artists have started to take control of these images, whether they realize it or not. . . . You see these rap and hip hop artists wearing tiny little braids just like those stereotypical pickaninny pictures. But it's a statement of power instead of self-loathing. It's taking back our own mythology. It is subverting the perversion."[2] James's own subversions continue when he further jars us in his disclaimer, which reads, "Negrophobia is a work of fiction, a product of the author's imagination. Any resemblance to any person, living or dead, is purely coincidental. Negrophobia is a work of fiction. Every word is true. Fuck you. The Author."[3] From this point, the novel delves into an irreverent pastiche of graphic sexual, racial, racist, scatological, and grotesque images designed to offend readers of all the positions named in the opening plate. The novel opens with a pseudo-citation from a new book on "voodoo's" ability to adapt to

---

1. C. Carr, *On Edge: Performance at the End of the Twentieth Century* (Hanover, N.H.: Wesleyan University Press, 1993), 113.

2. Esther B. Fein, "Book Cover is Questioned: The Cover of Darius James' Novel, *Negrophobia*, Called Racist," *New York Times*, 17 June 1992.

3. Darius James, *Negrophobia: An Urban Parable* (New York: St. Martin's, 1992), viii.

new environments in the United States. Although it would be excrescent—in all senses of the word—to review too many examples of James's grotesque images, a few demand some attention. For example, when a "200-Pound Black Muslim" hawks bean pies by suggesting that it would be possible for consumers to "fart all four sides of Brutha Miles' Bitches Brew out dey butts" before he is torn apart by machine gun fire; Mickey Mouse and Walt Disney are superimposed over Nazi propaganda films; in an allusion to Ralph Ellison's *Invisible Man*, Bubbles sees a sign for the "BUSH MASTER PAINT FACTORY," scrawled in sperm; James includes several plates of caricatured stereotypes of African bushmen, of which one carries the caption "National Geographic Bush Babe of the Month"; a pamphlet warns against the problem of "exploding Negroes," the result of hundreds of years of continuous racial oppression; Bubbles encounters cesspools, numerous filthy restrooms, human genitals, winos, buffoons, "Sambos," remnants of the UNIA and the Civil Rights and Black Power movements, such as "H. Rap Remus"; and so on.

Both before and after publishing *Negrophobia* and *That's Blaxploitation!*, James wrote extensively on the process of writing itself, politics, film, and other issues. To date, critical analyses of James's novel have been rare. This author wrote on James in *African American Satire* (2001), and C. Carr mentions him briefly in *On Edge: Performance at the End of the Twentieth Century* (1993). The single best analysis of *Negrophobia* is Ronald A. T. Judy's close study in "Irony and the Asymptotes of the Hyperbola," *Boundary 2* 25, no. 1 (Spring 1998). A revealing interview with James may also be found online at http://users.rcn.com/scrypt/Darius_James_Int.html.

James, Kelvin Christopher (b. circa 1945, Port of Spain, Trinidad) Not unlike fellow Trinidadian Elizabeth Nunez-Harrell, novelist and short-story author Kelvin Christopher James writes about the island nation, its citizens, and its émigrés in the United States. His prose is marked by a remarkable ear for language, especially the rhythms of Trinidadian patois. His first collection of short stories, *Jumping Ship and Other Stories* (1992) is divided into three sets of narratives. The first takes place in Trinidad and foregrounds the traditions that inform its rich culture and difficult politics; the second tells of the journey to the United States that Trinidadian stowaways make; the third focuses upon the hardships of living in Harlem and the disappointment, hostility, and raw violence that Caribbean immigrants encounter in that community. The novel *Secrets* (1993) is set in Trinidad; it focuses upon the young girl, Uxann, who finds herself privy to her family's and friend's secrets and deciding how to maintain her loyalty to each party. *A Fling with a Demon Lover* (1996) tells of Harlem schoolteacher Sassela Jack, who is slowly seduced by her pupil, Ciam, especially after they both appear on the same Greek island for a vacation. The novel takes a twist into magical realism as Sassela and Ciam find their relationship compromised by a young mystic girl.

Johnson, Charles Richard (b. 1948, Evanston, Illinois) Charles Johnson has had an impressive career as a cartoonist, scholar-essayist, philosopher, and fiction author, although he is best known for the last role. Since the publication of *Faith and the Good Thing* (1974), Johnson has won voluminous praise for his novels' philosophical sophistication, original narrative voice, highly complex characters, and fresh, if occasionally controversial perspective upon contemporary African American issues. Johnson's influences are extremely diverse; he cites his Buddhist faith, authors John Gardner (who taught Johnson at Southern Illinois University), Ralph Ellison (a personal friend and mentor), James Baldwin, John A. Williams, Herman Melville, eighteenth-century satirist Jonathan Swift, Bishop George Berkeley, Plato's *Republic*, African and African American folklore, numerous strains of African, Asian, and classical European philosophy, and so on. Before starting a career in fiction, Johnson created and hosted a popular art instruction program on the Public Broadcasting Services network, *Charley's Pad*, which arose from his editorial cartooning, and wrote six as-yet-unpublished novels while working on a master's degree in philosophy at Southern Illinois. With Gardner's mentoring, Johnson wrote and published *Faith and the Good Thing*.

Faith and the Good Thing is a modern-day folktale about Faith Cross, a young Georgian woman who leaves her ancestral home for Chicago, where she later meets her doom in a brothel. All the while, she lives in two distinct worlds, the physical and the metaphysical-spiritual, each rich in characters and philosophical complexity. The conflict between Faith's physical and metaphysical selves is the crux of the novel's plot; its central question is where and when material needs compete with or trump spiritual ones, or vice versa. The novel points in favor of the latter, a sign of Johnson's consistent advocacy throughout his career of the individual's intellectual and spiritual development. As in Johnson's later fiction, the choices the individual makes on the journey from naïveté and innocence to maturity and experience are studied carefully, albeit great ambivalence.

Although *Faith and the Good Thing* received almost unanimous praise, *Oxherding Tale* (1982) represents a significant leap forward in Johnson's artistry. Fusing the slave narrative form with the folktale, *Oxherding Tale* is also highly comic in its mode, even as it introduces questions about the nature of reality and contemporary African American literature. Johnson consciously attempts to liberate both the slave narrative and the larger tradition it has helped to engender from the limits of the first-person narrative, incorporating phenomenological theory (especially as delineated by Maurice Merleau-Ponty)[1] and Johnson's larger philosophical background. The novel tells the story of fugitive slave Andrew Hawkins, who escapes from physical and sexual slavery to find an identity that transcends the normal limits of the physical self, using a Zen painting as its philosophical and artistic template.[2] *The Sorceror's Apprentice* (1986) is a collection of philosophical fiction that Johnson composed simultaneously with *Oxherding Tale*; it comprises eight short stories, moral tales, memoir, and fables unified by Johnson's desire to update Plato's dialogues with elements of African American folklore and conjuring motifs.[3]

Middle Passage (1990) is similar to *Oxherding Tale* in a number of ways. It is, once again, a slave narrative that parodies the form's conventions, including the typical emphasis on the importance of education in obtaining freedom. It is also a complex pastiche of numerous other genres popular in American literature, most notably the adventure story, the travel narrative, and such picaresque novels as *Adventures of Huckle-*

1. James W. Coleman, "Charles Johnson's Quest for Black Freedom in *Oxherding Tale*," *African American Review* 29, no. 4 (Winter 1995): 14.

2. Jennifer Hayward, "Something to Serve: Constructs of the Feminine in Charles Johnson's *Oxherding Tale*," *BALF* 25, no. 4 (Winter 1991): 690.

3. Frederick T. Griffiths, "'Sorcery Is Dialectical': Plato and Jean Toomer in Charles Johnson's *The Sorceror's Apprentice*," *African American Review* 30, no. 4 (Winter 1996): 528.

berry Finn. In its form and content, the text closely resembles Aphra Behn's *Oroonoko*, Jonathan Swift's *Gulliver's Travels*, and Melville's *Moby-Dick*, joining each of those texts in utilizing the conventions of the travel narrative order to allegorize the moral failings of its society. *Middle Passage* uses the horrors of a slave ship during the passage between Africa and America, as well as slavery itself, as intricate metaphors for American sociopolitical structures. Unlike its literary models, however, *Middle Passage* refuses to see slavery or the political conditions that engendered it as a totalizing institution that deprived its victims of their culture or humanity. Instead, Johnson offers us a black protagonist, Rutherford Calhoun, who is neither a stereotypical "noble savage" nor a victim. Calhoun is at best an antihero who eschews the virtues and morals of his society, except for those virtues of the carnival in his home of New Orleans. Calhoun is a true rogue, the classic picaro; the text's frequent use of the grotesque body and scatology (feces/excrement, urine, semen, homo- and heterosexual intercourse, vomiting, and so on) further signals it as a text that draws upon the satirical milieu of the carnival. Calhoun's adventures are marked by continuous references to his and others' bodily excretions, as well as the various foulnesses to be found aboard a nineteenth-century slave ship. Calhoun's status as a black picaro, however, does not preclude his status as a fully developed character; he is an illustration of Johnson's anti-essentialism, which argues against two-dimensional literary characters or considerations of African Americans in general. *Middle Passage*, then, foregrounds Johnson's efforts to keep Rutherford Calhoun from being delimited by essentialist assumptions about black life. Both within and outside of his role as a classic rogue, Calhoun is the text's metaphor for the everyman caught within American ambiguities surrounding racial and political issues.

Johnson's next novel, *Dreamer* (1997), imagines the last days of Dr. Martin Luther King Jr. before his assassination on April 4, 1968. As in his earlier novels, Johnson incorporates extensive references to philosophy, different strains of Christian theology, and political references into a Manichean structure. Matthew Bishop, the novel's narrator and King's mythical assistant, encounters a gentleman named Chaym Smith, who not only looks exactly like King himself but was born on the same day, albeit without any of the advantages King enjoyed as part of Atlanta's middle class. The hard life Chaym has endured underscores his symbolic value; the name "Chaym Smith," we are reminded later, is a double reference for Cain from Genesis. He therefore functions as King's doppelganger and, after he is hired as King's double, might have followed Cain's fate. The structure allows Johnson to reflect upon King's legacy and African American politics during and since the 1960s (Johnson lampoons Black Nationalists and Afrocentrists such as Maulana Ron Karenga and Leonard Jeffries with one thinly veiled character) in a strong attempt to show why King was important, why he was both loved and hated, and why the full, complex range of King's thoughts and ideas are still resonant today.

Johnson has received high recognition for his literary efforts. He won a National Book Award for *Middle Passage* (1990) and a MacArthur Foundation "Genius" grant in 1998. His oeuvre as a whole—including his earlier foray in cartooning—have received extensive critical treatment, with *Middle Passage* attracting the most attention, followed closely by *Oxherding Tale* and *Faith and the Good Thing*.

Scholarship on Johnson is extensive, with most consisting of journal articles. Johnson published excerpts from his major works of fiction in such journals as *Callaloo* and *AAR* and its earlier forms several months before each book appeared; he also published a critical essay, "Whole Sight: Notes on New Black Fiction" in *Callaloo* 22 (Autumn 1984). Two books studying Johnson's fiction exclusively have been published to date: William R. Nash, *Charles Johnson's Fiction* (2003) and Jonathan Little, *Charles Johnson's Spiritual Imagination* (1997). *AAR* devoted its Winter 1996 issue (vol. 30, no. 4) to Johnson's career, including his early work as a cartoonist; that issue remains arguably the best single-volume retrospective collection extant in terms of its breadth and depth. Other key journal articles include: Bill Brown, "Global Bodies/Postnationalities: Charles Johnson's Consumer Culture," *Representations* 58 (Spring 1997); Sonnet Retman, "'Nothing Was Lost in the Masquerade': The Protean Performance of Genre and Identity in Charles Johnson's *Oxherding Tale*," *AAR* 33, no. 3 (Autumn 1999); Ashraf H. A. Rushdy, "The Phenomenology of the Allmuseri: Charles Johnson and the Subject of the Narrative of Slavery," *AAR* 26, no. 3 (Autumn 1992); James W. Coleman, "Charles Johnson's Quest for Black Freedom in *Oxherding Tale*," *AAR* 29, no. 4 (Winter 1995); Barbara Z. Thaden, "Charles Johnson's *Middle Passage* as Historiographic Metafiction," *College English* 59, no. 7 (November 1997); S. X. Goudie, "'Leavin' a Mark on the Wor(l)d': Marksmen and Marked Men in *Middle Passage*," *AAR* 29, no. 1 (Spring 1995); Ken McCollough, "Reflections on Film, Philosophy, and Fiction: An Interview with Charles Johnson," *Callaloo* 4 (October 1978); Daniel M. Scott III, "Interrogating Identity: Appropriation and Transformation in *Middle Passage*," and Celestin Walby, "The African Sacrificial Kingship Ritual and Johnson's *Middle Passage*," *AAR* 29, no. 4 (Winter 1995); John Whalen-Bridge, "Waking Cain: The Poetics of Integration in Charles Johnson's *Dreamer*," *Callaloo* 26, no. 2 (Spring 2003); Jennifer Hayward, "Something to Serve: Constructs of the Feminine in Charles Johnson's *Oxherding Tale*," and William Gleason, "The Liberation of Perception: Charles Johnson's *Oxherding Tale*," *BALF* 25, no. 4 (Winter 1991); Charles H. Rowell and Charles Johnson, "An Interview with Charles Johnson," *Callaloo* 20, no. 3 (Summer 1997).

James Weldon Johnson Memorial Collection, Beinecke Library, Yale University The Johnson Memorial Collection is one of the two preeminent repositories of African American historical and cultural artifacts, artwork, and original manuscripts in the United States; the other is the Schomburg Center for Research in Black Culture in New York City's Harlem. Although the Johnson Memorial Collection's greatest strength is its holdings in manuscripts, music, and artwork dated well before the contemporary era (particularly from the "New Negro" or Harlem Renaissance), no small number of authors published since the 1970s have either had some of their materials archived therein, studied other holdings as graduate students and professors, or been heavily influenced by its most celebrated authors and works. The collection was founded in 1941 at the urging and with the considerable aid of Carl Van Vechten, a major patron and controversial author of the Harlem Renaissance. Van Vechten's purpose was to preserve the work of the era's writers and artists, especially those of his close friend, Langston Hughes. The collection's namesake, James Weldon Johnson, was an editor, musician, lyricist, author, critic, ambassador, professor, patron of the arts and civil rights leader who wielded an immense influence over the Harlem Renaissance through his novel *The Autobiography of an Ex-Coloured Man*, published anonymously in 1912 and reprinted in 1927, at the height of the Harlem Renaissance. Johnson's novel is one of the foundational works of twentieth-century African American literature, while his work with the National Association for the Advancement of Colored People as its field secretary was exemplary. Via both roles, Johnson's influence on African American literature includes a substantial portion of the work emerging in recent decades.

The Johnson collection includes manuscript collections, personal papers, organizational records, photography, and artwork of some two hundred writers, artists (graphic and plastic), scholars, critics, and organizations. Although most of the materials contained therein are dated well before the contemporary era, many of the individuals included are themselves major influences upon recent artists: W. E. B. Du Bois, Chester Himes, Langston Hughes, Zora Neale Hurston, Georgia Douglass Johnson, James Weldon Johnson, Claude McKay, Gertrude Stein, Wallace Thurman, Jean Toomer, Dorothy West, William Carlos Williams, and Richard Wright.

Access to the collection is restricted to scholars and students working on research projects. Finding aids for the collection are now online at http://webtext.library.yale .edu/finddocs/fadsear.htm.

Johnson, Mat (b. 1970, Philadelpha, Pennsylvania) Novelist Mat Johnson is part of the generation of authors who have been both part of and influenced by the sentiments of Trey Ellis's "New Black Aesthetic," to the extent that his works question the prevailing standards for and marketing of African American lives and fiction alike. His first novel, *Drop* (2000), is in part a satire upon the worlds of journalism and advertising. Protagonist and narrator Chris Jones lands a position as an advertising designer after many years struggling in West Philadelphia and in his college studies. Jones leaves the United States for Britain, only to return when he discovers that the Philadelphia neighborhood he'd attempted to escape and avoid is far more important than he could have realized.

Johnson's second novel, *Hunting in Harlem* (2003), lampoons both the process of gentrification that has changed present-day Harlem and the ways in which the publishing industry both markets and exploits African American authors for their ability to cater cynically to an African American audience that is not concerned with cerebral themes in its literature. Through a plot that balances both farce and detective fiction, the novel links the destruction of Harlem's old character to the facile marketing of black authors. In 2004, *Hunting in Harlem* won the Hurston/Wright Legacy Award in fiction.

Jones, Edward P. (b. 1950, Washington, D.C.) Short-story author and novelist Edward P. Jones published his first collection *Lost in the City*, in 1992. It was nominated that same year for a National Book Award; two years later, he won a Lannon Award for fiction. A former student of James Alan McPherson, Jones's stories of African American life in his hometown of Washington, D.C., in *Lost in the City* reflect his mentor's influence to the extent that they show how individual African Americans manage to survive some of the most difficult and horrific conditions within the nation. His characters are extremely diverse and often eccentric yet sustained by a determination not to let their spirits be broken. In 2003, Jones published his first novel, *The Known World*, about an African American family, the Townsends, who bought and kept their own slaves, despite once having been slaves themselves. *The Known World* attracted considerable attention for both its chosen subject matter and for Jones's superb writing. The following year, Jones's novel won the Pulitzer Prize for fiction, the National Book Critics Circle's award for fiction, and was a finalist for the 2003 National Book Award.

Jones, Gayl (b. November 23, 1949, Lexington, Kentucky) Novelist, short-story author, poet, and professor Gayl Jones stands with Octavia Butler, Toni Morrison, Toni Cade Bambara, Alice Walker, Sherley Anne Williams, Ntozake Shange, and Gloria Naylor as one of the most important African American women writers in the contemporary era. Her novels are extremely complex and challenging in their careful use of black vernacular voices and diction, withering denouncements of sexism, and probing of the legacies of slavery and other forms of oppression. In these ways, Jones shows the influence of her mentor, Toni Morrison, who helped to get Jones's first novel, *Corregidora* (1975) published, but her work is truly her own. Over the years, especially after her first novels and short-story collection appeared in the late 1970s, personal problems slowed Jones's output considerably. More than twenty years passed between the publication of Jones's short-story collection, *White Rat* (1977) and her most recent novels, *The Healing* (1998) and *Mosquito* (1999), the latter of which Toni Morrison edited while Jones convalesced in Kentucky's Eastern State Hospital after her husband's bizarre suicide in 1998. Jones's reclusive personal life and the troubled protagonists of her early novels have fueled speculation about her past, but she has consistently refused to answer such queries. In any case, Jones's early literary achievements are now almost uniformly considered undeniably brilliant.

Corregidora (see separate entry) is widely considered Jones's masterpiece and one of the most harrowing indictments of slavery yet written. It also qualifies as one of the "neo–slave narratives," which imagine what slavery was like from the perspective of contemporary politics. When she is but five years old, the protagonist, blues singer Ursa Corregidora, is pulled aside by her grandmother to be told how she and Ursa's great-grandmother, were raped and forced to act as concubines for the same slavemaster, Co-

rregidora, the family's namesake. Through his acts, *Corregidora* is both Ursa's grandfather and great-grandfather. If the horror of this situation weren't enough, Ursa discovers that many of the African American men she knows share some of Corregidora's contempt for women, if not his precise transgressions. Both sets of knowledge and experience inform the blues Ursa sings and show, by extension, the breadth and depth of African Americans' pain and the way it is passed on through the generations, usually by women and often against their will.

Jones's sophomore effort, *Eva's Man* (1976) also takes a challenging tack on sexual relationships, but whereas Ursa Corregidora's tragic personal and familial histories were slightly cushioned by her ability to sing the blues, *Eva's Man* eschews the relative warmth of African American traditions for a nearly unrivaled immediacy. The novel opens with Eva Medina Canada sitting in a prison cell after being convicted for castrating her lover, Davis, who was the last of a long string of men who had sexually assaulted and abused her. Her cellmate, Elvira, appears sympathetic at first but is soon revealed to be as dangerous and abusive as the men who had hurt her for so many years. The novel's attempt to narrate the plot in Eva's voice is both innovative and effective; Eva's point of view is simultaneously pathetic, ironic, and utterly shocking. Reviews of both *Corregidora* and *Eva's Man* were strong upon their initial release, although they also elicited a certain degree of backlash from male critics who objected to the relative dearth of positive images of African American men.

Jones's comeback novel, *The Healing* tells the story of a faith healer, Harlan Jane Eagleton, who entered that practice after trying her hand as a beautician and manager of a black female rock musician. Most of the novel consists of Eagleton's recounting of her journey from her earlier professions to her new one, in which she learns how to heal herself psychically as well as others physically. Her story reveals, in the end, that ordinary women can find the means to heal their own spirits. *The Healing* was nominated in 1998 for a National Book Award.

Mosquito is Jones's most ambitious work to date. Jones's friend, Toni Morrison, edited the sprawling novel while Jones was in the hospital for the nervous breakdown that followed her husband's suicide. The story of Jane Nadine Johnson—the eponymous hero—*Mosquito* is a pastiche of many different genres and narrative styles, although Mosquito's scattered narration dominates. It is in many respects a direct descendant of Laurence Sterne's *Tristram Shandy*, if only due to both books' being travel narratives with maddening digressions, genre-shattering techniques, and pastiches of different documents. Jones's novel, for example, contains a complete play that comes to Johnson's attention during her many adventures.

Jones is among the most heavily studied authors of the contemporary era, with most of the scholarship appearing in journal-article form. Jones herself has contributed to scholarship with her book *Liberating Voices: Oral Tradition in African American Literature* (1991). Readers interested in her short fiction would do well to peruse back issues of *Callaloo*, in which she frequently published. *Callaloo* number 16 (October 1982) contains a special section on Jones, including several critical essays on her work to date; issue 20 contains more fiction excerpts and short stories; vol. 17, no. 2, contains excerpts from Jones's fiction and literary criticism, as does vol. 24, no. 3.

To date, the following books in which Jones's fiction is discussed have appeared: Lillie Jones Broome, "Sex, Violence, and History: Images of Black Men in the Selected Fiction of Gayl Jones, Alice Walker, and Toni Morrison" (Ph.D. diss., Bowling Green State University, 1990); Sherri Lynn Burwell, "The

Soul of Black Women: The Hermeneutical Method of Analysis as Applied to the Novel *Corregidora* (Ph.D. diss., California School of Professional Psychology at Berkeley, 1979); Angelita T. Streeter, "Rebellious Women and Autonomous Intentions: Disrupting Patriarchy in Selected Novels by Gayl Jones" (Ph.D. diss., Florida State University, 2002); Saadi A. Simawe, ed., *Black Orpheus: Music in African American Fiction from the Harlem Renaissance to Toni Morrison* (2000); Judith Jackson Fossett and Jeffrey A. Tucker, eds., *Race Consciousness: African American Studies for the New Century* (1997); Gunilla Theander Kester, *Writing the Subject: Bildung and the African American Text* (1997); Stelamaris Coser, *Bridging the Americas: The Literature of Paule Marshall, Toni Morrison, and Gayl Jones* (1995); Françoise Lionnet, *Postcolonial Representations: Women, Literature, Identity* (1995); Sally Robinson, *Engendering the Subject: Gender and Self-Representation in Contemporary Women's Fiction* (1991); Madhu Dubey, *Winged, but Grounded: A Contextual Study of the Fiction of Toni Morrison and Gayl Jones* (1989).

Significant journal articles on Jones include: Carol Margaret Davidson, "'Love 'em and Lynch 'em': The Castration Motif in Gayl Jones's *Eva's Man*," *AAR* 29, no. 3 (Autumn 1995); Jerry W. Ward Jr., "Escape from Tremblum: The Fiction of Gayl Jones," and Trudier Harris, "A Spiritual Journey: Gayl Jones's *Song for Anninho*," *Callaloo* 16 (October 1982); Amy S. Gottfried, "Angry Arts: Silence, Speech, and Song in Gayl Jones's *Corregidora*," *AAR* 28, no. 4 (Winter 1994); Françoise Lionnet, "Geographies of Pain: Captive Bodies and Violent Acts in the Fictions of Myriam Warner-Vieyra, Gayl Jones, and Bessie Head," and Richard Jackson, "Remembering the 'Disremembered': Modern Black Writers and Slavery in Latin America," *Callaloo* 13, no. 1 (Winter 1990); Joyce Pettis, "'She Sung Back in Return': Literary

"(Re)vision and Transformation in Gayl Jones's *Corregidora*," *College English* 52, no. 7 (November 1990); Claudia C. Tate, "An Interview with Gayl Jones," *BALF* 13, no. 4 (Winter 1979); John Wideman, "Defining the Black Voice in Fiction," *BALF* 11, no. 3 (Autumn 1977); Elizabeth Swanson Goldberg, "Living the Legacy: Pain, Desire, and Narrative Time in Gayl Jones' *Corregidora*," *Callaloo* 26, no. 2 (Spring 2003); Charles H. Rowell, "An Interview with Gayl Jones," *Callaloo* 16 (October 1982); Donia Elizabeth Allen, "The Role of the Blues in Gayl Jones's *Corregidora*," *Callaloo* 25, no. 1 (Winter 2002); Gil Zehava Hochberg, "Mother, Memory, History: Maternal Genealogies in Gayl Jones's *Corregidora* and Simone Schwarz-Bart's *Pluie et Vent sur Telumee Miracle*," *Research in African Literatures* 34, no. 2 (Summer 2003); Biman Basu, "Public and Private Discourses and the Black Female Subject: Gayl Jones's *Eva's Man*," *Callaloo* 19, no. 1 (Winter 1996).

Jordan, June (b. July 9, 1936, New York City; d. June 14, 2002, Berkeley, California) Poet, essayist, critic, educator, and novelist June Jordan was one of the preeminent artists and intellectuals of the contemporary period. Jordan's difficult family life as she grew up in Harlem, as well as her later marriage, motherhood, divorce, and life as a single mother became the subjects of much of her poetic and critical material. Although known primarily for those two roles, Jordan's relatively small corpus of fiction, which was written specifically for a young adult audience, has been inarguably influential and groundbreaking. Jordan was a key player in the wave of writers who emerged during and after the Black Arts Movement, particularly the cohort of black feminists/womanists that wrote in response to the movement's sexism and heterosexism, such as Alice Walker, Barbara Smith, Audre Lorde, bell hooks, and Ntozake Shange, among many others. In pursuit of the goals of both the Black Arts and womanist movements, Jordan's work is marked by a sincere and sustained interest in writing in ways that are accessible to a wide array of contingents within the larger black audience, including young people and single black women, by writing in Black English Vernacular (BEV) and generally viewing the lives and experiences of working-class African Americans as sites of dignity rather than pathology.

Jordan's first novel, *His Own Where* (1971), was written in part with the aid of the Rockefeller Foundation grant she won for 1968 through 1970. The novel itself was nominated for a National Book Award in 1971 and won a place in the *New York Times* List of the Most Outstanding Books for that same year. It tells the story of teenagers Buddy Rivers and Angela Figueroa, lovers who run away from abusive home environments only to be caught up in a society and social institutions that are equally dangerous and violent. Their struggles to find freedom for their romance and the physical, sexual, and psychological liberation of all African Americans, especially women, find them confronting society's indifference to their needs and ideals. In this and all subsequent novels, Jordan applies her interests in restoring value to African American vernacular language to a place of dignity and value, and in the effects of urban environments on young people and the educational process. Jordan's subsequent works—all young people's fiction—share the same basic interests, with her training in primary and secondary education influencing the novels' arguments. They include: *Dry Victories* (1972); *New Life: New Room* (1975); and *Kimako's Story* (1981).

Most of the scholarship on Jordan concerns her work as a poet, essayist, and feminist critic, rather than as a fiction writer. The majority of these sources, however, are highly relevant to discussions of Jordan's fiction, as her philosophical and ideological stances are inextricable parts of her creative work. Key books would include Jordan's autobiography, *Soldier: A Poet's Childhood* (2000), and *Some of Us Did Not Die: New and Selected Essays of June Jordan* (2002). Relevant articles include: Scott MacPhail, "June Jordan and the New Black Intellectuals," *AAR* 33, no. 1 (Spring 1999); Calvin Hernton, "The Sexual Mountain and Black Women Writers," *BALF* 18, no. 4 (Winter 1984); Peter Erickson and June Jordan, "After Identity: A Conversation with June Jordan and Peter Erickson," *Transition* 63 (1994); Judy Richardson, "Black Children's Books: An Overview," *The Journal of Negro Education* 43, no. 3 (Summer 1974).

Juneteenth (1999) Ralph Ellison's second published novel emerged posthumously with extensive fanfare in both academia and the mainstream press. The attention was not unwarranted; since the publication of Ellison's masterwork, *Invisible Man* (1952), the literary world had eagerly anticipated the novel that Ellison had indicated would be his magnum opus in numerous interviews and via excerpts that made their way into magazines and journals. Heightening rampant speculation was the tragic loss of 360 pages of Ellison's original manuscript—he kept no copies—in a fire at Ellison's Plainfield, Massachusetts, house in 1967, which obviously devastated the author. To make matters worse, Ellison revealed that the manuscript was fairly close to completion when he lost it. Ellison worked extremely

hard to reconstruct the burned portion of his manuscript from memory, producing over two thousand manuscript and typescript pages between 1967 and his death in 1994, indicating all the while that the novel was near completion. Ultimately, however, Ellison was far from completing the work, despite producing enough material for at least three novels, or perhaps three volumes of one epic novel. Ellison left few notes indicating how the many bits and pieces of his manuscript were to be ordered and organized and apparently did not write the transitional sections that would have linked together the different sections of the manuscript into to a cohesive whole. In short, the second novel remained one of the great unfinished works in American literature, and perhaps in modern history.[1]

Despite this rather daunting situation, Ellison's friend and literary executor John Callahan undertook the Herculean effort of trying to salvage a publishable novel from Ellison's manuscript, with widow Fanny Ellison's blessing. Realizing that the reconstructed manuscript fragments were indeed far from completion, Callahan opted to edit a fraction of them into a second novel "that best stands alone as a single, self-contained volume."[2] Callahan edited Ellison's voluminous manuscripts and notes according to the logic they presented within their pages and the ideals, goals, and readings of American history and culture that Ellison had shared in dozens of essays and interviews, to say nothing of many conversations with Callahan and other friends and acquaintances.

The result, *Juneteenth*, represents the concatenation of Ellison's ideas about the inherently interracial nature of American

1. Christopher C. De Santis and John F. Callahan, "'Some cord of kinship stronger and deeper than blood': An Interview with John F. Callahan, Editor of Ralph Ellison's *Juneteenth*," *African American Review* 34, no. 4 (Winter 2000): 601, 608.

2. De Santis and Callahan, " 'Some cord of kinship," 601.

society that he had introduced in *Invisible Man* almost half a century earlier. It is an extension of *Invisible Man*'s closing line: "Who knows but that on the lower frequencies, I speak for you?"[1] Those lines represent Ellison's vision of American pluralism. Ellison had written and argued many times for "a pluralistic American culture" in which all members of the American body politic are both indebted to and responsible for one another and for attempting to bring the promises of democratic liberty found within the Declaration of Independence and the United States Constitution into reality.[2] The novel's title refers to June 19, 1865, when Union troops first read the Emancipation Proclamation to slaves and their masters in Galveston, Texas. That date has come to be celebrated by African Americans throughout the United States as the ending of slavery. It also represents, however, the delay of the promise of freedom for all that has been a part of American and African American experiences, as the original "Juneteenth" occurred over two years after Abraham Lincoln had issued the Emancipation Proclamation.

The novel *Juneteenth* centers on two primary characters: the African American preacher Alonzo Z. Hickman, a reformed gambler, who sits at the deathbed of the racist Senator Adam Sunraider, cut down by an assassin's bullets. It is quickly revealed that Sunraider began life as "Bliss," a child of nearly indeterminate racial background, who was raised from birth by Hickman and his congregation as a charismatic child preacher. The novel's main plot consists primarily of an extended conversation between Hickman and Sunraider. Hickman forces the former Bliss to confront his, and, by extension, America's biracial heritage in

often haunting, if flawed, dialogue. Sunraider's path from this existence as a direct beneficiary of the richness of African American culture and as a potential leader or messiah, to a race-baiting segregationist is the crux of the novel, which explores the ways that race or ethnicity, nationhood, identity, and definitions of democracy intertwine, shift, or are perverted over time.

To all appearances, Callahan was forced to extract this situation from many found within Ellison's papers, thereby excluding dozens of other major and minor characters, much to the consternation of reviewers. The fact that Callahan is white played some small part in the controversy surrounding the novel's publication, but more common was the opinion of such critics as Joanna Scott that Ellison's epic ambitions were necessarily but unfortunately reduced to a more intimate narrative, one full of beautiful prose and wrenching looks at the human condition in America but also occasionally dogged by "redundant" platitudes and "wearying" lectures. Contemporary reviews as a whole were somewhat mixed, with most negative criticisms concerning what Callahan had presumably omitted. Typical of the positive reviews is Max Brzezinski's brief review for *Antioch Review*, in which he compares *Juneteenth* to Fitzgerald's *The Last Tycoon* due to both being "incomplete American classic[s]" and concludes that the "poetically suggestive" novel is an "essential and vital read for anyone interested in the literature or history of America."[3] Brzezinski is echoed by such reviewers as John L. Brown in *World Literature Today* 74:1 (Winter 2000), Christopher C. De Santis (who later interviewed Callahan for *AAR*) in *The Review of Contemporary Fiction* 19, no. 3 (Fall 1999), Norman

---

1. Ralph Ellison, *Invisible Man* (1952; reprint, New York: Vintage, 1980), 581.

2. De Santis and Callahan, " 'Some cord of kinship," 601.

3. Max Brzezinski, review of *Juneteenth*, *Antioch Review* 58, no. 1 (Winter 2000): 119.

Podhoretz in *Commentary* 108, no. 1 (July 1999), and many others. Most of the negative reviews were, in fact, generally supportive of the project, but as Charles R. Larson notes in his review in *The World and I* 14, no. 7 (July 1999), "it is in [the] search or quest [for Sunraider's past] that the novel breaks down," making the novel "both unsatisfying and disappointing" for the many unanswered questions about his past. In the end, Larson concludes, "*Juneteenth* is no *Invisible Man*, despite innumerable parallels with and echoes of the earlier work."[1]

Callahan has promised to publish a scholar's edition of *Juneteenth* that contains most or all of the material he had to cut to maintain the trade edition's narrative unity. In the meantime, a smattering of scholarly discussions of the novel have just begun to emerge, but some of the best scholarly work may be found in many of the initial reviews. Of the former, most notable are Christopher C. De Santis's extensive, rich interview with John Callahan, found in *AAR* 34, no. 4 (Winter 2000), and S. Krishnamoorthy Aithal, "*Juneteenth*: A Novel for the New Millennium," *American Studies International* 38, no. 3 (October 2000), which argues that *Juneteenth* is a strong plea for racial reconciliation. Norman Podhoretz's aforementioned review is a studied consideration of Ellison's career more than an actual review of the novel, but it does highlight the issues that captivated Ellison and that inform both of his major works.[2] A portion of the Spring 1995 issue of *Callaloo* (18:2, 250–287) was dedicated to remembrances of Ellison's career by Callahan, Steve Cannon, Leon Forrest, Michael S. Harper, David Levin, Nathan A. Scott Jr., and Richard G. Stern, plus a revealing interview with Ellison by Keneth Kinnamon.

Kelley, William Melvin (b. 1937, New York City) Although William Melvin Kelley began writing and published his most celebrated works at the cusp and in the midst of the Black Arts Movement, his fiction tended to be far more surrealistic than much of the material emanating from that period, privileging aesthetics over politics, although all of Kelley's fiction contains political elements that clearly comment upon the larger issues regarding American history, especially the role of African Americans within that history. Kelley's renown as an author may be most easily attributed to *A Different Drummer* (1962), *dem* (1967), and, to a lesser degree, *A Drop of Patience* (1965), which has been out of print for most of the last forty years.

Kelley's early novels examine and satirize white America's dependence upon both white supremacy and the continued presence and labor of African Americans to create their identity within a falsely constructed white/black binary. *A Different Drummer*, for example, tells a story not unlike that of Douglas Turner Ward's play *A Day of Absence* (1965), as the African American populations of different mythical Southern towns disappear, thereby highlighting the extent to which American identity depends upon African Americans' existence and labor. *A Drop of Patience* is a *Künstlerroman* centering upon Ludlow Washington, a blind jazz musician who obviously cannot tell people's "race" by sight but nevertheless discovers and experiences racism and its effects. These are contrasted

1. Charles R. Larson, "When We Were Negroes," *The World and I* 14, no. 7 (July 1999): 300, 301.
2. Norman Podhoretz, "What Happened to Ralph Ellison," *Commentary* 108, no. 1 (July 1999): 46–59.

with the power of jazz music in ways that parallel Ralph Ellison's *Invisible Man* and precede such later works as Toni Morrison's *Jazz* (1992), Leon Forrest's *Divine Days* (1994), and Nathaniel Mackey's *From a Broken Bottle Traces of Perfume Still Emanate* trilogy (1986–2001). Kelley's third book, *dem*, finally, satirizes hypocritical American apprehensions regarding miscegenation in a complex fabliau.

The achievements of *A Different Drummer*, Kelley's short-story collection, *Dancers on the Shore* (1964), and *A Drop of Patience* earned Kelley the Richard and Hinda Rosenthal Award of the National Institute of Arts and Letters in 1963 and paved the way for the more consistent satirical milieu of *dem* and Kelley's last novel, *Dunfords Travels Everywheres* (1970). Since the publication of *Dunfords Travels Everywheres*, Harvard University graduate Kelley has devoted himself to nonfiction social and political commentary and to teaching literature and writing at several institutions, including the New School for Social Research in New York City, the State University of New York at Geneseo, the University of Paris, Nanterre, the Taos Institute of Art, and Sarah Lawrence College (1989–present).

As in the work of such influential antecedents as William Faulkner and Ralph Ellison, and such peers as Hal Bennett, Alice Walker, Toni Morrison, and John Edgar Wideman, Kelley's fiction meditates upon the interracial nature of much of American society and, in the case of his African American peers at the very least, the comic absurdities of racism. Kelley's early novels and short stories are either comedic or satiric, while those published since 1970 combine comedy and satire with the influence of James Joyce, especially *Finnegans Wake* (1939). *Dunfords Travels Everywheres* is heavily influenced by Joyce's magnum opus, taking cues from Joyce's experiments with language and plot structure to create a fantastic allegory about race. The plot concerns Chig Dunford, who lives in a land in which segregation is the norm based upon color schemes individuals choose on a given day, an ironic commentary upon the fluidity of identity in general but particularly in societies that depend upon racial polarization. When Dunford later travels back to the United States, his bizarre adventures serve only to highlight the absurdity of both racial categorizations and human behavior, especially in terms of sexual desire, which leads to the racial admixture that undermines the aforementioned categories. *Dunfords Travels Everywheres* also comprises a version of Kelley's 1968 short story "The Dentist's Wife."

Although critics have considered Kelley's novels to be among the finest to emerge from the Black Arts era, the amount of scholarly attention devoted to Kelley has not fully reflected this esteem, perhaps because Kelley has not published a novel since 1973 and has therefore fallen out of the critical consciousness. Most of the scholarship on Kelley may be found in publications from the 1970s. Greater attention came to his works by the 1990s, yet most of that scholarship analyzes *A Different Drummer* and occasionally *dem*, with very little attention paid to the later novels. Bernard W. Bell's reliable *Afro-American Novel and Its Tradition* (1987) has a subsection devoted to all of Kelley's novels. One of the few recent books that examines the later works is Aldon Lynn Nielsen, *Black Chant: Languages of African American Postmodernism* (1997), which argues that *Dunfords Travels Everywheres* is one of the great experiments in African American fiction that truly challenges the way readers define and perceive "black" and "white" language. Roger Rosenblatt's section on Kelley in *Black Fiction* (1974) is an informative retrospective of Kelley's career, as are Donald M. Weyl, "The Vision of Man in the Novels of William Melvin Kelley," *Critique* 15, no. 3 (1974); Jill Weyant, "The

Kelley Saga: Violence in America," *CLA Journal* 19 (1975); and Addison Gayle, *The Way of the New World: The Black Novel in America* (1976). More recent are W. Lawrence Hogue, *The African American Male, Writing, and Difference: A Polycentric Approach to African American Literature, Culture, and Theory* (2003), which devotes a chapter to Kelley's *A Different Drummer*, with some discussion of Kelley's far-too-neglected role in African American fiction; and James W. Coleman, *Black Male Fiction and the Legacy of Caliban* (2001), which rightly places Kelley among a group of African American authors who took Ralph Ellison as a key literary forebear. Charles Johnson, *Being and Race: Black Writing Since 1970* (1988), also briefly mentions *Dunfords Travels Everywheres* and Kelley's later works.

Significant journal articles on Kelley include: W. Lawrence Hogue, "Disrupting the White/Black Binary: William Melvin Kelley's *A Different Drummer*," *CLA Journal* 44, no. 1 (September 2000); Eric J. Sundquist, "Promised Lands: *A Different Drummer*," *TriQuarterly* 107–108 (Winter-Summer 2000); H. Nigel Thomas, "The Bad Nigger Figure in Selected Works of Richard Wright, William Melvin Kelley, and Ernest Gaines," *CLA Journal* 39, no. 2 (December 1995); Charles Alva Hoyt, "The Five Faces of Malcolm X" (includes helpful biographical information about Kelley's early career), *NALF* 4, no. 4 (Winter 1970); Stanley Schatt, "You Must Go Home Again: Today's Afro-American Expatriate Writers," *NALF* 7, no. 3 (Autumn 1973); John M. Reilly, "The Black Anti-Utopia," *BALF* 12, no. 3 (Autumn 1978); Elizabeth A. Schultz, "The Insistence Upon Community in the Contemporary Afro-American Novel," *College English* 41, no. 2 (October 1979); Sigmund Ro, "'Desecrators' and 'Necromancers': Black American Writers and Critics in the 1960s and the Third World Perspective," *Callaloo* 25 (Autumn 1985); Phyllis R. Klotman, "An Examination of the Black Confidence Man in Two Black Novels: *The Man Who Cried I Am* and *dem*," *American Literature* 44, no. 4 (January 1973).

Kenan, Randall (b. 1963, Brooklyn, New York) Novelist, short-story writer, and playwright Randall Kenan is one of the more prominent younger authors to emerge as part of the Post-Soul generation of African American authors and a major voice in gay and lesbian fiction. After working for several years as an editor in the offices of the Alfred A. Knopf publishing house, Kenan published his first novel, *A Visitation of Spirits* in 1989 to excellent reviews. The novel focuses upon the Cross family of Tim's Cross, North Carolina (which is based upon Kenan's hometown of Chinquapin, N.C.), especially teenage protagonist Horace Cross. Horace's realization that he is homosexual conflicts harshly with his family's and community's mores and precipitates the decay of his mind. Horace slowly goes insane as he seeks redemption through an imagined transformation into a hawk, and he eventually commits suicide.

The stories in *Let the Dead Bury Their Dead and Other Stories* (1992), Kenan's first collection of short fiction, are connected by their setting in Tim's Creek. The town's diverse characters are also united by their struggles with public and private selves; in more than one story, gay characters are either persecuted for their orientation and desires or forced to keep them secret. These struggles ultimately force most characters to live in deep loneliness and fear. Kenan also inserts his interest in African American historical figures and moments in such stories as "This Far," in which Tuskegee Institute President Booker T. Washington visits old friends living in Tim's Creek, or in the title story, which Kenan frames as the town's oral history. Kenan has also published his short fiction and essays in many different venues, including *Callaloo*: "Now Why Come That Is?" 21, no. 1 (Winter 1998); "The Boy Who Played Cards with the Devil," 23, no. 1 (Winter 2000).

Kenan has already received some scholarly attention in article form: Karla F. C. Holloway, "Cultural Narratives Passed On: African American Mourning Stories," *College English* 59, no. 1 (January 1997); David Bergman, "Race and the Violet Quill," *American Literary History* 9, no. 1 (Spring 1997); V. Hunt, "A Conversation with Randall Kenan," *AAR* 29, no. 3 (Autumn 1995); Charles H. Rowell, "An Interview with Randall Kenan," *Callaloo* 21, no. 1 (Winter 1998).

Killens, John Oliver (b. January 14, 1916, Macon, Georgia; d. October 20, 1987, Brooklyn, New York) Few contemporary African American novelists have been as inexplicably neglected as John Oliver Killens, who was a major influence in African American literature through four decades, both as an author of fiction and as a major critic and intellectual. His literary, scholarly, and political careers were coterminous, which led to his being an associate of such diverse figures as Malcolm X, Langston Hughes, Paul Robeson, Mari Evans, Ruby Dee, Ossie Davis, and Maya Angelou. As an instructor at Howard University, he could also boast that Thulani Davis, Arthur Flowers, Ntozake Shange, Elizabeth Nunez-Harrell, and Richard Perry were once his students. Killens cofounded the Harlem Writers Guild in 1950 with Dr. John Henrik Clarke, Rosa Guy, and Walter Christmas; later members included Maya Angelou, Ossie Davis, Audre Lorde, Terry McMillan, Lon Elder III, Paule Marshall, and Walter Dean Myers; the guild still meets to this day. From the late 1940s until his death in 1987, Killens was a prolific and formidable critic, although his greatest years of

influence were inarguably in the 1950s and 1960s. Although Killens's literary output from 1970 until his death did not equal that of the two prior decades in either quality or quantity, his oeuvre is fairly consistent in its critical outlook. In his work since 1970, though, Killens took on a perspective that was more Black Nationalist in its reading of African American culture and history, as seen in the characters (*The Cotillion*'s Ben Ali Lumumba) and historical personages (Denmark Vesey, John Henry, and Alexander Pushkin) featured in his novels. Despite his influence and prolific career, many of Killens's best works have gone out of print for long stretches, making access and appreciation difficult for readers and teachers alike. Fortunately, several publishers began reprinting Killens's work in the late 1990s and early 2000s.

Bernard W. Bell has identified Killens's fiction as the epitome of the "critical realism" school that developed out of the social realist and naturalist innovations of Richard Wright. Critical realism differs significantly from social realism, however, to the extent that the latter is not necessarily allied to leftist politics, whereas, according to Bell, the former is "a Marxist literary concept" that contains "a negative attitude toward capitalism and a readiness to respect the perspective of socialism and not condemn it out of hand."[1] Critical realism is willing to entertain the possibility of redistributing wealth (and other foundational socialist beliefs), largely because it perceives capitalism as generally harmful towards the masses. Critical realism may safely be said to be allied to the more ambitious goals of the modern Civil Rights movement that was developing as Killens began his career. His early works were certainly connected to his Civil Rights activism, insofar as he consistently incorpo-

1. Bernard W. Bell, *The Afro-American Novel and Its Tradition* (Amherst: University of Massachusetts Press, 1987), 247.

rated political themes into every work, albeit not for the purpose of simple protest. True to Professor Killens' calling as a teacher, his novels often educate their readers regarding African American historical and political figures in general and the lives and intragroup politics of Southern African Americans in particular, but they are seldom pedantic in the ways that 1940s and 1950s black protest literature could be at times. In fact, Killens's earlier novels, *Youngblood* (1954), *And Then We Heard the Thunder* (1962), and *'Sippi* (1967), while all politically charged dramatizations of Southern black lives, are imbued with fully rounded characters, frequent uses of and references to black folk culture, and a stronger sense of pathos, humor, and irony than many novels of the period. They were also very well received; Killens was nominated for the Pulitzer Prize for his first two novels and for *The Cotillion, or, One Good Bull Is Half the Herd* (1971). In the years that each of those three novels were nominated, though, the Pulitzer jury did not award prizes for fiction, which has occurred on only five other occasions between 1918 and 1976. Perhaps most suspect of all, when *And Then We Heard the Thunder* was nominated in 1964, it had no competition. The precise reasons for the absence of a prize are unknown, but a combination of the politically charged nature of Killens's fiction and the tense atmosphere of the Civil Rights era are not outside the realm of possibility.

As the Black Arts Movement and its concomitant black aesthetics emerged out of the conflicts within the Civil Rights Movement, though, Killens began to foreground an ideological alliance with black nationalism in his work. One novel of Killens's later period stands above the rest, largely because it is his best known, most humorous, and one of his most complex. *The Cotillion* locates itself well in the thick of African America's post–Civil Rights intraracial conflicts to concentrate primarily on the black community's own class divisions, which threaten to destroy it. *The Cotillion* represents the convergence of numerous literary and ideological aesthetics and conventions. Bernard W. Bell classifies the novel as part of Killens's attempt to "'change the world, to capture reality, to melt it down and forge it into something entirely different,'" via critical realism's "negative attitude toward capitalism and . . . readiness to respect the perspective of socialism and not condemn it out of hand."[1] Killens turns a skeptical, satirical eye turned toward the divisiveness of the class system within the African American community, specifically the yawning divide between, on the one hand, a petit-bourgeois black middle class that identifies and strives for assimilation with the white middle class and, on the other hand, unpretentious, working-class blacks. *The Cotillion*'s events are seen through the cynical eyes of Ben Ali Lumumba, the protagonist, who is taken with Yoruba Lovejoy, a beautiful young woman from a petit-bourgeois family. Lumumba's narrative voice continuously switches between straight, conventional narrative and African American "street" argot as well as between first-, second-, and third-person narrative, which marks him as a trickster. It is also his means of creating an inclusive text, one appealing to all types and classes of African Americans.

Most of the novel's tension and satirical thrust derives from the tensions between the bourgeois aspirations of Daphne Lovejoy (mother to Yoruba, and "a caricature of her own dear bourgeois self"), Lumumba's nationalism, and Yoruba's quest for independence from each of these positions. The

---

1. Bell, *The Afro-American Novel*, 248, 247. Bell quotes Killens, "The Black Writer vis-à-vis His Country," from his collection *Black Man's Burden* (New York: Trident, 1965), 34.

plot leads toward Daphne's ambitious plans for Yoruba's debut at the grand cotillion held every year by a group of upper-crust black women, the Femmes Fatales (or, in the words of Yoruba's father, Matthew Lovejoy, "Femmes Fattails"). The cotillion itself is modeled after those held in the deep South, down to an utterly offensive portrayal of black southerners. As an object of satiric attack, the cotillion serves to prove Lumumba's (and the novel's) essential belief about both Daphne and the black bourgeoisie: as Matthew says during the event, "'Like brother Malcolm said, [middle-class African Americans] don't want no liberation. They tryna sneak back on the old plantation'" (Killens, *Cotillion*, 245).

Killens's *Cotillion* thus stands as one of the finest examples of the satire emanating from the brand of black nationalism born in the 1960s and explored in *African America* in the 1970s. In fact, the relative obscurity surrounding the novel is indeed mysterious, given the force of its satirical message. In the last twenty years the novel has barely been mentioned at all in critical discourse, except for brief, pro forma mentions in surveys of African American novels. This obscurity, however, may be attributable to the novel's politics; though it speaks to a continuing problem within African America, it is immersed in a period in which black nationalism was a more palatable option for black progress. Fortunately, though, Coffee House Press reprinted *The Cotillion* in 2002, complete with a new introduction by novelist Alexs D. Pate.

Killens's next two works of fiction were written with a younger audience in mind, specifically a young black audience that might not have been familiar with the exemplary black revolutionaries Killens admired. *Great Gittin' Up Mornin'* (1972) is a fictionalization of the life of nineteenth-century slave insurrectionist Denmark Vesey that argues that obtaining freedom for African Americans is a process that inevitably and necessarily requires periodic bloodshed, no matter how tragic that outcome may be. *Great Gittin' Up Mornin'* may also be considered a response in fictional form to William Styron's highly controversial *Confessions of Nat Turner* (1967), which outraged many African American authors and intellectuals, including Killens, who published their arguments against the novel in *William Styron's Nat Turner: Ten Black Writers Respond* (1968). Equally notable is *A Man Ain't Nothing but a Man: The Adventures of John Henry* (1975), a retelling of the legend of John Henry, the African American folk hero who battles a steam drill in a tunnel-digging contest to prove both his strength and his dignity. It also predates and precedes Colson Whitehead's *John Henry Days* (2001) in both its subject matter and theme. Both novels treat John Henry as an elaborate metaphor for African Americans' struggles, albeit in dramatically different ways. Killens's novel recasts the folk figure in an imaginatively realistic setting, while Whitehead examines the soullessness of contemporary America. Killens is especially concerned with showing the need for African Americans to form cross-racial alliances—as exemplified in the characters George Lang Lee (a Chinese American of mixed heritage) and Big Ben Lawson, a poor Southern white—to free the working masses and defeat the worst excesses of the machine-driven Industrial Age and capitalism.

The scope of Killens's work is also well represented in two volumes published posthumously: *Great Black Russian: A Novel on the Life and Times of Alexander Pushkin* (1989) and *Black Southern Voices: An Anthology of Fiction, Poetry, Drama, Nonfiction, and Critical Essays* (1992). The former, which was accepted for publication mere weeks before his death from cancer on October 20, 1987, is an elaborate exploration of the significance of the father of Russian literature, who was of

African descent via his maternal grandfather, Hannibal, an Abyssinian (Ethiopian) prince. Rather than minimize Pushkin's African heritage, the novel questions why this aspect of the legendary author has been virtually ignored by all but a few historians, most of whom have been black. The novel also attempts to show all of Pushkin's personal complexities in order to make the legend real without sacrificing one iota of his essential role in the development of modern Russian literature. *Black Southern Voices* is one of the better collections of African American literature to emerge in the early 1990s. It highlights a group of African American writers (including Richard Wright, Maya Angelou, Frank Yerby, Zora Neale Hurston, Nikki Giovanni, James Weldon Johnson, Tom Dent, Kalamu Ya Salaam, and Martin Luther King Jr.) whose identities as Southerners in background and cultural outlook are highlighted in the selections chosen. Killens began editing it shortly before his death and contributed its introduction; it was completed by critic Jerry W. Ward, who also wrote the foreword. According to historian Louis Reyes Rivera, Killens was also working on a manuscript, "The Minister Primarily" at the time of his death. Reyes, who worked with Killens later in life, offers this description: a "comedy of errors in which an African American goes back to [Africa] and returns to the States . . . as a double for the Prime Minister of a small theretofore unknown nation, both of which [become] targets of international intrigues and counterplots. Here he [Killens] engages the search for a Pan-African self while exploring the pitfalls of our American lack of consciousness and the eagerness with which we grab at anything that runs counter to European models without sufficient thought

given to what we're being led into."[1] It has yet to be published.

Critical works on Killens, again, have been somewhat limited. The only book-length study of Killens widely available is Keith Gilyard, *Liberation Memories: The Rhetoric and Politics of John Oliver Killens* (2003). Several dissertations on Killens have emerged; none have yet been published in book form: Betty L. Hart, "The Black Aesthetic and the Novels of John Oliver Killens" (West Virginia University, 1974); Audrey Rouse Bell, "A Progression of Protest in Three Novels of John O. Killens" (master's thesis, University of North Carolina at Chapel Hill, 1976); Paul R. Lehman, "The Development of a Black Psyche in the Works of John Oliver Killens" (University of Michigan, 1976); Gatsinzi Basaninyenzi, "Ideology and Four Post-1960 Afro-American Novelists" (University of Iowa, 1986); and Stephen A. Cary, "Black Men's Du Boisian Relationships to Southern Social Institutions in the Novels of John Oliver Killens" (University of Texas at Dallas, 1992). All of these studies attempt to place Killens within his proper historical context, particularly as one of the premier authors of the 1950s through the early 1970s, but the reader will also note that only two dissertations have been written in the last twenty years, and only one since Killens's death. This author has also written on *The Cotillion* in *African American Satire: The Sacredly Profane Novel* (2001). Alexs D. Pate's aforementioned introduction to the 2002 reprint of *The Cotillion* is also a fine overview of Killens's career. William H. Wiggins Jr.'s entry on Killens in the *Dictionary of Literary Biography*, vol. 33, *Afro-American Fiction Writers after 1955* 144–52) is seminal, yet somewhat outdated; it was published in 1984, several years before Killens's death.

1. Louis Reyes Rivera, "John Oliver Killens: Lest We Forget," http://www.nathanielturner.com/joklestweforget .htm, August 3, 2003.

Kincaid, Jamaica (b. 1949, St. John's, Antigua) Jamaica Kincaid has enjoyed great literary accomplishments and critical admiration since the early 1970s. In 1965, she moved from her native Antigua to Scarsdale, New York, then to New York City, to work as an au pair. Within a decade of this migration, Kincaid was a regular contributor to the *New Yorker* magazine, and by the mid-1980s, had become an acclaimed fiction writer whose poetic nonfiction, short stories, and books earned her comparisons to Toni Morrison. Born Elaine Potter Richardson to "land peasant" parents in 1949 in Antigua, which was then under British colonial rule, Kincaid formed an identity not entirely uncommon among black writers of Caribbean descent: simultaneously British/Anglophone, African, and feminine, but ultimately humanistic. These influences are found in a rich mix throughout Kincaid's writing, insofar as they are both complementary and contradictory. As her literary biographer Diane Simmons has put it, "Kincaid's language may be the most powerful symbol of all for the themes of loss and betrayal in a world divided against itself."[1] Her sentences and paragraphs tend to follow a pattern of rhetorical questioning that seeks both to understand and to indict, as the case may warrant—and it may warrant it simultaneously. In addition, Kincaid incorporates a less narrative form of writing meant to emulate the workings of the conscious mind, as opposed to the artifices of fictional conventions. Two of her most profound artistic inspirations and models have been French author Alain Robbe-Grillet and the French film *La Jetée*, both examples of storytelling that eschew conventional narrative form.[2]

Kincaid's short stories and novels are also highly autobiographical and frequently concern conflicts with the mother or maternal figures, whose ability to exert powerful influence and control over their children causes deep conflicts and seriously affects the tenor and direction of other relationships, especially romantic ones. In addition, Kincaid writes extensively against the oppression and cultural deracination that typically result from colonialism, especially in current and former British possessions. Kincaid finds distinct parallels and analogues in the forms of oppression that extend from matriarchs and colonialists alike; they are two of her crucial and most damning metaphors. The counter to such undue influences and controls is artistic creation, particularly writing. Kincaid's first collection of stories, *At the Bottom of the River* (1983), for example, contains one of her best pieces, "My Mother," which queries the role of a nearly omnipotent mother over her young daughter and is based heavily upon Kincaid's own experiences. Her first novel, *Annie John* (1985) continues in the same vein, albeit with a slightly more conventional narrative style, and shifts its focus to the adolescent years and the loss of innocence and naïveté that comes with that crucial transition. It was originally published in the preceding years in the *New Yorker*, as was Kincaid's second novel, *Lucy* (1990). The latter continues the narrative and (auto)biographical arc begun in its predecessor, albeit with a different female protagonist, and attention focused upon the struggles of young adulthood. *Autobiography of My Mother* (1994) is a novel about Xuela, a seventy-year-old woman whose mother died in childbirth. This event becomes a metaphor for the lack of connection Xuela has to most people, objects, and ideas in her life ranging from her mother, to love, and to her homeland or a sense of home in general.

---

1. Diane Simmons, *Jamaica Kincaid* (New York: Twayne, 1994), 4.
2. Simmons, *Jamaica Kincaid*, 16.

Several notable books that study Kincaid's work, usually in conjunction with other African Diasporic women authors, have been published in the 1990s and 2000s: Victoria Burrows, *Whiteness and Trauma: The Mother-Daughter Knot in the Fiction of Jean Rhys, Jamaica Kincaid, and Toni Morrison* (2004); Antonia MacDonald-Smythe, *Making Homes in the West/Indies: Constructions of Subjectivity in the Writings of Michelle Cliff and Jamaica Kincaid* (2001); Lizabeth Paravisini-Gebert, *Jamaica Kincaid: A Critical Companion* (1999); Harold Bloom, *Jamaica Kincaid* (1998), part of Chelsea's Modern Critical Views series; Moira Ferguson, *Jamaica Kincaid: Where the Land Meets the Body* (1994), and *Colonialism and Gender From Mary Wollstonecraft to Jamaica Kincaid* (1994); and the aforementioned Diane Simmons, *Jamaica Kincaid* (1994).

L

Lamar, Jake (b. 1962, Bronx, New York) Novelist and journalist Jake Lamar's three extant novels, *The Last Integrationist* (1996), *Close to the Bone* (1999), and *If 6 Were 9* (2001) play off of the themes and ideas Lamar introduced in his 1991 memoir, *Bourgeois Blues*, one of the better meditations upon the strange position occupied by African Americans born into the post–Civil Rights generation vis-à-vis their history, legacy, and the larger American culture. Put simply, Lamar is interested in the lives of the group of predominantly middle-class African Americans Trey Ellis called "cultural mulattoes," those living lives within a zone between the "black" and "white" worlds made possible by the advances of the Civil Rights movement. His characters' struggles with America's continued entrenched racism arise from their realization that the Civil Rights movement was indeed a movement of ideals that could not be brought to fruition easily, especially in view of the backlash that followed each of the movement's achievements. Some of Lamar's characters, such as *The Last Integrationist*'s black Attorney General Melvin Hutchinson, a neoconservative ideologue, help give such backlashes momentum, but also come to realize that "race" and racism cannot be easily transcended.

Close to the Bone resembles Terry McMillan's landmark bestseller *Waiting to Exhale* (1992) as a character study of several successful African Americans. The differences are that Lamar's characters are all men and all struggle with their identities as black men, particularly with regard to their connection to African American culture. The first, Hal Hardaway, must come to terms with the interracial relationship in which he is enmeshed. His friend Walker DuPree, on the other hand, is the *offspring* of an interracial relationship and feels divided between the complex branches of his biracial heritage. Dr. Emmett Mercy is a psychologist who has built his career upon books his wife, whom he neglects emotionally, has ghostwritten.

If 6 Were 9 is a thriller in which professor and former black activist Reggie Brogus becomes entangled in a murder mystery that involves his colleague Clay Robinette. Along the way, Lamar lampoons academic life and creates a novel that may be compared favorably to Alexs Pate's *Multiculti-boho Sideshow* (1999) or Ishmael Reed's *Japanese by Spring* (1993).

LaValle, Victor D. (b. 1972, Flushing, New York) Novelist and short-story author Victor D. LaValle, who received his Master of Fine Arts degree from Columbia University, published his first collection of short stories, *Slapboxing with Jesus*, in 1999 to excellent reviews and reception; Barnes & Noble Booksellers picked the collection as part of its Discover Great New Writers Series that year, and it also won the PEN Open Book Award (2002). All of the stories in the volume are set in New York City and feature African American and Latino youths whose lives are guided, and frequently *misguided*, by the choices they make with their circumstances and opportunities. His stories are marked by their reliance upon the characters' points of view and authentic language and slang. In 2002, LaValle published his first novel, *The Ecstatic*, a picaresque work that has been compared favorably to Ralph Ellison's *Invisible Man* (1952).

Lee, Helen Elaine (b. 1959, Detroit, Michigan) Novelist Helen Elaine Lee began writing fiction in the 1990s towards the end of a career as an attorney following her matriculation at Harvard Law School. Her debut novel, *The Serpent's Gift* (1994), won immediate critical acclaim from the *Washington Post Book World* and the *New York Times* and comparisons to the best work of Toni Morrison and Gloria Naylor. These comparisons are due primarily to Lee's richly lyrical style and attention to the types of stories, cultures, and lives within the African American community that are often left out of history. *The Serpent's Gift* centers on two Midwestern African American families, the Smalls and the Staples, who merge to maintain bloodlines and traditions after the deaths of the Small family patriarch in 1910. The novel logs the families' many challenges from that point until the present, touching upon many of the major events in American and African American history in the twentieth century. *Water Marked* (1999) studies the lives of sisters Delta and Sunday Owens, who have spent over four decades trying to make sense of their father's apparent suicide. As clues emerge that cast doubt upon the reality of his death, the sisters discover more about themselves and their family's secrets and intimacies. *Water Marked* won more critical praise for its style and language but was also criticized for a slow, pedantic plot.

Little, Benilde (b. 1958, Newark, New Jersey) Novelist Benilde Little stands among a large class of young authors of popular fiction who debuted in the latter half of the 1990s. This class includes such bestsellers as Omar Tyree, Eric Jerome Dickey, E. Lynn Harris, and Sheneska Jackson. Like her peers, Little uses her accessible style to address social issues that concern many African Americans while focusing upon familial and romantic relationships, although Little's novels should not be confused with formulaic romances. Her explorations of social issues are integrated fully into her plots and unpacked carefully and thoughtfully. They are also designed to appeal to the middle-class African American women Little courted as part of her former editorial position at the highly popular *Essence* magazine, whose articles frequently seek ways to address the audience's concerns about health, wealth, relationships, education, and other current events and issues.

Little's first novel, *Good Hair* (1996) was a major best-seller about Alice Lee, a middle-class African American woman who finds herself attracted to male members of Boston's black bourgeoisie, many of whom hold antiquated and elitist views of their own class status within the larger African American community and hold other blacks at great physical and social distances. Lee is forced to confront her own beliefs about these class strata; the novel's title refers to the still-common notion that "good" hair is that which is straight or most like Caucasian hair. It also refers, metaphorically, to Alice's desire to maintain and enhance her class status in much the same way that many African American women and men seek "good" hair. *Good Hair* was selected as one of the Los Angeles *Times*' best books of 1996. Little's second novel, *The Itch* (1998), covers much the same territory as the first, although it has a more satirical bite as it points out the follies of the bourgeois lifestyle.

Lorde, Audre (b. February 18, 1934, New York City; d. November 17, 1992, New York City) At first glance, Audre Lorde might seem an odd member of this volume. In the strictest terms, Lorde was not a fiction writer; her most substantive contributions to African American literature were in the areas of poetry, and in feminist, cultural, and literary criticism. Lorde's books *The First Cities* (1968), *The Cancer Journals* (1980; memoir), and *Sister Outsider* (1984) are now considered classics in poetry, memoir, and feminist criticism, respectively. She was also a founding member of Women of Color Press, a major feminist academic and literary publishing concern, and an internationally recognized activist for women's issues. Upon these achievements alone, Lorde is a major voice in contemporary African American literature and culture.

Lorde's *Zami: A New Spelling of My Name: A Biomythography* (1982), however, is difficult to classify. Not unlike Chinese American author Maxine Hong Kingston's classic *Woman Warrior: Memoirs of a Girlhood Among Ghosts* (1976), *Zami* may be read either as an autobiography or a novel, as it makes extensive use of the conventions of the latter form and is narrated from the perspective of a narrator who may or may not be Lorde. Hence Lorde's subtitle, "A Biomythography," which connotes the process of mythmaking in which Lorde engages. Lorde herself allowed in an interview that she considered Zami a novel despite its clearly autobiographical content; many of its reviewers and critics have read it as such.

Zami resembles Lorde's earlier *Cancer Journals*, which chronicles her struggles with breast cancer (the eventual cause of her death), in that it is as concerned with the process of personal growth that comes from struggling with a deadly disease as it is with women's bodies and the ways in which they have been historically neglected. It is also a narrative of cultural clashes, specifically between the Caribbean (Barbadian/Grenadian) background that Lorde and her narrator share, and the United States. Lorde's narrator tries to find a home in the United States, despite the fact that her parents do not consider it to be a true home. This functions as a metaphor for the narrator's search for her identity as a woman, a mother, a lesbian, and an activist for women's rights. To become "Zami," means becoming a mix of all these identities while maintaining the ability to criticize them.

Macarthur "Genius" Grants These John D. and Catherine T. MacArthur Foundation Fellowships—currently $500,000 paid over five years—are awarded annually (twice annually until 1984) to persons judged to possess extraordinary talent and potential in their given fields in the arts, sciences, humanities, and nonprofit organizations. Although the foundation keeps the deliberations that lead to individuals being nominated and selected a closely guarded secret and contends that its grants should not be considered "rewards" for work its recipients have completed, countless grants have clearly gone to those who have garnered significant notice due to one or more outstanding works or products. According to the official literature, "the MacArthur Fellows Program awards unrestricted fellowships to talented individuals who have shown extraordinary originality and dedication in their creative pursuits and a marked capacity for self-direction. There are three criteria for selection of Fellows: exceptional creativity, promise for important future advances based on a track record of significant accomplishment, and potential for the fellowship to facilitate subsequent creative work."[1] All fellowships come with no strings attached; that is to say, for the duration of the individual's program, he or she is not required to file any reports, attend any conferences, produce any work, or otherwise answer to anyone regarding the way the funds were used.

Since the program's inception in 1981, many African American fiction writers and critics have benefited from its largesse. They are, by year: James Alan McPherson and Henry Louis Gates Jr. (1981); Arnold Rampersad (1991); Stanley Crouch and John Edgar Wideman (1993); Octavia Butler and Virginia Hamilton (1995); Charles Johnson and Ishmael Reed (1998); Jacqueline Jones (1999); Patricia J. Williams (2000); and Colson Whitehead (2002). More information on all African Americans, in all fields of endeavor, who have been granted the award as of 1998 may be found in *The Journal of Blacks in Higher Education* 20 (Summer 1998): 30–31.

Mackey, Nathaniel (b. 1947, Miami, Florida) Nathaniel Mackey has written an extensive amount of poetry, prose fiction, essays, and criticism over four decades as a professor at the University of Southern California (1976–1979) and the University of California at Santa Cruz (1979–present). Mackey's work tends to focus on jazz, both as a musical form in his criticism and as a metaphor in the other genres in which he works. Mackey is heavily influenced by the poetry, fiction, nonfiction, and music of such authors and composers as Amiri Baraka, Ishmael Reed, Denise Levertov, Aimé Césaire, William Carlos Williams, Robert Duncan, Pharoah Sanders, and Anthony Braxton. His first two novels, *Bedouin Hornbook* (1986) and *Djbot Baghostus's Run* (1993), are part of From a Broken Bottle Traces of Perfume Still Emanate, a trilogy (thus far) continued with *Atet A.D.* (2001). Each novel is epistolary, comprising letters from complex, ironic characters—often jazz musicians—to the "Angel of Dust," who is deeply immersed in the world of music, including the exploitative industry that surrounds it. Various excerpts from the novels were published in different journals and magazines prior to their collection and publication in book form.

Many of the novels' letters focus on the history and meaning of jazz and the artists who shaped its development and made it a centerpiece of African American and American culture. For Mackey and his characters, jazz is very much an intellectual concern that has the power to invade the soul and transform the individual, but its intellectualism rarely, if ever, stands in the way of its spirituality and warmth. As Mackey indicated in one interview, music "includes so much: it's social, it's religious, it's metaphysical, it's aesthetic, it's expressive, it's creative, it's destructive. It just covers so much. It's the biggest, most inclusive thing that [he] could put forth if [he] were to choose one single thing."[2] Mackey's novels are thus populated with punningly named characters derived from African American and world folklore (e.g., the Angel of Dust, Aunt Nancy, the *djinns* Djeannine and Djbot

---

1. John D. and Catherine T. MacArthur Foundation, "The MacArthur Fellows Program," http://www .macfound.org/programs/fel/fel_overview.htm.

2. Christopher Funkhouser, "An Interview with Nathaniel Mackey," *Callaloo* 18, no. 2 (Spring 1995): 321.

Baghostus [also known as Flaunted Fifth, Jarred Bottle, Djbouche, DB, etc.) as well as musical figures (Thelonious Monk, Duke Ellington, Rahsaan Roland Kirk, Yusef Lateef, Miles Davis, Charles Mingus, Pharoah Sanders, Sonny Rollins, Louis Armstrong, Albert Ayler, and innumerable others) whose compositions are analyzed and used to evoke moods, begin or end plot points, and as metaphors for different characters and their quirks. All of these characters and figures represent the possibilities found within music, literature, and intellectual thought that encompass all the areas Mackey speaks of in his interview. Mackey sees music as a vehicle for "challenging and questioning . . . categories" and for the mixing of "things that defy and redefine boundary lines," which are "very important in the literary politics, cultural politics, and marginalized social politics of the time we're living in."[1] Beyond his own fiction, Mackey's belief in jazz's power is reflected in his anthology, *Moment's Notice: Jazz in Poetry in Prose* (1993), coedited with Art Lange. The volume includes the work of many major writers, including Melvin Tolson, Langston Hughes, James Baldwin, Cecil Taylor, Abdullah Ibrahim (formerly known as Dollar Brand), Jack Kerouac, Frank O'Hara, Michael Ondaatje, Michael S. Harper, Ishmael Reed, Amiri Baraka, Ntozake Shange, and Quincy Troupe.

Critical and scholarly attention to Mackey's novels has not been prolific, but it is almost invariably positive, generous, and attentive to Mackey's extensive, if not exhaustive knowledge of jazz's history and cultural significance. The aforementioned interview with Mackey, found in *Callaloo* 18, no. 2 (Spring 1995), is one of the best introductions to Mackey's own thoughts about his prose and poetry, including his influ-

ences. A better, albeit slightly less accessible source is Mackey's own scholarly book, *Discrepant Engagement: Dissonance, Cross-Culturality, and Experimental Writing* (1993), which argues for the writing and reading of literature as a means to interpreting culture and allowing individual voices to speak and obtain agency.

Magical realism "Magical realism" refers to a literary mode that incorporates and fuses a number of different features. These include mixing of environments, such as the urban with the rural, the real with the fantastic, black/African with white/European, or the present with the past and potential future. A good number of works experiment radically with authorial perspective or narrative techniques and voices. Magical realism is best known for weaving elements of the supernatural and mystical seamlessly into texts that are otherwise realistic in their structure, organization, and content. When these supernatural elements take on human form, they coexist on this plane with the narrative's "real" characters, and frequently function as symbols for ideas elucidated elsewhere in the text. More often than not, these figures are the very embodiment of other notions or element.

The mode is most frequently associated with author Gabriel García Márquez, especially his masterpiece, *One Hundred Years of Solitude* (1967), but has found favor with the muses of quite a few African American authors, most prominently Gayl Jones (*Eva's Man* and *Corregidora*), Charles Johnson (*Middle Passage*), Paule Marshall (*Praisesong for the Widow*), Toni Morrison (*Song of Solomon, Beloved, Jazz,* and *Paradise*), Gloria Naylor (*Linden Hills* and *Mama Day*), Ishmael Reed (*Mumbo Jumbo, The Last Days of Louisiana Red, The Terrible Twos,* and *The*

1. Funkouser, "An Interview with Nathaniel Mackey," 330.

Terrible Threes), Tina McElroy Ansa (*Baby of the Family*), and John Edgar Wideman (*Damballah*).

For many of these authors, the mystical elements are drawn directly from mythological figures and folklore from Africa and the African Diaspora, especially tricksters and trickster gods, folk legends, creation myths, religions (particularly vodun/voodoo/hoodoo and Santería, or Regla de Ocha). Others blend African American folklore with European myths, motifs, and literary texts. This may be seen in Naylor's *Linden Hills* and *Mama Day*, which play off *The Divine Comedy* by Dante Alighieri (thirteenth century) and *The Tempest* by William Shakespeare (1611), and Charles Johnson's *Middle Passage*, a mix of Jonathan Swift, African religion, Plato's Republic, Benjamin Franklin's *Autobiography*, and many other texts.

These texts' uses of magical realism vary widely, but most attempt to compose allegories representing specific problems concerning either African American communities or America as a whole, especially in a postmodern era in which many past values are being reconsidered as new views of history and culture find their way into the mainstream. Many of these works might therefore be classified under the larger rubric of postmodernism, although postmodern works are not normally associated with the supernatural.

Major, Clarence (b. 1936; Atlanta, Georgia) Any careful, complete discussion of postmodern African American literature must eventually mention Clarence Major. As Bernard Bell attests, Major stands, along with Toni Morrison, Charles Johnson, Toni Cade Bambara, John Edgar Wideman, and Ishmael Reed, as one of the African American "modernists and postmodernists" who are "rediscovering and reaffirming the power and wisdom of their own vernacular expressive tradition: African American ways of seeing, knowing, and expressing reality" that simultaneously diverge from and converge with the philosophical and literary traditions that inform postmodernity (6). Like Reed in particular, Major's short stories and novels have both perplexed and delighted critics and students with their complexity, their often seamless and ubiquitous references to popular cultural icons and history, and their attention to hidden histories. Major has not, however, enjoyed the same degree of familiarity and popularity among African American and academic audiences as other experimental contemporaries, despite his founding of *Coercion Review*, cofounding of the Fiction Collective publishing house, and his eight novels, thirteen poetry collections, a collection of short stories, and hundreds of poems and short stories in various journals and magazines spanning more than five decades. This relative dearth of attention may be attributed to the challenge that Major's metafictional innovations tend to pose to the casual reader.

Major's fiction is marked by its tacit avoidance of social realist conventions. While it would be highly inaccurate to say that Major's fiction is apolitical, ideological considerations are clearly second to the fictive world's own logic and organization, both of which reflect the feelings and thoughts of the narrators and their voices. Language's power to enable or obscure our perception of reality is the focus of his fiction in much the same way that an expressionist painter foregrounds the possibilities and limits of the paint medium. Fittingly, Major is also an accomplished painter in the expressionist style; his early artistic influences were divided almost equally between such painters as Cézanne, Munch, Degas, van Gogh, and Picasso; such writers as Richard Wright, Jean Toomer, Willard Motley, Chester Himes, and Rimbaud; and jazz music.[1] Major's artistic philosophy is therefore quite consistent, inasmuch as he has emphasized repeatedly that his works are designed to keep the reader "constantly focused on the page" and the narrative voice.[2] His novels in particular take on their "own reality and [are] really independent of anything outside [themselves]," and they need not be "reflection[s] of anything" outside the text's world.[3]

This focus upon the page, of the text's status qua text, is the hallmark of the metafiction or surfiction movements of the 1960s and 1970s. In *No* (1973), Major's second novel (*All Night Visitors* was his first, in 1969) the narrator/protagonist attempts to come to grips with his identity as a developing adult, particularly in terms of his evolution as a sexual being. In Major's conscious attempt to incorporate a reading of Sigmund Freud's Oedipus complex theory, it is difficult to tell the narrator from his father. Both are called by the same name at various points, and the narrator simply finds himself struggling with his father's legacies— particularly the father's murder of his own family in order to save them from suffering in a world of bigotry and prejudice. In the process, Major pushes the bounds of the narrator's linguistic abilities and consciousness.

In what is arguably his most challenging novel, *Reflex and Bone Structure* (1975), Major highlights the narrator's role as the creator and controller of the every last component within the narrative by creating a world in which the utterly fantastic and the realistic exist side by side, with few indications that this reality is unreal. One charac-

ter, Canada, may just as easily be the narrator's alter ego as not, and the characters and their fates are equally controlled by the author as by the characters. *Emergency Exit* (1979) is equally challenging. It combines a narrative about personal relationships with twenty-six of Major's own paintings, defying generic conventions of both media, especially since, according to Major, the paintings were selected for their ability to move or delay the narrative's rhythm and momentum; they do not intentionally illustrate any particular scenes within the written narrative.[4]

My Amputations (1986) builds upon *Emergency Exit*'s experiments, concerned as the former is with Major's interest in the barriers that divide artistic genres, cultural and artistic traditions, identities, and parts of the individual's psyche from one another. The protagonist, Mason Ellis, is an African American expatriate artist living in Europe (as Major did for much of the first half of the 1980s) who confronts all of the influences that have contributed to his personal and artistic identity. *Painted Turtle: Woman with Guitar* (1988), in turn, plays upon its predecessor; it is an experimental novel that expands the story of Painted Turtle, the Zuni (Native American) folksinger who originally appeared in *My Amputations*. Her struggles to maintain her cultural and artistic integrity in the face of cultural change form the novel's crux. The narrative experiments both with form and with subject matter; it is one of very few depictions of a

1. Bernard W. Bell, "Introduction: Clarence Major's Transgressive Voice and Double Consciousness as an African American Postmodernist Artist," in *Clarence Major and His Art*, ed. Bernard W. Bell (Chapel Hill: University of North Carolina Press, 2001), 1.

2. Larry McCaffery and Jerzy Kutznik, "'I Follow My Eyes': An Interview with Clarence Major," in *Clarence Major and His Art*, ed. Bernard W. Bell (Chapel Hill: University of North Carolina Press, 2001), 88.

3. Jerome Klinkowitz, "Clarence Major's Innovative Fiction," in *Clarence Major and His Art*, ed. Bernard W. Bell (Chapel Hill: University of North Carolina Press, 2001), 151.

4. Lisa C. Roney, "The Double Vision of Clarence Major, Painter and Writer," *African American Review* 28, no. 1 (Spring 1994): 67.

Native American culture and life by someone outside that culture that rings true, according to an authoritative contemporary review,[1] via its attention to cultural traditions and its refusal to condescend to different Native American cultures. *Painted Turtle* also won the honor of being a *New York Times Book Review* Notable Book of the Year. *Fun and Games: Short Fictions* (1990) is Major's first collection of its kind. Most of the stories are again experimental, with the subject matter focusing largely upon semi-autobiographical tales of personal growth, with no small amount of wry, yet sympathetic humor.

Not all of Major's texts are as challenging as his earlier, experimental fiction. Since the 1980s, Major's prolific fiction output has been more accessible but never pedestrian. Each novel or short story experiments in some way with voice, temporality, folk culture, and various political issues. Two of his more recent efforts, *Such Was the Season* (1987) and *Dirty Bird Blues* (1996), are more conventional in their style and subject matter, taking as their foci the resonance of folk idioms, especially the blues, in African Americans' life and culture. The plots concern attempts to reconnect with cultural roots and a blues musician's struggles for survival and meaning in America, respectively. These two novels may be Major's most accessible works, but they are still challenging in their attempt to plumb the complex relationship between a people's existence and their artistic creations.

The critical response to Major's work has been at once extensive and impressive. This response primarily comprises journal articles and book chapters, but critic Bernard Bell recently collected many of these into one volume, *Clarence Major and His Art*

(2001), easily the best introduction to the numerous readings of his work that have emerged in the last thirty years of the millennium. It includes selections from Major's poetry, excerpts from his fiction, interviews, and critical essays on all aspects of his artistic endeavors. Most of the critical essays included were first published in *AAR* 28, no. 1 (Spring 1994), a special issue devoted to Major. The most appropriate companion to Bell's collection is Major's own gathering of his nonfiction, *Necessary Distance: Essays and Criticism* (2001). In October 2002, the University Press of Mississippi published an essential collection of interviews, *Conversations with Clarence Major*, edited by Nancy Bunge.

Major has generated an extensive corpus of scholarly journal articles. Besides the aforementioned special issue of *AAR* and the other essays included in Bell's volume (many of which were published as journal articles in other issues of *AAR*), the Summer 1979 issue of *BALF* (vol. 13, issue 2) is also devoted to Major's work, including a bibliography of his published work compiled by Joe Weixlmann. The following articles are also among the most helpful and significant: Joe Weixlmann, "African American Deconstruction of the Novel in the Work of Ishmael Reed and Clarence Major," *MELUS* 17, no. 4 (Winter 1991–1992); Larry D. Bradfield, "Beyond Mimetic Exhaustion: The *Reflex and Bone Structure* Experiment," *BALF* 17, no. 3 (Autumn 1983).

Marshall, Paule (b. Valenza Pauline Burke, 1929, Brooklyn, New York) Paule Marshall's career as a writer began in 1959, when her first novel, *Brown Girl, Brownstones* was published at a time when very few African American women authors had their works

---

1. Deborah Fairman Browning, review for *Painted Turtle: Woman with Guitar*, by Clarence Major, *MELUS* 16, no. 4 (Winter 1989): 133–36.

in print.[1] She has since published many works of short fiction (including two collections) and four additional novels; all have received extensive praise and critical attention. She is one of many African American authors of Caribbean descent—Marshall's parents were second-generation Barbadian immigrants—who have repeatedly tried to reconcile that heritage with the situation of Americans of African descent in their fiction. In this regard, she may be compared to Jamaica Kincaid, Audre Lorde and Edwidge Danticat, all of whom emerged as major writers since 1970.

While her earlier work is certainly excellent and groundbreaking, Marshall's work since 1970—*Praisesong for the Widow* (1983), *Reena and Other Stories* (1983), *Daughters* (1991), and *The Fisher King* (2000)—have received the most attention. *Praisesong for the Widow* is perhaps Marshall's masterpiece and is the novel that scholars have studied most frequently, particularly in the late 1990s and early 2000s. It also won the Before Columbus Foundation's American Book Award in 1984. *Praisesong* is a neo–slave narrative (see separate entry) that tells the story of Avatara "Avey" Johnson, a middle-class African American woman who finds herself drawn to the Caribbean island of Carriacou while on a cruise to Grenada. Once she arrives on Grenada, Avey begins to recall her life with her deceased husband Jerome "Jay" Johnson, which went from a relationship of love and affection to coldness, miserliness, and distrust as they moved upward economically. She then books passage on an excursion to Carriacou, where she connects with her African roots by channeling the spirits of her African ancestors in the Big Drum ceremony on the island. This helps Avey see the links between her African ancestors and her

hometown in South Carolina. In deeply moving prose, Marshall revisits her project of drawing links between the peoples of the African Diaspora that began with *Brown Girl, Brownstones*. Marshall also published *Reena and Other Stories* in 1983, short stories about West Indian women, especially Marshall's grandmother (a.k.a. Da-Duh), who displayed strength and determination in the face of racial and sexual oppression. Her best known short story, "To Da-Duh, in Memoriam," is found here, along with Marshall's landmark introductory essay, "From the Poets in the Kitchen."

Daughters (1991) is the story of Ursa McKenzie, a consumer researcher living in Manhattan and the daughter of an influential politician on the mythical Caribbean island of Triunion. In a parallel reference to the island nation's name, three plots dominate the novel: the corruption of Ursa's father as he caves in to the offers of white developers; the similar corruption of a black politician in a city where Ursa had conducted a study; Ursa's own struggle with the decision to have an abortion after her mother had had many miscarriages before giving birth to Ursa, her only child. Each plot concerns situations in which individuals have to deal with the legacy and burden of the sacrifices made on their behalf in the past, raising questions of their responsibilities, whether real or perceived, to those who went before them or who may follow.

The Fisher King (2000) is set in Brooklyn and Paris of the 1940s through the 1980s. It is the saga of the McCullum and Payne families, whose matriarchs, Florence McCullum and Ulene Payne, are drawn together in part due to the pride they have for their respective musical children, Cherisse McCullum and Everett "Sonny-Rett" Payne. Cherisse

---

1. Keith Bernard Mitchell, "Paule Marshall," in *The Concise Oxford Companion to African American Literature*, ed. William L. Andrews, Frances Smith Foster, and Trudier Harris (London: Oxford University Press, 2001), 274.

and Sonny-Rett later reject their classical training in favor of jazz, much to the chagrin of their families, marry each other, and flee to Paris to escape the wrath their choices engender, as well as the racism that jazz musicians could expect in America. In the meantime, the two families break apart and begin a bitter forty-year feud, blaming each other for the children's departure from both the United States and their classical discipline. Eventually the families resolve their differences with the help of Sonny-Rett and Cherisse's grandson and a performance of Sonny-Rett's great music. The novel ultimately celebrates family ties, the richness of Caribbean heritage, the redemptive power of love, and especially jazz music.

Scholarship on Marshall is extensive, having grown tremendously since the publication of *Praisesong for the Widow*. Notable books include: Stelamaris Coser, *Bridging the Americas: The Literature of Paule Marshall, Toni Morrison, and Gayl Jones* (1995); Dorothy Hamer Denniston, *The Fiction of Paule Marshall: Reconstructions of History, Culture, and Gender* (1995); Simone A. James Alexander, *Mother Imagery in the Novels of Afro-Caribbean Women* (2001); Eugenia C. DeLamotte, *Places of Silence, Journeys of Freedom: The Fiction of Paule Marshall* (1998). Notable journal articles include: Harihar Kulkarni, "Paule Marshall: A Bibliography," *Callaloo* 16, no. 1 (Winter 1993); Linda Pannill, "From the 'Wordshop': The Fiction of Paule Marshall," *MELUS* 12, no. 2 (Summer 1985); Missy Dehn Kubitschek, "Paule Marshall's Women on Quest," *BALF* 21, nos. 1–2 (Spring-Summer 1987); Jane Olmsted, "The Pull to Memory and the Language of Place in Paule Marshall's *The Chosen Place, The Timeless People* and *Praisesong for the Widow*," *AAR* 31, no. 2 (Summer 1997).

McElroy, Colleen (b. Colleen Johnson, 1935, St. Louis, Missouri) Colleen McElroy is best known for her poetry, which she has been publishing since 1968. In that capacity, she has been called "the best, most balanced black woman poet working today."[1] Her short fiction, however, has garnered limited but respectable reviews. McElroy has authored two short-story collections: *Jesus and Fat Tuesday and Other Short Stories* (1987) and *Driving Under the Cardboard Pines and Other Stories* (1990). The former contains fourteen stories set in the American Midwest, with African American protagonists—often women—that discover the possibilities of imagination when the physical world becomes too limiting for them. The stories in *Driving Under* follow the same eclectic pattern as the first collection, with an emphasis on piercing cross-cultural boundaries. McElroy's style is reminiscent of her stunning poetry, with languid lines that match the openness of the characters' minds as they tap into their creative energies. McElroy has won fellowships from the National Endowment for the Arts, the Rockefeller Foundation (to aid in the writing of her 1999 travel memoir, *Over the Lip of the World: Among the Storytellers of Madagascar*), and a Fulbright Creative Writing Fellowship.

McElroy's works are anthologized in Gloria Naylor, ed., *Children of the Night: The Best Short Stories by Black Writers, 1967 to the Present* (1995); Bill Mullen, ed., *Revolutionary Tales: African American Women's Short Stories: From the First Story to the Present* (1995); Terry McMillan, ed., *Breaking Ice: An Anthology of Contemporary African American Fiction* (1990); and Craig Lesley, ed., *Dreamers and Desperadoes: Contemporary Short Fiction of the American West* (1993). Very little scholarly attention has been paid to McEl-

---

1. Charles Johnson, "Whole Sight: Notes on New Black Fiction," *Callaloo* 22 (Autumn 1984), 6.

roy's work, unfortunately, but she is profiled in Lynda Koolish, *African American Writers: Portraits and Visions* (2001); and Joyce Owens Pettis, *African American Poets: Lives, Works, and Sources* (2002). McElroy, a professor of creative writing at the University of Washington, has also edited the *Seattle Review*.

McKnight, Reginald (b. 1956, Germany) Reginald McKnight built a respectable place for himself among contemporary writers with stories he began publishing in the late 1980s, which were represented in his first book, *Moustapha's Eclipse* (1988), the winner of the Drue Heinze Literature Prize for that year. McKnight's stories and novels are eclectic in their subject matter; he attempts to write characters from many different groups, backgrounds, and perspectives, with a special ear for their speech patterns and idiosyncrasies. In the case of African Americans, McKnight actively and consciously avoids falling into common stereotypes, literary or otherwise, regarding black lives and identities. The same may be said of most of his characters, many of whom frequently find themselves forced to reconsider their prejudgments. In the ten stories in *Moustapha's Eclipse*, for example, several different types of Americans discover that the ways they expected people from other ethnic groups or cultures to behave were based in simplistic understandings of those cultures. The truth is far more complex, with identity determined less by biology than by circumstance.

Similarly, in McKnight's first novel, *I Get on the Bus* (1990), African American Evan Norris travels to Senegal to rediscover a black identity lost in pursuit of a middle-class lifestyle and subsequently finds that identity cannot be acquired or reshaped by mere travel; he must grasp the fact that African cultures are highly complicated and

nuanced. McKnight's second short-story collection, *The Kind of Light That Shines on Texas* (1991) comprises seven stories that force a reconsideration of everything from the Civil Rights Movement and Great Society programs of President Lyndon B. Johnson to crack addiction, to sexuality and art. In addition to the Drue Heinze Literature Prize, McKnight has won fellowships from the National Endowment for the Arts and the Thomas J. Watson Foundation, two *Kenyon Review* Awards for Literary Excellence (1989 and 1992), a Pushcart Prize, the PEN/Hemingway Special Citation, the O. Henry Award (1990), and a Whiting Writer's Award.

Interest in McKnight, scholarly or otherwise, has grown with each book. His work has been heavily anthologized; it may be found in Charles H. Rowell, ed., *Ancestral House: the Black Short Story in the Americas and Europe* (1995); Don Belton, ed., *Speak My Name: Black Men on Masculinity and the American Dream* (1995); and Gloria Naylor, ed., *Calling the Wind: Twentieth Century African American Short Stories* (1993). Relevant articles include: Bertram D. Ashe, "'Under the Umbrella of Black Civilization': A Conversation with Reginald McKnight," *AAR* 35, no. 3 (Fall 2001).

McMillan, Rosalyn (b. 1954, Port Huron, Michigan) Novelist Rosalyn McMillan is the younger sister of bestselling Terry McMillan and a highly popular author in her own right. Her novels' main strengths are in their depiction of male-female relationships; both *Knowing* (1994) and *One Better* (1997) plumb this territory in ways similar to other African American writers who emerged in the mid-1990s with novels about African Americans' relationships. That is to say, McMillan weaves the complexities of romantic relationships and such social problems as drug abuse, domestic violence, prostitution, and poverty into the lives of the black professionals who populate her novels. McMillan's later novels, however, foreground social ills to a greater degree, with mixed results. *Blue Collar Blues* (1998), for example, is based directly upon the twenty years McMillan spent working in a Ford Motors plant prior to her writing career. Her portrait of the conflicts between labor and management highlights class issues not only within American society in general but also within African American communities. The two principals, Thyme Tyler and Khan Davis, are a manager and blue-collar worker, respectively, in an automobile plant, which tests the limits of their friendship when labor disputes arise. *The Flip Side of Sin* (2000) is McMillan's most ambitious novel. It tells the story of Isaac Coleman, a musician and journalist who attempts to reconcile with his estranged wife, Kennedy (who becomes a police officer in Isaac's absence), and teenage son after spending twelve years in prison for vehicular manslaughter. The novel generally places romantic elements deeply in the background for a complex dose of social realism that examines the inequities and inadequacies of the justice system.

McMillan, Terry (b. October 18, 1951, Port Huron, Michigan) When novelist and editor Terry McMillan's third novel, *Waiting to Exhale* (1992; see separate entry) was published, the popular response it generated inarguably changed the direction and reception of African American literature for the rest of the 1990s. *Waiting to Exhale* touched a demographic segment of the American populace—primarily middle-class, professional women of varied ethnic and "racial" backgrounds—that found their experiences and thoughts about modern relationships reflected in McMillan's characters. The novel became a publishing sensation, selling over 2.5 million copies and enlivening the black

reading audience. These developments moved major publishers—many of whom previously considered African Americans to be nonreaders at worst and a generally moribund market at best—actively to seek out and publish the manuscripts of black writers, especially those of the Sister or "Girlfriend" Novel subgenre (see separate entry), at an unprecedented rate. Although McMillan herself exploited this trend to some extent with the largely autobiographical *How Stella Got Her Groove Back* (1996), each of her novels is distinct in both style and substance. McMillan also played a crucial role in opening the public to the new wave of African American fiction with the publication of her anthology, *Breaking Ice: An Anthology of Contemporary African American Fiction* (1990), featuring most of the major and minor talents of the 1980s and 1990s.

Although not quite the sensation that *Waiting to Exhale* would become, McMillan's *Mama* (1987) was a bestseller even before its initial publication due to the author's aggressive marketing and promotional skills. Protagonist Mildred Peacock's story is held together by this mother's attempts to keep her relationships with her immediate and larger family intact, but it is also a retrospective on the Civil Rights and Black Power eras, as well as upon African Americans' quests for cultural identities in the wake of those movements. Mildred's struggle is to transcend the roles with which a patriarchal society would circumscribe her, especially after so many individuals and groups had sought to liberate women like her.

Disappearing Acts (1989) is a romance between protagonists Zora Banks and Franklin Swift set in an urban environment. It is an inspired revision of Zora Neale Hurston's *Their Eyes Were Watching God* (1937) to the extent that it tries to expand the vocabulary of love for African Americans in contemporary society by using the voices and perspectives of the principals as sympathetically as possible. *Disappearing Acts* helps illustrate McMillan's skill with everyday vernacular language, although it is quite explicit. *Waiting to Exhale* takes this explicitness even further, as the four principals, all professional, middle-class black women with failed or broken relationships with husbands and other male partners, discuss frankly the heartache they have encountered. *How Stella Got Her Groove Back* tells, in a controversial stream-of-consciousness style, of forty-two-year-old protagonist Stella's journey to Jamaica, where she finds herself revitalized by a relationship with a man twenty years her junior. In addition to offering hope to women working through heartache, the novel questions societal double standards regarding age in relationships.

Beyond book reviews, scholarship on McMillan has been relatively limited and restricted to journal articles and book chapters. What presently exists, however, is generally sympathetic to McMillan's projects: E. Shelley Reid, "Beyond Morrison and Walker: Looking Good and Looking Forward in Contemporary Black Women's Stories," *AAR* 34, no. 2 (Summer 2000); Rita B. Dandridge, "Debunking the Motherhood Myth in Terry McMillan's *Mama*," *CLA Journal* 41, no. 4 (June 1998); Janet Mason Ellerby, "Deposing the Man of the House: Terry McMillan Rewrites the Family," *MELUS* 22, no. 2 (Summer 1997).

McPherson, James Alan (b. 1943, Savannah, Georgia) Short-story writer and essayist James Alan McPherson made his first significant mark on the literary scene with his collection *Hue and Cry* (1969), which explores the effects of racism upon the principal characters, who frequently suffer from loneliness and alienation in a culture and nation that fails to affirm their possibilities. These themes may be found throughout the majority of the Harvard Law School gradu-

ate's stories and essays, particularly the essay "On Becoming an American Writer," published in *The Atlantic Monthly* (December 1978). That essay was published immediately after McPherson's star truly began to rise with the publication of *Elbow Room* (1977), for which he won the Pulitzer Prize in Fiction (1978). The twelve stories in *Elbow Room* quietly decry definitions of American identity that deny the centrality of African Americans to the nation's identity, and the book vigorously asserts African Americans' American-ness. Since *Elbow Room*'s publication, McPherson's literary output has been restricted to essays and editing; McPherson edited the Fall 1985 and Fall 1990 fiction issues of the journal *Ploughshares*. McPherson also won a Guggenheim Fellowship in 1973–74 and was inducted in the American Academy of Arts and Sciences in 1995.

Critical scholarship on McPherson has focused greatly upon his essays, but he is frequently mentioned as a major figure in African American literature due to *Elbow Room*'s prestige and popularity. Key books include McPherson's autobiography, *Crabcakes* (1998), his book of essays, *A Region Not Home: Reflections from Exile* (2000), and Herman Beavers's *Wrestling Angels into Song: The Fictions of Ernest J. Gaines and James Alan McPherson* (1995). Key journal articles include: Herman Beavers, "I Yam What You Is and You Is What I Yam: Rhetorical Invisibility in James Alan McPherson's 'The Story of a Dead Man,'" *Callaloo* 29 (Autumn 1986); and Jon Wallace, "The Politics of Style in Three Stories by James Alan McPherson," *Modern Fiction Studies* 34, no. 1 (Spring 1988).

Morrison, Toni (b. Chloe Anthony Wofford, February 18, 1931, Lorain, Ohio) Toni Morrison's novels have been highly praised for their lyricism and tendency to reify and "evoke [African American] folklore and

[African American] mythology, as well as recodings of Black oral traditions" in order to preserve them.[1] Concomitantly, Morrison's fiction is notable for its understated subversion of totalizing African American mythologies, especially those of African American communities from the urban North to the rural Midwest or South. Rather than being a fixed ontology, identity in Morrison's novels is formed and revised by a nondeterministic process in which one cause does not necessarily lead to a specific effect. As Melvin Dixon argues, "her novels are bildungsromans of entire communities and racial idioms rather than the voice of a single individual," with a central protagonist developing only after interactions with larger communities.[2] Once those interactions have been completed, though, these texts defer the necessity to declare one narrative voice authoritative. To do so would mean Morrison's African American characters reproducing the hegemonic power of racism rather than dispersing and defying it, an outcome that would lead to the destruction of both communities and individuals, engendering what Orlando Patterson has called "social death."[3]

Morrison's first novel, *The Bluest Eye* (see separate entry) was a stunning debut that has inspired debate over the many issues it discovers in contemporary African American politics. Its depiction of Pecola Breedlove, a young African American girl driven to an insane love of blue eyes and white features after being emotionally neglected by her mother and molested by her father, raises as many questions about internal hatreds found within African American communities as it does about the system of white supremacy that engendered them.

Morrison's second novel, *Sula* (1974) is set in the small Ohio town of Medallion, where the African American population lives in a community called the Bottom. The protagonists, Sula Peace and her friend Nel Wright, come from very different classes but have bonds as deep as they are unspoken. As they grow into women, Nel and Sula's friendship becomes strained by secret shames, shared resentment, and the chasm of class that stands between their families. Nel enters into a stale, domesticated marriage, while Sula travels around the country, returning to become a pariah in the Bottom for her many sexual relationships with the town's men, regardless of their marital status.

Sula epitomizes Morrison's desire to focus on women's friendships and nonsexual relationships outside of a homosexual context, and it is a perfect illustration of the womanism (see separate entry) that author Alice Walker champions. Both Sula and Nel are troubled and damaged by their respective paths, yet the novel never treats them as pathological symbols. They are fully *human* in all of their desires and actions and, true to the rest of Morrison's characters, can never be reduced to stereotypes, even as the novel tempts us to do so. Morrison does her characters justice by giving them the ability to remember and compare their past and present. From these memories come identities that constantly evolve to the novel's end.

Song of Solomon (1977; see separate entry), first brought Morrison major national attention and acclaim. It won the National Book Critics Circle Award in 1978,

1. Elliott Butler-Evans, *Race, Gender, and Desire: Narrative Strategies in the Fiction of Toni Cade Bambara, Toni Morrison, and Alice Walker* (Philadelphia: Temple University Press, 1989), 59.

2. Melvin Dixon, *Ride Out the Wilderness: Geography and Identity in Afro-American Literature* (Urbana: University of Illinois Press, 1987), 164; italics in the original.

3. Orlando Patterson, *Slavery and Social Death: A Comparative Study* (Cambridge, Mass.: Harvard University Press, 1982).

sold tremendously well, and began her long career as a favorite on college reading lists, an honor soon extended to her earlier and subsequent works. Only *Beloved* (1987) has rivaled *Song of Solomon* in terms of essays, citations, and sheer influence.

Song of Solomon is the saga of Macon "Milkman" Dead and his middle-class family, which contains and represses a number of secrets not unlike those found within Morrison's earlier works. By rediscovering the legacy of the Dead family's mythical African ancestors, Milkman eventually confronts his own membership in a staunchly patriarchal lineage, thereby learning to appreciate the cultural riches and complexity of African American history. Milkman is the third Macon Dead, but he earns his nickname after one of the family's tenants witnesses him suckling at his mother's breast when he is eight years old. That act, along with the violent relationship between Milkman and Hagar, the lover he spurned, signify the desire the novel's women have to find intimate connections to their own womanhood and humanity in a community that systematically attempts to consign them to irrelevancy. Milkman's father, the second Macon Dead, takes pains to distance himself emotionally from other African Americans, his own past, his sister Pilate, and his family, most notably his wife and daughters, who desperately seek sustaining love elsewhere. The Dead family's name thus acts as a trope for the potential death of African American communities' history and bonds unless they are nurtured through memory and celebration. Milkman leaves his Great Lakes community for Virginia in search of a rumored lost family treasure that his father and Pilate, Milkman's aunt, had hidden in their youth. Along the way, Milkman slowly picks up clues to his heritage, eventually discovering that he is descended from the same Africans found in a traditional folktale about Africans who could once fly, but lost their ability in slavery. Milkman learns greater respect for other people, especially women, and a greater sense of his connection to a larger community of African Americans.

Tar Baby (1981) centers upon fashion model Jadine "Jade" Childs's desire for an authentic African American identity after she encounters and enters into a tempestuous relationship with William "Son" Green, who possesses and taunts Jadine with the authenticity she lacks. Jadine is the niece of Ondine and Sydney Childs, who raised her fully in the ideals of white society as they worked for retired confectioner Valerian Street and his wife Margaret—both white— on the mythical Isle de Chevaliers in the Caribbean. As Son, who had fled service on a merchant ship, becomes a part of the Street household, he confronts Jadine for failing to understand and appreciate the particularly Floridian African American culture in which he is deeply immersed, while she berates him for his failure to succeed in the "white" world as represented by cosmopolitan New York City. Their arguments form the crux of the novel and open a space for Morrison to explore the stereotypes that whites, blacks, women, and men hold about one another and often apply to themselves to limit their horizons and personal growth.

Until recently, *Tar Baby* held the dubious honor as the least-studied of Morrison's novels, particularly compared to the novels that immediately preceded and followed it. Some of the reasons for this neglect may be found in contemporary reviews, which found the novel different from Morrison's previous work and therefore inferior. Critics commonly cited the prominence of dialogue and intrusive narration, complaining that these elements replaced the lyricism for which Morrison had earned so much praise and did not serve as well to move the plot and convey the novel's symbolic value. The dialogue, however, resounds with issues as complex and irresolvable as those found anywhere in Morrison's oeuvre. The difficulty of the novel's bold exploration of racial stereotypes and hypocrisy might have discouraged scholars for a while, but by the 1990s *Tar Baby* had come into its own as the object of careful study.

"Recitatif" (1983), is Morrison's only published short story, but it matches her novels in both ambition and complexity. Situated midway between the publication of two of Morrison's novels, it extends *Tar Baby*'s inquiry into the nature of stereotypes and heralds the ambiguity at the heart of *Beloved* (1987). It follows the lives of two young women, Roberta and Twyla, who meet after their respective mothers deposit them in an orphanage and grow up and apart. One is white, the other black, but the story never identifies clearly which one is which. Instead, Morrison bestows the characters and their situations with numerous cultural markers and stereotypes that whites and blacks frequently hold about each other regarding hair textures, dancing, sexuality, music, political and social issues, and so on. The story's title refers to a vocal mode in opera that conveys skeletal information of the performance's plot, leaving the details to the aria to follow. Similarly, "Recitatif" leaves out the markers that would allow readers the comfort of easily identifying Twyla or Roberta's "race," thereby undermining many of the expectations those same readers might have about each culture or even about a story by African American author Toni Morrison. It purposefully undermines the identities of all these parties to force a reconsideration of our definitions of blackness and whiteness in the American context.

Beloved (see separate entry) is arguably Morrison's masterpiece, and one of the most celebrated and widely studied contemporary novels extant, African American or otherwise. *Beloved* won the Pulitzer Prize for

fiction in 1988 and in all likelihood earned Morrison the Nobel Prize in Literature in 1993. The novel remains extremely popular, especially on college and university campuses, and has inspired dozens of journal articles, book chapters, and even entire books. Although many of these discuss the novel in conjunction with other works, quite a few are devoted to the novel alone. Director Jonathan Demme also adapted it into a motion picture in 1998, to modest critical and commercial success.

Beloved is based upon the case of Margaret Garner, a runaway slave who slew her infant daughter and attempted to kill her young sons in 1856. The novel centers upon Sethe Suggs, who, like Garner, escaped while pregnant into Ohio from brutal, humiliating enslavement on a Kentucky farm, giving birth on the way. She obtains freedom but is pursued and discovered by her former slaveholder, "Schoolteacher." Again like her model, Sethe slays her infant daughter and attempts to kill her sons, who are saved by her husband's mother, and Sethe is jailed for her offense. Sethe is eventually freed from her physical prison, only to be confined to a psychological one by the ghost of her slain daughter. This spirit haunts Sethe's house, 124 Bluestone Road, and her fragmented family. When Paul D, whom Sethe knew as a fellow slave, comes to 124 and begins an intimate relationship with Sethe, he drives the spirit away temporarily, but it soon returns as a physical familiar, Beloved. Beloved soon manipulates Sethe into devoting all of her attentions to futile attempts at making amends with her daughter. This effort slowly devours Sethe until the townsfolk help drive the spirit away.

One of the crucial controversies within and surrounding the novel centers upon whether Beloved is real or, more likely, a multivalent metaphor for several issues that may haunt African Americans collectively: the legacy of slavery, generational conflicts, the difficulty of progress, the intractability of racism, self-hatred, the silencing of African American voices, women's struggles within the larger African American community, and the struggle to create new possibilities in the face of all of these adversities. The novel may also be read as Morrison's apocalyptic fictional meditation upon the successes and failures of either postbellum black America or of the Civil Rights and Black Power eras, to the extent that each period was a turning point for African Americans, rife with ambiguity and ambivalence. Similarly, each of the novel's characters wishes to confront and overcome the horrors of the past and present yet struggles with her or his desire to nurse pain and hatred, even if it is self-destructive.

Like *Tar Baby* before it, the critical community either neglected or avoided *Jazz* (1992) as it tried to unpack its many complexities and challenges. It arguably stands as Morrison's most artistically ambitious work to date, save perhaps for "Recitatif." It is the second book in the trilogy comprising *Beloved* and *Paradise* (1997), linked to the others via its tracing of a crucial period of African American history extending from slavery through the Harlem, or "New Negro" Renaissance of the 1920s and 1930s, the novel's present. This act of tracing finds a symbol in one of the main characters, Joe Trace, who was born of a wild woman who, according to some convincing interpretations, bears a passing resemblance to the ghost of the Sethe's murdered baby in *Beloved*. The novel never makes that connection unequivocally clear, in part because the story itself is told by a narrator whose identity is equally ambiguous and who flits between the first-, second-, and third-person perspectives. Several signs in the text indicate that the narrator may very well be the *novel* itself, highlighting one of the novel's central questions: Is it possible for African Americans to agree upon a single interpretation or understanding of black experiences and identities, whether through art or other means?

Despite this unreliable narrator, the text establishes two plots: that of the novel's protagonists, Joe and Violet Trace, and that of our expectations about the possibilities surrounding African Americans' political future. In both plots, Morrison writes against the idea of African American identity and its characterization as sets of discrete, yet predictable ontological positions. Joe and Violet Trace's relationship is troubled but not destroyed by the middle-aged Joe's affair with a young woman, Dorcas, whom he later murders when he discovers her in the company of a younger man. The narrative proper begins, in fact, with an account of Violet's assault upon Dorcas's body at her funeral. This particular plot begins as simple melodrama but immediately becomes layered with histories of the main characters that twist, turn, and reach back to antebellum times until shifts and generic conventions that fall well outside those of melodrama, beginning with the characters. Joe and Violet Trace's marriage and later actions cannot comfortably be reduced to stereotypes, dismissed, or underestimated, acts far too tempting for both the narrator and perhaps the reader. Joe and Violet's migration from their original Virginia to New York is at once a romance, a tragedy, and an allegory of the progress of African American identities in their time and ours.

Morrison also published *Playing in the Dark: Whiteness and the Literary Imagination* in 1992. The book comprises a series of lectures Morrison delivered at Harvard to address what she perceived as academics' reluctance to address fully the centrality of the black presence in American culture. She calls for an "American Africanism," a method of creating black literary figures who allow readers to explore America in all of its contradictions. *Playing in the Dark* has since become an influential analysis of American fiction.

Paradise (1997) extends *Jazz's* probe into the nature of "racial" progress by positing Ruby, Oklahoma, a fictional black town founded in the aftermath of the Civil War. Like the historical all-black settlements upon which it was based, the formerly enslaved people who founded the town of Haven (later renamed Ruby for a resident who died when Haven was moved to its present location) envisioned it as a potential Eden, a paradise on Earth that would free and shelter them from the oppression and racism in the larger American society. These freedoms come with high prices: a growing intolerance for dissent and diversity and the widespread oppression of women by the town's men. In the novel's present, that intolerance has fostered a rift between Ruby's older generation, which would preserve their perception of the town's legacy, and the younger generation seeking a more progressive and militant future. Their conflict revolves around the meaning of the obscured words inscribed on the town's communal oven, the preeminent symbol of its past, present, and future. Ironically, these conflicts have transformed the former Haven into Babel, with the inhabitants unable to speak to each other in any common language besides physical and psychological violence. A convent headed by the mysterious and magical Consolata on Ruby's outskirts serves as its only haven and true communal center, although this role can never be acknowledged: the convent's occupants are women, after all, and Ruby's elder men cannot allow such a site to exist unmolested. Ultimately, the town's factions must confront their own tensions or be destroyed. As the third book in the trilogy begun by *Beloved*, *Paradise* offers a cautionary tale regarding any and all utopias: they can never last.

Love (2003) is set in the seaside resort town of Silk, Florida, where middle- and upper-class African Americans go to vacation. The resort's main hotel was once run by the late, ingenious Bill "Papa" Cosey, who had many affairs with women who visited his hotel. The various facets of Cosey's personality that these women and his family witnessed form the plot and structure. The people who knew Cosey find that they saw remarkably different facets of his character, leading them to ponder the extent to which one charismatic man had affected their lives and friendships. This leads to the novel's multivalent lesson about the imprecision, frustration, mystery, and beauty of love.

Since Morrison won the Nobel Prize in Literature in 1993, critics have scrutinized her work as never before, often with an unforgiving eye. Neither *Paradise* nor *Love* earned the initial praise that Morrison's earlier works had. Nevertheless, both sold tremendously well, and *Paradise* has begun to find acceptance in the academy, notably more quickly than *Tar Baby* did.

The student of Toni Morrison's fiction has nothing less than an embarrassment of riches at her or his fingertips. Critical studies of Morrison's fiction, ranging from journal articles to theses, dissertations, essay collections, book chapters, and monographs, have appeared steadily since *Song of Solomon* won the National Book Critics Circle Award for fiction in 1978. The number of studies, as well as the rate at which they have appeared, have been increasing at a geometric rate since *Beloved* won the Pulitzer Prize in 1988, and the awarding of the Nobel Prize in 1993 turned this stream into a flood. As of the late 1990s, an article touching upon some portion or other of Morrison's oeuvre appeared somewhere every month. As of late 2004, more than 48 monographs, 475 dissertations, 10 essay collections, and 550 journal articles focusing upon Morrison's essays, short stories, and novels have been published. Many of these discuss Morrison's writings in tandem with her contemporaries in African American or postmodern fiction, including Alice Walker, Gloria Naylor, Jamaica Kincaid, Clarence Major, Charles Johnson, Ishmael Reed, and countless others. Even more numerous are the materials that make mention of Morrison at some point in their pages but that do not devote entire chapters to her. In short, again, a Morrison aficionado will never lack resources, although some of Morrison's novels have attracted more attention than others.

Inasmuch as it earned Morrison the Pulitzer Prize and was arguably the catalyst for her being awarded the Nobel Prize, *Beloved* is easily the most popular work among Morrison's critics, followed by *Song of Solomon* and *The Bluest Eye*. This is not to say that a dearth of material exists for *Sula*, *Tar Baby*, *Jazz*, *Paradise*, and *Love*; on the contrary, each has dozens of articles and book chapters devoted to it, with *Paradise* and *Love* possessing the least only because they are Morrison's most recent novels and therefore are still making an impression on Morrison's critics. In fact, the budding Morrison scholar would generally be well advised to seek out the essay collections and surveys of Morrison's fiction devoted almost entirely to her. It is nearly impossible to develop an appreciation of Morrison's craft without placing it within historical contexts, and very few of these studies divorce her from the history surrounding either the author or her characters.

It is worth noting that Morrison has expressed her desire for students of her work to focus more on her texts than on critical studies of them.[1] Indeed, Morrison can be a highly challenging read best enjoyed by many rereadings. Her dismay notwithstanding, though, Morrison is also well served by many of her most sympathetic critics, who tend to explicate their subject well, albeit with a great deal of duplication. This is to be expected, of course: scholars of major authors almost inevitably follow the tracks of their predecessors, and Morrison scholars are not excepted from this rule.

Missy Dehn Kubitschek, *Toni Morrison: A Critical Companion* (1998), offers essential synopses of Morrison's life, literary contexts, and the thematic issues that tend to concern the majority of Morrison's critics and admirers in all of Morrison's novels to date; it is one of the best introductions to Morrison's work. In addition, Nellie Y. McKay, *Critical Essays on Toni Morrison* (1988) is exemplary but obviously outdated for those interested in Morrison's later works. More up to date is David L. Middleton, *Toni Morrison's Fiction: Contemporary Criticism* (1997), which collects solid representative essays on every novel up to *Jazz*. His earlier *Toni Morrison: An Annotated Bibliography* (1987) is out of date but still a valuable resource. Better, perhaps, is Henry Louis Gates Jr. and K. A. Appiah's. eds., *Toni Morrison: Critical Perspectives Past and Present* (1993). Gloria G. Roberson, *The World of Toni Morrison: A Guide to Characters and Places in Her Novels* (2003) is an invaluable glossary to the Morrison oeuvre.

Other helpful volumes include Carl Plasa, ed., *Toni Morrison: Beloved* (1998); Naomi R. Rand, *Silko, Morrison, and Roth: Studies in Survival* (1999); Patricia McKee, *Producing American Races: Henry James, William Faulkner, Toni Morrison* (1999); Marc C. Conner, ed., *The Aesthetics of Toni Morrison: Speaking the Unspeakable* (2000).

To date, several hundred articles on Morrison have appeared in refereed scholarly

---

1. Missy Dehn Kubitschek, *Toni Morrison: A Critical Companion* (Westport, Conn.: Greenwood Press, 1998), 10–11.

journals alone. Most articles discuss one or two of Morrison's novels; others trace a particular thematic problem through all of Morrison's fiction; still others discuss Morrison in comparison with several different authors. Some of the most prominent journal articles on Morrison in general include: Mary Paniccia Carden, "Models of Memory and Romance: The Dual Endings of Toni Morrison's *Beloved*," *Twentieth Century Literature* 45, no. 4 (Winter 1999); Michael Nowlin, "Toni Morrison's *Jazz* and the Racial Dreams of the American Writer," *American Literature* 71, no. 1 (March 1999); Kimberly Chabot Davis, "'Postmodern Blackness': Toni Morrison's *Beloved* and the End of History," *Twentieth Century Literature* 44, no. 2 (Summer 1998); Harold T. Shapiro, Robert Fagles, Nell Irvin Painter, Claudia Brodsky Lacour, Russell Banks, and Arnold Rampersand, "Nobelist Professor Toni Morrison: An Academic Celebration," *The Journal of Blacks in Higher Education* 2 (Winter 1993–1994); Timothy B. Powell, "Toni Morrison: The Struggle to Depict the Black Figure on the White Page," *BALF* 24, no. 4 (Winter 1990); Nancy Jesser, "Violence, Home, and Community in Toni Morrison's *Beloved*" *AAR* 33, no. 2 (Summer 1999); Malin Walther Pereira, "Periodizing Toni Morrison's Work from *The Bluest Eye* to *Jazz*: The Importance of *Tar Baby*," *MELUS* 22, no. 3 (Autumn 1997); Jane S. Bakerman, "Failures of Love: Female Initiation in the Novels of Toni Morrison," *American Literature* 52, no. 4 (January 1981); Carolyn M. Jones, "Traces and Cracks: Identity and Narrative in Toni Morrison's *Jazz*," *AAR* 31, no. 3 (Autumn 1997); Lynda Koolish, "Fictive Strategies and Cinematic Representations in Toni Morrison's *Beloved*: Postcolonial Theory/Postcolonial Text," *AAR* 29, no. 3 (Autumn 1995); Cecil Brown, "Interview with Toni Morrison," *The Massachusetts Review* 36 (1995).

Mowry, Jess (b. March 27, 1960, near Starkville, Mississippi) Jess Mowry is best known for his fictional portrayal of the struggles of inner-city youth, particularly in the difficult conditions that emerged in the 1980s and 1990s. His stories and novels consciously attempt to remain current with the realities of the youths he depicts and to be as true to his subjects as possible; most are based upon the lives of youths Mowry counsels in Oakland, California. Each work also shares a number of common themes: American society is almost completely indifferent to the lives of young African Americans, particularly males, in its inner cities; these same young people are forced to work so hard for survival that it is nearly impossible to see a way out of the maze of guns, drugs, and gangs; the most viable way out is the redemptive power of love and friendship.

Mowry's first book, *Rats in the Trees* (1990), is a collection of stories about Robby, a young African American boy who travels from Fresno, California, to West Oakland and is almost immediately recruited into a gang, the Animals. The gang members' exploits and confrontations with a rival gang form the crux of the plot, but they also provide a stage for many ruminations upon the world and its corruptions as Robby and the other gang members see them. Mowry's first novel, *Children of the Night* (1991) is the story of Ryo, a thirteen-year-old black youth living in West Oakland. Ryo's mother, Tracy, gives him a great deal of love and affection to help protect him from the temptations of the streets, but her efforts are compromised by the distractions of her jobs. Ryo begins working for a local drug dealer to provide funds for his mother and himself but soon finds the work horrifying. He later destroys the dealer and joins with others in the community who help show him how to think and work affirmatively towards a more stable future. Although *Children of the Night* is still in print, its distribution by the small publisher Holloway House makes it somewhat difficult to find.

Way Past Cool (1992) is again set in West Oakland and concerns the lives of street gang members. Two rival gangs, the Friends and the Crew, find themselves manipulated into a gang war by Deek, a local drug dealer vying for their turf until they discover his machinations. They then join forces to hunt down and trap Deek, leading to even greater violence. Mowry paints a portrait of bleakness for his subjects, mitigated only by the redemptive power of love and friendship, even as he refuses to dismiss their lives and lifestyles. *Way Past Cool* also attracted attention upon its publication due to Mowry's refusal to sell the lucrative film rights—and therefore creative control—at the height of the "gangsta" trend in rap music and film.

Six Out Seven (1994) has the same setting as Mowry's previous works, focusing on thirteen-year-old Mississippian émigré Corbitt Wainwright, who befriends local resident Lactameon upon his arrival in Oakland. The two boys start to investigate the origins of the conditions in which Oakland's black residents, to say nothing of other African American communities beset by the destruction of the trade in guns and drugs. It is Mowry's strongest indictment of white Americans' indifference to African Americans in the inner cities and also alleges that more powerful forces in the United States government and elsewhere fuel these plagues.

Ghost Train (1996) is juvenile fiction set in World War II Oakland. Two teens, Haitian immigrant Remi DuMont and his friend Niya discover a ghost train haunting the city's streets in the wake of a murder Remi witnesses. The novel is equally concerned with suspense as with showing how the two friends from different cultural backgrounds can learn to work together. *Babylon*

Boyz (1999) may also be considered juvenile fiction, although it covers much of the same territory as the earlier, more adult novels. It concerns three young West Oakland teens, Dante, Pook, and Wyatt, who discover a cache of pure cocaine that could be their ticket out of poverty, but they find that trying to sell the drugs is more trouble than they had anticipated.

Mosley, Walter (b. January 12, 1952, Los Angeles) Walter's Mosley is the best-selling author of numerous celebrated detective novels and science (or speculative) fiction. He is also quite prolific, with nearly twenty books to his credit as of 2004, including thirteen novels, three short-story collections, and two books of social criticism. Although he has won acclaim for most of his efforts, Mosley is best known as a mystery author. His initial series of detective novels are easily his most famous, largely due to their clever yet vulnerable and sympathetic protagonist, Ezekiel "Easy" Rawlins. Via Rawlins, Mosley created a body of detective fiction that carved out its own distinctive niche while consciously working in the tradition of African American detective established by Harlem Renaissance author Rudolph Fisher with *The Conjure-Man Dies* (1932) and continued by Chester Himes (1909–1984), whose death left a significant gap that Mosley has seamlessly filled. Himes's novels, featuring "Gravedigger" Jones and "Coffin" Ed Johnson, were at once excellent entries in the detective tradition, influential commentaries upon the state of African America, and commercially successful. Coincidentally, both authors also wrote novels set in 1940s Los Angeles, although those of Himes were not in the detective genre.

Beginning with *Devil in a Blue Dress* (1990), Mosley revived and continued to generate massive interest in African American detective fiction. *Devil* introduces "Easy" Rawlins, a southerner and veteran of World War II who establishes roots in South Central Los Angeles, only to find himself drawn against his will into investigating the disappearance of a politician's fiancée, all while dodging the harassment and threats of the Los Angeles Police Department and the city's underworld. The novel also introduces Easy's childhood friend, Raymond "Mouse" Alexander, who functions as both his foil and as a decidedly violent doppelgänger. The duo's misadventures in this and subsequent entries in the series are marked by a few notable differences from the conventional detective genre and unusual elements that have endeared him to a wide audience. First, Rawlins is obviously intelligent and street-smart but not the nearly superhuman genius frequently found in mystery novels. Second, he is a highly reluctant, if ultimately successful detective, almost invariably forced to investigate various crimes against his better judgment. Third, throughout his exploits, Rawlins frequently and unabashedly offers insight into mid-twentieth-century African Americans' lives, especially in and around Los Angeles. The latter element allows Mosley's readers to see the extent to which both the Great Migration of African Americans from the South in the early to mid-twentieth century and wartime politics affected the economic and social situation of African Americans in southern California, while also musing on definitions of race, miscegenation, and intraracial conflicts. *Devil in a Blue Dress* was also made into a popular film in 1995.

Mosley's next few novels continue Easy Rawlins's saga in chronological order, part of the author's long-term plan to document the stages of his popular hero's life. Each stage is thoroughly based in historical realities, allowing Mosley to provide simultaneously a document of the changes that transformed his native Los Angeles in the latter half of the twentieth century. Perhaps equally important, Easy Rawlins also gains and occasionally loses more of the real estate he believes can save his cherished adopted community. In *A Red Death* (1991), Easy Rawlins and Mouse find themselves investigating the congregation of a black church in 1953 Los Angeles and later being threatened with murder charges themselves. In *White Butterfly* (1992), Los Angeles detectives press the now-married father Rawlins of 1956 into investigating the murder of a white female college student turned exotic dancer, despite the fact that the police have simultaneously ignored the rapes and murders of young African American women. *Black Betty* (1994) takes place in 1961, a transitional time for black Los Angeles, as urban decay began to erode some of the community's stability, which eventually led to the Watts uprising of 1965. Rawlins is recruited to find Black Betty, an African American housekeeper with whom he'd been stricken many years earlier, providing the novel with an opportunity to explore the many class and racial divisions among Angelenos. *A Little Yellow Dog* (1996) finds Rawlins working as a high school janitor in 1963, trying to leave behind the intense adventures stemming from his close connection to the streets, a goal that the heretofore extremely violent Mouse shares, at least initially. When he is asked to care for a small dog owned by one of the school's teachers (who also becomes a short-lived paramour), Easy soon finds himself involved in local gang and drug warfare. *Gone Fishin'* (1997) is a prequel to the other books of the series, tracking the early days of Easy and Mouse's friendship in Houston, Texas, in 1939, when the hero was but nineteen years old. A seventh installment in the Rawlins series, *Bad Boy Brawly Brown* (2002), follows *A Little Yellow Dog* chronologically in 1964, when racial tensions and talk of revolution in black Los Angeles began to rise precipitously. Finally, a collection of Easy Rawlins short stories, *Six Easy Pieces: Easy Rawlins Stories* (2003) was culled from earlier reprints of the original novels in the series.

Although Easy Rawlins is inarguably Mosley's most popular character, he has also written mysteries with different protagonists, science fiction novels, and dramatic narratives that transcend categorization. *RL's Dream* (1995) falls into the latter group; it introduces Atwater "Soupspoon" Wise, an elderly, southern African American blues musician who has fallen down on his luck on Manhattan's Lower East Side. When Soupspoon is evicted from his apartment, another Southerner, Kiki Waters, a white woman suffering from years of sexual abuse, helps him get back on his feet. They initiate a complex, symbiotic friendship that allows each to confront the trauma of her or his respective past, without easy solutions or platitudes. *Always Outnumbered, Always Outgunned* (1998) is a short-story collection revolving around street philosopher Socrates Fortlow, a former convict and resident of Watts, who unpacks the complexities of personal and moral issues he encounters in his struggle to create a post-prison life. Each story poses a thorny philosophical problem that Fortlow must attempt to apply to a community and world that is being consumed by nihilistic violence. Mosley also developed selections from *Always Outnumbered, Always Outgunned* into a teleplay produced and aired in 1998. Socrates Fortlow reappears as the protagonist of *Walkin' the Dog* (2000), an equally sophisticated meditation on the frequently blurred lines between good and evil, love and hate, freedom and enslavement, and other dichotomies. Fortlow attempts to resist the torments and temptations of his past as he continues his struggle for a new life and a new view of his past and possible future.

With *Blue Light* (1999), Mosley ventured into science fiction for the first time, garnering the sort of attention, if not the praise, that is normally accorded to Octavia Butler and Samuel R. Delany. Mosley also introduced his audience to another strong mystery series with *Fearless Jones* (2001) and *Fear Itself* (2003). The former's eponymous character is the foil of the true protagonist, Paris Minton, a shrewdly intellectual African American bookstore owner in Watts.

Mumbo Jumbo (1972) Ishmael Reed's third novel is arguably his masterwork, the one with which he is most easily identifiable and which best represents his creative powers. It is a satire upon the Western world and the concomitant aesthetics that denigrate the history, culture, literature, and lives of people of color. Most pointedly, it satirizes strictures, whether well meaning or not, that white and black critics place upon African Americans' creativity. The narrative's central metaphor is Jes Grew (the name is taken from several sources, including Harriet Beecher Stowe's *Uncle Tom's Cabin* and African American folklore), a pandemic that causes those infected to begin dancing and acting creatively against their will and cultural upbringing. The disease, it is later revealed, originated in Africa, passed through New Orleans (traditionally considered the birthplace of jazz), and was carried by people of African descent to all other points in the United States.

Jes Grew has several meanings: jazz and blues music, which played essential roles in transforming American culture in the twentieth century, especially during the Harlem Renaissance, also known as the "Jazz Age"; artistic freedom; the migration of African Americans that began in the early twentieth century; vibrant multiculturalism; and polytheistic, syncretic non-Western cultures of the world. The plot centers around protagonist and "HooDoo Detective" Papa LaBas (whose name comes from a vodun, or voodoo/voudou/hoodoo *loa*, or deity), who is trying to determine, first, why Jes Grew has arisen and, second, where it is headed. LaBas later discovers that Jes Grew is seeking its "text," the completed "Book of Thoth" (written by the ancient Egyptian god Osiris), which contains the land's syncopated dance moves and therefore the people's creativity. After the book was stolen from ancient Egypt, representatives of the ancient order of the Knights Templar divided it into fourteen pieces to prevent Jes Grew from having a focal point. Once Jes Grew finds its text, the millennia-long domination of monotheism and its concomitant monoculturalism will end.

Reed aims his satirical barbs at the sacred figures and ideas of Western cultures to force the reader to question their hegemony. In the process, he satirizes Christianity, Freemasonry, American Ivy League schools (the "Wallflower Order"), and Islam, showing how each is a form of or allied with monoculturalism and imperialism. In each case, these institutions and their official histories construct romantic narratives that elide any information that contradicts them in much the same way that Western societies have cast different peoples as Others to be marginalized or destroyed for the sake of expediency and greed. They also are what contribute to an American misreading of its history that sycophantically reveres Europe as the locus of "civilization," despite that region's overwhelming debt to non-Western cultures. The result is an America that hardly resembles its official history, which places white, European Americans at the center. Reed highlights this monoculturalism by making it part of the text's iconography; the number "1" is substituted for the

word one to show how an obsession with individual desires is the organizing principle of the West and of American society. *Mumbo Jumbo* calls for a continuous redefinition of "American" culture as a multicultural nation. It also argues against the more authoritarian views within the Black Arts Movement, as Reed points out in an interview in which he alleges that "there was a nonaggression pact signed between the traditional liberal critics and the black aesthetic critics. They were brought into the publishing companies about the same time that I was, about the same time that Doubleday . . . didn't renew my contract and this was about a week after I had been nominated for two National Book Awards, and then later I learned how these black aesthetic people had gone on . . . and I wasn't the only victim."[1] *Mumbo Jumbo* therefore represents the conflict between the "black aesthetic people"—representatives of one type of monocultural thinking—and other writers through a particular exchange between poet Major Young, Woodrow Wilson Jefferson and his patron, Hinckle Von Vampton. Jefferson not only serves as Von Vampton's personal servant; he is also the "Negro Viewpoint" for Von Vampton's paper, the "Benign Monster," a position which is designed to groom Jefferson for the role of the "Talking Android," one of the weapons against Jes Grew. When Jefferson misunderstands a bit of black vernacular, Von Vampton chides him to "Get with it, Jackson, maybe it will enliven your articles a bit. You still haven't made a transition from that Marxist rhetoric to the Jazz prose we want" (100). In this particular chastisement, Reed offers a somewhat thinly veiled attack on the ideology and rhetoric of some black aestheticians, specifically Amiri Baraka, whose work commonly followed the form of jazz then began to follow "Marxist

1. Reginald Martin, "An Interview with Ishmael Reed," *The Review of Contemporary Fiction* 4, no. 2 (1984): 177.

[/Maoist] blueprints" (Martin, "Interview" 177).[1]

With the possible exception of *Flight to Canada* (1976), *Mumbo Jumbo* is Reed's most frequently studied work, with at least a dozen articles studying the novel directly or mentioning it in brief since its initial publication. Most scholarship, however, emerged in the 1990s; in the ultimate chapter of *Figures in Black: Words, Signs, and the "Racial" Self* (1987), Henry Louis Gates Jr. offers a detailed analysis of *Mumbo Jumbo* that helped revive interest in Reed's work in the academy. Some of the most significant articles include Reginald Martin, "The Free-Lance Pallbearer Confronts the Terrible Threes: Ishmael Reed and the New Black Aesthetic Critics," *MELUS* 14, no. 2 (Summer 1987); Sharon A. Jesse, "Laughter and Identity in *Mumbo Jumbo*," *MELUS* 21, no. 4 (Winter 1996); Neil Schmitz, "Neo-HooDoo: The Experimental Fiction of Ishmael Reed," *Twentieth Century Literature* 20, no. 2 (April 1974); Sami Ludwig, "Ishmael Reed's Inductive Narratology of Detection," *AAR* 32, no. 3 (Autumn 1998); and Joe Weixlmann, "African American Deconstruction of the Novel in the Work of Ishmael Reed and Clarence Major," *MELUS* 17, no. 4 (Winter 1991–1992). Bruce Dick, *The Critical Response to Ishmael Reed* (1999), also collects a number of new and previously published essays, chapters, and articles on all of Reed's work, with significant attention given to *Mumbo Jumbo*.

Murray, Albert (b. 12 May, 1916, Nokomis, Alabama) Albert Murray is perhaps equally known as a novelist and a critic, although he has been considerably more prolific in the latter occupation. From the late 1940s until the present, Murray has written extensively and published essays on a wide variety of social and political issues, particularly concerning African Americans' ultimately American identities and the wealth that jazz has contributed to American culture. Murray has repeatedly and consistently asserted that most of what Americans of all backgrounds tell themselves about "race" is a harmful myth, which has meant that Murray has frequently run afoul of prevailing critical trends. He has eschewed in himself and opposed in others artificial and arbitrary limits on artistic boundaries. Murray greatly admires the genius of such jazz artists as Louis Armstrong, Duke Ellington, and Charlie Parker as much as the literary innovations and mythological aspirations of Thomas Mann, William Faulkner, James Joyce, and other modernists. Murray takes from all of these influences metaphors and symbols indicating the power of mythologies and referentiality, but it is from jazz that he derives arguably his greatest inspiration and the rubric for his own writing, regardless of genre.

It was not until the 1970s, however, that Murray began publishing his fiction, although he began the trilogy comprising *Train Whistle Guitar* (1974), *The Spyglass Tree* (1991) and *The Seven League Boots* (1996) in the mid-1940s. In all three installments, Murray evinces his determination to incorporate the rhythms and dynamics of blues and jazz performances into fiction with his late contemporary, correspondent, and good friend Ralph Ellison. The first novel, *Train*

1. Robert Elliot Fox, *Conscientious Sorcerers: The Black Postmodernist Fiction of LeRoi Jones/Amiri Baraka, Ishmael Reed, and Samuel R. Delany*, Contributions in Afro-American and African Studies 106 (Westport, Conn.: Greenwood, 1987), describes Baraka's jazz-inspired poetry as follows: "it is not the movement of, for example, Jack Kerouac's "bop prosody," which is as breathless and unpunctuated as the road itself; rather, it is an urban prose of jerky rhythms, full of starts and stops. It emphasizes the phrase, staccato notes. . . . I would analogize . . . Jones's [typewriter] to Lester Young's saxophone" (16).

Whistle Guitar, was instantly hailed as a modern classic; it is easily also Murray's highest and best-known achievement. It begins the saga of Scooter, born and raised in the American South, on an epic quest to appreciate simultaneously the importance of the individual's identity and personal freedom, on the one hand, and the individual's necessary reliance upon communal dynamics and improvisation for survival and success, on the other. Those dynamics are themselves a metaphor derived from jazz music, in which collective improvisation and imaginative individual soloing—at least since the innovations of trumpeter and cornetist Louis Armstrong in the 1920s—are the genre's sine qua non. The novel possesses a rich lyricism as well that is meant to emulate the cadences and syncopation of jazz and the blues. For Murray, freedom may be found within these forms of music, as they allow the performer and listener to transcend their present conditions by operating outside of the strict boundaries found in more traditional musical forms. In simpler terms, Scooter must find a way of balancing both official and homespun accounts of local and national history and then reconciling both to the experiences gained via adventures in an extraordinarily complex South.

While *Train Whistle Guitar* is primarily concerned with Scooter's childhood, adolescence, and teenage years, the second and third installments of the saga, *The Spyglass Tree* (1991) and *The Seven League Boots* (1996), cover his college years and a post-matriculation career as a jazz bassist, respectively.

Murray's thoughts on political and social issues have been collected in quite a few volumes, each of which mixes memoirs, essays, and music criticism in an enticing mix. They are, moreover, helpful counterparts to the novels' frequently rich yet dense investigations of history, culture, music, and ideology. The best of these may be *The Omni-*

Americans (1970), Murray's first book, which argues against the notion that African Americans are marginalized or pathological Others, as portrayed in much of the literature written by or about them, especially in sociological texts. Murray argues instead that African Americans are indeed the exemplars of American identity. *Stomping the Blues* (1976), which focuses upon jazz aesthetics, underscores Murray's stylistic influences and concerns, while *The Blue Devils of NADA* (1996) is largely a manifesto against artistic chaos.

Scholarship on Murray's fiction is extensive, including many book chapters and journal articles that frequently compare him to other popular authors of the era. Notable books include: Murray's autobiography, *South to a Very Old Place* (1971); *Trading Twelves: The Selected Letters of Ralph Ellison and Albert Murray* (2000), edited by Murray and John F. Callahan; Roberta S. Maguire, ed., *Conversations with Albert Murray* (1997); Lynda Koolish, *African American Writers, Portraits and Visions* (2001). Journal articles include: Warren Carson, "Albert Murray: Literary Reconstruction of the Vernacular Community," *AAR* 27, no. 2 (Summer 1993); Charles H. Rowell, "'An All-Purpose, All-American Literary Intellectual': An Interview with Albert Murray," *Callaloo* 20, no. 2 (Spring 1997); Albert Murray, "Regional Particulars and Universal Statement in Southern Writing," *Callaloo* 38 (Winter 1989).

Myers, Walter Dean (a.k.a. Walter M. Myers; b. 1937, New York, New York) Novelist, poet, and editor Walter Dean Myers is best known for his prodigious catalogue of juvenile fiction and nonfiction published from the 1960s until the present. To date, he has published over sixty books, including thirty-seven works of fiction. A former affiliate of the Harlem Writers' Workshop, Myers writes about a diverse set of subjects in African

American history and culture, often setting his works within a distinct historical context. A substantial number of his fictional books, however, are set in Harlem, where Myers grew to adulthood. His works in that setting tend to focus upon the richness of life in Harlem, rather than the images of pathology that sociologists and the mass media normally apply to that community.

Myers has won virtually every major award for young people's fiction available for the following titles:

> *Somewhere in the Darkness* (1992): the *Boston Globe/Horn* Book (1992), *Booklist* Editors' Choice (1992), Newbery Honor Book (1993), ALA Best Books for Young Adults (1993), and Coretta Scott King (1993) Awards
>
> *The Righteous Revenge of Artemis Bonner* (1992): ALA Best Books for Young Adults Award (1993)
>
> *The Mouse Rap* (1990): IRA Children's Choice, (1991)
>
> *Scorpions* (1988): ALA Notable Book Citation (1988) and Newbery Honor Book (1989)
>
> *Fallen Angels* (1988): ALA Best Books for Young Adults, Coretta Scott King, and Parents' Choice Awards (all 1988)
>
> *Motown and Didi: A Love Story* (1987): Coretta Scott King Award for Fiction (1985)
>
> *The Outside Shot* (1984): Parents' Choice Award (1984)
>
> *Hoops* (1981): Edgar Allen Pie Award Runner-up (1982) and ALA Best Books for Young Adults Citation (1982)
>
> *The Legend of Tarik* (1981): ALA Best Books for Young Adults Citation (1981) and Trade Book in the Field of Social Studies, National Council for Social Studies and the Children's Book Council (1982)
>
> *The Young Landlords* (1979): ALA Notable Book and Best Books for Young Adults Citations (1979) and Coretta Scott King Award for Fiction (1980)
>
> *It Ain't All for Nothin'* (1978): ALA Notable Book and Best Books for Young Adults Citations (1978)
>
> *Fast Sam, Cool Clyde, and Stuff* (1975): ALA Notable Book (1975)
>
> *The Dancers* (1972): Child Study Association of America's Children's Book of the Year (1972)
>
> *Where Does the Day Go?* (1969): Council on Interracial Books for Children Award (1969)

Myers's other fictional works include: *Fly, Jimmy, Fly!* (1974); *Brainstorm* (1977; science fiction); *Mojo and the Russians* (1977); *Victory for Jamie* (1977); *The Black Pearl and the Ghost; or, One Mystery After Another* (1980; juvenile adventure/mystery); *The Golden Serpent* (1980; juvenile adventure/ mystery); *The Nicholas Factor* (1983); *Tales of a Dead King* (1983); *Mr. Monkey and the Gotcha Bird* (1984); *Sweet Illusions* (1986); *Crystal* (1987); *Me, Mop, and the Moondance Kid* (1988); *Mop, Moondance, and the Nagasaki Knights* (1992); *Darnell Rock Reporting* (1994); *The Glory Field* (1994); *The Dragon Takes a Wife* (1995); *Shadow of the Red Moon* (1995); *The Story of the Three Kingdoms* (1995); *How Mr. Monkey Saw the Whole World* (1996); *Slam!* (1996); *Smiffy Blue: Ace Crime Detective: The Case of the Missing Ruby and Other Stories* (1996); *Monster* (1999); *145th Street: Short Stories* (2000).

As a major author of young people's fiction, Myers has also received considerable scholarly attention. Relevant books include Myers's own *Bad Boy: A Memoir* (2001) and Rudine Sims Bishop, *Presenting Walter Dean Myers* (1991). Related articles include: Violet J. Harris, "African American Children's Literature: The First One Hundred Years," *The*

Journal of Negro Education 59, no. 4 (Autumn 1990); R. D. Lane, "'Keepin' it Real': Walter Dean Myers and the Promise of African-American Children's Literature," and Elizabeth Schafer, "'I'm Gonna Glory in Learnin': Academic Aspirations of African American Characters in Children's Literature," and Nina Mikkelsen, "Insiders, Outsiders, and the Question of Authenticity: Who Shall Write for African American Children?" in *AAR* 32, no. 1 (Spring 1998). That entire issue of *African American Review*, in fact, is devoted to young people's fiction, including Myers's work.

National Association of African American Studies The National Association of African American Studies (NAAAS) was formed as an interdisciplinary gathering and scholarly group in 1992 at Virginia State University's School of Humanities and Social Sciences by that school's dean, Dr. Lemuel E. Berry Jr. Since February 1993, it has held a five-day annual conference; most conferences have converged on Houston, Texas. The membership comprises scholars and artists from the humanities (particularly in English, modern language, and history departments), the social sciences (primarily sociology, psychology, and anthropology), physical sciences (biology), and the arts (including dance, graphic arts, and theatre). In 1995 NAAS began affiliating itself officially with the National Association of Hispanic and Latino Studies (NAHLS), National Association of Native American Studies (NANAS), and the International Association of Asian Studies (IAAS). Since 2000, NAAS has also published an annual journal, the *Journal of Intercultural Disciplines*.

Due to its interdisciplinary nature, the panels at NAAAS conferences cover an extremely diverse set of topics. The group also serves as a source of mentoring for newer or younger faculty of color, especially those who work in nontraditional disciplines or fields. Membership information may be found online at www.naaas.org.

Naylor, Gloria (b. January 25, 1950, New York City) With the publication of her first novel, *The Women of Brewster Place* (1982), Gloria Naylor quickly became one of African American literature's most respected and studied authors. Her work follows closely in the footsteps of Toni Morrison, the author whose work first inspired her to pursue seriously a literary career. Naylor was entranced with the written word from an early age, but it was not until after she had converted to and later left the Jehovah's Witness faith (1968–1975) that Naylor revisited her passion for writing. She entered Brooklyn College in 1976, earned a B.A. in English in 1981, and a M.A. in Afro-American studies at Yale in 1983, for which she wrote a master's thesis that later became her second novel, *Linden Hills*. While at Brooklyn College, Naylor read Morrison's *The Bluest Eye* (1970), which showed Naylor how an African American woman's experiences could be validated in the most eloquent terms.

Naylor has made that eloquence her own in five novels to date—*The Women of Brewster Place* (1982), *Linden Hills* (1985), *Mama Day* (1988), *Bailey's Café* (1992), and *The Men of Brewster Place* (1998)—most of which closely resemble the work of Morrison, her artistic mentor, in content and approach. Each offers a searching critique of contemporary African American cultural issues and frequently combines such genres as magical realism, urban realism, and the romantic novel, while weaving in the folk culture of various traditions within the African Diaspora, including vodun/voodoo/hoodoo and trickster tales. Naylor's work, however, is not simply derivative of Morrison; she has managed to connect all of her novels into a complex weave, sharing characters, settings, and situations to an extent matched only by Faulkner's Yoknapatawpha County. Naylor simultaneously revises some of the most significant texts from European literary traditions, including William Shakespeare's *Tempest* (*Mama Day*) and Dante Alighieri's *Inferno* (*Linden Hills*). At its best, Naylor's often lyrical prose and shifting narrative voices open her texts and characters to rich ambiguity while still arguing for the need for African American community solidarity and unity of purpose. In her less inspiring moments—most notably in her *Brewster Place* novels—Naylor is susceptible to occasional demonizations of her characters on both sides of the gender divide as she struggles to reconcile tensions between black men and women. In addition, her political messages sometimes slip from their lyrical couching and may seem rather heavy-handed.

Despite these relatively minor flaws, Naylor has enjoyed an overwhelmingly kind critical and popular reception, winning an American Book Award (1983) for *The Women of Brewster Place*, which was adapted for a television film in 1989, numerous favorable reviews and top sales for all of her subsequent novels, and Guggenheim and National Endowment for the Arts fellowships. She has also taught at George Washington University, Princeton, the University of Pennsylvania, New York University, Boston University, Brandeis, and Cornell. Several high-quality critical studies and essay collections of Naylor's work have already emerged: *The Critical Response to Gloria Naylor*, ed. Sharon Felton and Michelle C. Loris (1997); *Gloria Naylor's Early Novels*, ed. Margot Anne Kelley (1999); *Conversations with Gloria Naylor*, ed. Maxine Laron Montgomery (2004); and *Understanding Gloria Naylor*, by Margaret Earley Whitt (1999). Henry Louis Gates Jr. and Kwame Anthony Appiah have collected and edited some of the best reviews and critical essays on Naylor in *Gloria Naylor: Critical Perspectives Past and Present* (1993). Finally, Naylor has also contributed to African American scholarship through her collection *Children of the Night: The Best Short Stories by Black Writers, 1967 to the Present* (1995).

Négritude The négritude movement in literature traces its origins to in a series of conversations in 1930s Paris cafes between three writers and intellectuals: Martinican writer Aimé Césaire, Senegalese intellectual Léopold Sédar Senghor (later the first elected president of that country), and French Guianan Léon Damas. Their conversations were intended to find ways to lift the stigma of inferiority that has been cast upon the artistic and intellectual abilities of people of Africa and the African Diaspora for hundreds of years. They were inspired by the example of the Harlem Renaissance (especially the Jamaican poet Claude McKay, a major figure of that movement) to find ways to turn racist views of African peoples on their head. Instead of viewing African or African-derived customs, cultural traditions, religions, art, and literature as inferior or derivative, the progenitors of négritude argued that these forms were products of a unique experience and richly deserving of value on their own terms. Later, a more essentialist version of this argument would emerge, with Senghor in particular arguing that African peoples possessed in common a naturally superior essence. The goal of the movement as a whole, however, was to counteract deeply entrenched beliefs in

African inferiority as espoused by such philosophers as Kant and Hegel. The theories, arguments, and movements of such figures as W. E. B. Du Bois, Marcus Garvey, Martin Delany, and William Blyden were particularly helpful in négritude's development, while the writings of McKay, Richard Wright, Countee Cullen, Jean-Paul Sartre, and Frantz Fanon were extremely influential as the movement developed over the next four decades.

In African American fiction, négritude had a significant impact in the way it helped bring to light the strong connections between cultural practices developed among the African Diaspora and continuous traditions on the African continent itself. Négritude was also nationalistic at its core and therefore resonated among American Black Nationalists and Black Arts Movement writers and intellectuals interested in rediscovering and revaluing African and syncretic traditions with traceable African origins. Its influence may be seen in the work of Alice Walker, especially *The Color Purple* (1983) and *Possessing the Secret of Joy* (1992) and *By the Light of My Father's Smile* (1998); John Oliver Killens; Toni Morrison; Gloria Naylor, especially *Mama Day* (1998); Ishmael Reed, particularly *Mumbo Jumbo* (1972) and *The Last Days of Louisiana Red* (1974); John Edgar Wideman; and many others.

Negro American Literature Forum. See *African American Review.*

Negro Digest/Black World (1942–1976) *Negro Digest/Black World* was arguably the most important periodical of the Black Arts Movement, to the extent that it offered a prime venue for the Civil Rights/Black Power era's intellectuals and writers. Toward the end of its existence, it became, through its editor, Hoyt Fuller, the vehicle for the articulation of the black aesthetic. It is nei-

ther insignificant nor coincidental that *Negro Digest* became *Black World* in May 1970, near the apex of the Black Arts Movement and at the beginning of the contemporary period. Other major publications of the time, including John Henrik Clarke's *Harlem* (1969) and Addison Gayle's *Black Aesthetic* (1971), owe their geneses to *Negro Digest/Black World.* It was also a direct ancestor to the journal *Callaloo,* whose editorial direction and philosophy were highly similar and that began publication in 1976, the same year that Johnson Publications cancelled *Black World.*

Negro Digest's evolution into a conduit for African American intellectualism and creativity is fairly curious, since its original purpose served more conservative ends. It began in 1942 as African American entrepreneur John H. Johnson's first foray into periodical publishing, inspired by the absence of a publication similar to *Life* magazine or *Reader's Digest.* It was in many respects the forebear to Johnson's most famous magazines, *Ebony* and *Jet,* especially in its goal of making news by and about African Americans palatable to the black masses without losing the attention or support of the black middle class. In its initial decade-long run, it emulated the best-selling *Reader's Digest* in both title and format, except that its condensed stories kept African Americans apprised of national events that directly affected them and it was decidedly more liberal politically than its model. Its list of editors and contributors in that period included virtually all major and not a few minor African American authors, including Zora Neale Hurston, Langston Hughes, Paul Robeson, W. E. B. Du Bois, Ruth Benedict, Walter White, George Schuyler, Fannie Hurst, Arna Bontemps, Sterling Brown, Alain Locke, and many others. The magazine's quality was eventually rewarded via advertising from corporate sponsors, a circulation peak around 100,000, and the U.S.

government's willingness to ship it to black GIs overseas.[1]

After Johnson introduced *Ebony* in 1945 as a more politically mainstream version of *Negro Digest*, he turned less of his attention and support to his first magazine, and it suspended publication in 1951. Johnson revived it in 1961 largely as a response to two imperatives: the momentum of the Civil Rights movement and the relative dearth of publication outlets for young writers, to say nothing of his desire to capitalize upon the mood within his targeted middle-class black audience.[2] Johnson picked Hoyt Fuller, who had briefly worked for *Ebony* in 1954, as the journal's new editor to address these imperatives, despite the fact that Fuller was far less convinced of the integrationist Civil Rights movement's ultimate success than Johnson. Nevertheless, the new *Negro Digest* did not immediately become a bulwark of radical thought. As Fuller rapidly became comfortable with the editorial reins and his relationship with Johnson, he soon disposed of the digest format and began soliciting work from young, progressive, and increasingly nationalist black artists and critics. A typical issue contained about eight articles, a few short stories and poems, Fuller's concatenation of cultural events and information, and a short editorial.

As the Civil Rights movement began to encounter more entrenched forms of racism, such as the attempts by national politicians to undermine the struggle, more young African Americans began to lose their faith in the promise of American democracy. The violent urban uprisings of the "long, hot summers" of 1964 and 1965, along with the assassination of former Nation of Islam minister Malcolm X (el-Hajj Malik el-Shabazz) in February 1965 and the compromises of Civil Rights leaders helped radicalize this generation. This mood shift extended deeply into such young African American artists as LeRoi Jones and Don L. Lee, whose work began to reflect this new skepticism via an embracing of black nationalism in general, and black cultural nationalism in particular.

Most important, Fuller shared this new mood, leading to substantial changes in *Negro Digest*'s content and direction; black cultural nationalism inarguably dominated the journal by the latter part of the 1960s. Unlike the more explicitly radical "little magazines," including *Liberator*, *Umbra*, *Soulbook*, *Black Dialogue*, *Journal of Black Poetry*, *Kitabu Cha Jua*, and *Black Creation*, *Negro Digest* maintained an editorial stance of tolerance toward integrationist perspectives, even if many of its more nationalistic contributors tended to discredit and denounce them at every opportunity. This stance was as much a product of Hoyt Fuller's judiciousness as John S. Johnson's ultimate editorial control.[3] The result was a list of contributors comprising most major and many minor African American intellectuals of the 1960s and 1970s: Amiri Baraka (né LeRoi Jones), Arna Bontemps, Gwendolyn Brooks, Henry Dumas, Mari Evans, Ronald Fair, Julia Fields, John Hope Franklin, E. Franklin Frazier, Sam Greenlee,

---

1. James C. Hall, "On Sale at Your Favorite Newsstand: *Negro Digest/Black World* and the 1960s," in *The Black Press: New Literary and Historical Essays*, ed. Todd Vogel (New Brunswick, N.J.: Rutgers University Press, 2001), 191–93. Hall notes that the magazine's popularity came despite the fact that its original editor was Ben Burns, who was both white and a communist at a time when African American publications steered clear of editors with either of those identities. Burns, however, was not listed on *Negro Digest*'s masthead until years after the magazine was established.

2. Hall, "On Sale at Your Favorite Newsstand," 195.

3. Hall, "On Sale at Your Favorite Newsstand," 198–200.

Nathan Hare, Robert Hayden, Langston Hughes, Maulana Ron Karenga, Etheridge Knight, Don L. Lee (later Haki Madhubuti), Audre Lorde, Clarence Major, Julian Mayfield, Louise Meriwether, Dudley Randall, Leopold Senghor, Wole Soyinka, Wyatt T. Walker, and John A. Williams, among many others.[1]

By the close of the 1960s, though, *Negro Digest* no longer possessed any appreciable ties to its original purpose and looked entirely different than it did near the decade's beginning. As African Americans began rejecting the label "Negro" as a reflection of slavery and oppression, the journal's title looked increasingly antiquated and offensive, which led to the May 1970 title change. The new title was meant to reflect the common nationalistic argument that African Americans shared a history and cultural solidarity with other black people around the world, especially in sub-Saharan Africa. Fuller had concluded years earlier that the responsibility of the black artist was to raise the consciousness of black people, rather than to pursue art for art's sake, and this became the magazine's overarching vision. Like its rivals, *Negro Digest/Black World* attempted to "[break] with the West" and advocate cultural nationalism and economic separatism so that a new, independent black mythos might emerge.[2]

The magazine shared a fate similar to that of its rivals. The decreasing interest in nationalism in the 1970s led to a great deal of self-criticism in the pages of the black literary magazines, *Black World* not excluded. Amiri Baraka, for example, rejected black cultural nationalism for Marxism and consequently "faulted black nationalists, including himself in earlier years, for an indiscriminate emphasis on Africa" and for "attempting to reject everything white."[3] Similarly, Nathan Hare found the emphasis upon the symbols of west African cultures in lieu of substantive political struggle "pathological."[4] These types of contributions led Hoyt Fuller to reflect, mere months before the journal was cancelled, that the solutions to African Americans' problems that he and other radical black intellectuals had embraced in the 1960s no longer seemed as viable as they had but a few years earlier.[5] Nevertheless, no other single magazine or editor was as crucial as Fuller in developing the Black Arts Movement, inasmuch as it had the largest circulation— about 30,000 per issue—of the black literary magazines. When this support dropped off significantly by the middle of the 1970s, John Johnson suddenly cancelled the magazine, apparently deeming it increasingly irrelevant.

In the absence of finding the complete run of *Negro Digest/Black World* in a library, those interested in the history and impact of the journal would be best advised to find Abby Arthur Johnson and Ronald Maberry Johnson, *Propaganda and Aesthetics: The Literary Politics of African American Magazines in the Twentieth Century* (1979, reprinted with a new preface in 1991), which devotes an excellent, long chapter to the Black Arts Movement and concomitant black aesthetic as expressed in the little magazines. More recent, and more complete

1. Hall, "On Sale at Your Favorite Newsstand," 198–99.

2. Carolyn Gerard, quoted in Abby Arth Johnson and Ronald Maberry Johnson, *Propaganda and Aesthetics: The Literary Politics of African American Magazines in the Twentieth Century* (Amherst: University of Massachusetts Press, 1979), 165.

3. Amiri Baraka, quoted in Johnson and Johnson, *Propaganda and Aesthetics*, 195.

4. Nathan Hare, quoted in Johnson and Johnson, *Propaganda and Aesthetics*, ibid.

5. Johnson and Johnson, *Propaganda and Aesthetics*, 196.

in terms of careful examination of *Negro Digest/Black World* from its inception to its demise, is James C. Hall's chapter, "On Sale at Your Favorite Newsstand: *Negro Digest/Black World* and the 1960s," in *The Black Press: New Literary and Historical Essays*, edited by Todd Vogel (2001).

Neorealism/urban realism Realism, by definition, presents life as it is actually lived rather than an idealized portrait of our surroundings. It tends to highlight the material nature of the world as it appears at a particular moment via a narrator or protagonist who makes a more objective appraisal of her or his environment. In *The Afro-American Novel and Its Tradition*, Bernard W. Bell defines earlier (that is, pre-1970s) realistic African American novels as narratives that "used the conventional linear, closed plot and combined elements of the slave narratives, historical romance, and genteel realism … which attacked racial discrimination while embracing middle-class values." Neorealism falls under this same basic rubric, but it also takes a critical stance toward middle-class values and eschews the nihilism of some realistic texts, especially those of the existentialists. Instead, Bell writes, African American neorealists "assume that man is a social being who ought not to be separated from the social and historical context … in which he [*sic*] finds his significance and develops his potential as an individual. … . There is more hope for humanity and the world expressed in [African American] neorealism." Bell goes on to divide most African American realism into two major subcategories: critical realism, which openly criticizes the dangers of capitalism, and poetic realism, which "uses regional and racial matter in a poetic manner."[1]

Urban realism may fall into either of these subcategories, but as the name implies, it is defined by urban settings that offer critical or poetic readings of the world of the city dweller. Most texts in this subcategory have special emphases on the unique outlook of a city's or community's denizens and the pressures of their environment. In the contemporary period, African American neorealism in all its forms has generally served the purpose of offering reflections of life in African American communities in different regions or within specific cities. Contemporary realism is also distinguished from earlier forms by signs that clearly mark and foreground the narrative's location, whether rural or urban, thereby lending a strong sense of authenticity. These signs may include everything from actual street names to detailed descriptions of historical events that occurred at the time the narrative is set. The social and historical context of the narrative is therefore never far from the reader's mind, lending the narrative more immediacy.

The overwhelming majority of African American authors since 1970 either write within the realistic mode or use some of its techniques. The authors most frequently associated with neorealism, however, include: John Oliver Killens, Toni Morrison, John Edgar Wideman, Alice Walker, John A. Williams, Ann Petry, Gloria Naylor, James Baldwin, Jess Mowry, Donald Goines, Jamaica Kincaid, Toni Cade Bambara, James Alan McPherson, Bebe Moore Campbell, J. California Cooper, Edwidge Danticat, Sapphire, Walter Mosley, and Al Young.

Neo–slave narrative Scholar and critic Bernard W. Bell coined the term "neoslave narrative" to describe a particular subgenre of the novel that emerged in African Ameri-

1. Bernard W. Bell, *The Afro-American Novel and Its Tradition* (Amherst: University of Massachusetts Press), 246.

can fiction in the late 1960s in his *Afro-American Novel and Its Tradition* (1987), while Ashraf H. A. Rushdy altered Bell's term to "neo-slave narrative" and expanded Bell's definition to include a wider variety of texts. Whereas Bell defines the neoslave narrative as a novel that combines "elements of fable, legend, and slave narrative to protest racism and justify the deeds, struggles, migrations, and spirit of black people, Rushdy defines neo–slave narratives as "contemporary novels that assume the form, adopt the conventions, and take on the first-person voice of the antebellum slave narrative," often to make a number of arguments about the ways in which history and individuals' personal stories are recorded, interpreted, and frequently misunderstood.[1]

Since their emergence, neo–slave narratives have been written by some of the finest writers in the African American literary tradition. Many neo–slave narratives written after 1968 have been in part responses to the controversy surrounding William Styron's *Confessions of Nat Turner* (1967). Numerous African American writers and critics roundly condemned Styron's novel for its reading of Nat Turner's original testimony by focusing upon a questionable reconstruction of his psyche, sexual proclivities, and the marked absence of his historical wife.[2] At issue in the controversy was whether white writers and critics have the right or authority to appropriate or revise African American history and culture for their own purposes, given the ways in which both have been distorted or silenced throughout the history of the Afrian Diaspora. In addition, white critics' clear disdain for Black Power politics and African Americans' attempts to take ownership of their history caused many to dismiss the valid criticisms of Styron's novel.[3]

In contrast, neo–slave narratives are meant to imagine and approximate the views and experiences of slaves based upon a combination of authentic historical documents, oral histories, and the author's intelligence and creative powers, albeit with fairly sympathetic views of those experiences or, at the very least, with more historically accurate views and careful attention to the complexities of African American cultures. Rushdy and Bell consider the first neo–slave narratives to be Margaret Walker's *Jubilee* (1966) and John Oliver Killens's *Slaves* (1969), although an argument might be made that portions of William Melvin Kelley's *A Different Drummer* (1962) qualify. In any case, virtually all of the novels that might either be classified as neo–slave narratives or that comprise neo–slave narratives within their pages have been published since 1970. A partial listing follows in chronological order:

Ernest Gaines, *The Autobiography of Miss Jane Pittman* (1971)

Gayl Jones, *Corregidora* (1975)

Lucille Clifton, *Generations: A Memoir* (1976)

Alex Haley, *Roots* (1976)

Ishmael Reed, *Flight to Canada* (1976)

Barbara Chase-Riboud, *Sally Hemings* (1979)

David Bradley, *The Chaneysville Incident* (1981)

John Edgar Wideman, *Damballah* (1981)

Charles Johnson, *Oxherding Tale* (1982)

1. Bell, *The Afro-American Novel*, 285; Ashraf H. A. Rushdy, *Neo-Slave Narratives: Studies in the Social Logic of a Literary Form* (New York: Oxford University Press, 1999), 3.

2. Rushdy, *Neo-Slave Narratives*, 54, 61ff.

3. Rushdy, *Neo-Slave Narratives*, 61.

Sherley Anne Williams, *Dessa Rose*
(1986)

Toni Morrison, *Beloved* (1987)

Barbara Chase-Riboud, *Echo of Lions*
(1989)

Charles Johnson, *Middle Passage*
(1990)

J. California Cooper, *Family* (1991)

Toni Morrison, *Jazz* (1992)

Caryl Phillips, *Crossing the River* (1993)

J. California Cooper, *In Search of Satisfaction* (1994)

Louise Meriwether, *Fragments of the
Ark* (1994)

Barbara Chase-Riboud, *The President's
Daughter* (1994)

Fred D'Aguiar, *The Longest Memory*
(1994)

Alice Randall, *The Wind Done Gone*
(2001)

Neo-soul. *See* **new black aesthetic.**

New black aesthetic The term "new black
aesthetic," or NBA, is the invention of
author Trey Ellis as the concatenation of the
critical and social outlooks of "cultural
mulattoes": African Americans raised in
white, middle-class suburbs, frequently misunderstood by both the white and black
worlds (234). Ellis first put his definition of
the term forward in an eponymous 1989
essay and manifesto published in *Callaloo*
12, no. 1. That issue also included critical
responses from Tera Hunter and Eric Lott,
as well as Ellis's responses to his critics.

Ellis's definition of the new black aesthetic riffs equally off of Langston Hughes's
declaration of artistic independence nearly
sixty-five years earlier in "The Negro Artist
and the Racial Mountain" and the many
debates over the responsibilities of African

American artists to their community that
have dominated African American literary
criticism ever since, but especially the
debates of the 1960s and 1970s. Ellis argues
in "The New Black Aesthetic" that contemporary black artists and writers should be
free to pursue artistic projects that reflect all
of their influences, rather than trying to
accommodate a single, overarching vision of
"blackness" or black progress. To paraphrase Henry Louis Gates Jr.'s foreword to
Greg Tate's *Flyboy in the Buttermilk*, new
black aestheticians feel but resist "the temptation to romanticize black culture [and]
can parody black nationalism because [they
have] a real measure of sympathy for it." By
the same token, these artists and intellectuals have also learned much from feminism,
the gay rights movement, other liberation
struggles, and their own immersion in the
complexities of black culture either to
"apologize" for it, or to excuse the fallacies
of its past proponents.[1]

Ellis's argument in "The New Black Aesthetic" stems from the fact that one segment
of the first generation of African Americans
born during or after the modern Civil
Rights movement—the "Post-Soul" generation—has benefited from the new opportunities that the movement engendered by
learning how to move between two cultures:
the dominant, or "white," defined by rock 'n'
roll music and Caucasian cultural and literary icons; and "black," as defined by rap/hip-
hop, jazz, African American literature and
history, and so on. The healthy "cultural
mulattoes," the core of the NBA, are sufficiently "torn between two worlds to finally
go out and create [their] own" (236). The
resulting world would be the site of a cultural rapprochement not unlike the balance
that W. E. B. Du Bois sought while describ-

---

1. Henry Louis Gates Jr., foreword to *Flyboy in the Buttermilk: Essays on Contemporary America*, by Greg Tate,
(New York: Simon & Schuster, 1992), 14.

ing double-consciousness in *The Souls of Black Folk* (1903): "He would not bleach his Negro soul in a flood of white Americanism, for he knows that Negro blood has a message for the world. He simply wishes to make it possible for a man to be both a Negro and an American, without having the doors of Opportunity closed roughly in his face."[1] The difference between Du Bois's generation and Ellis's, of course, is that the latter's is formed of African Americans in an unprecedented situation, given their access to middle-class privileges, employment opportunities, and cultural cachet of which Du Bois could scarcely dream. In fact, the very goal of this rapprochement for new black aestheticians is to show how much African Americans have already given their "message to the world" or, more accurately, to the world's culture.

Ellis's definition of the new black aesthetic and its most receptive audience is not without its problems either. Ellis privileges the experiences of suburban, often middle-class blacks who attended predominantly white colleges and universities as exemplary developers and keepers of this aesthetic. Yet as Mark Anthony Neal points out, "with the intense commodification of black popular culture in the post–civil rights era and unprecedented access to it within mainstream commercial culture, young blacks were connected to mainstream commercial culture in ways that previous generations had not been," and this includes those black youths not living in white suburbia.[2] Neal also quotes Tera Hunter's response to Ellis, in which she asks, "If one has to attend an elite, predominately white university to live among black people for the first time, to

what extent is [Ellis] talking about an aesthetic that is homegrown in black culture?"[3] Ellis's definition, in other words, too glibly assumes that access to mainstream, or "white" culture, comes from a physical or class location.

Neal cites Greg Tate's essays, "Nobody Loves a Genius Child: Jean Michel Basquiat, Flyboy in the Buttermilk" and "Cult-Nats Meet Freaky-Deke" from Tate's collection *Flyboy in the Buttermilk*, as more trenchant and theoretically sophisticated facets of the new black aesthetic. Tate parses the ways in which younger African American artists simultaneously and paradoxically embrace black cultural nationalism and corporate capitalism. Put simply, most new black aestheticians want to be "black" in the sense of 1960s and 1970s black nationalism, without its sexism, homophobia, or myopia, but they also want to enjoy freely every aspect of American culture that is not self-destructive. The combined affinity for and skepticism of an earlier generation's nationalism that many of these artists held has also earned them the label "neo-soul" or "Post-Soul." The former term, incidentally is most often used to describe one style of R&B music that pays homage to 1970s soul while combining hip-hop beats and rhythms.

In literary terms, the new black aesthetic found expression most obviously in the "new black renaissance" of the 1980s and 1990s. Although most of the authors in this volume born after 1965 would qualify (as would some born earlier in the decade), the fiction authors that best represent the aesthetic are: Eric Jerome Dickey, Tananarive Due, Trey Ellis, Darius James, Darryl Pinckney, Danzy Senna, Sister Souljah, Omar

---

1. W. E. B. Du Bois, *The Souls of Black Folk* (1903; reprint, New York: Knopf, 1993), 9.

2. Mark Anthony Neal, *Soul Babies: Black Popular Culture and the Post-Soul Aesthetic* (New York: Routledge, 2002), 112.

3. Tera Hunter, "'It's a Man's Man's Man's World': Specters of the Old Renewed in Afro-American Culture and Criticism," *Callaloo* 12, no. 1 (Winter 1989): 247.

Tyree, Colson Whitehead, and Monique Wright.

"New black renaissance" The "new black renaissance" has a number of different meanings, depending upon who is employing the term. One could justifiably identify the surge of writing by African Americans, especially women, beginning in the mid-1970s as the beginnings of a new renaissance, but the wave of young artists who began publishing in the late 1980s has usurped the title, thanks to a combination of the "new black aesthetic," which Trey Ellis, Greg Tate, and others developed in the 1980s, and the revival of traditional, acoustic jazz spearheaded by an alliance of trumpeter Wynton Marsalis and cultural critic Stanley Crouch.

New breed or new fiction These are terms used to describe African American authors who either began publishing or achieved prominence in the late 1970s and early 1980s, including David Bradley, Virginia Hamilton, Charles Johnson, Clarence Major, Gloria Naylor, Alice Walker, and John Edgar Wideman. These authors were often cited as the beginning of the new black renaissance as a result of their challenging, often experimental fiction.

Nobel Prize in Literature Although it is almost universally regarded as the highest honor any author might receive for a lifetime of literary achievement, the Nobel Prize in Literature has thus far been bestowed upon only one African American author, novelist Toni Morrison, who received it in October 1993. This accolade did not come without considerable controversy. Morrison's most vocal critics, including Charles R. Johnson and Stanley Crouch,

among others, decried what they viewed as an award given more for political reasons than for literary merit. Johnson and Crouch in particular favored Ralph Ellison as the most deserving recipient.[1]

While it may be true that Morrison's Nobel Prize was awarded in part to end a rather resoundingly inexplicable absence of African Americans among the exclusive club of recipients, many of her critics conveniently ignored the fact that the Nobel Prizes in Literature have never been divorced from politics. Charles Johnson's advocacy of Ralph Ellison and *Invisible Man* as better candidates for the prize similarly ignores the fact that the prize has historically been awarded for a lifetime of achievement. Brilliant as Ellison was, at the time of Morrison's award he had still published only one novel—albeit one of the most impressive and revered in modern literary history—the only in his lifetime. Morrison, on the other hand, published six novels in the nearly twenty-five years between *The Bluest Eye*'s appearance in 1970 and the awarding of the Nobel. Each of these has become the subject of extensive scholarly scrutiny and, with the exception of *Tar Baby*, great popular acclaim.

The controversy over Morrison's award reveals, perhaps to the same extent as the controversy over Alice Walker's novel *The Color Purple* in the early 1980s, how the rise and dominance of African American women authors has led to some black male authors' resentment toward the power of the critical establishment, especially feminists within that larger group. It also reveals general antipathy toward the inroads African Americans and their literature and culture have made in mainstream America, further reflecting the ways the face of African American literature has changed along with its popular acceptance since 1970.

---

1. Courtland Milloy, "For Morrison, a Song of Sour Grapes," *Washington Post*, October 10, 1993.

Norton Anthology of African American Literature (1996) As the most heralded anthology of African American literature to be published in recent years, the *Norton Anthology of African American Literature* (1996) stands as one of the finest collections for classroom and personal use. Although hundreds of anthologies of African American literature have been published since the nineteenth century, perhaps none was so widely and eagerly anticipated as the *Norton Anthology of African American Literature*, whose general editors were Henry Louis Gates Jr. and Nellie Y. McKay. The other editors, each of whom was responsible for a major segment of the text, were selected from the most eminent scholars of African American literature in the latter part of the century. They included: William L. Andrews, Houston A. Baker Jr., Barbara T. Christian, Frances Smith Foster, Deborah E. McDowell, Robert G. O'Meally, Arnold Rampersad, Hortense Spillers, and Richard Yarborough. The *Norton Anthology* preceded into print by several months Houghton Mifflin's *Call and Response: The Riverside Anthology of the African American Literary Tradition*, for which Patricia Liggins Hill was the general editor. The anthologies inevitably competed with each other, and are, for different reasons, virtually equal in their merits. Due in large part to a decade of aggressive advance publicity, savvy marketing, and name recognition, though, the *Norton Anthology* has become the most commonly used anthology and is likely to remain so for the foreseeable future.

The *Norton Anthology*'s significance and eminence stem from its fulfillment of several critical needs in African American literary studies:

1) It was the first comprehensive and fully updated anthology since Richard Barksdale's and Keneth Kinnamon's *Black Writers of America* (1972)

2) It was published by W. W. Norton & Co., which produces many of the most popular and widely respected literary anthologies used on college campuses

3) It helped advance the project of canon building that earlier anthologies had attempted to complete

4) It was relatively affordable and, with 127 discrete writers and orators represented, as well as eighty folktales, sermons, work songs, spirituals, jazz and blues songs, toasts, and raps, it had a broader selection of artists than Barksdale and Kinnamon's, or any other previous anthology

5) Of the artists represented, fifty-one were women, far more than had ever been included in earlier collections

6) Not only were song lyrics included, but a compact disc of songs, rhymes, speeches, and poems—many read or performed by the original artists—also accompanied the anthology. For all of these reasons, the anthology sold dramatically

Clearly, the publication of *Norton Anthology of African American Literature* was a major event. It began with a proposal that Henry Louis Gates Jr. made in 1986 to M. H. Abrams, a preeminent literary critic of the United States and the general editor of the *Norton Anthology of English Literature*. Abrams and editors at Norton gave their enthusiastic support, and Gates began assembling the editorial team and resources to construct the anthology. Its editorial philosophy focused upon the thesis that African American literature had always already been part of American literature but had been excluded from mainstream recognition by the academy and the general public due to a combination of racism and paternalism. Such exclusions had the effect of silencing African American voices for much of the nation's history, effectively placing black people, their identities, and their thoughts under erasure. The anthology is also meant to benefit the unprecedented demand for African American literature courses and their teachers in black studies and English programs and departments that developed in the 1980s and 1990s in particular.

The anthology's greatest virtues are its richly detailed biographies and histories that accompany each author's entry and its extensive bibliography, timeline, and index. All of these resources make it about as close to a self-sufficient study guide for African American literature as any editor could hope to get. Each historical era, individual author, or movement has a list of related books, articles, stories, recordings, and other media sources that the interested student would find invaluable. The timeline, "African American Literature in Context," begins at 1492, when Pedro Alonzo Nino, an explorer of African descent, sailed with Christopher Columbus and ends with a list of major publications of 1996. In the intervening years, the timeline lists major events and publications that influenced or changed the direction of African American literature, culture, and history.

The essays that preface individual historical sections are, per the editors' wishes, written mostly in the singular voices of the individual editors, with due uniformity of format and objective. This has the benefit of creating a diverse, rich blend of perspectives and ideological positions, and most of these essays are both thorough and perceptive. A few, however, veer too far into the more esoteric language and theoretical analyses that might be transparent to the teacher but that are likely to be opaque to the beginning student. In addition, the volume arguably contains too little of the strongest contemporary fiction—especially examples of urban realism—opting instead to include the entirety of Toni Morrison's *Sula*. While the latter is certainly one of Morrison's finest

works, and therefore a worthy addition to the volume, one wonders how many other authors and stories could have been included. Of course, this is a problem that no anthology can realistically hope to avoid, and most of the anthology's lapses are visible mostly to the more experienced reader of African American literature. Nonetheless, a comparison of the *Norton Anthology of African American Literature* to some of the other volumes that have been published in its wake would reveal just how much more diversity may be found among the builders of an African American canon. In late 2003, the second edition of the anthology appeared, without *Sula* and with a broader representation of contemporary authors.

Nunez, Elizabeth (b. 1944, Cocorite, Trinidad) Novelist Elizabeth Nunez is one of the founders of the National Black Writers Conference, which she directed from 1986 to 2000. Nunez wrote a series of novels in the 1990s that are set in and inspired by her homeland of Trinidad. Each of these novels reflects Nunez's specific concern with the effects of colonialism on Trinidad and other Caribbean nations, particularly their black populations. Her first novel, *When Rocks Dance* (1986, republished 1992; Nunez's name is given as Elizabeth Nunez-Harrell), focuses upon Christopher Columbus's voyages to the Americas and the destruction wrought by Columbus and the conquerors and merchants that followed him. *Bruised Hibiscus* (1994) is based upon real events in the Trinidad of the 1950s, where protagonists Rosa and Zuela seek answers regarding a gruesome murder that brings to light a number of long-simmering issues of racial and gender inequality. Although Nunez was criticized for the novel's treatment of men, particularly black men, it was also roundly applauded for its discovery of the tensions within Trinidadian society along racial and gender lines. Sara Edgehill, the protagonist of *Beyond the Limbo Silence* (1998), wins a scholarship to a women's college in Wisconsin and faces several challenges simultaneously: the paternalism of the school's officials towards people of African descent; the pain of the racial and class divide between Sara and her white classmates, which is barely ameliorated by the friendship of the school's few other Caribbean students; and the impact of the Civil Rights movement's most harrowingly momentous events upon Sara's consciousness and life.

Due in no small part to her major contribution to contemporary literature by and about people from Caribbean nations, Nunez's novels should soon generate considerable scholarly interest. In the meantime, Nunez's own contributions to the scholarship on this area will suffice. She is the author of "Could Shakespeare Have Known," *The Journal of Negro Education* 45, no. 2 (Spring 1976); (as Elizabeth Nunez-Harrell) "The Paradoxes of Belonging: The White West Indian in Fiction," *Modern Fiction Studies* 31, no. 2 (Summer 1985); and she is coauthor, with Brenda M. Greene, of "The Big Nommo: The Writer as Prophet," in their edited collection *Defining Ourselves: Black Writers in the 90s* (1999).

O

Oprah Winfrey's Book Club One of the most remarkable phenomena to emerge in the wake of Terry McMillan's popular hit *Waiting to Exhale* (1992) was a marked increase in the number of African American readers, which led in turn to the establishment of local reading groups, book clubs, and literary salons devoted almost exclusively to African American literature. These gatherings could be found virtually anywhere a sizeable black population existed but particularly thrived in major cities. These clubs were so ubiquitous that popular television talk show host Oprah Winfrey, already a voracious reader, began featuring her favorite books and authors, African American and otherwise, on her show, and she produced numerous special programs in which Winfrey invited several of her viewers to dine with a featured author and discuss her or his works.

Winfrey's regular viewing audience numbered over 22 million households by 1996, when Winfrey began devoting part or all of her shows to featured books and authors on a regular basis as part of her book club. Whenever Winfrey featured a book, any book, on the program, that book's sales were guaranteed to increase exponentially after the program aired; many books with previously modest to abysmal sales became bestsellers literally overnight. Publishers soon capitalized upon this opportunity, emblazoning those titles that Winfrey had given the nod with stickers and emblems proclaiming their connection to the show. In some cases, Winfrey's show helped bring out of print titles back into print and encouraged publishers to put otherwise endangered titles through additional printings. Since Winfrey also made a point of featuring many African American authors on the show, she was therefore responsible for bringing invaluable publicity to many new and established authors. Among the latter, Toni Morrison was easily among the greatest beneficiaries; Winfrey discussed Morrison's books seriously numerous times on her daytime show, hosted two specials, and bought the rights to several of Morrison's novels. One of these acquisitions was Morrison's masterpiece, *Beloved*, which Winfrey produced as a major motion picture in 1998, giving herself a starring role as the protagonist, Sethe, in the process.

The book club was not without some controversy. Winfrey's choices for the book club were occasionally criticized for featuring titles whose quality or artistic merit was questionable, but Winfrey was criticized most often simply for wielding so much power and influence over the publishing industry via her personal tastes and sizeable built-in following. Perhaps most controversial was the aforementioned film version of *Beloved*, which performed poorly at the box office and received mixed reviews. In addition, it was not entirely clear that Winfrey's club expanded the American reading audience as a whole, despite having a positive effect upon individual titles' success and upon the reading habits of the public. Winfrey certainly helped to introduce both new and established African American authors to the American public, thereby boosting attention to others and encouraging publishers to find ways to market their books to exploit the attention. Also clear is the fact that when Winfrey announced in 2002 that she was canceling the Book Club's operations, the outcry and notice from both her fans and the general public was enormous, and a year later the book club was reinstated with great fanfare and an endorsement of John Steinbeck's *East of Eden* (1952).

P

Packer, ZZ (Zuwena; b. 1973, Chicago, Illinois) From the moment her story "Drinking Coffee Elsewhere" appeared in *The New Yorker* magazine's Debut Fiction issue in 2000, ZZ Packer generated extensive buzz in the literary world. Although this was not Packer's first published work—she had appeared in the collection *Twenty-five and Under/Fiction* (1997) and in *Seventeen* magazine, for example—the buzz grew to murmurings of a new, great talent on the scene as

she published other stories over the next couple of years in *Harper's*, *Ploughshares*, *The Best American Short Stories of 2000*, and other outlets. When Packer published her first collection, also entitled *Drinking Coffee Elsewhere* (2003), those murmurings became ecstatic shouts. The book drew almost universal acclaim, and Packer began to gather such laurels as a Jones Lectureship at Stanford University. (Packer was a Stegner Fellow at Stanford for 1999–2000.) Earlier in her career, Packer also won the Whiting Foundation Writers' Award (1999) and a Rona Jaffe Foundation Writers' Award (1997).

The stories in *Drinking Coffee Elsewhere* feature African American characters, but this is almost incidental to the stories' content. They are more concerned with the harshness and cruelty of growing up in a world in which silence and exclusion are common responses to those who fail to conform. If Packer's stories lampoon black churches, pimps, and hustlers and skewer African American communities' silence regarding sexuality and black gays and lesbians in particular, these institutions and figures are not condemned as pathological or otherwise terribly different from the rest of American society; they are simply part of humanity's baseness, no more, no less. The first story, "Brownies," is a perfect example; it centers upon the conflict between black and white members of the Girl Scouts organization, but neither side of the "racial" divide comes out clean in the end. Packer has drawn as many comparisons to such authors as Flannery O'Connor as she has to Percival Everett and James Alan McPherson. The latter two writers are African American, but their fiction defies the usual stereotypes applied to African American fiction in general.

Pate, Alexs D. (b. 1950, Philadelphia, Pennsylvania) Award-winning novelist Alexs Pate authored a number of novels in the 1990s that attracted respectable attention nationwide but especially in Minnesota, the site of his residence and the setting for several of his novels. *Losing Absalom* (1994) is a character study of protagonist Abraham Goodman, whose children are forced to confront the unsatisfying paths they have taken in life when they return home to be by their dying father's bedside. *Losing Absalom* won the First Novel Award of the American Library Association Black Caucus and the Minnesota Book Award (both 1994). *Finding Makeba* (1996) centers upon novelist Ben Crestfield and his daughter Makeba, whom he abandoned along with her mother many years earlier. When Ben encounters Makeba at a book signing for the novel that is about his failed marriage, the narrative evolves into a mixture of Ben's novel and Makeba's journal, allowing for their widely divergent accounts of their personal history to be revealed. *The Multicultiboho Sideshow* (1999) is a satire in which young writer Ichabod Word holds a policeman hostage so he can recount the elaborate story that led him to the desperate moment. Word's misadventures with a group of glib, multicultural, bohemian writers and intellectuals—hence the novel's title—provide a scathing indictment of the cynical side of multiculturalism as practiced by those who wear their ethnic identities on their sleeves.

Journal articles on Pate include: Katherine Link, "'Illuminating the Darkened Corridors': An Interview with Alexs Pate," *AAR* 36, no. 4 (Winter 2002). Pate also authored an article on African Americans who die of natural causes, "The Invisible Black Family Man," in *The Journal of Blacks in Higher Education* 4 (Summer 1994).

Perry, Phyllis Alesia (b. 1961, Atlanta, Georgia) Journalist and novelist Phyllis Alesia Perry entered the national literary scene with the publication of her first novel, *Stigmata* (1998), which was compared to the best work of Toni Morrison, Alice Walker, Octavia But-

ler, Tananarive Due, and other authors who tell the undertold stories of African American women's lives, particularly under slavery and other forms of oppression, through the lens of fantasy. These comparisons have their foundation in *Stigmata*'s plot, which concerns Lizzie DuBose, who inherits a trunk full of her late grandmother's effects, including a quilt that contains her family's complex history within its patches and intricately woven thread. Just as the other authors' essays and novels argue that women's creativity may be found in other forms than the printed page, in *Stigmata* Lizzie eventually has to create her own quilt—and therefore her own history—to understand her history and to come to terms with it. She learns about her great-great-grandmother Ayo's torment during the horrific Middle Passage between Africa and Americas and as an enslaved woman in the United States. As Lizzie discovers this history, her body manifests the physical pain that her ancestors endured. Perry won high praise for the novel's gorgeous yet disciplined language. In 2003, Perry published her second novel, *A Sunday in June*, which concerns a middle-class African American family living in Alabama in the early 1900s. As in *Stigmata*, the Mobley family includes young women, Grace, Eva, and Mary Nell, who possess mystic powers that enable their relatives to open and appreciate their African past and the turmoil of the present.

Perry is among a small handful of younger African American authors whose work attracted nearly immediate scholarly interest. To date, *Stigmata* has earned one article: Lisa A. Long, "A Relative Pain: The Rape of History in Octavia Butler's *Kindred* and Phyllis Alesia Perry's *Stigmata*," *College English* (March 2002).

Petry, Ann Lane (b. October 12, 1908, Old Saybrook, Connecticut; d. April 28, 1997, Old Saybrook, Connecticut) Novelist, poet, and short-story author Ann Petry became a major figure of twentieth-century African American literature on the basis of her classic novel of urban realism, *The Street*, which was originally published in 1946. Beyond being universally hailed by critics, *The Street* is also a best-seller, having sold well over two million copies.[1] Between the great success following *The Street*'s publication and 1969, Petry continued to write at a steady clip—she had been writing since at least the early 1930s—including the excellent *Country Place* (1947), *The Narrows* (1953), and several works of fiction for children and young adults. Save for many reprints and anthologies of her work, though, Petry wrote only a handful of fictional works, primarily for a juvenile audience: *Legends of the Saints* (1970), a collection of profiles of major religious figures, including an African American;[2] *Miss Muriel and Other Stories* (1971), is a solid collection that is accessible to both juvenile and adult audiences and comparable in quality to Petry's novels. In 1988, Petry published "The Moses Project," a short story on the effects of house arrest.

Critical scholarship on Petry is extensive, albeit focused almost exclusively on her career prior to 1970. Hilary Holladay, *Ann Petry* (1996) is the most current biography extant, while Hazel Arnett Ervin, *Ann Petry: A Bio-bibliography* (1993) offers a complete annotated bibliographic record of Petry's career, including an excellent biographical sketch. Other major articles on Petry's later work include Gladys J. Washington, "A World Made Cunningly: A Closer Look at Ann Petry's Short Fiction," in *CLA Journal* 30 (September 1986). General essays include: Calvin Herton, "The Significance of Ann Petry," in his *The Sexual Mountain and Black Women Writers: Adventures in Sex, Lit-*

erature, and Real Life (1987); Vernon E. Lattin, "Ann Petry and the American Dream," *BALF* 12, no. 2 (Summer 1978); Margaret McDowell, "*The Narrows*: A Fuller View of Ann Petry," *BALF* 14, no. 4 (Winter 1980); and Keith Clark, "A Distaff Dream Deferred? Ann Petry and the Art of Subversion," *AAR* 26, no. 3 (Autumn 1992).

Phillips, Caryl (b. 1958, St. Kitts) In the early 1980s, novelist, essayist, playwright, and poet Caryl Phillips quickly established himself as one of the most poetic and incisive chroniclers of the postcolonial legacy in the Caribbean. Phillips was born in St. Kitts but raised from infancy in England, returning many years later to his West Indian roots. Many of his five novels published between 1984 and 2000 are semiautobiographical; all reflect in some way on the problem of displacement among people of the African Diaspora, especially in the Caribbean and Great Britain. Phillips is consistently interested in investigating the way such displacement occurs over vast stretches of time divided into several sections within some novels. Some of his fictional works thus read as short-story collections, but ultimately come together thematically as unified wholes.

Phillips's first novel, *The Final Passage* (1985), is his first major fictional investigation of the journey of black Caribbeans to England in search of new opportunities in education and employment, the passage named in the title. Protagonist Leila Preston, her son, and her errant husband make the trek after her mother falls ill and needs better medical attention. The blatant racism they encounter upon arrival speaks to the legacy of British imperialism for those from Commonwealth nations, especially the Bri-

1. Hazel Arnett Ervin, "Petry, Ann," *The Concise Oxford Companion to African American Literature* (New York: Oxford University Press, 2003), 324.
2. Ibid.

tish West Indies. *A State of Independence* (1986) looks at the postcolonial subject's conundrums as he attempts to return to his newly independent nation. Bertram Francis's impressions during his sojourn and return to the West Indian island of his birth explode many of the romantic notions about independence and freedom; those states either create or perpetuate the class and political strata installed under colonial rule.

Higher Ground (1989) comprises three stories about individuals struggling to find dignity and selfhood in an alienating world. The first story is a semi-allegorical tale about an African who is spared many of the indignities of the institution by aiding the enslavers, at the cost of his humanity; the second revolves around Rudi Williams, an African American prisoner in the South who tries to maintain his humanity by drawing inspiration from the Black Power Movement; the third tells of Irina, a Jewish refugee from wartime Poland and the Holocaust nearly driven mad by her experiences. Set in the nineteenth century, *Cambridge* (1991) examines postabolition England and its Caribbean plantations. When Emily Cartwright, the daughter of a wealthy English plantation owner is sent to her father's property to inspect its status, she encounters numerous tensions along social, sexual, religious, and class lines that delineate the divide between Anglo and African cultures. Similar to *Higher Ground* in structure, *Crossing the River* (1993) comprises three interconnected stories of the different paths that African slaves brought to the United States took historically as a way of tracing slavery's extensive legacy. *The Nature of Blood* (1997) again interweaves stories about people (Jews and Africans) across time (the sixteenth century, World War II, and the postwar period) and location (Venice, Ethiopia, Israel, Germany) that are at once disparate yet tightly connected.

Phillips's fiction has won the Malcolm X Prize for Literature (1984) for *The Final Passage*; a Guggenheim Foundation Fellowship (1992); the (London) *Sunday Times* Young Writer of the Year Award (1992) for *Cambridge*; a Rockefeller Foundation Bellagio Residency (1994); the James Tait Black Memorial Prize (1994) for *Crossing the River*; a Lannan Literary Award (1994); the University of the West Indies Humanities Scholar of the Year (1999); a fellowship with the Royal Society of Literature (2000). He was also short-listed for the Booker Prize in 1993 for *Crossing the River*.

Scholarly books on Phillips include: Bénédicte Ledent, *Caryl Phillips* (2002); Darryl Pinckney, *Out There: Mavericks of Black Literature* (2002), which features a section on Phillips's work; and Phillips's own *The European Tribe* (1987), a memoir of sorts that discusses his encounters as an exile in European locales. Journal articles include: Charles P. Sarvan and Hasan Marhama, "The Fictional Works of Caryl Phillips: An Introduction," *World Literature Today* 65, no. 1 (Winter 1991); Evelyn O'Callaghan, "Historical Fiction and Fictional History: Caryl Phillips' *Cambridge*," *The Journal of Commonwealth Literature* 28, no. 2 (December 1993); Bénédicte Ledent, "'Overlapping Territories, Intertwined Histories': Cross-culturality in Caryl Phillips's *Crossing the River*," *The Journal of Commonwealth Literature* 30, no. 1 (Winter 1995); Gail Low, "'A Chorus of Common Memory': Slavery and Redemption in Caryl Phillips's *Cambridge* and *Crossing the River*," *Research in African Literatures* (Winter 1998); Horace I. Goddard, "Travel Discourse in Caryl Phillips' *The Final Passage* and *A State of Independence*," *Kola* 14, no. 2 (Autumn 2002).

Pinckney, Darryl (b. 1953, Indianapolis, Indiana) Novelist and literary critic Darryl Pinckney caused a splash with the publication of his semiautobiographical novel *High Cotton* (1992). With its unnamed narrator, picaresque form, and eloquent lyricism, *High Cotton* takes a cue from Ralph Ellison's classic *Invisible Man*, albeit with a then-unusual focus upon the African American upper middle class that grew and came into prominence during and after the Civil Rights era. In contrast to Ellison's narrator, Pinckney's grows up in suburbia in a very well-to-do family and toggles between his devout Anglophilia, nerdiness, militancy, and an overarching desire to find a viable identity as an African American. His travels to New York eventually bring him into comical encounters with everything that is noble or farcical within contemporary African American culture, resulting finally in a choice to remain true to himself rather than to any particular ideology.

Postmodernism While no single definition of postmodernism could ever suffice to describe it fully, in its broadest possible application to fiction it refers to contents, strategies, and styles of writing in which the ways that history, culture, language, identity, knowledge, and often the very idea of the written text itself are called into question within the narrative. Most of the texts now identified as postmodern were composed after World War II, when many in the West found themselves in a world under the threat of nuclear annihilation, full of wild changes in the social order (the modern Civil Rights movement; attacks upon communists and other political radicals; etc.), paranoia, and the triple threat of the rise of the suburban middle class, consumer culture, and widespread social conformity. The resultant alienation led to widespread questioning of the very same "grand narratives" of history and culture that allowed modern

society to function. In general, though, the height of postmodernism in literature was the 1960s and 1970s, when the experimental surfiction and black humor of such non–African American authors as Thomas Pynchon, Robert Coover, Kurt Vonnegut, Donald Barthelme, John Barth, William Gaddis, Ronald Sukenick, and William Gass became popular.

Linda Hutcheon's definition is also helpful. Hutcheon argues that postmodernism is "a contradictory phenomenon, one that uses and abuses, installs and then subverts, the very concepts it challenges," which means that the text often undermines itself even as it is trying to subvert specific concepts. Hutcheon posits this as an ultimately ironic relationship in which the text or author is fully conscious of the difficulty her or his text may have in creating meaning or an unequivocal argument.[1] Postmodernism, then, is a rubric in which the dominant myths of and about the past and history, in all their manifestations, are subjected to critical and often ironic scrutiny, questioned at their very bases.

In African American literature, a number of authors have been defined as postmodern due to texts that do at least one of the following: question the way mainstream or Western versions of history have been constructed and by whom; revise, update, or parody such traditional literary forms as the travel narrative, slave narrative, romance, tragedy, and so on for the purpose of expanding these forms or showing how they have limited African American forms of expression; construct experimental texts that dispense with many literary conventions, including linear plots, rules about the mechanical arrangement of text and other media, and the obligation of the author to help the reader construct meaning. Some

1. Linda Hutcheon, *A Poetics of Postmodernism: History, Theory, Fiction* (New York: Routledge, 1988), 3–4.

authors, such as Ishmael Reed, reject the label of "postmodern." In Reed's case, he sees the term as too limiting, inasmuch as the sort of maneuvers postmodernism makes in revising and subverting systems are not at all unlike the critical work that traditional African American folk figures have performed for centuries.[1] By the same token, postmodernism does not differ significantly from what African American intellectuals have done by continually calling for American society to take a revised look at its myths and legends about its greatness that would include the viewpoints of peoples of color as subjects, rather than as objects of history.

Despite Reed's objections to the label of being a postmodern writer, he is one of many African American authors whose novels from the 1970s until the present provide excellent examples of theories of postmodernism at work. In fact, most of the novels of one such author, Clarence Major, are often considered key postmodernist texts. Others who have either been discussed as postmodern or might justifiably earn the label include: Toni Morrison, Gayl Jones, Leon Forrest, Paul Beatty, Darius James, Hal Bennett, Fran Ross, John Edgar Wideman, Ernest J. Gaines, William Melvin Kelley, Charles S. Wright, Ronald Fair, and Toni Cade Bambara.

Post-Soul The term "Post-Soul" was coined as a way of describing the works emerging from the generation of writers that were born during or after the Civil Rights/Black Power eras or who reached personal and artistic maturity from the late 1970s forward.

It is virtually synonymous with the new black aesthetic that author Trey Ellis outlines in his 1989 *Callaloo* essay of the same name (see the separate entry, new black aesthetic).

Post-Soul most accurately refers to the ambivalent outlook that the post–Civil Rights generation has toward its literary and political predecessors, specifically the cultural nationalism to which many black intellectuals adhered. "Soul" means, quite simply, "the essence of blackness . . . black authenticity . . . African-American culture" or "cultural truth or validity."[2] While this definition might make "Post-Soul" seem superfluous, it is meant to evoke the younger generation's desire to transcend the definitions of the older, to rise above while being posterior. It indicates doubts about whether "black authenticity" may ever be achieved or whether it may be defined clearly at all. Of course, such a position may be achieved only by simplifying "soul" itself, but this is merely a reaction to perceived oversimplifications of "cultural truth." Post-Soul writers, then, tend to look upon black cultural nationalism with an ironic, skeptical eye, never fully accepting an overarching definition of blackness. Post-Soul writers may demonstrate how "blackness" is always already complicated through binaries—biraciality, bisexuality, biculturality—or other identities, such as one's gender, region, sexuality, culture, age, or politics. All of these, presumably, may become part of "blackness," rather than compromise it.

Many writers would fit easily under this term, but some of the better examples would be Paul Beatty, Stephen Carter, Trey Ellis, Darius James, Randall Kenan, Darryl Pinck-

1. See Reginald Martin's "An Interview with Ishmael Reed," *The Review of Contemporary Fiction* 4, no. 2 (1984). In this interview Reed argues that most of the labels American critics have used to describe African American literature have been inadequate; they often rely upon Western notions that do not allow for the type of inclusion that African religions and philosophies posit.

2. Clarence Major, *From Juba to Jive: A Dictionary of African-American Slang* (New York: Penguin, 1994), 434.

ney, Sapphire, Danzy Senna, Greg Tate, Philippe Wamba, and Colson Whitehead.

Powell, Kevin (b. 1966, Jersey City, New Jersey) Journalist, writer, and editor Kevin Powell is a leading voice among the younger generation of African American writers that came into its own in the 1990s and 2000s. Although he first gained fame as one of the original cast members of MTV's "The Real World" show, Powell has racked up an extensive and impressive résumé at such magazines and newspapers as *Vibe, Ms., Rolling Stone, Essence, The Washington Post,* and many others. His work for these magazines helped bring Powell into contact with many of the authors who populate his two anthologies of writing by younger African American and African Diasporic authors: *In the Tradition: An Anthology of Young Black Writers* (1993; coedited with Ras Baraka); and *Step Into a World: A Global Anthology of the New Black Literature* (2000). The former is one of the first major collections to focus primarily on African American writers born since the mid-1960s, while the latter extends the reach of its predecessor by including writers of African descent from Africa, Britain, Canada, and the Caribbean. Although only the fourth of *Step Into a World*'s six parts is devoted solely to fiction, the entire collection is invaluable; the other sections are "Essays," "Hip-hop Journalism," "Criticism," "Poetry," and "Dialogue," with the sections of criticism and journalism arguably being the most relevant to the fiction reader. The anthology also includes short author autobiographies, which are both informative and entertaining. The selected fiction authors include Paul Beatty, Edwidge Danticat, Tananarive Due, Christopher John Farley, Jake Lamar, Ben Okri, Phyllis Alesia Perry, Patricia Powell, Danzy Senna, Zadie Smith, and Colson Whitehead.

Race Relations Institute, Fisk University The Race Relations Institute was founded in 1942 by Dr. Charles S. Johnson, a famed sociologist and the founding editor of the National Urban League's official organ, *Opportunity: A Journal of Negro Life*, where he worked from 1923 to 1928. The institute began as a series of seminars Johnson inaugurated as forums for social scientists, educators, clergy, and other leaders to discuss ways to advance racial equality and the issue of race vis-à-vis economics, employment, education, housing, and so on. Its stated mission is "to heighten awareness among all people about the divisive and insidious nature of racism."[1] Beyond the annual one-week seminars on race that carry its name, the institute also holds lectures, symposia, community forums, and workshops and connects scholars via its WILDER (World Institute for Learning, Discussing, and Evaluating Race Relationships) Internet listserv. It is also responsible for the HOLDINGS Project (Holding Our Library Documents Insures Nobility, Greatness, and Strength), the Du Bois/Nash Lecture series, and other gatherings as current events demand. Under the psychologist Dr. Raymond A. Winbush in the 1990s, the institute took a more Afrocentric turn, focusing on current pressing issues in the development and deterioration of African American communities. The RRI has consulted widely with organizations such as the U.S. Justice Department, the United Auto Workers, numerous universities and colleges, InterMedia, Inc., and the U.S. Army, the U.S. Congress, and the White House. Dr. Winbush left the institute for Morgan State's Institute for Urban Research in 2003.

1. Fisk University, "About the Race Relations Institute," http://www.fisk.edu/index.asp?cat=24&pid=203.

Reed, Ishmael (b. February 22, 1938, Chattanooga, Tennessee) Ishmael Reed's output, influence, and controversy are nearly unequaled in post-1970 African American literature. He has authored nine novels, five books of poetry, and three plays. He has also edited five anthologies, three compilations of his own essays, one retrospective of his career to date (*The Reed Reader*, 2000), and numerous compilations of his and other writers' fiction, poetry, and essays. Equally important, Reed has been instrumental in starting or furthering the careers of both new and established African American authors, including Al Young, Gloria Naylor, Edwidge Danticat, Toni Cade Bambara, Jill Nelson, Nelson George, Terry McMillan, Toni Morrison, and many others. All of these authors have either been published in Reed's magazines, including *The Yardbird Reader* (1972–76), *Y'Bird* (1977), *Quilt* (1981), *Konch* (1991–present), or have been the recipients of the American Book Award, which is bestowed by the Before Columbus Foundation, an organization devoted to promoting the art of American multicultural writers that Reed cofounded in 1976. Moreover, Reed has been a consistent advocate for a number of African American authors whose work has not gained as much notice as it might deserve, including Cecil Brown, John A. Williams, and John Oliver Killens; he also publishes *Vines* magazine (1999–present), which serves as an outlet for college students' publications. It would be fair, therefore, to argue that Reed has been as important in shaping contemporary African American literature as Toni Morrison, in her capacity as an editor at Random House, despite the controversy Reed has garnered over the years.

Much of this controversy stems from several key factors that touch upon the whole of the contemporary period. First, Reed is nothing if not an iconoclast, a description that guarantees that he will, and does, offend many. Second, Reed's ideological positions on various issues are often shifting and difficult to determine. He has been quite consistent, however, in defending the culture, literature, and lives of the African Diaspora from monoculturalists' assaults. In the 1980s and 1990s especially, Reed has defended black male figures as different as Clarence Thomas, O. J. Simpson, and Rodney King from attacks that bear the imprimatur of racists and their stereotypes about black men and their sexuality, the same stereotypes that destroyed lives and careers since the beginning of chattel slavery. As Bruce Dick has put it, Reed "has received more critical attention than almost any other contemporary African American male writer" due to his "contentions and changing position as a black man in a traditionally hostile, racist environment," and these changes can befuddle anyone trying to create an overarching view of his career.[1]

Third, Reed has become notorious for his relentless criticism of contemporary feminists and has engaged in long battles with Michele Wallace, Susan Brown Miller, Alice Walker, Gloria Steinem, and many others. Reed accuses these critics and authors of being complicit, even actively interested, in destroying the images and work of African American males. Finally, Reed's primary mode of writing, if the number and content of his books are of any account, is as a satirist, which ensures that he will court controversy and outrage.

These factors notwithstanding, it would be impossible either to overestimate or to dismiss Reed's body of work, particularly his early novels. He has earned a number of awards and fellowships for his work, includ-

1. Bruce Allen Dick and Pavel Zemliansky, *The Critical Response to Ishmael Reed*, Critical Responses in Arts and Letters 31 (Westport, Conn.: Greenwood, 1999), xix.

ing a MacArthur Foundation Fellowship (1996), and was nominated in 1973 for two categories of the National Book Award, in fiction for *Mumbo Jumbo* (1972) and in poetry for *Chattanooga* (1973). *Chattanooga* was also nominated the same year for the Pulitzer Prize. His papers from 1964 to 1995 are now housed in the University of Delaware's library.

Reed has steadfastly refused to fit within prevalent notions of what an African American author should write about, both as a creative artist and cultural critic, especially when faced with criticism from the African American critical community. Reed considers the "average Afro-American" to be living "in an ideological cloud. What's happening in New York and New England is a power struggle . . . over [white] liberal patronage among Afro-American writers and intellectuals."[1] *Mumbo Jumbo* (1972; see separate entry) represents Reed's largely satirical interpretation of this power struggle as it manifested itself in both the 1960s and during the Harlem Renaissance, including the effects it has had on African American life, art, and culture. Reed sees a reproduction of the monocultural impulse ingrained in Western cultures in the black aesthetic's developments in the early 1970s that threatens to curb intellectual, cultural, and artistic freedom. Although Reed was an advocate of the black aesthetic's more inclusive approach to African American art, his novel reveals the extent to which this approach was being stifled by ideological orthodoxy. One of Reed's key arguments is that African American radicals, like other revolutionaries before and since, are just as susceptible to the temptations of the society they struggle against, primarily because they are still very much part of those societies. Complete separatism is virtually impossible, so long as the cultural and political ideologies of the oppressive society remain within the minds of the separatists.

Even if separatism is not a viable option, finding an aesthetic that allows for true artistic freedom is an excruciatingly slow and complex process. One ironic trope in *Mumbo Jumbo* concerns the practically inevitable ideological compromises that follow when African Americans in a new cultural phase try to find their place by seeking white patronage. This is a trope that touches many characters, scenes, and actions within the text. Through such characters as Abdul Sufi Hamid, Hinckle Von Vampton, Woodrow Wilson Jefferson, and Papa LaBas, Reed satirizes such time-honored ideological constructs as Black Nationalism and Western dualism as the cultural bases for racism. *Mumbo Jumbo* succeeds partially because the satirical spirit is not without some ambivalence. Though Reed satirizes the above ideologies, he also lends each at least a small degree of veracity, if only to demonstrate the ambivalence found within any culture. His objection is to the idea that any single staid, immutable ideology is capable of resolving social problems; in fact, any such ideology is doomed to fail, since it does not allow for new input.

In the place of monoculturalism, Reed substitutes his "Neo-HooDoo aesthetic," modeled upon the syncretism of vodun/voodoo. Hoodoo is one of the names for the religions people of African descent practice throughout Diaspora based upon West African religions, especially Yoruban forms. It combines the pantheons of gods and spirits—loa—of these religions with the basic structure of Roman Catholicism; it also incorporates the mysticism and magical rites of both religions. The vodun/hoodoo pantheon is generally divided into two major categories: the Rada and Petro loa. The former are generally benevolent and

1. Peter Nazareth, "An Interview with Ishmael Reed," *Iowa Review* 13, no. 2, 126.

warm; the latter are more mysterious but may range from malevolent to the benevolent. The Petro loa include a number of tricksters, most prominently Legba Attibon, sometimes called Papa Legba or Papa LaBas; all are translations of the Yoruban trickster god Esu-elegbara into the terms of African Diasporic peoples. In Zora Neale Hurston's[1] analysis of Haitian "VooDoo" mythology, Legba/LaBas is "the god of the gate" who holds "the way to all things . . . in his hands" (Hurston, *Tell My Horse* [(1938) New York: Perennial, 1990], 128). "Every service to whatever loa for whatever purpose," therefore, "must be preceded by a service to Legba" (Hurston, *Tell My Horse*, 128). Papa LaBas serves a similar purpose in *Mumbo Jumbo* as the hoodoo trickster. His goal in the novel is to help "Jes Grew"[2] find its text. Jes Grew is a new loa and pandemic disease that causes its carriers to begin dancing, singing, and generally appreciating black folk culture.

The Last Days of Louisiana Red (1974) is a fantastic novel extending many of the motifs found in *Mumbo Jumbo*, as Reed uses the protagonist Ed Yellings to indict revolutionary groups of the Black Power era for their insincerity, violent rhetoric and tactics, and occasional criminal behavior. Papa LaBas reprises his role as a hoodoo detective trying to bring the anarchic advocates of Moochism/"Louisiana Red"—Reed's euphemism for questionable ideologies and their followers—to mend their ways and return to the hoodoo aesthetic of antideterminism that Reed generally advocates. *Last Days* is also the novel that brought a substantial degree of criticism from feminists, black and white alike, for its often mean-spirited lampooning and stereotyping of the contemporary women's movement and its members.

Flight to Canada (1976) is, after *Mumbo Jumbo*, arguably Reed's greatest achievement, a mix of fantasy, science fiction, and postmodern irreverence for generic boundaries and conventions. One of the many neo–slave narratives published since 1970, *Flight to Canada* is a direct response to Harriet Beecher Stowe's historic *Uncle Tom's Cabin*, whose story, Reed demonstrates, was stolen from an African American. This act is Reed's metaphor for the ways in which African Americans have seen their voices, ideas, and achievements appropriated, co-opted, or stolen outright. The protagonist, Raven Quickskill, is a poet and former slave who seeks his own Canada, a metaphor for fleeting and ultimately unreachable freedom and justice. Over the course of the novel's plot, Reed satirizes traditional readings of American history (especially the iconic place of Abraham Lincoln), Richard Nixon, literary critics, Black Nationalism, and even the protest strategies of the same slave narratives whence Reed draws his inspiration.

Despite Reed's objections to the label of being a "postmodern" writer, his novels in the 1970s provide excellent examples of both ironic revision and theories of postmodernism at work, insofar as they revise vast swathes of history using pastiche, parody, irony, and satire. Reed would rather be called a "neo-hoodoo" artist; that is, an artist whose work syncretically draws upon the characters, cultures, and morals of the pantheons of African Diasporic religions, especially vodun, as well as "European . . . African,

---

1. Reed includes Hurston, *Voodoo Gods: An Inquiry into the Native Myths and Magic in Jamaica and Haiti* (London: Dent, 1939), in his "Partial Bibliography" for *Mumbo Jumbo*.

2. Reed takes the name of "Jes Grew" from a name James Weldon Johnson assigned to the earliest ragtime songs in his preface to *The Book of American Negro Poetry* (1922). Ishmael Reed, *Mumbo Jumbo* (1972; New York: Athaneum, 1988), 11.

Native-American [and] Afro-American" influences.[1] Via these figures, Reed's early novels challenge us to look past Western epistemologies to perceive, appreciate, and adopt the social and ethical systems of the Diaspora, thus allowing us glimpses into entirely new and richly referential views of history. Reed's novels of the 1980s and 1990s, however, differ in slight but noticeable ways in style and content from his earlier work. Reed is less concerned with inserting countless references to mythical and historical events and figures that populate *Mumbo Jumbo* and *Flight to Canada*, nor does he utilize the "neo-hoodoo Aesthetic" at the same level of consistency as his earlier novels. Reed's attacks upon numerous enemies—real or imagined—escalate in these works, fueled by criticism of ideological issues within Reed's work and confrontations he has had with various feminists and literary critics of different stripes, all of which are reflected in his critical essays, reviews, and interviews of a particular moment. While he is still clearly concerned with the problem of Western ideas dominating American intellectual and cultural discourse, Reed's later novels concentrate upon two general topics: first, the advent of neoconservatism in recent years and its effects on racial and cultural politics; second, the philosophical relativism that can result when the concept of multiculturalism is misapplied by inept academicians. These later works are products of what Reed calls the "Writin' is Fightin'" stage of his career, a phrase that comes from the title of one of Reed's essay collections, which is in turn a quotation from boxer Muhammad Ali, who realized the importance, as did countless African Americans before him, of the potential of words to become weapons. As a result of this shift, the line between Reed's polemical essays and his fiction

became more blurred with each subsequent novel. Lengthy, biting diatribes against racists on the Left and Right, radical feminists, and monoculturalists could be found in Reed's novels and essays of this period. Set in the 1980s, *The Terrible Twos* (1982) and its sequel *The Terrible Threes* (1989) form an extended, elaborate vision of American political conservatism as a reductio ad absurdum. In the novels' contexts, the principles underlying American politics, most prominently capitalism and jingoism, are stripped of their coded manifestations and placed within characters who cynically understand what the American mainstream really wants and are relatively successful at satisfying those demands. Put simply, the American people (and, by extension, their leaders) are the equivalent of two-year-olds throwing tantrums and in need of stern—or at least satiric—discipline (*Terrible Twos*, 23–24). The metaphor of the two-year-old as representative of American political and social concerns continually resurfaces throughout the text, primarily through the presence of Dean Clift (a composite character whose name is taken from the 1950s matinee idols James Dean and Montgomery Clift, and who is based in part on Presidents Ronald Reagan and John F. Kennedy), a former actor elected to the United States vice presidency not for his political skills, which are nonexistent, but for his good looks. When his running mate, former General Walter Scott dies in office, Clift succeeds to the presidency and subsequently finds himself acting as a figurehead for the reactionary politicians who bankrolled his election campaign. They then write the platform undergirding Clift's presidency, which becomes the novel's central concern and the primary site for exploration of American racial politics. "Operation Two Birds" is a wildly elabo-

---

1. Reginald Martin, "An Interview with Ishmael Reed," *The Review of Contemporary Fiction* 4, no. 2 (1984): 186.

rate conspiracy that would consolidate power for a small, fascist elite of white men by convincing the American public that the "surps," or surplus people (read: people of color) are destroying both the country and the world.[1] *The Terrible Twos* tracks the unraveling of this plot and the efforts of numerous characters to derail it; *The Terrible Threes* is the chronicle of the plotters' attempts to hide the plot from the public, who were exposed to it at the end of the former novel. Darryl Pinckney argues that "Reed's campaign to mention everything that has gone wrong in America results in a narrative that is all over the place, as if he were trying to work in everything from crime against the environment to offenses against the homeless. Instead of suspense or satire one is confronted with an extended editorial rebuttal."[2]

Reckless Eyeballing (1986), which was published between the *Terribles* and *Japanese by Spring* (1993), is another satirical extension of Reed's discourses on American politics practiced in his essays and articles in *Writin' is Fightin'* and is easily his most controversial novel. Reed satirizes certain feminists—including, in a very thinly veiled pseudonym, Alice Walker—as cynical, manipulative women, equally as enthralled by misanthropy and racist images of black men as the men they critique are enthralled by misogyny. Upon its publication, *Reckless Eyeballing* stoked an uproar and backlash against his work that continues to the present. The novel chronicles the exploits of Ian Ball and Tremonisha Smarts, two black writers trying to court the favor of the feminists currently in vogue and in power. Their desire for fortune and fame lead them to assimila-

tion and, consequently, the evisceration of their cultural backgrounds. The most galling part of this move is that Ball and Smarts are assimilating into an artistic world that is condescending toward them at best and contemptuous at worst. Again, Reed issued similar warnings previously in *Yellow Back Radio Broke-Down* and *Mumbo Jumbo*, but here the enemy is not Black Nationalism; rather, it is the materialism of the black middle class in the post–Civil Rights era and the crass materialism of the 1980s that indirectly causes black art and culture to suffer. This is best expressed through Reed's thinly veiled caricature of Alice Walker, Tremonisha Smarts, who reveals that many of the critics who praised her play about abusive black men "took some of these characters and made them out to be all black men" and therefore used the characters as excuses "to hate all black men" (129–30).

Through its updating of the problems of academic racism and intellectual co-optation for the 1990s, *Japanese by Spring* is largely a revision of *Reckless Eyeballing*. It makes Reed's ideology increasingly explicit via the introduction of Reed himself as an eponymous character, one who actively contributes invective material to the novel's plot and discursive strategies. Reed confronts the reader with the same type of hard historical evidence that buoys his previous novels but without the subtler mediative function that his other characters have served. Moreover, the eponymic stratagem may be a sardonic attempt to make Reed's personal views entirely lucid to a critical audience that has frequently attacked his satire, especially *Reckless Eyeballing*. *Japanese By Spring* represents Ishmael Reed's concatenation of the

---

1. Jay Boyer, *Ishmael Reed* (Boise, Idaho: Boise State University Press, 1993), 36.

2. Roger Matuz et al., eds., *Contemporary Literary Criticism: Excerpts from Criticism of the Works of Today's Novelists, Poets, Playwrights, Short Story Writers, and Other Creative Writers*, 70 vols. (Detroit: Gale Research, 1990), 60:314.

intensely fierce debates over the meaning of multiculturalism in U.S. academia in the late 1980s and early 1990s, offering in novel form Reed's vision of what a productive, transcendent multiculturalism should be, as opposed to what it has become in the face of American cynicism. The novel's setting, fictional Jack London College in Oakland, California, is ultimately a synecdochal representation of American academia, in which established, nearly unquestioned racist beliefs, as well as a marked lack of moral courage and minimal intelligence, undergird some of the multicultural debates' primary players. The solution to these debates is for the public at large to realize how mainstream American culture is always already multicultural. Via his eponymous character, Reed posits a multiculturalism that is neither faddish nor materialistic, which will help restore the integrity and strength of progressive racial and cultural politics.

Scholarship on Reed is nearly as voluminous as his own fictional, poetic, and critical output, despite his periodic claims that his work has been ignored or persecuted. Reed is mentioned or discussed in virtually every major book-length work on contemporary African American fiction published (see bibliography). In addition, his work has been collected several times over. The best and most recent such collection is Reed's own *The Reed Reader* (2000), which contains an incendiary introduction that reviews Reed's career to date, excerpts from all of his novels, plays, poetry, and books of essays. *The Reed Reader*'s natural complement may be found in two recent books: *Conversations with Ishmael Reed* (1995; interviews coedited by Bruce Dick and Amritjit Singh) and *The Critical Response to Ishmael Reed* (1998; reviews and critical essays edited by Bruce Dick with the assistance of Pavel Zemliansky). Elizabeth and Thomas Settle, *Ishmael Reed: A Primary and*

Secondary Bibliography (1982), remains the most exhaustive bibliography of Reed's career published in book form, although it is clearly outdated.

Critical studies include: Robert Elliot Fox, *Conscientious Sorcerers: The Black Postmodernist Fiction of LeRoi Jones/Amiri Baraka, Ishmael Reed, and Samuel R. Delany* (1987); Reginald Martin, *Ishmael Reed and the New Black Aesthetic Critics* (1988); Santiago Juan-Navarro, *Re-contextualizing Historiographic Metafiction in the Americas: The Examples of Carlos Fuentes, Ishmael Reed, Julio Cortázar, and E. L. Doctorow* (1995); Patrick McGee, *Ishmael Reed and the Ends of Race* (1997).

Notable journal articles include: Joe Weixlmann, "African American Deconstruction of the Novel in the Work of Ishmael Reed and Clarence Major," *MELUS* 17, no. 4 (Winter 1991–1992); Sami Ludwig, "Ishmael Reed's Inductive Narratology of Detection," *AAR* 32, no. 3 (Autumn 1998); Daniel Punday, "Ishmael Reed's Rhetorical Turn: Uses of 'Signifying' in *Reckless Eyeballing*," *College English* 54, no. 4 (April 1992); Neil Schmitz, "Neo-HooDoo: The Experimental Fiction of Ishmael Reed," *Twentieth Century Literature* 20, no. 2 (April 1974); Chester J. Fontenot, "Ishmael Reed and the Politics of Aesthetics, or Shake Hands and Come Out Conjuring," *BALF* 12, no. 1 (Spring 1978); James Lindroth, "Images of Subversion: Ishmael Reed and the HooDoo Trickster," *AAR* 30, no. 2 (Summer 1996); Sharon Jessee, "Ishmael Reed's Multi-Culture: The Production of Cultural Perspective," *MELUS* 13, nos. 3–4 (Autumn-Winter 1986) and "Laughter and Identity in Ishmael Reed's *Mumbo Jumbo*," *MELUS* 21, no. 4 (Winter 1996); Carol Siri Johnson, "The Limbs of Osiris: Reed's *Mumbo Jumbo* and Hollywood's *The Mummy*," *MELUS* 17, no. 4 (Winter 1991–1992); Madge Ambler, "Ishmael Reed: Whose Radio Broke Down?" *NALF* 6, no. 4 (Winter 1972); Ann duCille,

"Phallus(ies) of Interpretation: Toward Engendering the Black Critical 'I,'" *Callaloo* 16, no. 3 (Summer 1993). Finally, *Callaloo* 17, no. 4 (Autumn 1994) contains a special section on Reed.

Rhodes, Jewell Parker (b. February 12, 1954, Pittsburgh, Pennsylvania) Novelist and short-fiction author Jewell Parker Rhodes is a professor of creative writing at Arizona State University, where she used to head its MFA program. She started publishing her work in the late 1980s; she has been included in such anthologies as Gloria Naylor's *Children of the Night: The Best Short Stories by Black Writers, 1967 to the Present* (1995) and Charles Rowell's *Ancestral House: The Black Short Story in the Americas and Europe* (1995). Her stories and novels focus upon a diverse set of topics, but all are characterized by deeply introspective and fully drawn characters Her first novel, *Voodoo Dreams* (1995), retells the life of legendary New Orleans voodoo/hoodoo practitioner Marie Laveau. *Magic City* (1998) is a fictionalized retelling of the Tulsa Riot of 1921, in which the African American community of Deep Greenwood was bombed from the air. The narrative centers upon Joe Samuels, an African American man who tries to escape from the mob attempting to lynch him after he is falsely accused of raping a white woman. He is aided by another white woman, Mary Keane, which leads to a number of tensions as each comes to terms with his or her respective identity. In the process, Rhodes gives immediacy to one of the worst and least known incidents of racial violence in U.S. history.

The masterpiece of Rhodes' career thus far is her 2002 historical novel, *Douglass' Women* [*sic*], which won the Before Columbus Foundation American Book award (2003), the PEN Oakland/Josephine Miles award (2003), and the Black Caucus of the American Library Association award for fiction (2003). It was also a finalist for the Hurston/Wright Legacy award for fiction (2002). It explores and imagines the lives and emotions of Anna Murray Douglass and Ottilie Assing, the two most significant women in the life of fugitive slave and abolitionist Frederick Douglass. Anna, a free woman of color who became Douglass's first wife once he was free, was a key player in his ultimate attempt to escape from slavery, yet she is scarcely mentioned in Douglass's three autobiographies. Assing, on the other hand, was a German heiress who joined the abolitionist movement and became one of Douglass's closest confidantes and mistress for many years, yet she similarly received little notice in Douglass's published writings. *Douglass' Women* has been roundly and justifiably praised for its sensitivity to the lives of two women who were instrumental in making Douglass into a legendary figure yet were nearly forgotten and silenced by history.

A special section of *Callaloo* 20, no. 2 (Spring 1997) was devoted to Rhodes's work, including an excerpt from *Magic City* and an interview. She was also interviewed in *AAR* 29, no. 4 (Winter 1995). Other essays and short fiction appear in: *Creative Nonfiction*, *Calyx*, *The Seattle Review*, *Feminist Studies*, *CITYAZ*, and *Hayden's Ferry Review*. Rhodes has also received a Yaddo Creative Writing Fellowship and the National Endowment of the Arts Award in Fiction, and she was selected as writer-in-residence for the National Writer's Voice Project.

Ross, Fran (Frances Dolores; b. June 25, 1935, Philadelphia, Pennsylvania; d. September 17, 1985, New York City) Novelist, screenwriter, and editor Fran Ross was almost entirely unknown until Northwestern University Press reprinted her only novel, *Oreo* (1974) in November 2000 with a new preface by

Harryette Mullen. The novel received a smattering of reviews and recognition by such talents as comedian Richard Pryor—for whom Ross wrote briefly in 1977—after its initial publication, but it went out of print shortly thereafter, and Ross disappeared into obscurity as a freelance writer until her death.

Oreo stands as one of very few satirical novels written by an African American woman. The eponymous narrator, whose (ironic) birth name is Christine Schwartz, is the child of a Jewish father and African American mother. Her nickname is derived in part from a slang term in African American communities for a black person who is "white" on the inside, like the famous cookie. The novel, however, satirizes such characterizations, as well as various aspects of African American, Jewish American, and simply American culture and literature, with the ancient Greek myth of Theseus as its template. To that end, it defies the sorts of aesthetic principles defined by the Black Arts Movement, which might help explain its obscurity.

Since *Oreo* came back into print very recently and received no scholarly notice to speak of in the interim, the scholarship is quite limited: Harryette Mullen, " 'Apple Pie with Oreo Crust': Fran Ross's Recipe for an Idiosyncratic American Novel," *MELUS* 27, no. 1 (Spring 2002); Tobe Levin, "The Challenge to Identity in Jeannette Lander and Fran Ross," in *Commonwealth and American Women's Discourse: Essays in Criticism*, ed. A. L. McLeod (New Delhi: Sterling, 1998).

S

Sapphire (b. Ramona Lofton, 1950, Fort Ord, California) Sapphire is one of the most con-troversial and startlingly innovative authors to emerge since 1970. Not unlike such predecessors as Gayl Jones, Alice Walker, and Toni Morrison, Sapphire's work and reputation have rested upon her pushing the boundaries of acceptable discourse about the secrets and secret histories within African American families.

Sapphire's first book, *American Dreams* (1994), is a largely autobiographical poetic account of the sexual abuse she suffered as a child at the hands of her father and of the later discovery of her sexuality. While the poetic narrative cannot be called a novel in the strictest sense, it bears much of the continuity and realism commonly associated with the novel form. It is, nonetheless, an extremely graphic and ultimately—purposely—disturbing indictment of the ways in which the pursuit of the American dream, or at least the *image* thereof, is horribly destructive in both psychic and physical ways. Arguably, the most distressing element within Sapphire's/the protagonist's narrative is the degree to which the mother in the family aids and abets the father's abuse for the sake of maintaining the image of middle-class respectability.

One particular passage from a later vignette in the book is worth mentioning primarily because its image of Jesus Christ performing fellatio was among many that angered conservative politicians to the point of starting a backlash against the National Endowment for the Arts, leading to that agency's struggle for survival in the 1990s and early 2000s.

Sapphire's second book, *Push* (1996), continues the same subject matter and thematics as the first but is written as a novel. Its protagonist is Claireece Precious Jones, a poor, functionally illiterate, obese, and HIV-positive young girl abused by her mother and raped by her father. Her harrowing narration of her suffering and methods used to cope with it is written in a dialect that is difficult at first but ultimately moving and utterly devastating. *Push* earned Sapphire even greater accolades, attention, and controversy, making her one of the most important writers of the late 1990s. Since *Push*, Sapphire has published *Black Wings and Blind Angels*, a book of poetry that has also received strong reviews.

Schomburg Center for Research in Black Culture Located in the heart of New York City's Harlem community, the Schomburg Center is the preeminent research center in the United States for anyone interested in the African Diaspora, especially African, African American, and Afro-Caribbean history and culture. It comprises five divisions: Art and Artifacts (paintings, sculptures, historical and archeological artifacts); General Research and Reference (holdings in African, Caribbean, and African American literature and newspapers); Manuscripts, Archives, and Rare Books; Moving Image and Recorded Sound; and Photographs and Prints. All of these divisions hold extremely impressive and invaluable materials, but the Schomburg is best known for its holdings in African American literature, manuscripts, and photographs. Arguably, the only other facility that exceeds the Schomburg's manuscript holdings is the James Weldon Johnson Collection in Yale's Beinecke Rare Book and Manuscript Library. The Schomburg Center is also part of the New York Public Library system and therefore enjoys the benefits of being partially supported by one of the best public library systems in the world.

The Schomburg Center began as the private book collection of Arthur A. Schomburg, a bank messenger, ardent bibliophile, and significant figure of the "New Negro" or Harlem Renaissance, interested in proving the worthiness and cultural wealth of the peoples of the African Diaspora. In 1926, one year after the 135th Street branch of the New York Public Library opened, the Carnegie Corporation bought Schomburg's collection and, six years later, designated him curator. After Schomburg died in 1940, the collection was renamed in his honor. It has since amassed over five million pieces classified under the five separate divisions. The collection now includes books, manuscripts, newspapers, magazines, films, photographs, paintings, drawings, sculptures, anthropological artifacts, organizational records and archives, and the personal papers of many famous figures in African American history, favoring those who lived or otherwise played crucial roles in New York, particularly black Harlem. When all of its holdings are considered together, the Schomburg stands as the single largest collection of materials documenting the achievements of the African Diaspora in the world. For scholars interested in contemporary African American fiction, the collection's holdings in original manuscripts of authors of Black Arts Movement are invaluable, as are the many scholarly books contained therein. Although the collection is open to the public, access to archival materials is restricted to scholars working on research projects.

Science/speculative fiction and fantasy The genre of science, or speculative fiction is defined broadly by narratives "that represent an imagined reality that is radically different in its nature and functioning from the world of our ordinary experience," with the setting often the Earth of the future or another world with a history or society resembling Earth's.[1] The "science" and "speculative" parts of the term refer to the possible or real inventions resulting from

---

1. M. H. Abrams, *A Glossary of Literary Terms*, 7th ed. (New York: Harcourt, Brace, 1999), 278–79.

the application of scientific inquiry, used to make fantastic elements in the genre's stories plausible. Science/speculative fiction thereby offers *speculation* on what the future or present might hold if science or history were to develop or had developed in various ways. While fantasy is closely related to science fiction, it does not always rely upon scientific plausibility, assuming instead that the uncanny elements within the narratives are plausible in their own right.[1] Each genre has a number of subgenres, including space opera (e.g., the *Star Wars* franchise, "Flash Gordon," and the like), sword-and-sorcery (*Conan the Barbarian*, *John Carter, Warlord of Mars*, Anne McCaffrey's Pern series, and so on), cyberpunk (concerned with the impact of computer technology, computer networks, and the culture they have spawned, as delineated in the novels of William Gibson and selected works of Samuel R. Delany), among many others. Ultimately, however, both science/speculative fiction and fantasy are very difficult to define precisely, as they frequently cross generic boundaries and vary widely in quality and purpose.

Historically, very few African American authors have publicly succeeded in the genre, which is dominated by white males, who also make up the majority of the audience. Since the late 1960s, however, at least two authors have established themselves as major voices in science fiction: Octavia E. Butler and Samuel R. Delany (see separate entries). Both have won the highest awards (the Hugo and the Nebula) in the field, loyal audiences, and impressive sales. Several other authors have also contributed to the field as well, albeit not as prolifically as Butler and Delany. These authors include Jewelle Gomez (see separate entry), who attracted high praise for her novel *The Gilda*

Stories (1991) and short-story collection, *Don't Explain* (1998), both of which have been read as science fiction and fantasy; Walter Mosley (see separate entry), who has also made a recent foray into the field with his novel *Blue Light* (1999); Tananarive Due, whose first novel, *The Between* (1995) relies heavily on science fiction conventions; Steven Barnes (Due's husband), who has written or cowritten (with Larry Niven) half a dozen fantasy novels since 1981; Charles R. Saunders, who wrote several fantasy novels in the Imaro series during the early to mid-1980s.

Scott, Darieck (b. August 7, 1964, Fort Knox, Kentucky) Novelist Darieck Scott is among the group of younger black authors whose fiction openly questions many of the divisions and silences within African American communities. He is also a prominent figure in contemporary black gay fiction. Scott's first novel, *Traitor to the Race* (1995), is an experimental novel about African American actor Kenneth Gabriel and his white lover, Evan, a soap opera star. Their complex relationship is filled with sexual role-playing games and broken cultural taboos (hence the title) that are linked symbolically to other events in the text, particularly the murder of Kenneth's brother Hammett. Kenneth finds himself having to deal with the intersections of "race," sexuality, class, gay politics, the AIDS epidemic, and many other issues. The novel received good reviews upon its initial publication, with a few reviewers wishing that Scott had sacrificed either some of the issues he wished to tackle or some of the text's experiments.

Scott's short stories have also been published in *Callaloo* 17, no. 4 (Fall 1994); 21, no. 1 (Winter 1998); 23, no. 1 (Winter 2000) and in the anthologies *Ancestral House: The*

1. Abrams, *Glossary*, 279.

Black Short Story in the Americas and Europe (1995) and *Giant Steps: The New Generation of African American Writers* (2000).

Senna, Danzy (b. 1970, Boston, Massachusetts) Danzy Senna may rightfully be considered among the most talented of the "neo-soul" or "Post-Soul" generation of African American authors born during or after the modern Civil Rights Movement. As is true of many of her contemporaries, she is a product of that movement and of various cultural influences, including historically "white" institutions of higher education (B.A., Stanford University; M.F.A., University of California at Irvine). She teaches at College of the Holy Cross in Worcester, Massachusetts.

The bulk of Senna's work has been a number of brilliant essays and short stories that blend the barrier between the two genres and a major debut novel, *Caucasia* (1998). Although her output has not been extremely prolific, it has been consistent in its quality and provocative nature. Senna focuses primarily upon the complexities of life for the children of biracial unions, but she never slips into the cliché of the "tragic mulatto" stereotype, except to satirize it.

This description befits her strongest short story/essay, "The Mulatto Millennium," which debuted in *Utne* magazine's September/October 1998 issue and was later collected in Claudine C. O'Hearn's acclaimed anthology, *Half and Half: Writers on Growing Up Biracial and Bicultural* (1998). Senna's story riffs on the late-1990s fad of claiming multiracial or -cultural status in the wake of multiracial golfer Tiger Wood's spectacular and unprecedented celebrity. Senna invents a number of hilarious neologisms for bicultural classifications (e.g., "Jewlato" for half-Jewish, half-black; "Gelato" for half-Italian, half-black; and so on) as she simultaneously reaffirms the fact of race as a social phenom-

enon while highlighting the absurdity of racial classifications.

Caucasia earned Senna enthusiastic accolades from numerous mainstream sources, including trade journals and the major American news magazines. *Caucasia* is a semiautobiographical narrative about Birdie Lee, the younger—and lighter-skinned—daughter of a black male intellectual and white activist descended from Eastern bluebloods. When her parents split up, Birdie travels the countryside with her mother under a Jewish pseudonym, attempting to stave off her sense of invisibility in the absence of her father's and sister's connections to African American culture. Birdie's struggle to find her racial and cultural identity is both engaging and compelling, peppered liberally with references to Ralph Ellison's *Invisible Man*, Fyodor Dostoevsky's *Notes from Underground* and *Crime and Punishment*, and James Baldwin's *Giovanni's Room*, the texts to which it owes much of its thematic content.

Since Senna's work is so new, no critical articles or books have yet emerged, save for initial book reviews, which were mostly positive. Senna's second novel, *Symptomatic*, appeared in 2004.

Shange, Ntozake (b. Paulette Williams, 1948, Trenton, New Jersey) Ntozake Shange is best known as a prolific and controversial playwright and poet. Her landmark play, the "choreopoem" *for colored girls who have considered suicide / when the rainbow was enuf* (1977) first elevated her as one of the strongest playwrights of the 1970s and 1980s. Her work is routinely discussed in the same breath as the major novels and stories of Toni Morrison, Alice Walker, Audre Lorde, and Sonia Sanchez for its complex weaving of feminist themes and African American cultural politics. Shange consistently calls for women, particularly African American women, to learn how to free themselves from their dependence upon men in order to develop fully as individuals. This applies equally to Shange's style as a poet and writer. Shange plays with spelling and punctuation conventions to create rhythm and timbre that suggest the sound and structure of everyday speech. Her novels push the boundaries of the genre, reading more like extended poems than traditional prose.

Although the quantity of Shange's output in fiction ranks well below that of her poetry and plays, it reflects her commitment to the aesthetics of poetry. Shange's first major prose work, *Sassafrass: A Novella* (1976) contains prose that resembles poetic verse in its rhythm, cadence, and physical setting on the page. The novella's eponymous and semiautobiographical heroine recounts the many obstacles she has encountered on the way to developing her artistic sensibility as a weaver. Shange later expanded *Sassafrass* into *Sassafrass, Cypress, and Indigo* (1982), in which Sassafrass joins and interacts with her sisters, who also practice arts that require improvisation and intuition: Cypress is a dancer, while Indigo is a midwife. Through a complex, blues-based dialogue, each searches for her creative muse and the expressive forms that will allow her to realize her artistic identity. In the process, each learns the difficulties of abusive personal relationships, which leads in turn to lessons about the artist's need for independence from material trappings or societal norms. The novel garnered some controversy for its portrayal of both black males and lesbian relationships, but it remains the strongest and most popular of Shange's novels. The titular protagonist of *Betsey Brown* (1985) is a young African American girl who becomes the first to attend an all-white school. Although the novel's plot is based upon school integration events of the Civil Rights era, it is concerned

more with the way Betsey's encounter with her school affects her family and her sense of personal identity. To that end, it may be considered another semiautobiographical work. *Liliane* (1994) is the story of Liliane Lincoln, a painter who struggles to express herself through her vivid, colorful art. Her story is narrated through a mix of voices and settings, including Liliane's own voice, that of her lovers, and sessions with her analyst. It also continues Shange's experiments with form, as chunks of the narration are formatted as pure dialogue, as if written for a play.

Most of the scholarship on Shange focuses upon her work as a playwright and poet rather than her fiction. Since her novels frequently evoke the format and rhythm of her dramatic works and frequently cover the same themes, at least some of the scholarship may safely be applied to Shange's novels. The only book-length study of Shange's fiction extant is Teshie Jones's master's thesis, "Uncovering African Retentions: Traditional West African Religions and Philosophy in Gloria Naylor's *Mama Day* and Ntozake Shange's *Sassafrass, Cypress, and Indigo*" (Florida State University, 1998); it is not yet available in book form. Neal A. Lester, *Ntozake Shange: A Critical Study of the Plays* (1995), focuses exclusively on Shange's drama, as do Phillip Effiong, *In Search of a Model for African-American Drama: A Study of Selected Plays by Lorraine Hansberry, Amiri Baraka, and Ntozake Shange* (2000), and Tejumola Olaniyan, *Scars of Conquest/Masks of Resistance: The Invention of Cultural Identities in African-American and Caribbean Drama* (1995). Claudia Tate's interview collection, *Black Women Writers at Work* (1983) also contains and interview with Shange about her art and the critical response to it.

Journal articles on Shange's fiction are more plentiful: Arlene Elder, "*Sassafrass, Cypress, and Indigo*: Ntozake Shange's Neo-

Slave/Blues Narrative," *AAR* 26, no. 1 (Spring 1992); Henry Blackwell, "An Interview with Ntozake Shange," *BALF* 13, no. 4 (Winter 1979); Neal A. Lester, "At the Heart of Shange's Feminism: An Interview," *BALF* 24, no. 4 (Winter 1990); Karla F. C. Holloway, "Revision and (Re)membrance: A Theory of Literary Structures in Literature by African-American Women Writers," *BALF* 24, no. 4 (Winter 1990); Charles Johnson, "Whole Sight: Notes on New Black Fiction," *Callaloo* 22 (Autumn 1986).

Signifying Monkey, The: A Theory of African-American Literary Criticism Henry Louis Gates Jr.'s seminal 1988 volume is one of a handful that transformed African American literary studies in the 1980s and 1990s. Gates became the preeminent scholar of African American literature in the United States largely upon the wide acceptance and success of this book, considered Gates's most significant contribution to African American literary theory. Although a substantial portion of the material reprises and revises Gates's first book, *Figures in Black: Words, Signs, and the "Racial" Self* (1987), a collection of papers and essays Gates had presented and published beginning in the late 1970s, *The Signifying Monkey* is mostly distinctive from its predecessor, to the extent that it expands one of Gates's central theories.

Fittingly, Gates combines the methods and approaches of structuralist and post-structuralist theories, hermeneutics, and phenomenology to argue that African American literature consists of a tradition in which each author effectively revises the work of those who went before her or him.

Gates calls this practice a form of "signifying," or troping, whereby one author acknowledges a previous author's contributions to the tradition yet simultaneously pays homage to and alters the meaning of her or his literary antecedents' phrases, ideas, or entire texts. "Signifying," in African American vernacular discursive communities, is a verbal behavior used for a number of purposes. It may describe a type of verbal jousting consisting of insults and trickery used to create a clever, often subtly devastating critique of a particular person, idea, or object. According to Roger D. Abrahams, signifying can mean several things, including "the propensity to talk around a subject, never quite coming to the point . . . ; making fun of a person or situation; . . . speaking with the hands and eyes," and so on.[1] Equally instructive is Claudia Mitchell-Kernan's suggestion that signifying is "a way of encoding messages or meanings which involves, in most cases, an element of indirection," which "might best be viewed as an alternative message form, selected for its artistic merit, and may occur embedded in a variety of discourse."[2] The fact that signifying is occurring may be deeply buried within those forms of discourse, including literary texts, to such a degree that all but the more informed reader—or at least one attuned to African American cultural traditions—may be completely unaware of it. Signifying is thus a way for an author to make use of her or his influences and models while remaining true to her or his own vision and identity as an author. It "puts one over" on the uninformed or naïve reader or critic in much the same way that peoples of the African Diaspora have been forced to

---

1. Roger D. Abrahams, *Deep Down in the Jungle: Negro Narrative Folklore from the Streets of Philadelphia* (Chicago: Aldine, 1970), 52.

2. Claudia Mitchell-Kernan, "Language Behavior in a Black Urban Community" (Ph.D. diss., University of California at Berkeley, 1971), 87.

speak with double voices over the course of their history, beginning in sub-Saharan Africa but especially in slavery and the century of legal segregation that followed it. *The Signifying Monkey*'s title itself refers to the trickster featured in African American rhyming "toasts," who signifies upon those unable to comprehend that he is indeed "putting one over."

Gates also devotes an entire chapter to one particular form of signifying, the trope of the "Talking Book," a figure found throughout the African American literary tradition. The "Talking Book" signifies the clash between oral traditions, which are crucial to expression in most black African cultures, and the written text, which is privileged by Western or European cultures. When it appears in the African American literary tradition, whether in literal books that characters or authors expect to "talk" or in more figurative manifestations, such as the pandemic "Jes Grew" in Ishmael Reed's masterpiece *Mumbo Jumbo*, the Talking Book signifies the ways in which cultural differences can be both illuminating and confusing.

Gates's tracing of the Talking Book's place in the African American literary tradition is arguably *The Signifying Monkey*'s most original contribution to African American literary theory. Less original, but no less influential, is Gates's theory of signifying; it is itself a signification upon prior musings regarding the importance of different influential figures to such individual African American authors as Gwendolyn Brooks, George S. Schuyler, Langston Hughes, Wallace Thurman, Zora Neale Hurston, W. E. B. Du Bois, Alain Locke, Jean Toomer, Richard Wright, Ralph Ellison, Ishmael Reed, Amiri Baraka,

Addison Gayle, Houston A. Baker Jr., and Hoyt Fuller. Indeed, countless essays on the subject of African American literature since the Harlem Renaissance and through the Black Arts Movement have touched upon the topic of African American literature being both a collusion and collision of multiple cultural influences, with the African portion often dominating. It would be more accurate to say, therefore, that Gates's text is a concatenation of all that has gone before; it is the literal fulfillment of his theory, an end that Gates undoubtedly intended.

Gates and *The Signifying Monkey* have since come under some criticism for minimizing the place of women within this tradition, although *The Signifying Monkey* improves upon *Figures in Black* in this regard. To the extent that Gates is attempting to fuse poststructuralism with a more Afrocentric approach via his privileging of African American vernacular language and culture, it may also be said that the theory depends too heavily upon a forced syncretism that differs markedly from what his text describes. Critical reviews of the theory have reflected the problematic aspects of the theory, such as Barbara Johnson's response to one crucial presentation of Gates's ideas.[1]

Nonetheless, no one could possibly deny that Gates's arguments dominated African American literary studies for the better part of the 1990s. *The Signifying Monkey* was not only assigned frequently to graduate students and reviewed in the mainstream press but also cited in countless studies of African American literature that followed it. In addition, it brought enormous attention and influence to its author, who was courted by many major American universities. Gates eventually settled at Harvard University,

---

1. Barbara E. Johnson, response to Henry Louis Gates Jr.'s essay "Canon-Formation and the Afro-American Tradition: From the Seen to the Told," in *Afro-American Literary Study in the 1990s*, ed. Houston A. Baker Jr. and Patricia Redmond (Chicago: University of Chicago Press, 1989), 39–44.

where he revitalized its African American Studies department by attracting a "dream team" of major black intellectuals, including philosophers Cornel West and Kwame Anthony Appiah, sociologist William Julius Wilson, and critical scholars Patricia Williams, Lani Guinier, and Evelyn Higginbotham.

Sinclair, April (b. 1953, Chicago, Illinois) April Sinclair's three novels written in the 1990s stand out among the works published in the wave of interest in African American fiction that began swelling in the middle of that decade. This is not to imply that Sinclair simply rode the wave; on the contrary, her works reflect several influences at once: the Black Arts Movement, her activist spirit, a feminist outlook, and an interest in intelligently and accessibly raising difficult issues among African American women. Sinclair manages to keep these issues in the forefront of her novels without being pedantic or losing her robust sense of humor, an achievement made more impressive by the fact that each novel is semiautobiographical.

Sinclair's *Coffee Will Make You Black* (1994) was her breakthrough novel, attracting both respectable sales and strong critical support. It is a semiautobiographical narrative set in Chicago during the latter half of the 1960s, when the protagonist, Jean "Stevie" Stevenson, attempts to wade through the tense intra- and interracial politics of the time. As she moves from intermediate through high school, Stevie is bewildered by the transformation of African Americans of her generation into militant advocates of Black Nationalism who are still haunted by the self-hatred that defined their lives before blackness became beautiful. Stevie finds herself confronting both racist oppressors and black militants who are more interested in radical chic even as she discovers her own bisexuality. *Ain't Gonna Be the Same Fool Twice* (1995), the sequel to *Coffee Will Make*

You Black, finds Stevie leaving Chicago for college, then San Francisco, where she stays and explores the bisexuality she began accepting at home. In the process, Stevie negotiates the tensions and complexities of black and gay politics of the 1970s with humor and irony. *I Left My Back Door Open* (1999) moves away from some of Sinclair's autobiographical material to focus on Chicago deejay Daphne "Dee Dee" Dupree, who struggles with her weight, bulimia, and difficulty with romantic relationships that stem from repressed memories of an abusive childhood. Dee Dee is eventually forced to confront her memories and learn to love herself as she is before she can enter into a healthy, loving relationship with her friend Skylar.

Sister Novel This is one term (another is "Girlfriends' book") describing the subgenre of African American fiction that became popular in the early 1990s, especially after the publication of Terry McMillan's *Waiting to Exhale* (1992). "Sister" or "sistah" is a term of endearment for an African American woman. The plot of a sister novel usually revolves around a small, close-knit group of women who may be of various ages but are frequently middle-class professionals in pursuit of romance and marriage, family stability, career advancement, sexual satisfaction, and spiritual peace. Along the way, the women have at least a few witty, engaging discussions of their partners' strengths and shortcomings and highlight the difficulty of finding personal fulfillment in communities undergoing significant change.

These novels are notable for the immense popularity they have enjoyed and the influence they have inarguably had upon African American fiction. Their appeal comes from the authors' willingness to speak sympathetically and almost exclusively to black, predominantly female audiences and their experiences and to affirm their thoughts and feelings.

Key authors who might be classified in this vein would be Terry McMillan, Venise Berry, Connie Briscoe, Eric Jerome Dickey, E. Lynn Harris, Sheneska Jackson, Benilde Little, Omar Tyree, Lolita Files, April Sinclair, and Rosalyn McMillan. As with any such classification, though, the reader is cautioned against pigeonholing any of these authors, equating one's work with another's, or otherwise discounting these works' intrinsic value. None are bereft of valid social commentary or artistic merit, even if some might adhere more closely to formulaic plots and subplots.

Song of Solomon Toni Morrison's third novel, published in 1977, first brought her major national attention, especially after it won the National Book Critics Circle Award. When Morrison won the Nobel Prize in literature in 1993, the Nobel jury cited *Song of Solomon* as her strongest work. Accordingly, it has been studied and cited most often in the many books and articles devoted to Morrison's work, edging out Morrison's equally powerful *Beloved*.

Song of Solomon is the saga of Macon "Milkman" Dead and his family, which contains and represses a number of secrets that threaten to tear them apart. Milkman is forced to confront his own disdain for family, community, and African American history, which stems from his middle-class status, his father's fear of his own humanity, and the ways in which women are expected to revere men uncritically. Milkman is the third Macon Dead; he earns his nickname after one of the family's tenants witnesses his mother breastfeeding her eight-year-old son. Milkman's birth name and nickname alone evoke several of the novel's many complex themes. The surname was given when the first Macon Dead, a freedman, had his original name replaced when a drunken Freedmen's Bureau clerk construed his report that he was from Macon, Georgia, and that his father was dead to mean that his name was Macon Dead. Because the first Macon Dead could not read—a product of the slave system—and a white person had no regard or respect for him, his origins and, consequently, his future progeny's heritage, began to be shrouded in mystery. Moreover, an old identity *died* at that moment, yet the family's definite connection to the South remained, as will be revealed later in the plot. Furthermore, each succeeding male generation of the family becomes increasingly alienated from these same origins, which means a spiritual and cultural *death* is passed on from generation to generation. The second Macon Dead, Milkman's father, takes pains to distance himself emotionally from other African Americans, his own past, his sister Pilate, and his family, most notably his wife and daughters, who desperately seek out sustaining love elsewhere. Macon Dead thus openly rejects virtually all of the markers of his African or African American cultural heritage, which has a direct effect upon Milkman's outlook, one that is as "white" as the substance buried in his nickname.

Milkman's spiritual death is manifested as complete disregard for the emotional lives of anyone besides himself, but especially for any and all women in his family and in his love life. His second cousin and paramour, Hagar, an avatar for the Biblical character, loses her grip on reality after Milkman casts her aside when she seeks a closer connection to him, while his utter indifference toward his sisters (First Corinthians and Magdalena, called Lena) and mother earns his siblings' enmity. After his aunt, Pilate Dead, reveals that she might have the key to a treasure that she and Milkman's father stumbled across as children, both Macon and Milkman's close friend Guitar goad (for markedly different reasons) Milkman to return to the family's

Southern roots and ancestral home in Virginia to discover the treasure's whereabouts. Along the way, Milkman slowly picks up clues to his heritage, eventually discovering that he is descended from the same Africans found in a well known folktale about Africans who were once able to fly but who lost this ability in slavery. Equally important, Milkman learns greater respect for other people, especially women, and a greater sense of his connection to a larger community of African Americans.

Song of Solomon is now routinely praised as the culmination of Morrison's creative powers. It is an accessible novel that is rich in haunting imagery, multivalent symbols, and Morrison's trademark lyricism. It also received a substantial boost in sales and revived interest after Oprah Winfrey featured *Song of Solomon* in her nationally syndicated book club. Accordingly, *Song of Solomon* has been written about more often than any other in her body of work, although most scholarly interest came well before Winfrey helped revive the book. Beyond the listing of books, chapters, and articles found in the bibliography accompanying Morrison's separate entry, the following are among the most helpful resources.

Over thirty major journal articles have been written on *Song of Solomon* since its publication. Of these, Bertram Ashe, "'Why Don't He Like My Hair?': Constructing African-American Standards of Beauty in Toni Morrison's *Song of Solomon* and Zora Neale Hurston's *Their Eyes Were Watching God*," *AAR* 29, no. 4 (Winter 1995), offers a comparative study that traces the ways that intraracial beauty standards have defined African American women's literature, especially the chosen texts. Ann E. Imbrie, "'What Shalimar Knew': Toni Morrison's *Song of Solomon* as a Pastoral Novel," *College English* 55, no. 5 (September 1993), is a somewhat conventional reading that places Morrison into a larger generic category, but it is

still quite useful as an examination of Morrison's project. A more Afrocentric perspective may be found in Betty Taylor Thompson's recent "Common Bonds from Africa to the U.S.: Africana Womanist Literary Analysis," *Western Journal of Black Studies* 25, no. 3 (Fall 2001), which draws connections between *Song of Solomon*, *Beloved*, Gloria Naylor's *Bailey's Café*, and three African authors (Flora Nwapa, Mariama Ba, and Tsitsi Dangarembga). David Cowart, "Faulkner and Joyce in Morrison's *Song of Solomon*," *American Literature* 62, no. 1 (March 1990), connects Morrison to two of the writers with whom she is most frequently compared (especially Faulkner, upon whom Morrison wrote her master's thesis). Finally, Nellie Y. McKay and Kathryn Earle, *Approaches to Teaching the Novels of Toni Morrison* (1997), bears another endorsement, as does Missy Dean Kubitschek, *Toni Morrison: A Critical Companion* (1998).

Souljah, Sister (b. Lisa Williamson, 1964, New York City) Sister Souljah is perhaps better known as a political activist and performer than as an author of fiction, but she has won substantial acclaim in the last occupation. She attended Cornell and Rutgers, where she obtained degrees in African history and a sharp political consciousness that shaped her subsequent career.

Souljah first gained attention for her activism, which led to a charter membership of the hip-hop group Public Enemy in 1991 and her own recording contract. The following year, Souljah was thrust into the national spotlight when Arkansas governor and U.S. presidential candidate Bill Clinton publicly lambasted Souljah for controversial remarks about race relations she made on a New York radio program. This temporarily improved sales of her recording, *360 Degrees of Power*, and breathed new life into Clinton's candidacy, but the notoriety and its benefits to Souljah's recording career were extremely short-lived. Nevertheless, she earned the respect of many African Americans, especially disadvantaged young women of her native Bronx, whom she has mentored and aided for many years.

Souljah's career gained new life after she published her intensely personal memoir, *No Disrespect*, in 1995. Not only does the book contain devastating accounts of Souljah's difficult life and of the Bronx's heartbreaking conditions, it also establishes Souljah as a writer more than capable of seamlessly combining immense storytelling skills with astute, impassioned political observations and arguments. In the book tour and public appearances that followed, Souljah won over a new audience. Her first novel, *The Coldest Winter Ever* (1999), is semiautobiographical in its approach, with some events similar to those in Souljah's life and memoir. The novel, however, stands on its own as an accomplished work of fiction. It revolves around Winter Santiaga, the daughter of a Brooklyn drug dealer who tries to maintain her family's grip on power in general and in the drug trade in particular after her mother is murdered and her father is sent to prison. The novel's graphic language and contents offer a gripping and horrifying moral play on the seductiveness of money, materialism, and power at the individual, communal, and societal levels.

Tarpley, Natasha (b. 1971, Chicago, Illinois) Most of Natasha Tarpley's contributions to African American literature have been poetry and nonfiction, although she has brought the conventions of fiction to the latter genre. She is, therefore, part of the recent "creative nonfiction" movement in American literature. Her major contribution in this area is *Girl in the Mirror: Three Generations of Black Women in Motion* (1999), an extensive memoir of her family's history. *Girl in the Mirror* was roundly praised for its lyrical invocation of her ancestor's voices, which most reviewers rightly found closer to a novel in most respects. It therefore resembles Audre Lorde's *Zami* (1982), which also blends the autobiographical with the conventions of the novel.

Tarpley is also well known for her children's book, *I Love My Hair!*, which encourages young African American girls to take pride in their hair and appearance. Recently, Tarpley has also published proper fiction in a few venues, notably her story "All of Me," found in Carol Taylor's collection, *Brown Sugar: A Collection of Erotic Black Fiction* (2001). To date, though, no critical articles on Tarpley's work have emerged.

Taylor, Mildred (b. 1943, Jackson, Mississippi) Although Mildred Taylor is known primarily as an author of young people's fiction, several books within her body of work are now recognized classics in the field and assigned frequently in primary school classes. Her books are based upon incidents in Taylor's childhood in Mississippi, whence her family fled to avoid a violent and potentially deadly confrontation between her father and a white man.[1] The novella *Song of the Trees* (1975), which won first place in the Council on Interracial Books for Children's competition in 1973, is a history of the Logan family from slavery to freedom and life in the twentieth century. The family's saga is continued in *Roll of Thunder, Hear My Cry* (1976), a universally acclaimed and assigned

---

1. Nagueyalti Warren, "Taylor, Mildred D.," *The Concise Oxford Companion to African American Literature* (New York: Oxford University Press, 2003), 386.

classic that explores the insidiousness of personal racial prejudice and systematic racism through the eyes of young Cassie Logan. It won the Newbery Medal in 1977. *Let the Circle be Unbroken* (1981), which won the Coretta Scott King Award in 1984, and *The Road to Memphis* (1990) both continue Taylor's analysis of the successes and failures of the Civil Rights movement through the Logans, especially Cassie. *The Gold Cadillac* (1987) is the story of an African American family traveling to the South in a gaudy car; *The Friendship* (1987) is based upon the incident that preceded the Taylor family's flight from Mississippi.

This Bridge Called My Back: Writings by Radical Women of Color This 1981 essay collection, edited by Chicana writers Cherríe Moraga and Gloria Anzaldúa, holds a permanent place as one of the foundations of contemporary intellectual thought by feminists of color, rivaled only by *All the Women Are White, All the Blacks Are Men, But Some of Us Are Brave: Black Women's Studies* (1982), edited by Gloria T. Hull, Patricia Bell Scott, and Barbara Smith.

This Bridge Called My Back represents Moraga's and Anzaldúa's desire to provide a collection by and about feminists of color, as the subtitle indicates, and in this it is highly successful. Although it is not dominated by African American women's concerns, the anthology contains several indispensable essays that advanced the development of African American women's studies, including the Combahee River Collective, "A Black Feminist Statement"; Audre Lorde, "The Master's Tools Will Never Dismantle the Master's House"; Barbara and Beverly Smith, "Across the Kitchen Table: A Sister-to-Sister Dialogue"; and Cheryl Clarke, "Lesbianism: An Act of Resistance." Other African American authors of note are Gabrielle Daniels, Hattie Gossett, and Toni Cade Bambara, who provided the foreword.

The essays are not by any means uniform in focus, content, or direction, beyond the overarching editorial goal of giving voice to silenced women, and it is precisely this goal which gives the volume its power. Each writer addresses a subject that either the greater American society or the mainstream women's movement has labeled a taboo. By broaching these boundaries, the essayists have inspired a generation of women of color to be more outspoken, whether in writing or in other public forums, and helped to ensure that the modern women's movement neither exclude nor minimize the views of women of color to the degree that it did in the past. This is due largely to *This Bridge*'s frequent assignment in innumerable women's studies courses, whether in whole or in part. It also won the Before Columbus Foundation's American Book Award (1986). Unfortunately, the volume also frequently goes out of print, despite being an unqualified classic in its field. Interested readers and instructors are encouraged to seek second-hand and library copies.

Thomas, Joyce Carol (b. 1938, Ponce City, Oklahoma) Novelist, poet, and playwright Joyce Carol Thomas is best known as the author of many books of poetry and young people's fiction. Although her first novel, *Marked by Fire* (1982), is also placed in that category, it is considered her finest work and a landmark in the field for its luxuriously poetic prose. It introduces Abyssinia "Abby" Jackson, a young African American girl with a gift for storytelling and poetry. Over the course of the novel and its sequels, Abby is forced to deal with many trials stemming from a horrific tornado that hits her community, in addition to the threats posed by jealous, bigoted, and otherwise disturbed members of that community and the rest of her Oklahoma town. *Marked by Fire* garnered an American Book Award (1982), the National Book Award, a designation as an

"Outstanding Book of the Year" from the *New York Times*, and a TABA Children's Books Award, all in 1983. Thomas's other young-adult novels include *Bright Shadow* (1983), winner of the Coretta Scott King Honor Book Award from the American Library Association (1984); *Water Girl* (1986); *The Golden Pasture* (1986), winner of Pick of the List distinction from the American Booksellers Association that year; *Journey* (1988); and *When the Nightingale Sings* (1992). In 2001, Thomas also published *House of Light*, her first novel for a more adult audience.

Thomas was one of the authors featured in *AAR*'s special issue on "Children's and Young Adult Literature" (32, no. 1; Spring 1998). Darwin L. Henderson and Anthony L. Manna's "Evoking the 'Holy and the Terrible': Conversations with Joyce Carol Thomas" in that volume is particularly trenchant.

Transition (1961–1974; 1975–1976; 1991–2003)
Transition was founded in Uganda in late 1960 by Indian graduate student Rajat Neogy as a medium for intellectual debate primarily about the future of the African continent. At the time, many African states were either in the process of obtaining or had already obtained their independence from colonial European powers. Each issue focused considerable attention on political issues within specific African countries, but *Transition* was also well known as an outlet for poetry, fiction, plays, and essays discussing cultural and artistic questions relevant to the continent. Some of the many famous contributors to the magazine's first incarnation included Nadine Gordimer, Wole Soyinka, Chinua Achebe, Bessie Head, Christopher Okigbo, Ngugi wa Thiong'o, V. S. Naipaul, D. J. Enright, David Gill, Paul Theroux, James Baldwin, Martin Luther King Jr., Langston Hughes, and Julius Nyerere. By the late 1960s, and with the help of financing from the Congress for Cultural Freedom (CCF), it was arguably the best magazine published in and about Africa, but it also came under fire from the Ugandan government for being subversive, resulting in editor and publisher Neogy being jailed for sedition in late 1968. After his release in 1969, Neogy moved the magazine to Ghana but soon found the magazine again persecuted by the government. To avoid imprisonment and losing the magazine again, Neogy resigned his position in 1972. Wole Soyinka became the editor from 1972 to its 1975/1976 issue (which was intended to be both the ultimate issue of the magazine and the premier of a new title, *Ch'indaba*), with an editorial policy that was more black nationalist in outlook and clearly focused upon the "black revolution" in Africa and among the African Diaspora, especially the United States. Contributors to this incarnation included Henry Louis Gates Jr. (one of Soyinka's former graduate students), Ted Joans, Eldridge Cleaver, and Kofi Awoonor. After Soyinka cut off the magazine's funding from the Ford Foundation in response to reader's criticisms that the magazine was funded by neocolonialist forces, only the 1975/1976 issue saw print. It lay fallow until 1991, when Gates and Kwame Anthony Appiah revived *Transition* at Harvard University in the same spirit as its earlier incarnations, albeit with more attention paid to American and African American issues concerning race, culture, and public policy. Some of the many contributors between 1991 and 2003 included Soyinka, Gates, Appiah, Ken Burns, Angela Y. Davis, Cornel West, Patricia J. Williams, Robert O'Meally, Lindsay Waters, Darius James, Houston A. Baker Jr., Julie Dash, Ali Mazrui, Walter Benn Michaels, George Elliott Clarke, Rita Dove, Robert Elliot Fox, Manthia Diawara, Ice Cube, Martin Bernal, Kathleen Cleaver, Naipaul, Marjorie Garber, William Julius Wilson, Caryl Phillips, Philippe Wamba, and Eric Lott.

Tyree, Omar Rashad (b. 1969, Philadelphia, Pennsylvania) Omar Tyree is among the more prolific and successful authors riding the new wave of African American popular fiction that swelled in the 1990s and an enterprising advocate of other black writers, both new and established. Since 1996, he has published eight novels, as well as a screenplay and some poetry. Tyree's appeal to his rather sizeable audience stems largely from his attempts to portray the lives and thoughts of everyday African Americans realistically while addressing a number of political and social issues. Critical reception of his work has been lukewarm; many critics have found Tyree's plotting cumbersome and repetitive but have appreciated his desire to give a voice to a generation of African Americans whose stories have been written only within the last dozen years of the twentieth century. The concerns of the Post-Soul/post–Civil Rights era are Tyree's forte, particularly the personal relationships that bind its members to one another. Tyree has emphatically declared that while his novels do explore some of the complexities of relationships among African Americans, he does not intend "to follow . . . [Terry McMillan's] lead in writing about the continuous bedroom issues of African-American men and women." Rather, he wishes "to create new literature about those countless other subjects in [the African American] community that need to be explored from a fresh voice and perspective," a literature that does not eschew complexity and confrontation of challenging issues (www.omartyree.com/mission.html).

This mission is arguably most prominent in his debut, *Flyy Girl* (1996), a morality tale focusing upon the life of Philadelphian Tracy Ellison, who seeks a largely material and superficial lifestyle until this search brings various forms of hardship, including drugs, poor relationships, and violence into her life. As Tracy learns the art of self-discovery, she slowly extricates herself from the emptiest and most dangerous situations in her life. Her surname is not coincidental; similar to Ralph Ellison's Invisible Man, Tracy is forced to go beyond superficial meanings and values to transcend her world, if only temporarily. In addition, like many of Tyree's protagonists and major characters, she is meant to embody a significant part of her generation, particularly those who grew up immersed in the music and culture of hip-hop. Her saga is continued in *For the Love of Money* (2000), in which the teenage Ellison has grown into a successful young author chronicling her life story (her first novel is entitled *Flyy Girl*). *A Do Right Man* (1998) tells of a young professional disc jockey, Bobby Dallas, who struggles to find a satisfying romantic relationship while keeping his principles. *Single Mom* (1998) chronicles the travails of Denise Stewart, who finds herself trying to establish a life for herself, her children, and a prospective husband, even as the children's fathers try to reenter her life.

Verdelle, A. J. (b. 1960, Washington, D.C.) A. J. Verdelle was born and raised in Washington, D.C., and later earned degrees in political science, statistics, and writing, and chose the second field as her steady vocation. Her debut novel, *The Good Negress* (1996) earned major accolades and several prizes upon its publication, including a Whiting Award for fiction (1996), the American Academy of Arts and Letters Vursell Award for Distinguished Prose, a Literary Honor Award from the Black Caucus of the American Library Association, and finalist honors for the PEN/Faulkner and 1995 *Los Angeles Times* Book Awards, Bunting and NEA Fellowships, and IMPAC Dublin International Fiction Prize. Verdelle wrote the preface for the 1998 reprint of Julia Peterkins's 1928 novel *Scarlet Sister Mary*. Verdelle has also published critical articles on the Ebonics controversy in *The Nation*; on the photography of Roy DeCavara in Miwon Kwon's collection *Tracing Cultures: Art History, Criticism, Critical Fiction* (1994); and an essay, "The Half Light of Manumission," in Ellen Dugan's 1996 collection, *Picturing the South: 1860 to the Present: Photographers and Writers*. In 1997 and 1998, Verdelle lectured in Princeton University's Creative Writing Program.

The Good Negress easily fits within the bildungsroman tradition. Its protagonist, Denise Palms, is a young African American girl who must make the transition from life in rural Virginia to urban Detroit in the early 1960s. As her worldview is radically and irrevocably changed in the migration between regions, lifestyles, and states of education, Denise also finds that the language of her Southern upbringing is both an asset and a hindrance. She eventually learns how to find her voice and identity in the language and culture of her recent past, while accepting the new knowledge and language in her new environment. In the process, she discovers her self and her agency. The novel's genius lies in Verdelle's ability to make Denise's language a natural, unobtrusive form of narration, one that never condescends to her subject.

Most of the literature on Verdelle and *The Good Negress* consists of book reviews, but a few interviews and one critical essay have appeared, with more sure to follow. Of the latter, Lisa B. Day, "'I Reach to Where the Freedom Is': The Influence of the Slave Narrative Tradition on A.J. Verdelle's *The Good Negress*," *Critique* 41, no. 4 (Summer 2000), is an outstanding first contribution to schol-

arly criticism of this novel. Day shows how *The Good Negress* "both depends on and undermines the literary tradition of the slave narrative" (411). This makes the novel one of many in the contemporary period, including Gayl Jones's *Corregidora*, Toni Morrison's *Beloved*, David Bradley's *Chaneysville Incident*, and Sherley Anne Williams's *Dessa Rose*, that revise the form and function of the slave narrative. Day argues that Denise's diction, inasmuch as it is written to suggest an oral narrative, fuses communication modes in much the same way a slave narrator would. Day also notes, however, that *The Good Negress* also sidesteps or even questions many of the conventions of the slave narrative. Denise's freedom depends primarily upon finding her voice, not upon freedom from hard labor, a considerable shifting of the slave narrative's goals.

Waiting to Exhale Terry McMillan's 1992 novel may be considered nothing short of a publishing phenomenon and a major, albeit controversial, catalyst for African American authors' success in the 1990s. By the end of 2000, McMillan's third novel had sold approximately 800,000 hardcover and 1.75 million paperback copies. This is to say nothing of more than $120 million in worldwide box office and video-rental receipts ($100 million in the United States alone) for the 1995 film, 7 million copies of the film soundtrack album, and untold millions of dollars in accessories and merchandise linked to the book and film.[1] In short, *Waiting to Exhale*'s success easily dwarfs that of Richard Wright's *Native Son* (1940),

1. The Romance Reader, "Got to Be Real: Three Original Love Stories by E. Lynn Harris, Eric Jerome Dickey, Colin Channer and Marcus Major," http://www.theromancereader.com/harris-gotto.html.

which also had a major impact upon African American literature. It gave McMillan, whose first two novels, *Mama* (1987) and *Disappearing Acts* (1989), sold respectably and garnered favorable notices, the clout to demand million-dollar contracts for her subsequent works, *How Stella Got Her Groove Back* (1996) and *A Day Late and a Dollar Short* (2001); *Stella* was also made into a successful film in 1998.

Waiting to Exhale's success, however, extends far beyond McMillan's own fortune. It is widely credited for several major achievements: (1) attracting publishers to African American authors and therefore spawning a new flood of black fiction writing that continues to this day; (2) enlarging the African American reading audience and increasing white Americans' interest in African American literature in general; (3) pursuant to (2), inspiring the formation of thousands of book clubs and literature discussion groups nationwide, including Oprah Winfrey's Book Club; (4) giving an essential shot in the arm to the black romance genre; (5) prompting novels by male authors that respond to *Waiting*'s woman-centered plot. In short, most young African American authors who have published successfully since 1992 owe at least a small debt to McMillan's success. Rival publishers even imitated the novel's colorful cover art by Synthia Saint James for the covers of many African American authors' books, including such established writers as Bebe Moore Campbell, who was fairly successful long before *Waiting to Exhale* captured the reading public's imagination.

Although *Waiting to Exhale* has been an undeniable financial success story, its literary reputation has not come close to that stratospheric level. The novel centers around four middle-class African American women in their mid-thirties living in Phoenix, Arizona, whose bonds to one another are formed in part by their respective quests for true love, romance, and sexual fulfillment. Predictably, each woman is disappointed by the prospective romantic and sexual partners she encounters, and each shares her disgruntlement with her friends. The novel's writing is often quite funny and sardonic and clearly sympathetic to the concerns modern women, especially African American women, have regarding romantic possibilities. In a number of scenes, for example, the women individually or collectively lament the changes in African American demographics wrought by the events of the post–Civil Rights era, including the devastation of black communities by drugs, health problems, and even desegregation itself. This sympathetic quality, which is continuously blended with humorous general complaints about men, certainly accounts for the novel's general popularity, but it does not necessarily make for great literature. As Frances Stead Sellers put it in her *Times Literary Supplement* review, whereas "most black women writers are associated with a recognizable tradition of serious ideologically inspired black literature, written primarily for 'concerned' whites and black intellectuals, McMillan, however, has little truck with ideology of any kind. She writes to entertain, by providing the type of sexy, popular novel that has been making Jilly Cooper and Danielle Steele rich for years."[1]

To this extent, McMillan has helped redefine what African American fiction is expected to do or be and, arguably, helped make writing and publishing more lucrative for all African American writers. This does not mean, though, that *Waiting to Exhale* is

---

1. Frances Stead Sellers, review of *Waiting to Exhale*, by Terry McMillan, *Times Literary Supplement*, 6 November 1992, 20.

apolitical. In fact, it refers to the spread of AIDS, crack cocaine, single-parent families, and the growing number of African Americans under the care of the judicial system, all of which were and remain crucial issues in many African American communities and the concern of much of McMillan's readership. Moreover, in his review in the *New York Review of Books*, Darryl Pinckney points out that McMillan is both a part and a beneficiary of the wave of black women writers who emerged in the 1970s and 1980s, even if, as McMillan has allowed, she has not been fully embraced by those same authors.[1]

In all fairness, though, neither McMillan nor a sizeable portion of her audience were particularly concerned with *Waiting to Exhale*'s literary merits; its resonance with many women of all ages stems from its ability to touch an emotional center linked to the issues named above. Many of the criticisms that arose regarding *Waiting to Exhale* had much to do with the novel's distance in quality from McMillan's earlier novels, which had enabled her to win National Endowment for the Arts and Doubleday/Columbia University Fellowships, a National Book Award, and many other accolades. Nonetheless, if McMillan never achieves the same level of critical acclaim that her earlier novels gained, or even the same degree of success that *Waiting to Exhale* obtained, her third novel remains one of the most important in the history of African American literature.

Waiting to Exhale has not enjoyed the same amount of careful critical attention that its contemporaries have, but much of the attention it has received has been thoughtful. Tina M. Harris's 1998 article "'*Waiting to Exhale*' or 'Breath(ing) Again': A Search for Identity, Empowerment, and Love in the 1990s," focuses more on the way

that the film version of the novel counters many of the stereotypes about African American women in the cinema rather than on the novel itself, but it argues smartly that both the novel and the film have had greater social significance as exemplars of feminist thought than a first glance might reveal.

Walker, Alice (b. 1944, Eatonton, Georgia) Of the African American authors who began writing and publishing fiction in the late 1960s and early 1970s, perhaps only Toni Morrison has attracted more critical laurels and sustained academic analysis than Alice Walker. She is also one of the most controversial, especially since the publication of Walker's best-known novel, *The Color Purple* (1982; see the separate entry) and its production as a major film two years later. Walker is a novelist, short-story author, poet, and political activist who has worked within the Civil Rights movement and for various causes within the modern feminist movement. Walker's novels are, in turn, closely tied to her ideological underpinnings as displayed in many essays on feminism (or womanism, the term Walker prefers when discussing the experiences of African American women; see separate entry) literature, and the arts for *Ms.* magazine, to which she contributed regularly for over a decade, beginning in 1974.

Walker also played a crucial role in the development of African American literary studies since 1970: She almost single-handedly rescued Harlem Renaissance author Zora Neale Hurston from obscurity by working to get Hurston's *Their Eyes Were Watching God* (1937) back into print and back into scholarly attention. Eventually, through Walker's efforts all of Hurston's works returned to print and to popularity in

1. Darryl Pinckney, review of *Waiting to Exhale*, by Terry McMillan, *New York Review of Books*, 4 November 1993, 35; Esther Fein, "Fiction Vérité: Characters Ring True," *New York Times*, 1 July 1992.

both academic and popular circles, resulting in Hurston's becoming one of the most heavily (and deservedly) studied African American authors of the twentieth century, despite her dying penniless and outcast in 1961. Walker also taught one of the first African American women's literature courses at Wellesley College in 1977 and helped J. California Cooper publish her own novels and stories.

Walker's activities in reviving Hurston's career and beginning Cooper's reveal the crux of her own artistic sensibility, which may best be summarized as a colorful mosaic that both rescues and criticizes African American communities' virtues—rich oral and folk traditions and indomitable spiritual strength—and their shortcomings, especially sexism, intraracial racism or colorism, and homophobia. In this sense, Walker shares much with the generation of authors born and raised during and after the Civil Rights movement, to the extent that she believes strongly in the necessity of self-criticism within African America. From her first novel, *The Third Life of Grange Copeland* (1970) through *By the Light of My Father's Smile* (1998), to say nothing of her many essays, Walker persistently raises a number of disturbing issues within African American communities, particularly the oppression of black women at the hands of men, black and white, and other women who have learned to hate themselves and their sexuality. Walker attempts to end silence regarding taboo subjects in all of her major texts, consistent with the principles of feminism she developed before, during, and after her tenure at *Ms.* Walker built upon these principles to coin the term "womanism," which combines feminism with the peculiar situations in which African American women find themselves (see separate entry).

Walker also offers extensive criticism of racism, the sometimes superficial or paternalistic white liberalism that caused many

tensions during the Civil Rights movement, in which Walker was an activist, and the ways in which African American history, literature, and folk life have been silenced and marginalized. Walker's depiction of males', especially black males', transgressions toward black women, however, has tellingly been the focus of many of her critics. Walker has been accused of everything from ignoring, betraying, or minimizing black men's humanity to hating African American men altogether, primarily due to her character Mr. ——— in *The Color Purple*, her passionate campaign against female genital mutilation that began in *The Color Purple* and continued in *Possessing the Secret of Joy* (1992), and her identity as a bisexual, then lesbian woman. While Mr. ——— is indeed a problematic character to the extent that he resembles some of the worst stereotypes about African American men, it is also fair to note that Walker, similar to her contemporary Toni Morrison, always attempts to show how women and men can resolve the damage done in the worst of their relationships; she seldom consigns her characters to irrelevancy or incorrigibility. In trying to avoid this trap, Walker arguably tries too hard, but the more extreme acts of which she has been accused seem to ring hollow once her novels are read closely. In short, she does not create negative men for the sake of relaying a simplistic message; her novels are meant to show the possibilities available to women through communitarian values.

Walker's first novel, *The Third Life of Grange Copeland*, gained considerable notice and criticism upon its publication for its focus upon familial conflicts within African American communities, which went against calls for positive images of black communities that were common in 1970. In the autocratic character of Brownfield, it also contained an early version of the type of character that incited Walker's most hostile critics. The eponymous protagonist, however, represented the possibility of redemption not simply for men but also for anyone struggling to become more human and humane. The collection *In Love and Trouble: Stories of Black Women* (1973), represented some of Walker's strongest work, including "Everyday Use," one of the most frequently anthologized short stories; it is virtually a staple of first-year college writing courses, to say nothing of African American and American literature curricula. Its popularity may be attributed to Walker's use of implicit criticism of Black Nationalism through the character of Dee, who denies the richness of her black Southern heritage until she becomes radicalized during her first year in college. When Dee returns home, she fetishizes all of the homespun work her sister Maggie and mother (the narrator) have created, even though she had despised all of it mere months earlier. It is a cautionary tale against romanticizing African Americans' African past, on the one hand, and against uncritical valorization of selected hallmarks of "blackness," usually to the detriment of both family ties and a sense of reality, on the other. Through the painstakingly crafted quilt Maggie makes, the story also introduces the reader to Walker's ideas regarding the importance of quilts and other domestic objects as commonly neglected expressions of women's artistry. In these ways, "Everyday Use" is perhaps the best single representation of and introduction to Walker's art. Its influence and accessibility were enough to warrant a nearly exhaustive guidebook: *Everyday Use/Alice Walker* (1994), which was edited by Barbara T. Christian as part of Rutgers University Press's Women Writers: Texts and Contexts series. Christian includes interviews and essays by and about Walker that make the story's innovations and artistry more lucid for both beginning and advanced readers. The remainder of *In Love and In Trouble*, however, should not be neglected; upon its initial publication, all but a handful of the nearly thirty reviews it received were largely positive, faulting only occasional artistic failures among the stories.

Walker's second novel, *Meridian* (1976), is a semiautobiographical narrative based upon Walker's experience in the 1960s. It revolves around Meridian, who, like Walker, grew up in a small Georgia town, went to a historically black women's college that strictly regulated the students' lives and morals, dropped out because of a pregnancy, joined the Civil Rights movement, and struggled with the complex relations between black and white men and women of that time. Perhaps more than Walker's earlier stories and *Grange Copeland*, *Meridian* is her retrospective on the social, racial, and sexual upheavals that the Civil Rights and Black Power eras produced.

Some shifts in Walker's political and artistic outlook are reflected in the short-story collection *You Can't Keep a Good Woman Down: Stories* (1981). Whereas *In Love and In Trouble* was concerned more with showing how African American women have managed to create or find creative outlets in the face of racist and sexist oppression, the stories in *You Can't Keep a Good Woman Down* focus more acutely upon the pain and tragedy that black women experience as a result of both oppression and the eternal pursuit of love and sexual freedom. Each story shows how it is possible to transcend pain and to find love against all odds. The later collection's reviews were less generous than those for the earlier; while most acknowledged that Walker infused her short stories with engrossing lyricism, a few faulted her tendency to sacrifice art for ideology.

Walker's third novel, *The Color Purple* (see separate entry), builds upon the ideas developed in *You Can't Keep a Good Woman Down*. It is also easily Walker's most famous, celebrated, and controversial work. It is written in an epistolary format, in which the protagonist and narrator, Celie, writes to God and, later, her sister Nettie about her travails. Celie is raped by her stepfather (whom she believes to be her biological father at the time) and bears two children by him, both of whom he sends away for adoption. Celie is eventually married off to Mr. ——— (whose name is eventually revealed as Albert) when Nettie refuses Mr. ———'s advances. This marriage of convenience becomes entirely miserable for Celie after Nettie runs away to escape Mr. ———'s overtures. Celie eventually finds spiritual and sexual sustenance in her husband's former lover, Shug Avery, who helps her discover her sexuality, her voice, her identity, and consequently her will to leave Albert, start her own business, and, much later, reunite with Nettie and her long-lost children. As mentioned above, *The Color Purple*'s depiction of such men as Celie's stepfather and Albert, combined with Steven Spielberg's problematic 1984 interpretation of the novel, brought great controversy Walker's way. Criticism notwithstanding, *The Color Purple* also garnered extensive praise and the Pulitzer Prize in 1983. It soon became a staple of African American and women's literature courses.

The Temple of My Familiar (1989) was somewhat less successful, both artistically and in terms of its popular appeal, than *The Color Purple*, but it curried favor with many critics for its highly imaginative story of humanity's spiritual development. The novel is linked to *The Color Purple* via a few of the earlier work's primary characters (specifically Shug Avery and Fanny Nzingha, Celie's granddaughter) but in most other respects is a wholly independent work. The plot is a mythological fantasy about humanity's movement away from a close connection to the natural and spiritual worlds, symbolized through animal familiars (spirits assigned to guard and help individual human beings).

Walker imagines human development as having several ages. In the first, humans were in harmony with nature until the second age, when the appearance of cultural and racial distinctions and the desire for wealth began to corrupt humanity's relationship with its environment. In the next age, capitalism and organized religion have almost completely sapped humanity's ability to connect with its natural spiritualism. Although the novel's mysticism and emphasis on a fantastic spiritual past took some of her readers by surprise, the reviews of *The Temple of My Familiar* were generally positive, citing the novel's ability to construct an elaborate world, worldview, and history. It was occasionally derided for being *too* fantastic, and therefore divorced from reality and realistic solutions, as well as for its occasionally confusing mix of narrative techniques. Such articles as Bonnie Braendlin, "Alice Walker's *The Temple of My Familiar* as Pastiche," *American Literature* 68, no. 1 (March 1996); and Felipe Smith, "Alice Walker's Redemptive Art," *AAR* 26, no. 3 (Fall 1992) offer readings of *The Temple of My Familiar* that use theories of the postmodern and a history of spiritual movements to place the novel in a more sympathetic light.

Possessing the Secret of Joy (1992) earned nearly as much controversy upon its publication as *The Color Purple*. Extending that novel's brief mention of pharoanic circumcision, in which most parts of the vulva are removed and the vaginal entrance shown shut, Walker uses the ritual, which is still commonly practiced among some East African ethnic groups, as a metaphor for women's sexual oppression and repression. The controversy surrounding the novel came from its strong indictment of the practice. While many reviewers agreed with Walker and the novel that female circumcision was a brutal and humiliating ritual, it also raised the question of whether individuals from one culture have the right to criticize others' cultural traditions. Other critics, such as the one for *Publishers Weekly*, simply found the novel too "strident and polemical" and lacking careful structuring and development. Nevertheless, *Possessing the Secret of Joy* and Walker's subsequent activism are perhaps the two most important factors in bringing female circumcision to the world's consciousness. Both have attracted quite a few journal articles since the novel's publication, which seems to uphold Walker's dictum that the "real revolution is always concerned with the least glamorous stuff."[1]

By the Light of My Father's Smile (1998) earned Walker some of her least enthusiastic reviews, based largely upon a narrative style and content that some reviewers found too laconic and often too preachy, despite Walker's thematic ambitions. The narrative is an example of magical realism revolving around the Mundo (Spanish for "world"), a people created via the union of escaped slaves and Mexican Indians, who are studied by two black anthropologists posing as missionaries. The magical part of the plot stems from the ability of spirits and angels to view and narrate the action, most of which is concerned with the relationships between fathers and their daughters. More to the point, the novel explores the liberating power of human sexuality—in all its orientations—which is always threatened by the dual specters of patriarchy and traditional, organized religions. Walker wishes for fathers to be able to recognize and support their daughters' development, rather than

sheltering and protecting them from both their sexuality and the larger world. While reviewers generally acknowledged that Walker's attempt to build upon her earlier novels' arguments for women's freer sexual expression, some found the novel "deeply mired in New Age hocus-pocus and goddess religion baloney," and "predictable."[2] As of this writing, only book reviews have been published on *By the Light of My Father's Smile*, although Rudolph P. Byrd's review in *African American Review* is one of the best and most sympathetic.

Critical studies of Walker's novels, fiction, and poetry are plentiful in thesis, dissertation, book, or article form. Walker's classic collection *In Search of Our Mothers' Gardens* (1983) gathers together the best and most famous of her essays, interviews, and letters on such topics as womanism/feminism, the art of writing, politics, the Civil Rights movement and its legacy, and many others. Beyond Walker's early novels and short-story collections, it is the best introduction to her thoughts. Maria Lauret's *Alice Walker* (2000) links Walker's novels to her political and social activism and spirituality in a solid literary biography. *Alice Walker: Critical Perspectives Past and Present* (1993), edited by Henry Louis Gates Jr. and K. Anthony Appiah, is an excellent starting point for readers interested in the criticism and controversy surrounding Walker. This collection begins with contemporary, generally balanced reviews of Walker's novels, but it mostly consists of scholarly articles. Barbara Christian, *Black Women Novelists: The Development of a Tradition, 1892–1976*

---

1. Alice Walker, "The Unglamorous but Worthwhile Duties of the Black Revolutionary Artist, or of the Black Writer Who Simply Works and Writes," in *In Search of Our Mothers' Gardens: Womanist Prose* (New York: Harcourt Brace, 1984), 135.

2. Francine Prose, review of *By the Light of My Father's Smile*, by Alice Walker, *New York Times Book Review*, October 4, 1998; Richard Bernstein, review of *By the Light of My Father's Smile*, by Alice Walker, *New York Times* October 7, 1998.

(1980), is a comparative study that begins by tracing the history of African American novelists until the contemporary period. It culminates with chapters on Paule Marshall, Toni Morrison, and Walker and a conclusion linking the trio. The chapter on Walker became the basis of Smith's later book on Walker's "Everyday Use." Elliott Butler-Evans, *Race, Gender, and Desire: Narrative Strategies in the Fiction of Toni Cade Bambara, Toni Morrison, and Alice Walker* (1989), is another excellent comparative study; it offers a nuanced semiotic reading through contemporary feminist criticism. Butler-Evans's chapter devoted exclusively to Walker focuses primarily on *The Third Life of Grange Copeland, Meridian,* and *The Color Purple.* Ikenna Dieke, *Critical Essays on Alice Walker* (1999), is a highly diverse essay collection. Most of the essays are relatively short—under twenty pages—but each covers compelling subjects. The majority of essays are on *The Color Purple,* and a few focus upon Walker's poetry. Those that discuss Walker's other novels do so briefly, which makes the collection more valuable as a resource on her most famous single work. Louis H. Pratt and Darnell D. Pratt, *Alice Malsenior Walker: An Annotated Bibliography: 1968–1976,* is an outdated yet valuable resource listing works by and about Walker through the *Color Purple* controversy.

To date, approximately 225 dissertations and theses have been written about Walker's novels, short fiction, essays, and political activism, although Walker is usually one of several authors studied. The majority of those compare Walker to other African American authors, such as Zora Neale Hurston, Toni Morrison, Toni Cade Bambara, Gloria Naylor, Harriet Jacobs, or Gayl Jones, while many others compare Walker to other authors—often women—who write in the same genres she uses (autobiography/memoir, fantasy, epistolary novel, pastoral

novel, travel narrative, and so on) or to other explicitly political authors, including Margaret Atwood, Buchi Emecheta, James Baldwin, Louise Erdrich, and Joyce Carol Oates.

Similarly, Walker's work has received extensive treatment in no fewer than one hundred scholarly articles (excluding book reviews) since she emerged on the literary scene. While the majority discuss *The Color Purple,* Walker's short fiction and first two novels also receive extensive treatment. *Callaloo* in particular devoted a special section to Walker: issue 39, Spring 1989. The more prominent articles are: Philip M. Royster, "In Search of Our Fathers' Arms: Alice Walker's Persona of the Alienated Darling," *BALF* 20, no. 4 (Winter 1986); Jacqueline Bobo, "Sifting Through the Controversy: Reading *The Color Purple,*" *Callaloo* 39 (Spring 1989); Roberta M. Hendrickson, "Remembering the Dream: Alice Walker, *Meridian,* and the Civil Rights Movement," *MELUS* 24, no. 3 (Autumn 1999); Bonnie Braendlin, "Alice Walker's *The Temple of My Familiar* as Pastiche," *American Literature* 68, no. 1 (March 1996); Deborah E. Barker, "Visual Markers: Art and Mass Media in Alice Walker's *Meridian,*" *AAR* 31, no. 3 (Autumn 1997); Felipe Smith, "Alice Walker's Redemptive Art," and Ikenna Dieke, "Toward a Monastic Realism: The Thematics of Alice Walker's *The Temple of My Familiar,*" *AAR* 26, no. 3 (Autumn 1992); Maria V. Johnson, "'You Just Can't Keep a Good Woman Down': Alice Walker Sings the Blues," and Angeletta K. M. Gourdine, "Postmodern Ethnography and the Womanist Mission: Postcolonial Sensibilities in *Possessing the Secret of Joy,*" *AAR* 30, no. 2 (Summer 1996); Deborah E. McDowell, "'The Changing Same': Generational Connections and Black Women Novelists," *New Literary History* 18, no. 2 (Winter 1987); Ann duCille, "Phallus(ies) of Interpretation: Toward Engendering the Black Critical 'I,'" *Callaloo*

16, no. 3 (Summer 1993); Lynn Pifer, "Coming to Voice in Alice Walker's *Meridian*: Speaking Out for the Revolution," and James C. Hall, "Towards a Map of Mis(Sed) Reading: The Presence of Absence in *The Color Purple*," *AAR* 26, no. 1 (Spring 1992); Karen F. Stein, "*Meridian*: Alice Walker's Critique of Revolution," and Harold Hellenbrand, "Speech, After Silence: Alice Walker's *The Third Life of Grange Copeland*," *BALF* 20, nos. 1–2 (Spring–Summer 1986); Deborah E. McDowell, "New Directions for Black Feminist Criticism," *BALF* 14, no. 4 (Winter 1980); Anne M. Downey, " 'A Broken and Bloody Hoop': The Intertextuality of *Black Elk Speaks* and Alice Walker's *Meridian*," *MELUS* 19, no. 3 (Autumn 1994); Cynthia Hamilton, "Alice Walker's Politics or the Politics of *The Color Purple*," *Journal of Black Studies* 18, no. 3 (March 1988); Trudier Harris, "On *The Color Purple*, Stereotypes, and Silence" and Calvin Hernton, "The Sexual Mountain and Black Women Writers," *BALF* 18, no. 4 (Winter 1984); Trudier Harris, "Folklore in the Fiction of Alice Walker: A Perpetuation of Historical and Literary Traditions," *BALF* 11, no. 1 (Spring 1977); Patricia Sharpe, F. E. Mascia-Lees, and C. B. Cohen, "White Women and Black Men: Differential Responses to Reading Black Women's Texts," *College English* 52, no. 2 (February 1990); Joseph A. Brown, " 'All Saints Should Walk Away': The Mystical Pilgrimage of *Meridian*," *Callaloo* 39 (Spring 1989); King-Kok Cheung, " 'Don't Tell': Imposed Silences in *The Color Purple* and *The Woman Warrior*," *PMLA* 103, no. 2 (March 1988); Mary Jane Lupton, "Clothes and Closure in Three Novels by Black Women," *BALF* 20, no. 4 (Winter 1986); W. Lawrence Hogue, "History, the Feminist Discourse, and Alice Walker's *The Third Life of Grange Copeland*," *MELUS* 12, no. 2 (Summer 1985); Lynn Pifer and Tricia Slusser, " 'Looking at the Back of Your Head': Mirroring Scenes in Alice Walker's *The Color Purple* and *Possessing the Secret of Joy*," *MELUS* 23, no. 4 (Winter 1998).

Weaver, Afaa Michael (b. Michael S. Weaver, Baltimore, Maryland, 1951) Afaa M. Weaver is best known and most accomplished as a poet. Several of his short stories, however, have been published. The best—and best known—of these are "By the Way of Morning Fire," found in Gloria Naylor's collection *Children of the Night* (1995), and "Honey Boy," found in Maria Mazziotti Gillan and Jennifer Gillan's *Growing Up Ethnic in America: Contemporary Fiction About Learning to be American* (1999). Beyond his six books of poetry, Weaver has also edited *These Hands I Know: African-American Writers on Family* (2002). He is profiled in Lynda Koolish's *African American Writers: Portraits and Visions* (2001).

Whitehead, Colson (b. 1969, New York City) In the wake of Ralph Ellison's achievements in *Invisible Man* (1952), critics and aficionados of African American literature have habitually hailed the advent of purported successors to Ellison's intellectual and literary achievements. These pronouncements are invariably as problematic as they are premature; in the long view, an author is rarely well served by being compared to a canonized icon. Nevertheless, when Colson Whitehead's first novel, *The Intuitionist* (1999), emerged, it was almost universally praised as a work comparable to *Invisible Man*, Toni Morrison's *Bluest Eye* (1970), and the best work of Thomas Pynchon, Kurt Vonnegut, and Don DeLillo in terms of its genius and scope. It made the *New York Times* Notable Books and the *San Francisco Chronicle* Best Books of the Year lists and was among the finalists for the PEN/Faulkner Award in 1999. Whitehead's second novel, *John Henry Days* (2001), received even higher accolades and was a finalist for the

National Book Critics Circle Award, thereby avoiding the sophomore jinx and indicating that Whitehead may be one of the few authors for whom the hyperbole nearly matches the reality.

Whitehead's interviews have revealed his significant interest in popular culture, not uncommon among the post–Civil Rights generation. This interest led to a job writing music, television, and book reviews at the *Village Voice* in 1991. His first, and as yet unpublished, novel was, per his own description, "a kind of pop-culture-heavy book about a child-genius cherub, Michael Jackson–Gary Coleman type" who is forced to play various stereotypical roles.[1] When this manuscript was rejected over two dozen times, leading to Whitehead's agent abandoning him, Whitehead stumbled upon the idea of writing about elevator inspectors in a major city that closely resembles New York. The result, *The Intuitionist*, is an elaborate allegory exploring at once several crises of American modernity: the insidiousness of racism; the conflict between scientific knowledge and intuitive belief, especially the ways in which that struggle plays out in academic careerism; and the progress and regress of African Americans within the body politic. Set either in the near future or recent past, the elevator operators in question are divided between the Empiricists, who inspect elevators with scientific precision, and the Intuitionists, who complete their task through intuition and improvisation. Whitehead describes each faction as if it were a religious sect vying for control of the church, with each side ascribing heresy to the other.

This central conflict takes on a number of philosophical issues that defined tensions within critical discourse in the 1980s and 1990s. Questions of how scientific and other forms of knowledge are obtained, mastered, and become definitive—the cruces of epistemology—are the novel's central concerns, closely connected to inter- and intraracial tensions. The protagonist, Lila Mae, is the leading Intuitionist, as she is blessed with the ability to detect problems within elevators simply by standing inside them. The Empiricists find Lila Mae and her ilk threatening precisely because their methods lack a structure that can be easily adapted and therefore co-opted by the Empiricist majority. When an elevator that Lila Mae inspected fails immediately after she has given her approval, she and other Intuitionists are immediately accused of being irresponsible charlatans. The Intuitionists charge in return that Empiricists are closed to new methods. Lila Mae is caught in the middle of this epistemological holy war as she attempts to clear her name and the worldview she represents.

Outside of its sophisticated meditations on differences between the material and the physical, the novel's strengths are its irony, which is dispensed via the extremely witty and sardonic narrative voice, and its near-flawless weaving of pop culture references, contemporary history, and reflections on racial politics since the Civil Rights movement. Many of these same elements may be found in *John Henry Days*, albeit with a broader focus. That novel is a vast, picaresque epic featuring J. Sutter, as its nominal protagonist. He is an African American journalist, and his investigative reporting focuses on the United States Postal Service's new commemorative John Henry stamp. The true center of the novel is the John Henry legend itself, which Whitehead uses as a riff to delve into the intricate corners of America's postmodern, pop-cultural wasteland. The novel consists of a series of loosely connected vignettes, many wildly humorous

---

1. Christopher Mari, "Whitehead, Colson." *2001 Current Biography Yearbook* (New York: H. W. Wilson, 2001), 593–95.

and devastatingly ironic, that are as much about race in the post–Civil Rights era as they are about the larger American milieu itself. *John Henry Days* has been widely praised as a messy masterpiece comparable to recent works by Don DeLillo and David Foster Wallace, and it certainly deserves this esteemed company.

To date, little has been published on Whitehead's fiction in major literary journals, but this is likely to change in short order as it passes through academic writing and publishing cycles. This is not to say that it has not attracted academic interest; Candra K. Gill wrote a thesis, "Beyond Boundaries: Counter-Discourse and Intertextuality in Nalo Hopkinson's *Brown Girl in the Ring* and Colson Whitehead's *The Intuitionist*," in 2002 (master's thesis, Northern Michigan University). That same year, Whitehead was named a recipient of a MacArthur Fellowship, most likely based upon the achievements of his first two novels. In the meantime, Whitehead has given a number of interviews that help illuminate his artistic vision, and his novels have received some of the most thoughtful reviews that a contemporary author, African American or otherwise, could want. Perhaps most promising is the frequency with which Whitehead has been featured in such popular magazines as *Time* and *Newsweek*, which may help bring more attention to similar authors.

Wideman, Daniel Jerome (b. 1968; Philadelphia, Pennsylvania) Wideman is the son of prominent African American novelist John Edgar Wideman and Judy Ann Goldman. After attending Brown University, traveling abroad, and graduate work at Northwestern University, Wideman coedited the anthology *Soulfires: Young Black Men on Love and Violence* (1996) with Rohan B. Preston. His work has since been published in the journal *Callaloo* and the anthologies *Outside the Law: Narratives of Justice in America, Black*

Texts and Textuality, and *Giant Steps*. Of these three outlets, only *Outside the Law* contains actual fiction, the story "Free Papers."

Readers of the senior Wideman will find that Wideman *fils* compares well to his father yet possesses his own conversational, probing, and haunting voice that is equally captivating and delightful to read. His essay "Your Friendly Neighborhood Jungle" does hint at the degree to which he inherited some of his father's skills, but the essay and the rest of the younger Wideman's output are more remarkable for their painstaking explorations of African Americans' cultural identities, specifically their links to the African continent, its cultural riches, and the legacies of slavery. In addition, he tends to focus on more contemporary issues of identity, specifically those of the Post-Soul generation.

Wideman, John Edgar (b. June 14, 1941, Washington, D.C.) Although novelist, essayist, and passionate basketball aficionado John Edgar Wideman was born in Washington, D.C., his mature work has been focused primarily on his memories of life in Pittsburgh, Pennsylvania, where he spent his formative years. His earliest years were spent in Pittsburgh's predominantly black Homewood neighborhood, but he later moved to Shadyside, one of the city's predominantly white, affluent areas. This act of moving from a predominantly African American area to a white one would be repeated in Wideman's life and would also become one of his dominant metaphors. He won a scholarship to the University of Pennsylvania, where he studied psychology and English and was a star player on the school's basketball team. In 1963, Wideman became only the second African American to win a Rhodes Scholarship to Oxford University; Harlem Renaissance luminary Alain Locke was the first. At Oxford he studied eighteenth-century literature, earning a bachelor of philosophy degree in 1966. He then attended the Creative Writing Workshop at the University of Iowa from 1966 to 1967 as a Kent Fellow before accepting an appointment at the University of Pennsylvania (1967 to 1973). Since 1973, Wideman has been a professor of literature at the University of Wyoming. That state's dearth of African American culture and the ways in which Wideman and his family have coped with it have been extensive sources of inspiration and material in Wideman's later fiction, which is easily his best.

Wideman's stories and novels repeatedly plumb the depths of the African Diaspora's anguish as its members have been forced, whether physically or by economic need, or have chosen to become deracinated from their own Homewoods: the areas, cultures, ideas, and lives into which they were born. Wideman is equally fascinated by definitions of manhood within African American communities, the innumerable ways in which American culture perceives black males as threats, and how the quest for black manhood can be both self-destructive and liberating. This particular issue continuously bubbles beneath the surface or explodes outright in the overwhelming majority of Wideman's work. Such interests should not be confused, however, with the overt political content of the Black Arts Movement, which was in ascendance as Wideman's artistic career began with the publication of his first novel, *A Glance Away*, in 1967. Wideman has a strong interest in investigating the human condition in general, which has earned him praise from critics wary of political agendas in African American literature. Without a doubt, though, Wideman has garnered success and praise from the widest possible spectrum of critics.

Wideman's first two novels, *A Glance Away* (1967) and *Hurry Home* (1969), are existential explorations of the identity that feature an interracial mix of protagonists and consciously eschew a specific focus upon race as a discrete category. In that respect, they stand apart from many African American works of the Black Power/Arts/ aesthetic era. *The Lynchers* (1973) is the first of Wideman's novels in which concerns about race and racism play prominent roles in the plot. It opens with a long catalogue of brutal lynching accounts from the late nineteenth and twentieth centuries before launching into the main plot, a "blend of realism and surrealism" in which Willie "Littleman" Hall attempts to launch a scheme that would end in a white policeman being publicly lynched by the black community of Philadelphia's South Side.[1] Hall's plan is meant to release the community of its fear of white people—specifically of *killing* whites—and is inspired in part by the splintering and collapse of Orin and Bernice Wilkerson's family. Their son, Thomas, is interested in Littleman's plan, but in an increasingly complex sequence of events, he finds that the prospect of communal and nationalistic revolution embodied in the lynching plot is far more difficult than he had determined. In the course of executing the narrative, Wideman experiments with many different techniques and points of view, creating the best of his early works.

Arguably, the crowning achievement of Wideman's oeuvre is his Homewood Trilogy: *Damballah* (1981, short stories), *Hiding Place* (1981, novel) and *Sent for You Yesterday* (1983, novel), published eight years after Wideman's last major work, *The Lynchers*. The trilogy not only included a PEN/ Faulkner award winner in *Sent for You Yes-*

---

1. Bernard W. Bell, *The Afro-American Novel and Its Tradition* (Amherst: University of Massachusetts Press, 1987), 309.

terday, but it also placed Homewood clearly on the literary map. Wideman's Homewood may be compared favorably to Faulkner's Yoknapatawpha County or Joyce's Dublin in terms of vibrancy and complexity, although it is perhaps more emotionally devastating than either. *Damballah* contains some of Wideman's best short stories. One of the finest is the heavily anthologized title story, an account of the enslaved—but never subjugated—griot Orion, who keeps African traditions, especially reverence for the god Damballah, alive and inspires a young boy to maintain them. *Damballah*'s vignettes blend tragedy, cultural confrontations, myth, and mysticism to discover how Homewood came to have its history and sense of community. *Reuben* (1987) follows the lives of three characters living in Homewood: Reuben, a self-styled lawyer of sorts for the community; Kwansa, who recruits Reuben in the search for her five-year-old son; and the murderous Wally, a college scout. The novel explores the nature of personal tragedies and how individual characters find the means to cope and live with those tragedies; those who do not find themselves destroyed physically and psychically. Wideman furthers his experiments with vernacular language and point of view begun in his earlier Homewood stories and novels as well.

Fever (1990) collects twelve short stories about a wide variety of subjects, including Wideman's own writing. The story "Surfiction," for example, parodies Wideman's most difficult fiction, consciously playing with his longtime readers' expectations. That same year, Wideman published *Philadelphia Fire*, an extraordinary novel that both concerns and is inspired by the May 13, 1985, firebombing of the West Philadelphia neighborhood in which the controversial MOVE organization was headquartered. The bombing resulted in the deaths of 6 adults and 5 children and the destruction of 53 houses, which left 262 people homeless.

The novel is not so much about the event as it is a lyrical chronicling of the complexities of black neighborhoods whose demographics, politics, and culture shifted and decayed in the crises of the 1980s. *All Stories Are True* (1992), a collection of stories excerpted from the previous year's *The Stories of John Edgar Wideman* (1992), consists of ten stories drawn from the author's vision of Homewood and academe, and it is one of the better introductions to his craft.

Finally, Wideman's epistolary memoir *Brothers and Keepers* (1984), although technically nonfiction, ranks among his best work. It is an extended, wrenching meditation on the differences between Wideman's great artistic and personal success and the fate of his brother Robby, who was sent to prison in 1976 for armed robbery and murder. Wideman succeeds in blending, in his words, "memory, imagination, feeling, and fact" into a frank yet compassionate account of the brothers' emotional and physical strife.

Wideman's work has earned him an extensive list of awards, fellowships, and honors. He has been a Rhodes Scholar (1963), Kent Fellow (1966–67), and was the recipient of the PEN/Faulkner award twice, in 1984 for *Sent for You Yesterday* and in 1991 for *Philadelphia Fire*. In 1993, Wideman received a MacArthur Fellow, the so-called Genius Grant.

To date, book-length critical studies of Wideman's work have been limited. Bonnie TuSmith edited *Conversations with John Edgar Wideman* (1998), an invaluable source of Wideman's own thoughts on his fiction and related issues. But only three books on Wideman alone are currently in print: Keith Byerman, *John Edgar Wideman: A Study of the Short Fiction* (1998); James William Coleman, *Blackness and Modernism: The Literary Development of John Edgar Wideman* (1989); and Doreatha D. Mbalia, *John Edgar Wideman: Reclaiming the African Per-*

sonality (1995). Each of these books has great merit on its own terms, but all are quite limited in their scope and outlook for various reasons. Byerman's, of course, looks only at the short fiction, while Coleman's places Wideman in the context of modernism, which many critics have noted over the years. Mbalia's is arguably the most inventive, but its focus on African elements necessarily excludes many other considerations.

Readers of Wideman's fiction, therefore, might do better by seeking studies not devoted solely to his work. Philip Auger, *Native Sons in No Man's Land: Rewriting Afro-American Manhood in the Novels of Baldwin, Walker, Wideman, and Gaines* (2000), is especially valuable for its attention to a theme that torments Wideman's most memorable characters. Of the more than two dozen extant critical essays on Wideman, several stand out for their creative perspectives: Ashraf Rushdy, "Fraternal Blues: John Edgar Wideman's Homewood Trilogy," *Contemporary Literature* 32, no. 3 (Fall 1991); Madhu Dubey, "Literature and Urban Crisis: John Edgar Wideman's *Philadelphia Fire*," *AAR* 32, no. 4 (Winter 1998); Heather Andrade, "'Mosaic Memory': Auto/biographical Contexts in John Edgar Wideman's Brothers and Keepers," *The Massachusetts Review* 40, no. 3 (Autumn 1999); and Mumia Abu-Jamal, "The Fictive Realism of John Edgar Wideman," *The Black Scholar* 28, no. 1 (Spring 1998), which is unique in that activist and journalist Abu-Jamal is a longtime advocate for the MOVE organization, featured in *Philadelphia Fire*. Finally, the entire Summer 1999 issue of *Callaloo* was devoted to Wideman's work and represents the most diverse collection of essays on his work currently in print.

Williams, John Alfred (b. 1925, Hinds County, Mississippi) Novelist, journalist, and essayist John A. Williams is one of the most enduring and prolific authors to begin a writing career in the 1960s. Over the course of eleven novels, as well as six nonfiction books, three anthologies of both his own and others' writing, a play, and hundreds of essays, Williams has maintained an intensely political focus upon African Americans' experiences that usually manages to avoid pedantry. He is best known as the author of *The Man Who Cried I Am* (1967), a landmark book of social-realist fiction that frequently has been compared to Richard Wright's *Native Son* (1940) and Ralph Ellison's *Invisible Man* (1952). Since 1970, Williams has continued to write and publish often, although only one novel, *Captain Blackman* (1972), has approached the popularity of *The Man Who Cried I Am*, although it is in many ways more artistically successful than its predecessor. Williams has also played a significant role as an editor; he coedited the seminal anthologies *Amistad* (1970) and *Amistad II* (1971) with Charles F. Harris and compiled *Yardbird No. 1* (1979), which reprinted material from Ishmael Reed and Al Young's *Yardbird Reader* magazine. In addition, Williams edited a key textbook of the 1980s, *Introduction to Literature* (1984).

Most of Williams's novels fit the definition of the useful art that the Black Arts Movement demanded, to the extent that they draw upon Williams's own life experiences as well as those of many others within African American communities. One of Williams's most harrowing and foundational experiences came from his time in the United States Navy, in which he enlisted in 1943 after growing up in Syracuse, New York. Williams witnessed firsthand the racism inherent both in the rigidly segregated armed forces and in the conduct of the Pacific Theater of World War II. His stint involved, in fact, a stretch in the brig for violating the Navy's rules regarding segregation.[1] These experiences in the Navy and with other forms of legal and customary segregation while growing up in Syracuse, New York, and working in New York City's publishing industry formed Williams's continuing belief in the exploitative nature of American society, especially along racial lines. His early novels—*The Angry Ones* (1956; republished 1969; later republished as *One for New York*—Williams's original title—in 1975), *Night Song* (1961), *Sissie* (1963), *The Man Who Cried I Am* (1967), and *Sons of Darkness, Sons of Light* (1969)—all deal with the difficulties African Americans encounter as they try to sidestep America's racial barriers to find gainful, fulfilling employment. Although they are not the sort of seminal characters as Richard Wright's Bigger Thomas from *Native Son* (1940), Williams's early protagonists share that creation's frustration with the policies and practices of the color line.

Yet Williams's abiding interest has also been to educate his audience regarding African American history and to get that audience to identify with his protagonists. Paradoxically, each of Williams's novels seems to build upon the achievements of its predecessor, yet *Captain Blackman* is perhaps the culmination of Williams's attempts to create heroic yet sympathetic characters. The novel, Williams's sixth, is the third in a triptych beginning with *The Man Who Cried I Am* and continuing with *Sons of Darkness, Sons of Light*. Each of these novels faetures a plot that ultimately turns apocalyptic, positing the possibility that a devastating race war is the likely result of the duplicity of the U.S. government, to say nothing of the general public's complicity. In the case of *Captain Blackman*, the U.S. comes under specific indictment. It is the story of Abraham Blackman, a captain in the U.S. Army

during the Vietnam War who, after being wounded in battle, is transported back in time to every major military conflict in U.S. history through the delirium caused by his injuries. All of these conflicts involved African Americans in one way or another—often in prominent or pivotal roles—and it is into the lives and experiences of earlier black soldiers that Blackman and the men in his unit are transported. Through their experiences in the past, Blackman and his integrated platoon learn about the many ways in which African Americans have been exploited in American military history, which symbolizes the way that power has been denied African Americans in general. Their ultimate plan is to obtain freedom through power. In the course of reaching this plan, Williams offers unflinching portrayals of the brutality and complexities of war, which is linked symbolically to the complex oppression African Americans have both endured and participated in, whether willfully and wittingly or not. The novel's crux is the question of the origins and means of obtaining agency and power.

Power or its absence, therefore, ultimately occupies Williams' artistic focus. To be more specific, he is interested in the myriad ways African American historical figures and artists have pursued and been denied agency and power and the methods by which they were denied their dreams and opportunities. In *!Click Song* (1982), Williams's autobiographical protagonist is novelist William Cato Douglass, who finds himself improving as a writer as he becomes more sophisticated and perspicacious with regard to both his art and his racial identity but is also increasingly ignored by critics, reviewers, and academics. Douglass simultaneously descends into despair and finds sustenance and meaning in his writing, which most others fail to com-

---

1. James L. de Jongh, "John A. Williams," *DLB* 51:280.

prehend. The novel's title, in fact, refers to black South African songs and languages that were for many years beyond the ken of European ears and sensibilities in much the same way that Douglass's/Williams's novels are incomprehensible to a critical establishment that long ago lost interest in a highly talented, accomplished, yet challenging author.

The Berhama Account (1985) tells of an elaborate assassination plot against the head of a small Caribbean nation that eventually leads to extensive social reforms. *Jacob's Ladder* (1989) is a novel about Pandemi, a mythical African nation that aspires to obtain true independence by eschewing the aid of both the United States and the Soviet bloc. It functions as an extended meditation on the state of former colonized states on the African continent, arguing that colonialism never ended; it was merely transformed into new forms of financial and material dependence. *Clifford's Blues* (1999) is a book of travel fiction that is based upon Williams's own travels.

Despite his eminence in the history of African American letters, Williams's corpus of fiction arguably has not been studied to the extent it should merit, given its breadth, its depth, and Williams's enormous influence. On the other hand, Williams has not been ignored, either. His papers have been stored in the University of Rochester's library since 1987, and several books examining Williams's works and career, especially his early novels, have been published, along with many excellent comparative articles. Of the former, a first choice should be Gilbert Muller, *John A. Williams* (1984), from Twayne Publishers' United States Authors series, if only because Muller is one of Williams's close friends and collaborators. Earl Cash's earlier—and therefore significantly outdated—*John A. Williams: Evolution of a Black Writer* (1975) is valuable primarily because of its extensive and balanced

analysis of Williams's life and work through *Captain Blackman.*

Williams, Sherley Anne (b. 1944, Bakersfield, California; d. 1999, San Diego, California) Sherley Anne Williams's literary reputation has rested primarily upon two major components of her oeuvre. The longtime Fresno, California, resident is one of the more accomplished poets to emerge from the Black Arts Movement era, and her first novel, *Dessa Rose* (1986), stands as one of the finest to be published in the 1980s. Her poetic accomplishments have been celebrated elsewhere, but it is worth mentioning that Williams's first book of poetry, *The Peacock Poems* (1975), was nominated for both a National Book Award and the Pulitzer Prize in 1976. Williams's poetry and fiction have drawn on a number of strong influences, including poets Langston Hughes, Philip Levine (one of Williams's professors at Fresno State College, now Fresno State University, where she earned her B.A.), Amiri Baraka, and Sterling Brown. The fictional and nonfictional works of authors Richard Wright and Eartha Kitt were also extremely important, as were the lyrical content and rhythms of the blues, which can be seen throughout Williams's work. After completing graduate work at Howard University, Williams earned her M.A. at Brown University in 1972 and began a long tenure at the University of California at San Diego until her death in 1999.

Williams began writing and publishing short stories in the late 1960s; the first of these is "Tell Marth Not to Moan," which shows Williams's blues influences; it has since been widely anthologized. Save for a book of criticism, *Give Birth to Brightness* (1972), however, Williams concentrated most of her efforts in poetry until *Dessa Rose.* Its story is based upon two actual historical incidents: a pregnant, enslaved woman's rebellion on a coffle (a line of slaves chained together for transportation to a slave auction) in Kentucky in 1829, and a white woman who gave sanctuary to runaway slaves on her North Carolina farm in 1830. Williams's novel imagines what would have occurred had these women met. It is an example of what Ashraf Rushdy calls a neo–slave narrative, "contemporary novels that assume the form, adopt the conventions, and take on the first-person voice of the antebellum slave narrative," often to make a number of arguments about the ways in which history and individuals' personal stories are recorded, interpreted, and frequently misunderstood.[1] Many neo–slave narratives are partially responses to the controversy surrounding William Styron's *Confessions of Nat Turner* (1967), which many African American writers and critics roundly condemned for its interpreting Nat Turner's original testimony by focusing upon a questionable reconstruction of his psyche and sexual proclivities, as well as the marked absence of his historical wife.[2] Thus while the story of the enslaved woman, Dessa Rose, is told primarily through her own voice, it also comprises the narrative viewpoint of Nemi, an unreliable white male amanuensis who refers to Dessa as a "darky," and Miss Rufel, a white female plantation owner, who is considerably more sympathetic to Dessa but still problematic as a narrator due to her idealism. The plot tells of Dessa's life on a plantation, the path that led to her motherhood, the growth of her desires for freedom and her own voices, and her subsequent escape with Miss Rufel's aid. As in Williams's earlier work, the story of loss and survival that is essential in the blues informs every aspect of Dessa's narration. In many respects, Williams's gestures in re-creating Dessa's story prefigure and

parallel Toni Morrison's masterpiece, *Beloved* (1987), which is based upon the history of Margaret Garner, an enslaved woman who attempted to kill her children—succeeding with one—and herself rather than return to slavery. In fact, Anne E. Goldman fully makes the argument via her comparative essay, "'I Made the Ink': (Literary) Production and Reproduction in *Dessa Rose* and *Beloved*."

Although a substantial portion of the critical work on Williams has focused on her poetry, *Dessa Rose* has received a wealth of attention as well. Besides Rushdy's *Neo-slave Narratives* (1999), Mary Kemp Davis, "Everybody Knows Her Name: The Recovery of the Past in Sherley Anne Williams's *Dessa Rose*," *Callaloo* 40, no. 1 (Spring 1989) offers a meticulous discussion of the importance of the neo–slave narrative form and *Dessa Rose*'s place within the tradition. Shirley M. Jordan's exquisite biography of Williams may be found in Claudia Tate's *Black Women Writers at Work* (1983), while Jordan's interview with Williams may be found in Jordan's collection *Broken Silences: Interviews with Black and White Women Writers* (1993). Mae Henderson, "(W)riting *The Work* and Working the Rites," *BALF* 23, no. 4 (Winter 1989), is a detailed analysis of the relationship of *Dessa Rose* to Styron and to African American cultural rituals and forms, including the blues; Henderson's essay on the novel's erotic elements and subversive qualities may be found in *Female Subjects in Black and White: Race, Psychoanalysis, Feminism* (1997), edited by Elizabeth Abel, Barbara Christian, and Helene Moglen. Farah Jasmine Griffin, "Textual Healing: Claiming Black Women's Bodies, the Erotic, and Resistance in Contemporary Novels of Slavery," *Callaloo* 19, no. 2 (Spring 1996) follows a similar tack,

1. Rushdy, *Neo-slave Narratives: Studies in the Social Logic of a Literary Form* (New York: Oxford University Press, 1999), 3.

2. Rushdy, *Neo-slave Narratives*, 54, 61ff.

230 A–Z Guide to Contemporary African American Fiction

with special emphasis on how *Dessa Rose* and other neo–slave narratives portray African American women as fully human subjects, complete with sexual identities and desires, rather than as objects. Marta E. Sanchez, "The Estrangement Effect in Sherley Anne Williams' *Dessa Rose*," *Genders* 15 (Winter 1992), examines the novel's narrative technique and voices.

Womanism "Womanism" is a term that author Alice Walker coined to help define a way for African American women to be feminists in ways relevant to Black people. The best definition may be found in Walker's *In Search of Our Mother's Gardens: Womanist Prose* (1984):

> Womanist 1. From *womanish*. (Opp. of "girlish," i.e., frivolous, irresponsible, not serious.) A black feminist or feminist of color. From the black folk expression of mothers to female children, "You acting womanish," i.e., like a woman. Usually referring to outrageous, audacious, courageous or *willful* behavior. Wanting to know more and in greater depth than is considered "good" for one. Interested in grown-up doings. Acting grown up. Being grown up. Interchangeable with another black folk expression: "You trying to be grown." Responsible. In charge. *Serious*.
> 2. *Also*: A woman who loves other women, sexually and/or nonsexually. Appreciates and prefers women's culture, women's emotional flexibility (values tears as natural counterbalance of laughter), and women's strength. Sometimes loves individual men, sexually and/or nonsexually. Committed to survival and wholeness of entire people, male *and* female. Not a separatist, except periodically, for health. Tradi-

tionally universalist, as in: "Mama, why are we brown, pink, and yellow, and our cousins are white, beige, and black?" Ans.: "Well, you know the colored race is just like a flower garden, with every color flower represented." Traditionally capable, as in: "Mama, I'm walking to Canada and I'm taking you and a bunch of other slaves with me." Reply: "It wouldn't be the first time."[1]

Walker posited the concept of womanism to distinguish the struggles African American women have faced from those of the mainstream—that is, white—women's rights movement, which has sometimes been oblivious, insensitive, or even hostile to African American women's history and concerns. Walker, as an editor for and frequent contributor to the pro-woman/feminist magazine *Ms.*, wrote many articles criticizing modern feminism's blind spots. Her main argument is that African American women have historically been less concerned with entering the workplace, since they have always been forced to work, whether because of enslavement or necessity. A feminism that fails to recognize this fact is therefore inadequate, inasmuch as it is tailored more for middle-class white women. A secondary complaint may be found within the definition above. Specifically, African American women, while strong and independent, are not likely to be gender separatists. They appreciate their womanhood but do not necessarily subscribe to the converse: antipathy towards men qua men. Instead, African American women/womanists desire economic independence and mutually beneficial relationships with men. A womanist would understand, for example, that one of her goals is "to assure understanding among black women, and that understanding among

---

1. Alice Walker, *In Search of Our Mothers' Gardens: Womanist Prose* (New York: Harcourt Brace, 1984), xi.

women is not a threat to anyone who intends to treat women fairly."[1]

To the extent that Walker's theory attempts to inscribe a strong, consistent critique of sexism and racism into African American intellectual discourse, womanism's precepts bear a strong resemblance to those of the Combahee River Collective, whose 1977 statement also asserts the possibilities for liberation found in black women's identities, voices, and political work. As Walker outlines in her essay, "Duties of the Black Revolutionary Artist," the "real revolution is always concerned with the least glamorous stuff. With raising a reading level from second grade to third. With simplifying history and writing it down (or reciting it) for the old folks. With helping illiterates fill out food-stamp forms—for they must eat, revolution or not. The dull, frustrating work with our people is the work of the black revolutionary artist."[2] Such revolutionary work includes helping women and men to find and appreciate their voices and ways to express themselves that may range from the written, to the verbal, to expressive artistic forms that transcend the verbal.[3]

Walker thus envisions womanism as she does her other ideal political positions: firmly based in grassroots activism and therefore focused on individual and contingent needs rather than on concerns and strategies strictly circumscribed by ideology. The goal is to eschew hierarchies constructed by men for men, in favor of inclusive pluralities and a pantheism that stands in sharp contradistinction to traditional religions. It requires women making full use of their voices and their creative capacities, however they might be manifested. In African American fiction, especially Walker's own, such

possibilities may be offered either by portraying them in imagined worlds or positing them through the words and actions of pivotal characters. This is especially true of Walker's later works, especially *The Color Purple, The Temple of My Familiar*, and *Possessing the Secret of Joy*. Walker demonstrates the double burden of racism and sexism that African American women bear throughout her novels and short stories, but if womanism may be considered an aesthetic, it is best illustrated in the later selections.

As one might expect, Walker's womanism lacks neither precedents nor fellow travelers. The poetry, novels, and stories of Toni Cade Bambara, Bebe Moore Campbell, Edwidge Danticat, Gayl Jones, Jamaica Kincaid, Audre Lorde, Paule Marshall, Toni Morrison, Gloria Naylor, Sonia Sanchez, Sapphire, Ntozake Shange, Sherley Anne Williams, and many others are frequently cited as exemplars of a womanist aesthetic. Even if they were not influenced directly by Walker's work—and many were—these authors have either professed strong desires to give voice to frequently silenced women's concerns via their fiction or to encourage others to do so. This may involve citing a matrilineal string of influences ranging from archetypal or legendary African women, to everyday women and pioneering African American women of letters.

Analyses of womanism and its role in African American literature may be found throughout African American literary criticism since the late 1970s, but a few books and essays have distinguished themselves in their complexity and sensitivity to the subject. Among them are: Tuzyline Jita Allan, *Womanist and Feminist Aesthetics: A Comparative Review* (1995), which includes a chapter on Walker's *Color Purple*; Elliott

1. Walker, "A Letter to the Editor of *Ms.*," in *In Search of Our Mothers' Gardens*, 273.
2. Walker, "Duties of the Black Revolutionary Artist," in *In Search of Our Mothers' Gardens*, 135.
3. See Walker, "In Search of Our Mothers' Gardens," in *In Search of Our Mothers' Gardens*, pages 231–43.

Butler-Evans, *Race, Gender, and Desire: Narrative Strategies in the Fiction of Toni Cade Bambara, Toni Morrison, and Alice Walker* (1989), whose definition of womanism is particularly accessible, especially when applied to the authors named in the title; Lean'tin L. Bracks, *Writings on Black Women of the Diaspora: History, Language, and Identity* (1998), a monograph that includes chapters on Toni Morrison, Alice Walker, and Paule Marshall.

Equally important would be the major books of essays on African American feminism and feminism among people of color, including *All the Women Are White, All the Blacks Are Men, But Some of Us Are Brave: Black Women's Studies* (1982), and *This Bridge Called My Back: Writings by Radical Women of Color* (1981).

Young, Al (b. 1939, Ocean Springs, Mississippi) Novelist and editor Al Young published five novels between 1970 and 2000, all of which were well received. The Mississippian's close affiliation with Ishmael Reed has also yielded a number of major publishing projects that helped push African American literature forward during the same period. Through their eponymously named publishing company, Young and Reed coedited *Yardbird Reader*, a magazine devoted to multicultural fiction, poetry, and criticism. Young also edited *African American Literature: A Brief Introduction and Anthology* (1996), one of many anthologies of African American literature to hit the market in the wake of the *Norton Anthology of African American Literature* (1996), as part of publisher Harper Collins' Literary Mosaic series, edited by Ishmael Reed.

Young's first novel, *Snakes* (1970) is a *Künstlerroman* (novel of artistic and personal growth) set during one year in the ghettoes of Detroit, Michigan, where MC, a young guitarist who forms a band with his friends Champ and Shakes. Champ functions as MC's mentor as the latter tries to escape both his own limits and those found within the ghetto through his music and reflection. In the process, MC is forced to choose between his girlfriend, Donna Lee; his friends, especially Champ, who becomes involved in the illicit drug trade; and his grandmother, Claude. Each of these characters is a force that alternates between being inspirational and fulfilling to MC and being a hindrance to his personal and musical growth. Eventually he leaves Detroit for New York City on the path to freedom, growth, and fulfillment. *Who is Angelina?* (1975) is similar to *Snakes* in many ways, with the protagonist in search of her own identity through her friends and romantic encounters. Angelina seeks sophistication in her life and finds eventually that many of her friends and acquaintances are too busy trying to escape the world than live in it. By the end of the novel, she discovers that personal fulfillment comes from one's own inner strength and resolve.

Sitting Pretty (1976) is the story of Sidney J. Prettymon, also known as Sitting Pretty or "Sit," a father, former husband, ladies' man, and rogue down on his luck due to his drinking and philandering. His adventures in the San Francisco Bay Area with his friends and family allow him many opportunities to wax philosophically upon life as a black man in America, particularly in eclectic and multicultural northern California. *Ask Me Now* (1980) revolves around Durwood Knight, a retired professional basketball player who rediscovers himself as a man and as a father once he leaves the world of sports. *Seduction by Light* (1988) recounts the life of Mamie Franklin, a former singer and actor who works as a part-time maid for a rich family in Beverly Hills while maintaining a career as a psychic and mystic healer. Her struggles with the ghost of her former lover, Burley, and her sons offer a warm yet humorous insight into everything from family to race and class relations.

Young has received many awards for his work in both poetry and fiction: the San Francisco Foundation's Joseph Henry Jackson Award (1969); National Arts Council awards for editing and poetry (1968–1970); National Endowment for the Arts fellowships (1968, 1969, 1975); a Pushcart Prize (1980); a Guggenheim Foundation Fellowship (1974); a *New York Times* Outstanding Book of the Year citation (1980); a Before Columbus Foundation American Book Award (1982); and fellowships from the Wallace Stegner and Fulbright foundations. He has also received considerable scholarly attention for both his poetry and prose. He is profiled in Irv Broughton, ed., *The Writer's Mind: Interviews with American Authors*, vol. 3 (1990) and in Don L. Lee, "About Al Young," *Ploughshares* 19, no. 1 (Spring 1993). His work is also studied in the following articles: Douglass Bolling, "Artistry and Theme in Al Young's *Snakes*," *NALF* 8, no. 2 (Summer 1974); William J. Harris, "*The Yardbird Reader* and the Multi-Ethnic Spirit," *MELUS* 8, no. 2 (Summer 1981); Elizabeth A. Schultz, "The Insistence upon Community in the Contemporary Afro-American Novel," *College English* 41, no. 2 (October 1979).

Youngblood, Shay (b. 1959, Columbus, Georgia) Shay Youngblood is best known as an accomplished and award-winning playwright and poet, but she has also published many short stories to significant acclaim and two notable novels. Her short story "Born with Religion" won the Pushcart Prize, which is awarded to stories, poetry,

essays, and plays published in small presses. In 2002, Youngblood was named the University of Mississippi's John Grisham writer-in-residence.

Youngblood's fiction has made a significant impact in women's literature circles, particularly in the gay and lesbian communities. Her work cannot, however, be pigeonholed in those categories, as it focuses at least as often upon life in the deep South, with which Youngblood is intimately familiar. Youngblood's fiction is concerned with issues of loss, definitions of family and motherhood, the resonance and resilience of African American communities, and how black women form the linchpins of those same communities. Youngblood's first collection of fiction, *The Big Mama Stories* (1989), centers around a protagonist who is orphaned at an early age—as Youngblood was—and finds herself raised and taught by several different women in her Southern African American community, the "Big Mamas" of the title. The wisdom they pass on to her about life and love allow her to discover, albeit painfully, her identity as a woman, her poetic voice as an author, and her sexuality. Youngblood's first novel, *Soul Kiss* (1997), covers ground similar to *The Big Mama Stories*, with the primary difference being that the protagonist, Mariah, is abandoned by her mother, Coral, at a young age and cared for by her aunts and later (and to a lesser degree) by her previously absent father, Matisse. Mariah learns, as does the protagonist of Big Mama Stories, about the pain that comes with the search for the type of sustained love that can help heal the feelings of abandonment and other forms of abuse she experiences. In her second novel, *Black Girl in Paris* (2000), Youngblood's largely autobiographical protagonist, Eden, travels to Paris in 1986 to find inspiration from the literary paths burned by James Baldwin, Richard Wright, and other African

American expatriate writers. Eden's sojourn revolves around her financial struggles and the cultural differences between the United States and France. Along the way, she makes extended observations about "race," politics, ethnicity, and sexuality.

Youngblood's strengths as a writer include her ability to explore her protagonist's inner world and the concomitant process of self-discovery they undergo, usually through language and the written word. Many reviewers of these two books found a substantial improvement between the first and the second to the extent that Youngblood drew more realistic and three-dimensional characters. While the reviewers for *Publishers Weekly* and the *New York Times Book Review* found *Black Girl in Paris*'s setting and characters either inaccurate or too full of unintentional and highly problematic national and ethnic stereotypes, other reviewers found Youngblood's ability to discuss sexuality frankly and intelligently powerful. As a result, *Black Girl in Paris* won a Lambda Literary Award for Lesbian Fiction in 2001.

Youngblood has not received any substantial scholarly treatment. Several insightful interviews exist, however. The best of these would be "Delicious, Forbidden: An Interview with Shay Youngblood," *Lambda Book Report* 6, no. 2 (September 1997).

Selected Bibliography

PRIMARY LITERATURE
Anthologies

Barksdale, Richard C. and Keneth Kinnamon, eds. *Black Writers of America: A Comprehensive Anthology*. New York: McMillan, 1972.

Cade, Toni, ed. *The Black Woman*. New York: New American Library, 1970.

Chapman, Abraham, ed. *New Black Voices: An Anthology of Contemporary Afro-American Literature*. New York: Mentor, 1972.

Donalson, Melvin, ed. *Cornerstones: An Anthology of African American Literature*. New York: St. Martin's, 1996.

Gates, Henry Louis, Jr., Nellie Y. McKay, et al., eds. *The Norton Anthology of African American Literature*. New York: Norton, 1996.

Hamer, Judith A., and Martin J. Hamer, eds. *Centers of the Self: Short Stories by Black American Women from the Nineteenth Century to the Present*. New York: Hill and Wang, 1994.

Hill, Patricia Liggins, Bernard W. Bell, Trudier Harris, et al., eds. *Call and Response: The Riverside Anthology of the African American Literary Tradition*. Boston: Houghton Mifflin, 1998.

James, Charles L., ed. *From the Roots: Short Stories by Black Americans*. New York: Dodd, Mead, 1970.

Koolish, Lynda, ed. *African American Writers: Portraits and Visions*. Jackson: University Press of Mississippi, 2001.

McMillan, Terry, ed. *Breaking Ice: An Anthology of Contemporary African-American Fiction*. New York: Penguin, 1990.

> Terry McMillan's anthology is one of the best documents of the wave of African American fiction writers who emerged in the 1970s and 1980s. Most of the contents are short stories, although a few novel chapters may be found within as well. Major authors include: McMillan, Ntozake Shange, Toni Morrison, Ishmael Reed, J. California Cooper, Alice Walker, Gloria Naylor, Darryl Pinckney, Trey Ellis, and John Edgar Wideman.

Major, Clarence, ed. *Calling the Wind: Twentieth Century African-American Short Stories*. New York: HarperPerennial, 1993.

Mullen, Bill. *Revolutionary Tales: African American Women's Short Stories, From the First Story to the Present*. New York: Laurel, 1995.

Naylor, Gloria, ed. *Children of the Night: The Best Short Stories by Black Writers, 1967 to the Present*. Boston: Little, Brown, 1995.

O'Hearn, Claudine Chiawei, ed. *Half and Half: Writers on Growing up Biracial and Bicultural*. New York: Pantheon, 1998.

Powell, Kevin, ed. *Step Into a World: A Global Anthology of the New Black Literature*. New York: Wiley, 2000.

Powell, Kevin, and Ras Baraka, eds. *In the Tradition: An Anthology of Young Black Writers*. New York: Harlem River Press, 1992.

Quashie, Kevin Everod, Joyce Lausch, and Keith D. Miller, eds. *New Bones: Contemporary Black Writers in America*. Upper Saddle, N.J.: Prentice Hall, 2001.

> *New Bones* features writers of fiction, poetry, drama, essays, criticism, autobiography, and philosophy from 1970 through 2001. One of the most thorough anthologies of its kind, as both new and more established authors are included, with helpful biographies accompanying each author's contributions.

Reed, Ishmael, ed. *19 Necromancers from Now*. Garden City, N.Y.: Anchor Books, 1970.

Reed gathers together many of the major voices in African American fiction of the late 1960s and early 1970s, with two Asian-American authors, Frank Chin and Shawn Wong, added to the mix. Its major weakness is the complete absence of women authors, despite the volume's mission to be an introduction to the experimental fiction of the era's writers of color. Nevertheless, the selections are consistently excellent and provocative. Featured authors include Reed, Cecil Brown, Ronald Fair, William Melvin Kelley, Clarence Major, John A. Williams, Charles Wright, and Al Young.

Reed, Ishmael, and Al Young, eds. *Yardbird Lives!* New York: Grove, 1978.

This is a compilation of poetry, fiction, and drama printed in *Yardbird Reader*, a magazine published and edited by novelist Ishmael Reed from 1972 to 1976. Contributing authors include Amiri Baraka, Cecil Brown, Claude Brown, Steve Cannon, Victor C. Cruz, Bob Fox, Colleen J. McElroy, Merceditas Manabat, E. Ethelbert Miller, Ibn Mukhtarr Mustapha, Francisco Newman, Thulani Nkabinde, Diana Rollins, Ntozake Shange, Lorenzo Thomas, Shawn Wong, and many others.

Reed, Ishmael, Kathryn Trueblood, and Shawn Wong, eds. *The Before Columbus Foundation Fiction Anthology: Selections from the American Book Awards, 1980–1990*. New York: Norton, 1992.

Robotham, Mary, ed. *Mending the World: Stories of Family by Contemporary Black Writers*. New York: Basic Civitas, 2003.

Rowell, Charles H., ed. *Ancestral House: The Black Short Story in the Americas and Europe*. Boulder, Colo.: Westview Press, 1995.

——, ed. *Making* Callaloo: *Twenty-five Years of Black Literature*. New York: St. Martin's Griffin, 2002.

Ruff, Shawn Stewart, ed. *Go the Way Your Blood Beats: An Anthology of Gay and Lesbian Fiction by African-American Writers*. New York: Henry Holt, 1996.

Smith, Rochelle, and Sharon L. Jones. *The Prentice Hall Anthology of African American Literature*. Upper Saddle River, N.J.: Prentice Hall, 2000.

Washington, Mary Helen. *Black-eyed Susans: Classic Stories by and About Black Women*. Garden City, N.Y.: Anchor Books, 1975.

Weaver, Afaa M., ed. *These Hands I Know: African-American Writers on Family*. Louisville, Ky.: Sarabande, 2002.

Worley, Demetrice A., and Jesse Perry Jr., eds. *African-American Literature: An Anthology*. 2nd ed. Lincolnwood, Ill.: NTC Publishing Group, 1998.

Young, Al, ed. *African American Literature: A Brief Introduction and Anthology*. New York: HarperCollins, 1996.

Young, Kevin, ed. *Giant Steps: The New Generation of African American Writers*. New York: Perennial, 2000.

Poet Young's anthology stands as one of the best collections of recent African American fiction, nonfiction, and poetry. As the subtitle indicates, all of the authors included are of the younger, "Post-Soul" generation: those born from the late 1950s through the early 1970s. Nearly the entire the volume is split between fiction and poetry, with the remaining space devoted to creative nonfiction or memoir. Fiction writers include: Edwidge Danticat, Carolyn Ferrell, Randall Kenan, Darieck Scott, Danzy Senna, Natasha Tarpley, Colson Whitehead, and Daniel Jerome Wideman.

SECONDARY LITERATURE
Books: Relevant Literary and Cultural Criticism

Abel, Elizabeth, Barbara Christian, and Helene Moglen, eds. *Female Subjects in Black and White: Race, Psychoanalysis, Feminism*. Berkeley: University of California Press, 1997.

Abrams, Meyer Howard. *A Glossary of Literary Terms*. 5th ed. New York: Holt, 1988.

Asante, Molefi Kete. *Afrocentricity*. 3d ed. Trenton, N.J.: Africa World Press, 1988.

Baker, Houston A., Jr. *Black Studies, Rap, and the Academy*. Black Literature and Culture. Chicago: University of Chicago Press, 1993.

——. *Blues, Ideology, and Afro-American Literature: A Vernacular Theory*. Chicago: University of Chicago Press, 1984.

——. *The Journey Back: Issues in Black Literature and Criticism*. Chicago: University of Chicago Press, 1980.

    Baker considers the major issues in African American literary studies since the 1950s, including a retrospective of the then-recent Black Arts Movement and black aesthetic.

——. *Long Black Song: Essays in Black American Literature and Culture*. Charlottesville: University Press of Virginia, 1972.

——. *Singers of Daybreak: Studies in Black American Literature*. Washington, D.C.: Howard University Press, 1974.

——. *Workings of the Spirit: The Poetics of Afro-American Women's Writing*. Chicago: University of Chicago Press, 1991.

    Baker assays a study of the importance of the autobiographical and spiritual elements in African American literature, especially that produced by key black women writers. Two of those, Toni Morrison and Ntozake Shange, are the subjects of the later chapters.

Baker, Houston A., Jr., and Patricia Redmond, eds. *Afro-American Literary Study in the 1990s*. Chicago: University of Chicago Press, 1989.

Banks, William M. *Black Intellectuals: Race and Responsibility in American Life*. New York: Norton, 1996.

Bell, Bernard W. *The Afro-American Novel and Its Tradition*. Amherst: University of Massachusetts Press, 1987.

    Bell provides one of the most complete reviews of the African American novel from its roots and antecedents in African oral traditions and abolitionist literature, through the early antebellum and postbellum novels, the pre–World War I period, the Harlem Renaissance, and Naturalism, ending in the contemporary period.

Bell, Derrick. *And We Are Not Saved: The Elusive Quest for Racial Justice*. New York: Basic, 1987.

——. *Confronting Authority: Reflections of an Ardent Protester*. Boston: Beacon, 1994.

——. *Faces at the Bottom of the Well: The Permanence of Racism*. New York: Basic, 1992.

——. *Gospel Choirs: Psalms of Survival for an Alien Land Called Home*. New York: Basic, 1996.

Bloom, Harold, ed. *Black American Women Fiction Writers*. New York: Chelsea House, 1995.

    Most of the authors discussed in this collection of biographies are from the contemporary period, including Maya Angelou, Toni Cade Bambara, Gayl Jones, June Jordan, Terry McMillan, Paule Marshall, Toni Morrison, Gloria Naylor, Ann Petry, and Alice Walker.

——, ed. *Contemporary Black American Fiction Writers*. New York: Chelsea House, 1995.

Bracks, Lean'tin L. *Writings on Black Women of the Diaspora: History, Language, and Identity*. New York: Garland, 1998.

Bruck, Peter, and Wolfgang Karrer, eds. *The Afro-American Novel Since 1960*. Amsterdam: B. R. Grüner, 1982.

Butler, Robert. *Contemporary African American Literature: The Open Journey*. Madison, N.J.: Fairleigh Dickinson University Press, 1998.

    This volume includes chapters on Hurston, Ellison, Walker's *Third Life of Grange Copeland*, Morrison's *Song of Solomon*, Johnson's *Faith and the Good Thing*, Reed's *Flight to Canada*, Williams's *Dessa Rose*, and Octavia E. Butler's *Parable of the Sower*.

Butler-Evans, Elliott. *Race, Gender, and Desire: Narrative Strategies in the Fiction of Toni Cade Bambara, Toni Morrison, and Alice Walker*. Philadelphia: Temple University Press, 1989.

Byerman, Keith. *Fingering the Jagged Grain: Tradition and Form in Recent Black Fiction*. Athens: University of Georgia Press, 1986.

Christian, Barbara. *Black Feminist Criticism: Perspectives on Black Women Writers*. 1985. Reprint: New York: Teachers College Press, 1997.

——. *Black Women Novelists: The Development of a Tradition, 1892–1976*. Westport, Conn.: Greenwood Press, 1980.

Cooke, Michael G. *Afro-American Literature in the Twentieth Century: The Achievement of Intimacy*. New Haven, Conn.: Yale University Press, 1984.

Dick, Bruce Allen, and Pavel Zemliansky. *The Critical Response to Ishmael Reed*. Critical Responses in Arts and Letters 31. Ed. Cameron Northouse. Westport, Conn.: Greenwood, 1999.

Dickson-Carr, Darryl. *African American Satire: The Sacredly Profane Novel*. Columbia: University of Missouri Press, 2001.

Dixon, Melvin. *Ride Out the Wilderness: Geography and Identity in Afro-American Literature*. Urbana: University of Illinois Press, 1987.

Dubey, Madhu. *Black Women Novelists and the Nationalist Aesthetic*. Bloomington: Indiana University Press, 1994.

——. *Signs and Cities: Black Literary Postmodernism*. Chicago: University of Chicago Press, 2003.

duCille, Ann. *The Coupling Convention: Sex, Text, and Tradition in Black Women's Fiction*. New York: Oxford University Press, 1993.

——. *Skin Trade*. Cambridge, Mass.: Harvard University Press, 1996.

   DuCille places greater emphasis here on popular culture and the academy than on literature per se, but her observations are as relevant to discussions of contemporary African American literature and culture as her earlier *The Coupling Convention*.

Ellison, Ralph. *Going to the Territory*. New York: Random House, 1986.

——. *Shadow and Act*. 1964. Reprint: New York: Vintage, 1995.

Ervin, Hazel Arnett. *African American Literary Criticism, 1773 to 2000*. New York: Twayne, 1999.

Fisher, Dexter, and Robert B. Stepto, eds. *Afro-American Literature: The Reconstruction of Instruction*. New York: Modern Language Association of America, 1979.

Fossett, Judith Jackson, and Jeffrey A. Tucker, eds. *Race Consciousness: African American Studies for the New Century*. New York: New York University Press, 1997.

Fox, Robert Elliot. *Conscientious Sorcerers: The Black Postmodernist Fiction of LeRoi Jones/Amiri Baraka, Ishmael Reed, and Samuel R. Delany*. Contributions in Afro-American and African Studies 106. Westport, Conn.: Greenwood, 1987.

Furman, Jan. *Toni Morrison's Fiction*. Understanding Contemporary American Literature. Ed. Matthew J. Bruccoli. Columbia: University of South Carolina Press, 1996.

Gaines, Kevin K. *Uplifting the Race: Black Leadership, Politics, and Culture in the Twentieth Century*. Chapel Hill: University of North Carolina Press, 1996.

Gates, Henry Louis, Jr. *Figures in Black: Words, Signs, and the "Racial" Self*. Oxford: Oxford University Press, 1987.

——, ed. *"Race," Writing, and Difference*. Chicago: University of Chicago Press, 1986.

——. *The Signifying Monkey: A Theory of African-American Literary Criticism*. Oxford: Oxford University Press, 1988.

Gates, Henry Louis, Jr., and Sunday Ogbonna Anozie, eds. *Black Literature and Literary Theory*. New York: Methuen, 1984.

Gayle, Addison, Jr., ed. *The Black Aesthetic*. Garden City, N.Y.: Doubleday, 1971.

——. *Bondage, Freedom, and Beyond: The Prose of Black Americans*. Garden City, N.Y.: Zenith Books, 1971.

——. *The Way of the New World: The Black Novel in America*. Garden City, N.Y.: Anchor/Doubleday, 1975.

Harper, Michael S., and Robert B. Stepto, eds. *Chant of Saints: A Gathering of Afro-American Literature, Art, and Scholarship*. Urbana: University of Illinois Press, 1979.

Higginbotham, Evelyn Brooks, Darlene Clark Hine, and Leon Litwack, eds., *The Harvard Guide to African-American History*. Cambridge, Mass.: Harvard University Press, 2001.

Hogue, W. Lawrence. *The African American Male, Writing, and Difference: A Polycentric Approach to African American Literature, Criticism, and Theory*. Albany: State University of New York Press, 2003.

——. *Discourse and the Other: The Production of the Afro-American Text*. Durham, N.C.: Duke University Press, 1986.

——. *Race, Modernity, Postmodernity: A Look at the History and the Literatures of People of Color Since the 1960s*. Albany: State University of New York Press, 1996.

Hubbard, Dolan. *The Sermon and the African American Literary Imagination*. Columbia: University of Missouri Press, 1994.

   Only the last chapter, on Toni Morrison's *Sula* and *Song of Solomon*, specifically concerns contemporary literature. Hubbard's larger theory, however, is generally applicable to contemporary fiction, especially neo–slave narratives.

Hull, Gloria T., Patricia Bell Scott, and Barbara Smith, eds. *All the Women Are White, All the Blacks Are Men, But Some of Us Are Brave: Black Women's Studies*. Old Westbury, N.Y.: Feminist Press, 1982.

James, Darius. *That's Blaxploitation: Roots of the Baadasssss 'Tude (Rated X by an All-Whyte Jury)*. New York: St. Martin's, 1995.

Jimoh, A. Yemisi. *Spiritual, Blues, and Jazz People in African American Fiction: Living in Paradox*. Knoxville: University of Tennessee Press, 2002.

Johnson, Charles. *Being and Race: Black Writing Since 1970*. Bloomington: Indiana University Press, 1988.

   Novelist Johnson's brief review of the arc of contemporary African American fiction begins with philosophical discussions of "race," fiction, and form as they developed in the post–Civil Rights era, then divides the remainder of his study into two long chapters (approximately thirty pages each) on "The Men" and "The Women" that offer short, critical assessments of specific major authors. While this division along gender lines is problematic, Johnson's text is otherwise a fine introduction to the major works of African American fiction in the period covered.

Jones, Gayl. *Liberating Voices: Oral Tradition in African American Literature*. Cambridge, Mass.: Harvard University Press, 1991.

Karenga, Maulana Ron. *Introduction to Black Studies*. Inglewood, Calif.: Kawaida Publications, 1982.

Kester, Gunilla Theander. *Writing the Subject: Bildung and the African American Text*. New York: Peter Lang, 1997.

Levine, Lawrence W. *Black Culture and Black Consciousness: Afro-American Folk Thought from Slavery to Freedom*. Oxford: Oxford University Press, 1977.

Mackey, Nathaniel. Discrepant Engagement: Dissonance, Cross-Culturality, and Experimental Writing. Cambridge: Cambridge University Press, 1993.

   Mackey's study is divided almost equally between poetry and fiction, but its focus is mostly contemporary and its emphasis is on the poetics of recent literature. Not all of the authors discussed are African American, although most are of African descent.

Martin, Reginald. *Ishmael Reed and the New Black Aesthetic Critics*. London: Macmillan, 1988.

Matus, Jan. *Toni Morrison*. Contemporary World Writers. Ed. John Thieme. Manchester: Manchester University Press, 1998.

McGee, Patrick. *Ishmael Reed and the Ends of Race*. New York: St. Martin's, 1997.

Mitchell, Angelyn, ed. *Within the Circle: An Anthology of African American Literary Criticism from the Harlem Renaissance to the Present*. Durham: Duke University Press, 1994.

Montgomery, Maxine Lavon. *The Apocalypse in African-American Fiction*. Gainesville: University Press of Florida, 1996.

Moraga, Cherríe L., and Gloria E. Anzaldúa, eds. *This Bridge Called My Back: Writings by Radical Women of Color*. Watertown, Mass.: Persephone Press, 1981.

Morrison, Toni. *Playing in the Dark: Whiteness and the Literary Imagination*. New York: Vintage, 1993.

Napier, Winston, ed. *African American Literary Theory: A Reader*. New York: New York University Press, 2000.

Neal, Mark Anthony. *Soul Babies: Black Popular Culture and the Post-Soul Aesthetic*. New York: Routledge, 2002.

Nielsen, Aldon L. *Black Chant: Languages of African-American Postmodernism*. New York: Cambridge University Press, 1996.

——. *Writing Between the Lines: Race and Intertextuality*. Athens: University of Georgia Press, 1994.

Nunez, Elizabeth, and Brenda M. Greene, eds. *Defining Ourselves: Black Writers in the 90s*. New York: Peter Lang, 1999.

   Defining Ourselves contains essays on the state of African American literature in the 1990s from such authors as Paule Marshall, Amiri Baraka, John A. Williams, Ishmael Reed, Walter

Mosley, Jill Nelson, Thulani Davis, Arthur Flowers, Bebe Moore Campbell, Brent Staples, Terry McMillan, Stanley Crouch, Houston A. Baker Jr., Barbara Christian, Karla F. C. Holloway, Marita Golden, and William W. Cook.

Page, Philip. *Reclaiming Community in Contemporary African American Fiction*. Jackson: University Press of Mississippi, 1999.

Patterson, Orlando, *Slavery and Social Death: A Comparative Study*. Cambridge, Mass.: Harvard University Press, 1982.

Pinckney, Darryl. *Out There: Mavericks of Black Literature*. New York: Basic Civitas, 2002.

Reed, Thomas Vernon. *Fifteen Jugglers, Five Believers: Literary Politics and the Poetics of American Social Movements*. Berkeley: University of California Press, 1992.

Roberts, John W. *From Trickster to Badman: The Black Folk Hero in Slavery and Freedom*. Philadelphia: University of Pennsylvania Press, 1989.

Rodriguez, Max. *Sacred Fire: The* QBR *100 Essential Black Books*. New York: Wiley, 1999.
      Lists, summarizes, and analyzes the most distinguished works in over two hundred years of African American literary history.

Rose, Tricia. *Black Noise: Rap Music and Black Culture in Contemporary America*. Middletown, Conn.: Wesleyan University Press, 1994.

Rushdy, Ashraf H. A. *Neo-slave Narratives: Studies in the Social Logic of a Literary Form*. New York: Oxford University Press, 1999.

Smith, Valerie. *Self-Discovery and Authority in Afro-American Narrative*. Cambridge, Mass.: Harvard University Press, 1987.

Soitos, Stephen F. *The Blues Detective: A Study of African American Detective Fiction*. Amherst: University of Massachusetts Press, 1996.

Stuckey, Sterling. *Going Through the Storm: The Influence of African American Art in History*. New York: Oxford University Press, 1994.

Sundquist, Eric J. *The Hammers of Creation: Folk Culture in Modern African-American Fiction*. Athens: University of Georgia Press, 1992.

——. *To Wake the Nations: Race in the Making of American Literature*. Cambridge, Mass.: Belknap Press of Harvard University Press, 1993.

——, ed. *Cultural Contexts for Ralph Ellison's* Invisible Man: *A Bedford Documentary Companion*. Boston: Bedford Books of St. Martin's Press, 1995.

Tate, Claudia. *Psychoanalysis and Black Novels: Desire and the Protocols of Race*. New York: Oxford University Press, 1998.

——, ed. *Black Women Writers at Work*. New York: Continuum, 1983.

Tate, Greg. *Flyboy in the Buttermilk: Essays on Contemporary America*. New York: Simon and Schuster, 1992.

Wall, Cheryl, ed. *Changing Our Own Words: Essays on Criticism, Theory, and Writing by Black Women*. New Brunswick, N.J.: Rutgers University Press, 1989.
      Features essays by Abena P. A. Busia, Barbara Christian, Mae Gwendolyn Henderson, Gloria T. Hull, Deborah E. McDowell, Valerie Smith, Hortense Spillers, Claudia Tate, and Susan Willis regarding key issues in criticism about African American women's literature and culture.

Watkins, Mel. *On the Real Side: Laughing, Lying, and Signifying—the Underground Tradition of African-American Humor That Transformed American Culture, from Slavery to Richard Pryor*. New York: Simon and Schuster, 1994.

Weisenburger, Steven. *Fables of Subversion: Satire and the American Novel, 1930–1980*. Athens: University of Georgia Press, 1995.

West, Cornel. *Race Matters*. Boston: Beacon, 1993.

Books: Biographies

Angelou, Maya. *I Know Why the Caged Bird Sings*. New York: Random House, 1969.

Baraka, Imamu Amiri. *The Autobiography of LeRoi Jones*. Chicago: Lawrence Hill, 1997.

Boyer, Jay. *Ishmael Reed*. Boise, Idaho: Boise State University Press, 1993.

Carroll, Rebecca. *Swing Low: Black Men Writing*. New York: Crown, 1995.

Leeming, David. *James Baldwin: A Biography*. New York: Knopf, 1994.

Smith, Valerie, Lea Baechler, A. Walton Litz, eds. *African American Writers*. New York: Charles Scribner's Sons, 1991; rev. ed., 2000.

Winchell, Donna Haisty. *Alice Walker*. New York: Twayne Publishers, 1992.

Journals and Magazines

African American Review, formerly *Negro American Literature Forum* (1967–76) and *Black American Literature Forum* (1976–1991).

American Literature

Amistad. Ed. John A. Williams and Charles Harris. New York: Random House, 1970–1971.

Callaloo (1976–)

CLA Journal (1957–)

MELUS (*Multi-Ethnic Literature in the United States*) 12, no. 2 (Summer 1985) is devoted to "Black American Literature."

Review of Contemporary Fiction

Journal Articles

Bergenholtz, Rita A. "Toni Morrison's *Sula*: A Satire on Binary Thinking," *African American Review* 30, no. 1 (1996), 89–98.

Blake, Susan L. "Ritual and Rationalization: Black Folklore in the Works of Ralph Ellison." *Publications of the Modern Language Association* 94, no. 2 (1979), 121–36.

Bryant, Jerry H. "Old Gods and New Demons: Ishmael Reed and his Fiction." *The Review of Contemporary Fiction* 4, no. 2 (1984): 195–202.

Ellis, Trey. "The New Black Aesthetic." *Callaloo* 12, no. 1 (Winter 1989): 233–46.

Harris, Norman. "The Black University in Contemporary Afro-American Fiction." *CLA Journal* 30 (1986): 1–13.

Lesoinne, Veronique. "Answer Jazz's Call: Experiencing Toni Morrison's *Jazz*." *MELUS* 22 (1997): 151–66.

Mason, Theodore O., Jr. "Performance, History, and Myth: The Problem of Ishmael Reed's *Mumbo Jumbo*." *Modern Fiction Studies* 34, no. 1 (1988): 97–109.

Mitchell, Angelyn. "'Sth, I Know That Woman': History, Gender, and the South in Toni Morrison's *Jazz*." *Studies in the Literary Imagination* 31, no. 2 (1998): 49–60.

Page, Phillip. "Traces of Derrida in Toni Morrison's *Jazz*." *African American Review* 29, no. 1 (Spring 1995): 55–66.

Ryan, Judylyn S., and Estella C. Májoza. "*Jazz* . . . on 'The Site of Memory.'" *Studies in the Literary Imagination* 31, no. 2 (1998): 125–52.

Wright, Richard. "Blueprint for Negro Writing." *The New Challenge: A Literary Quarterly* 2, no. 2 (1937).

Interviews

Carroll, Rebecca. *I Know What the Red Clay Looks Like: The Voice and Vision of Black Women Writers*. New York: Carol Southern, 1994.

Denard, Carolyn. "Blacks, Modernism, and the American South: An Interview with Toni Morrison." *Studies in the Literary Imagination* 31, no. 2 (1998): 1–16.

Martin, Reginald. "An Interview with Ishmael Reed." *The Review of Contemporary Fiction* 4, no. 2 (1984): 176–87.

Nazareth, Peter. "An Interview with Ishmael Reed." *Iowa Review* 13, no. 2:117–30.

Newman, Katharine. "An Evening with Hal Bennett: An Interview." *Black American Literature Forum* 21, no. 4 (Winter 1987): 357–78.

Reference Materials

Andrews, William L., Frances Smith Foster, and Trudier Harris, eds. *The Oxford Companion to African American Literature*. New York: Oxford University Press, 1997.

The *Oxford Companions* are arguably the *crème de la crème* of quick literary references, concerned as they are with providing brief biographies and concise assessments of an author's or text's significance. The introduction of this particular volume was as significant to scholars as the publication of the *Norton Anthology of African American Literature* the previous year was to both scholars and students.

———. *The Concise Oxford Companion to African American Literature*. New York: Oxford University Press, 2003.

As the title implies, this is a shorter, and therefore more portable version of the landmark 1997 *Companion*. Its conciseness is a result of the editors' decision to highlight "the writers and the writing that have made African American literature valuable and distinctive for more than 250 years," regardless of genre. It has also been updated and corrected, with entries noting the lives and works of newer authors.

Appiah, Kwame Anthony, and Henry Louis Gates Jr., eds. *Africana: The Encyclopedia of the African and African American Experience*. New York: Basic Civitas, 1999.

Appiah and Gates's magnum opus was both inspired by and meant to be the embodiment of the "Encyclopædia Africana" that legendary African American scholar W. E. B. Du Bois had dreamed of compiling for over five decades until his death in 1963. Du Bois envisioned his "Encyclopædia Africana" as the equivalent to the *Encyclopædia Britannica*, with the focus specifically on the history, culture, and works of the peoples of Africa and the African Diaspora. Despite some contemporary controversy about the volume's corporate funding and editorial direction, Appiah and Gates indeed created arguably the most comprehensive single-volume reference to all matters linked to Africans and people of African descent. It stands as an invaluable reference for both research and public libraries.

Davis, Thadious M., and Trudier Harris, eds. *Dictionary of Literary Biography*. 112 vols. Vol. 33, *Afro-American Fiction Writers After 1955*. Detroit: Gale Research, 1984.

Along with their later *Afro-American Dramatists and Prose Writers After 1955* (1985), the thirty-eighth volume in this series, Davis and Harris's collection is arguably the greatest reference source on contemporary African American authors published until its time. It comprises forty-nine author entries, the overwhelming majority of which are now major authors in African American literary tradition. It is, however, too expensive for most individuals, as it is meant to be purchased by research libraries. It is also now outdated, although most scholars will find its entries invaluable for an understanding of the lives and early careers of those writers who began publishing in the thirty year period the volume covers. Scholars should note that the prose writers in the subtitle of volume 38 are those who have written *nonfictional* prose.

Magill, Frank N., ed. *Masterpieces of African American Literature*. New York: HarperCollins, 1992.

Magill's collection, a companion to *Masterpieces of World Literature*, provides biographies and plot summaries to the most prominent authors and works in the African American literary tradition in a single, affordable volume.

Mason, Elizabeth B., and Louis M. Starr, eds. *The Oral History Collection of Columbia University*. New York: Oral History Research Office, 1979.

Matuz, Roger, et al., eds. *Contemporary Literary Criticism: Excerpts from Criticism of the Works of Today's Novelists, Poets, Playwrights, Short Story Writers and Other Creative Writers*. 70 vols. Detroit: Gale Research, 1990.

Schomburg Center for Research in Black Culture. *The New York Public Library African American Desk Reference*. New York: Wiley, 1999.

This compendium of historical facts, timelines, statistical data, organizational information, and bibliographies is one of the most accessible and affordable quick references for both lay and professional scholars of African American history, literature, and culture. It is divided into nineteen sections, such as "Education," "The Arts," "Family and Heritage," "The Diaspora," and "Literature and Language." Each section contains a short overview of its subject, followed by lists of organizations, outlets, notable figures or groups, and a bibliography for further reference.

Smith, Valerie, Lea Baechler and A. Walton Litz, eds. *African American Writers.* New York: Collier, 1993.

An excellent collection of literary biographies of the major writers in the African American literary tradition, including such contemporary authors as Alice Walker, Toni Morrison, Ishmael Reed, John Edgar Wideman, and Ralph Ellison.

Index